P9-DII-130

HTML5 and CSS3

Seventh Edition

ELIZABETH CASTRO • BRUCE HYSLOP

Peachpit Press

HTML5 and CSS3, Seventh Edition: Visual QuickStart Guide
Elizabeth Castro and Bruce Hyslop

Peachpit Press
1249 Eighth Street
Berkeley, CA 94710
510/524-2178
510/524-2221 (fax)

Find us on the Web at www.peachpit.com.

To report errors, please send a note to errata@peachpit.com.
Peachpit Press is a division of Pearson Education.

Copyright © 2012 by Elizabeth Castro and Bruce Hyslop

Editor: Clifford Colby
Development editor: Robyn G. Thomas
Production editor: Cory Borman
Compositor: David Van Ness
Copyeditor: Scout Festa
Proofreader: Nolan Hester
Technical editors: Michael Bester and Chris Casciano
Indexer: Valerie Haynes Perry
Cover design: RHDG/Riezebos Holzbaur Design Group, Peachpit Press
Interior design: Peachpit Press
Logo design: MINE™ www.minesf.com

ISBN-13:   978-0-321-71961-4
ISBN-10:   0-321-71961-1

9 8 7 6 5 4 3 2 1

Printed and bound in the United States of America

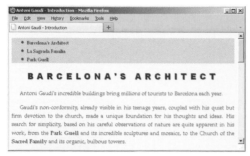

To decorate text:

1. Type **text-decoration:**.

2. Type **underline** after the colon (:) to underline text.

   Or type **overline** for a line above the text.

   Or type **line-through** to strike out the text.

To get rid of decorations:

Type **text-decoration: none;**.

TIP You can eliminate decorations from elements that normally have them (like a, del, or ins) or from elements that inherit decorations from their parents.

TIP While it's perfectly fine to remove underlines from links, be sure to distinguish them sufficiently from surrounding text another way, or visitors won't know they're actionable.

in Ayn Rand's *The Fountainhead*. Gaudí's munity whose residents would love where

in Ayn Rand's *The Fountainhead*. Gaudí's munity whose residents would love where

B In the top image, you can see that the underline is removed from all links, including those in the table of contents. Farther down the page is another link, which is in italics because it's the title of a book, so I marked it up with a **cite** element inside the link (default styling of **cite** is italic). The bottom image shows the underlining I added to links that are being hovered over to encourage the user to take action. I set the **a:hover** color to **#c3f** earlier in the chapter.

Decorating Text

Style sheets let you adorn your text with underlines and lines through the text (perhaps to indicate changes) (A).

(A) Here's the entire style sheet for the page (B), including the **text-decoration** changes to the links. However, you don't have to restrict underlining or other text decorations to **a** elements. They can be applied to other elements too.

```
body {
      background: #eef;
      color: #909;
      font: 100% "Palatino Linotype", Palatino,
      → serif;
}

h1,
h2 {
      color: navy;
      font: 1.375em "Arial Black", Arial,
      → sans-serif;
      letter-spacing: .4em;
      text-align: center;
}

h1 {
      text-transform: uppercase;
}

h2 {
      font-size: 1.15em;
      font-variant: small-caps;
}

p {
      font-size: .875em;
      line-height: 1.6;
      text-align: justify;
      text-indent: 1.5em;
}
```

```
em {
      font-weight: bold;
}

/* Links */
a:link {
      color: #74269d;
      font-weight: bold;
      text-decoration: none;
}

a:visited {
      color: #909;
      text-decoration: none;
}

a:hover {
      color: #c3f;
      font-weight: bold;
      text-decoration: underline;
}

/* Table of Contents navigation */
.toc {
      background: #ebc6f9;
}

.toc a {
      font-size: .75em;
}
```

code continues in next column

A I've changed **h2** to **small-caps** and have also taken the opportunity to bump up the font size a bit so it's in better proportion to the **h1** **B**. Don't forget the hyphen in both **font-variant** and **small-caps**.

```
body {
    background: #eef;
    color: #909;
    font: 100% "Palatino Linotype", Palatino,
    → serif;
}

h1,
h2 {
    color: navy;
    font: 1.375em "Arial Black", Arial,
    → sans-serif;
    letter-spacing: .4em;
    text-align: center;
}

h1 {
    text-transform: uppercase;
}

h2 {
    font-size: 1.15em;
    font-variant: small-caps;
}

... [rest of CSS] ...
```

B Now you see small caps for each **h2** letter. The rendering of small caps may vary a tiny bit from browser to browser.

Using Small Caps

Many fonts have a corresponding small caps variant that includes uppercase versions of the letters proportionately reduced to small caps size. You can invoke the small caps variant with the **font-variant** property **A**.

To use a small caps font:

Type **font-variant: small-caps**.

To remove small caps:

Type **font-variant: none**.

TIP Small caps are not quite as heavy as uppercase letters that have simply been reduced in size.

TIP Not all fonts have a corresponding small caps design. If the browser can't find such a design, it has a few choices. It can fake small caps by simply reducing the size of uppercase letters (which tends to make them look a bit squat), it can forget about small caps altogether and display the text in all uppercase (similar to **text-transform: uppercase**, as described earlier), or, theoretically, it can choose the next font in the list to see if it has a small caps design (though I've never seen this happen).

TIP The **font-variant** property is inherited.

Changing the Text Case

You can define the text case for your style by using the **text-transform** property 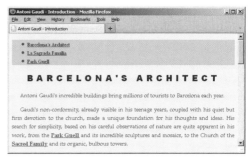. In this way, you can display the text with initial capital letters, with all capital letters 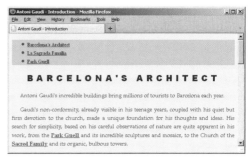, with all lowercase letters, or as it was typed.

To change the text case:

1. Type **text-transform:**.

2. Type **capitalize** after the colon (:) to put the first character of each word in uppercase.

   Or type **uppercase** to change all the letters to uppercase.

   Or type **lowercase** to change all the letters to lowercase.

   Or type **none** to leave the text as is (possibly canceling out an inherited value).

TIP The `capitalize` value has its limitations. It doesn't know when a language's word shouldn't be capitalized by convention, it just capitalizes every word. So, text in your HTML like "Jim Rice enters the Hall of Fame" would render as "Jim Rice Enters The Hall Of Fame."

TIP Why use `text-transform` if you can just change the text in the HTML? Well, sometimes the content is beyond your reach. For example, it could be stored in a database or pulled from another site's news feed. In those cases, you're dependent on adjusting the text case with CSS. Also, if you want text to be all caps, use `text-transform: uppercase` most of the time. Search engines typically index the text as it's typed in the HTML, and the text may be more legible in search results in standard case.

TIP The `lowercase` value can be useful for creating stylish headings (or if you're e.e. cummings).

TIP The `text-transform` property is inherited.

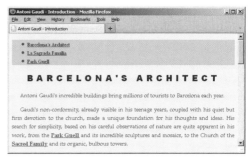 I've decided to display the level 1 heading in all uppercase letters for emphasis 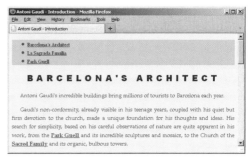.

```
body {
    background: #eef;
    color: #909;
    font: 100% "Palatino Linotype", Palatino,
    → serif;
}

h1,
h2 {
    color: navy;
    font: 1.375em "Arial Black", Arial,
    → sans-serif;
    letter-spacing: .4em;
    text-align: center;
}

h1 {
    text-transform: uppercase;
}

h2 {
    font-size: .9375em;
}

... [rest of CSS] ...
```

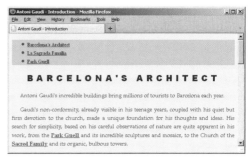 Now the heading really stands out.

B After the changes, the headings are centered, while the paragraph text is justified.

TIP If you choose to justify the text, be aware that the word spacing and letter spacing may be adversely affected. For more information, see "Controlling Spacing."

TIP Note that the `text-align` property can only be applied to elements that are set to `display: block` or `display: inline-block`. Elements like p and `div` are set to `display: block` by default. Prior to HTML5, those types of elements were known as block-level elements. Their default setting still holds in HTML5, but they aren't dubbed block-level anymore so as not to equate HTML semantics with appearance. So this point primarily applies to phrasing content ("inline" elements in pre-HTML5 days) such as `strong`, em, a, `cite`, and the others that appear within the context of sentences, headings, and so on. If you want to align *these* elements individually rather than along with their surrounding text, you must first override their default `display: inline` style with either `display: block` or `display: inline-block` and then set `text-align` accordingly. For those with `display: inline-block`, you may need to add a width to see the effect. In truth, the occasions you'll have a need to set `text-align` on "inline" content are pretty limited.

TIP The `text-align` property is inherited. Its default value is supposed to depend on the document's language and writing system, but in most cases it's indiscriminately set to `left`.

Aligning Text

You can set up text so that it always aligns right, left, center, or justified, as desired Ⓐ.

To align text:

1. Type **text-align:**.

2. Type **left** to align the text to the left.

   Or type **right** to align the text to the right.

   Or type **center** to center the text in the middle of the screen.

   Or type **justify** to align the text on both the right and the left.

Ⓐ The alignment of the heading and paragraph text is adjusted after these changes. Don't forget the hyphen in **text-align**.

```
body {
    background: #eef;
    color: #909;
    font: 100% "Palatino Linotype", Palatino,
    ⇢ serif;
}

h1,
h2 {
    color: navy;
    font: 1.375em "Arial Black", Arial,
    ⇢ sans-serif;
    letter-spacing: .4em;
    text-align: center;
}

h2 {
    font-size: .9375em;
}

p {
    font-size: .875em;
    line-height: 1.6;
    text-align: justify;
    text-indent: 1.5em;
}

... [rest of CSS] ...
```

B For demonstration purposes only, I've added an **intro** class so you can see how **nowrap** affects the display of the first paragraph.

```
...

<h1 id="gaudi">Barcelona's Architect</h1>

    <p class="intro">Antoni Gaudi's
    → incredible buildings bring millions of
    → tourists to Barcelona each year.</p>

    <p>Gaudi's non-conformity, already
    → visible in his teenage years, coupled
    → with his quiet but firm devotion to
    → the church, made a unique foundation
    → for his thoughts and ideas...</p>

...
```

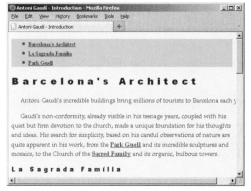

C The first paragraph won't wrap, even when the browser window is too narrow to display the entire line. As a result, a horizontal scrollbar appears.

As an example, I've shown how to apply the **nowrap** value to the first paragraph (**A** and **B**). As you can see, it prevents the line from wrapping **C**. However, since we don't really want this effect in our page, I'll omit the **class** and associated CSS from subsequent examples.

TIP The value of `pre` for the `white-space` property gets its name from the `pre` element, which displays text in a monospace font while maintaining all of its spaces and returns. The `pre` element, in turn, got its name from the word "pre-formatted." You can find more information about `pre` in Chapter 4.

TIP Note that the `pre` value for the `white-space` property has no effect on an element's font (in contrast with the `pre` element, which browsers display in a monospace font by default).

TIP You may use the `br` element to manually create line breaks in an element styled with `white-space:nowrap`. Having said that, it's best to avoid using `br` unless you have no alternative, because it mixes presentation with your HTML instead of letting CSS take care of it. For details about the `br` element, consult "Creating a Line Break" in Chapter 4.

Setting White Space Properties

By default, multiple spaces and returns in an HTML document are either displayed as a single space or ignored. If you want the browser to display those extra spaces, use the **white-space** property.

To set white space properties:

1. Type **white-space:**.

2. Type **pre** to have browsers display all the spaces and returns in the original text.

   Or type **nowrap** to treat all spaces as non-breaking.

   Or type **normal** to treat white space as usual.

Ⓐ The **nowrap** value for **white-space** treats spaces as non-breaking.

```
body {
     background: #eef;
     color: #909;
     font: 100% "Palatino Linotype", Palatino,
     → serif;
}

h1,
h2 {
     color: navy;
     font: 1.375em "Arial Black", Arial,
     → sans-serif;
     letter-spacing: .4em;
}

h2 {
     font-size: .9375em;
}

p {
     font-size: .875em;
     line-height: 1.6;
     text-indent: 1.5em;
}

.intro {
     white-space: nowrap;
}
... [rest of CSS] ...
```

Ⓐ This code adds a 1.5em indent to the **p** elements, which, since their font size is about 14 pixels, will be an indent of about 21 pixels **Ⓑ**.

```
body {
    background: #eef;
    color: #909;
    font: 100% "Palatino Linotype", Palatino,
    → serif;
}

h1,
h2 {
    color: navy;
    font: 1.375em "Arial Black", Arial,
    → sans-serif;
    letter-spacing: .4em;
}

h2 {
    font-size: .9375em;
}

p {
    font-size: .875em;
    line-height: 1.6;
    text-indent: 1.5em;
}
... [rest of CSS] ...
```

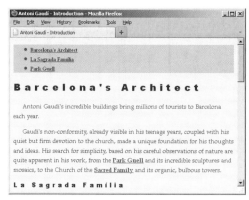

Ⓑ Each paragraph is indented 21 pixels.

Adding Indents

You can determine how much space should precede the first line of a paragraph by setting the **text-indent** property **Ⓐ**.

To add indents:

Type **text-indent:** *length*, where *length* is a number with units, as in **1.5em** or **18px**.

TIP A negative value creates a hanging indent. You may need to increase the padding or margins around a text box with a hanging indent in order to accommodate the overhanging text. (See "Adding Padding around an Element" and "Setting the Margins around an Element" in Chapter 11.)

TIP Em values, as usual, are calculated with respect to the element's font size. Percentages are calculated with respect to the width of the parent element.

TIP The **text-indent** property is inherited.

TIP If you use a percentage or an em value, only the resulting size (or "computed value") is inherited. So, if the parent is 300 pixels wide, a **text-indent** of 10% will be 30 pixels. And all child elements will also have their first lines indented 30 pixels, regardless of the width of their respective parents.

TIP Use a value of 0 to remove an inherited indent.

Layout with Styles

You can create a wide variety of layouts with CSS. This chapter demonstrates how to build a common layout type: a masthead on top, two columns of content, and a footer on the bottom Ⓐ (on the next page). However, you can apply the CSS properties you'll learn about to make vastly different layouts.

I won't show every line of CSS in this chapter. For instance, most of the text formatting was done ahead of time. Please see the complete code at www.bruceontheloose.com/htmlcss/ examples/chapter-11/finished-page.html. I also created a fixed-width (with no fluid interior) version called finished-page-fixed-width.html so you can see how that could be achieved. I've included a lot of comments in all of the files (especially the style sheets) to help explain the code.

In This Chapter

Considerations When Beginning a Layout

Here are a few things to help you along as you lay out your own sites and hone them before releasing them into the wild.

Separating content and presentation

- As a best practice, always separate your content (HTML) and presentation (CSS). You learned how to do this in Chapter 8 by linking to an external style sheet. If you do so from all your pages, they can all share the same layout and overall style. This also makes it easier to change the design of the whole site at a later date, simply by modifying the CSS file or files.

Browser considerations

- Not all visitors will use the same browser, operating system, or even device when accessing your site. So, in most cases, you will want to test your pages on a range of browsers before making them live on your server. I recommend testing a page in a few browsers periodically as you develop it so you'll have fewer issues to address at the end when you perform comprehensive testing. See "Testing Your Page" in Chapter 20 for information about both how to test your pages and the browsers in which to test them.

- Sometimes it is necessary to write CSS rules for specific versions of IE to fix display issues caused by IE's misbehavior. This is especially the case for IE6 and, to a lesser extent, IE7.

  There are a few ways to do this, but the best from a performance standpoint is to use conditional comments to create IE

A This page, with two fluid columns, a header, and a footer, was laid out with CSS. It is explained step by step throughout this chapter.

version-specific classes on the `html` element that you can leverage in your style sheets. See http://paulirish.com/2008/conditional-stylesheets-vs-css-hacks-answer-neither/ for details. There's a fair amount to parse there, so if you're wondering which code to use, it follows the "Throw it on the html tag" heading (read the notes after the code too). Another approach is to use conditional comments to deliver the IE patches in a separate style sheet or sheets.

I've provided an example of both techniques in the book site's code samples. The first approach is in finished-page.html (see this chapter's intro), and the second is in finished-page-conditional-stylesheets.html in the same directory. Learn more about conditional comments at www.quirksmode.org/css/condcom.html.

Layout approaches

There are several ways to do a layout.

- A *fixed* layout has pixel-based widths for the whole page and for each column of content. As its name suggests, its width doesn't change when viewed on smaller devices like mobile phones and tablets or when a desktop browser window is reduced. Chances are you've seen many fixed layouts when browsing the Web, particularly on corporate and big-brand sites. Fixed layouts are also the easiest to get the hang of when learning CSS.

- A *fluid* (or liquid) layout uses percentages for widths, allowing the page to shrink and expand depending on the viewing conditions. This approach has been enhanced of late to create *responsive* and *adaptive* layouts, which can not only shrink for phones and

tablets like traditional fluid layouts, but also shift their design in specific ways based on the screen size. This allows for tailoring the experience to mobile, tablet, and desktop users independently, but with the same HTML, not with three different sites. (Ethan Marcotte created the term "responsive Web design" and the package of techniques behind it. See his article on *A List Apart* to get a taste: www.alistapart.com/articles/responsive-web-design/. He goes into greater detail in his book *Responsive Web Design*, which I highly recommend. An adaptive layout uses some of the same techniques.)

- An *elastic* layout uses ems for both width and all other property sizes, so the page scales according to a user's font-size settings.

There is no single layout approach that is right for every circumstance, and, in fact, there are even hybrid approaches. This chapter teaches you how to make a hybrid of a fluid and fixed layout: the columns have fluid, percentage-based widths so they grow and shrink, but the overall page width has a fixed maximum width that limits how wide it can grow.

To family.

Acknowledgments

Writing the acknowledgments is one of the most daunting challenges of working on a book, because you want to be sure to convey your appreciation of everyone properly. This book is the result of the support, tireless work, and good spirits of a lot of people. I hope to do them all justice, and I hope that you'll indulge me for a bit while I thank them.

A most sincere thank you goes out to:

Nancy Aldrich-Ruenzel and Nancy Davis, for entrusting me with this edition of a book that has been important to Peachpit for many years.

Cliff Colby, for recommending me and making this possible; for his confidence in me and his patience, flexibility, and guidance; and for countless conversations and lots of laughs.

Robyn Thomas, for her tremendous effort in keeping us all on track, wrangling countless documents, making thoughtful edits and suggestions, and providing regular words of encouragement, which were always a boost.

Michael Bester, for all the spot-on feedback and suggestions, catching technical errors and omissions, and helping us get the right message across to readers. It was a real pleasure working with him on another book.

Chris Casciano, in the same vein, for all your technical expertise, suggestions, and crucial feedback. I really appreciated your joining us in the final weeks; we were lucky to have you.

Cory Borman, for expertly overseeing the production of the book and creating diagrams in a pinch, and for his good humor.

Scout Festa, for carefully correcting grammar and punctuation, tightening up language, ensuring the accuracy of figure and chapter references, and, overall, providing an all-important level of polish.

David Van Ness, for his great care laying out the pages and for his proficiency and attention to detail.

Nolan Hester, for lending his expertise to the effort of reviewing the laid-out pages.

Valerie Haynes Perry, for handling the critical task of creating an effective index on which readers will rely time and again.

The numerous marketing, sales, and other folks at Peachpit for working behind the scenes to make the book successful.

My family and friends, for checking in on my progress and providing occasional, welcome breaks from writing. Thanks to those friends in particular who probably tired of hearing me say often that I couldn't get together, but who kept asking anyway.

Robert Reinhardt, as always, for getting me started in writing books and for his guidance as I was embarking on this one.

The Web community, for your innovations and for sharing your knowledge so that others may benefit (I've cited many of you throughout the book).

To you readers, for your interest in learning about HTML and CSS and for selecting this book; I know you have a lot of others from which to choose. I hope the book serves you well.

Thank you so much to the following contributing authors. Readers have a more valuable book because of your efforts, for which I'm grateful. I'd also like to extend my apologies to Erik Vorhes that we weren't able to fit Appendixes A and B in the book. Readers who see them on the book's site will surely appreciate your work.

In alphabetical order by last name, the contributing authors are:

Scott Boms (Chapter 14)
Scott is an award-winning designer, writer, and speaker who has partnered with organizations such as PayPal, HSBC, Hyundai, DHL, XM Radio, *Toronto Life* magazine, and Masterfile during his more than 15 years of working on the Web. When he's away from the computer, you might find him shooting Polaroids; playing drums with his band, George; or enjoying time with his wonderful wife and two children. He's @scottboms on Twitter.

Ian Devlin (Chapter 17)
Ian Devlin is an Irish Web developer, blogger, and author who enjoys coding and writing about emerging Web technologies such as HTML5 and CSS3. In addition to front-end development, Ian also builds solutions with back-end technologies such as .NET and PHP. He has recently written a book, *HTML5 Multimedia: Develop and Design* (Peachpit Press, 2011).

Seth Lemoine (Chapters 5 and 16)
Seth Lemoine is a software developer and teacher in Atlanta. For over ten years, he's worked on challenging projects to see what's possible, with technologies from HTML, JavaScript, and CSS to Objective-C and Ruby. Whether it's finding innovative ways to teach HTML5 and CSS to his students or perfecting a Schezuan recipe in his outdoor wok, being creative is his passion.

Erik Vorhes (Appendixes A and B, available on the book's Web site)
Erik Vorhes creates things for the Web with VSA Partners and is managing editor for Typedia (http://typedia.com/). He lives and works in Chicago.

Brian Warren (Chapter 13)
Brian Warren is a senior designer at Happy Cog in Philadelphia. When he's not writing or designing, he spends his time playing with his beautiful family, listening to music, and brewing beer. He blogs, intermittently, at http://begoodnotbad.com.

And, finally, I'd like to extend a special thank you to Elizabeth Castro. She created the first edition of this book more than 15 years ago and nurtured her audience with each edition that followed. Her style of teaching has resonated with literally hundreds of thousands of readers over the years. I'm extremely grateful for the opportunity to be part of this book, and I was very mindful of doing right by both it and readers while working on this edition.

—Bruce

Contents at a Glance

Table of Contents

Introduction

Whether you are just beginning your venture into building Web sites or have built some before but want to ensure that your knowledge is current, you've come along at a very exciting time in the industry.

How we code and style pages, the browsers in which we view the pages, and the devices on which we view the browsers have all advanced substantially the past few years. Once limited to browsing the Web from our desktop computers or laptops, we can now take the Web with us on any number of devices: phones, tablets, and, yes, laptops and desktops, and more.

Which is as it should be, because the Web's promise has always been the dissolution of boundaries—the power to share and access information freely from any metropolis, rural community, or anywhere in between, from any Web-enabled device. In short, the Web's promise lies in its universality. And the Web's reach continues to expand as technology finds its ways to communities that were once shut out.

Adding to the Web's greatness is that anyone is free to create and launch a site. This book shows you how. It is ideal for the beginner with no knowledge of HTML or CSS who wants to begin to create Web pages. You'll find clear, easy-to-follow instructions that take you through the process of creating pages step by step. Lastly, the book is a helpful guide to keep handy. You can look up topics in the table of contents or index and consult just those subjects about which you need more information.

HTML and CSS in Brief

At the root of the Web's success is a simple, text-based markup language that is easy to learn and that any device with a basic Web browser can read: HTML. Every Web page requires at least some HTML; it wouldn't be a Web page without it.

As you will learn in greater detail as you move through this book, HTML is used to define your content's meaning, and CSS is used to define how your content and Web page will look. Both HTML pages and CSS files (*style sheets*) are text files, making them easy to edit. You can see snippets of HTML and CSS in "How This Book Works," near the end of this introduction.

You'll dive into learning a basic HTML page right off the bat in Chapter 1, and you'll begin to learn how to style your pages with CSS in Chapter 7. See "What this book will teach you" for an overview of all the chapters and a summary of the topics covered.

What is HTML5?

It helps to know some basics about the origins of HTML in order to understand HTML5. HTML began in the early 1990s as a short document that detailed a handful of elements used to build Web pages. Many of those elements were for describing Web page content such as headings, paragraphs, and lists. HTML's version number has increased as the language has evolved with the introduction of other elements and adjustments to its rules. The most current version is HTML5.

HTML5 is a natural evolution of earlier versions of HTML and strives to reflect the needs of both current and future Web sites. It inherits the vast majority of features from its predecessors, meaning that if you coded HTML before HTML5 came on the scene, you already know a lot of HTML5. This also means that much of HTML5 works in both old and new browsers; being backward compatible is a key design principle of HTML5 (see www.w3.org/TR/html-design-principles/).

HTML5 also adds a bevy of new features. Many are straightforward, such as additional elements (`article`, `section`, `figure`, and many more) that are used to describe content. Others are quite complex and aid in creating powerful Web applications. You'll need to have a firm grasp of creating Web pages before you can graduate to the more complicated features that HTML5 provides. HTML5 also introduces native audio and video playback to your Web pages, which the book also covers.

What is CSS3?

The first version of CSS didn't exist until after HTML had been around for a few years, becoming official in 1996. Like HTML5 and its relationship to earlier versions of HTML, CSS3 is a natural extension of the versions of CSS that preceded it.

CSS3 is more powerful than earlier versions of CSS and introduces numerous visual effects, such as drop shadows, text shadows, rounded corners, and gradients. (See "What this book will teach you" for details of what's covered.)

Web standards and specifications

You might be wondering who created HTML and CSS in the first place, and who continues to evolve them. The World Wide Web Consortium (W3C)—directed by the inventor of the Web and HTML, Tim Berners-Lee—is the organization responsible for shepherding the development of Web standards. *Specifications* (or *specs*, for short) are documents that define the parameters

(A) The W3C site is the industry's primary source of Web-standards specifications.

of languages like HTML and CSS. In other words, specs standardize the rules. Follow the W3C's activity at www.w3.org **(A)**.

For a variety of reasons, another organization—the Web Hypertext Application Technology Working Group (WHATWG, found at www.whatwg.org)—is developing the HTML5 specification. The W3C incorporates WHATWG's work into its official version of the in-progress spec.

With standards in place, we can build our pages from the agreed-upon set of rules, and browsers—like Chrome, Firefox, Internet Explorer (IE), Opera, and Safari—can be built to display our pages with those rules in mind. (On the whole, browsers implement the standards well. Older versions of IE, especially IE6, have some issues.)

Specifications go through several stages of development before they are considered final, at which point they are dubbed a *Recommendation* (www.w3.org/2005/10/Process-20051014/tr).

Parts of the HTML5 and CSS3 specs are still being finalized, but that doesn't mean you can't use them. It just takes time (literally years) for the standardization process to run its course. Browsers begin to implement a spec's features long before it becomes a Recommendation, because that informs the spec development process itself. So browsers already include a wide variety of features in HTML5 and CSS3, even though they aren't Recommendations yet.

On the whole, the features covered in this book are well entrenched in their respective specs, so the risk of their changing prior to becoming a Recommendation is minimal. Developers have been using many HTML5 and CSS3 features for some time. So can you.

Progressive Enhancement: A Best Practice

I began the introduction by speaking of the universality of the Web—the notion that information on the Web should be accessible to all. *Progressive enhancement* helps you build sites with universality in mind. It is not a language, rather it's an approach to building sites that Steve Champeon created in 2003 (http://en.wikipedia.org/wiki/Progressive_enhancement).

The idea is simple but powerful: Start your site with HTML content and behavior that is accessible to all visitors . To the *same* page, add your design with CSS **B** and add additional behavior with JavaScript, typically loading them from external files (you'll learn how to do this).

The result is that devices and browsers capable of accessing basic pages will get the simplified, default experience; devices and browsers capable of viewing more-robust sites will see the enhanced version. The experience on your site doesn't have to be the same for everyone, as long as your content is accessible. In essence, the idea behind progressive enhancement is that everyone wins.

photobarcelona... capturing barcelona's cultural treasures on film

- home
- about
- resources
- archives

Search: `architecture, Gaudí, etc.` [Go]

Recent Entries

Hospital Sant Pau

June 26, 2011

The Saint Paul Hospital at the top of Gaudí Avenue in the Sagrada Família neighborhood is an oft-overlooked gem of modernist architecture. Although the building was begun in 1902 under the direction of the architect Lluís Domènec i Montaner, the hospital itself dates from the 14th century. It serves some 34,000 inpatients yearly, along with more than 150,000 emergency room...

continued

A A basic HTML page with no custom CSS applied to it. This page may not look great, but the information is accessible—and that's what's important. Even browsers from near the inception of the Web more than 20 years ago can display this page; so too can the oldest of mobile phones with Web browsers. And *screen readers*, software that reads Web pages aloud to visually impaired visitors, will be able to navigate it easily.

B The same page as viewed in a browser that supports CSS. It's the same information, just presented differently. Users with more capable devices and browsers get an enhanced experience when visiting the page.

This book teaches you how to build progressively enhanced sites even if it doesn't always explicitly call that out while doing so. It's a natural result of the best practices imparted throughout the book.

However, Chapters 12 and 14 do address progressive enhancement head on. Take an early peek at those if you're interested in seeing how the principle of progressive enhancement helps you build a site that adapts its layout based on a device's screen size and browser capabilities, or how older browsers will display simplified designs while modern browsers will display ones enhanced with CSS3 effects.

Progressive enhancement is a key best practice that is at the heart of building sites for everyone.

Is This Book for You?

This book assumes no prior knowledge of building Web sites. So in that sense, it is for the absolute beginner. You will learn both HTML and CSS from the ground up. In the course of doing so, you will also learn about features that are new in HTML5 and CSS3, with an emphasis on the ones that designers and developers are using today in their daily work.

But even if you *are* familiar with HTML and CSS, you still stand to learn from this book, especially if you want to get up to speed on much of the latest in HTML5, CSS3, and best practices.

What this book will teach you

We've added approximately 125 pages to this book since the previous edition in order to bring you as much material as possible. (The very first edition of the book, published in 1996, had 176 pages *total*.) We've also made substantial updates to (or done complete rewrites of) nearly every previous page. In short, this Seventh Edition represents a major revision.

The chapters are organized like so:

- Chapters 1 through 6 and 15 through 18 cover the principles of creating HTML pages and the range of HTML elements at your disposal, clearly demonstrating when and how to use each one.

- Chapters 7 through 14 dive into CSS, all the way from creating your first style rule to applying enhanced visual effects with CSS3.

- Chapter 19 shows you how to add pre-written JavaScript to your pages.

- Chapter 20 tells you how to test and debug your pages before putting them on the Web.

- Chapter 21 explains how to secure your own domain name and then publish your site on the Web for all to see.

Expanding on that, some of the topics include:

- Creating, saving, and editing HTML and CSS files.

- What it means to write semantic HTML and why it is important.

- How to separate your page's content (that is, your HTML) from its presentation (that is, your CSS)—a key aspect of progressive enhancement.

- Structuring your content in a meaningful way by using HTML elements that have been around for years and ones that are new in HTML5.

- Improving your site's accessibility with ARIA landmark roles and other good coding practices.

- Adding images to your pages and optimizing them for the Web.

- Linking from one Web page to another page, or from one part of a page to another part.

- Styling text (size, color, bold, italics, and more); adding background colors and images; and implementing a fluid, multi-column layout that can shrink and expand to accommodate different screen sizes.

- Leveraging new selectors in CSS3 that allow you to target your styles in a wider range of ways than was previously possible.

- Learning your options for addressing visitors on mobile devices.

- Building a single site for all users—whether they are using a mobile phone, tablet, laptop, desktop computer, or other Web-enabled device—based on many of the principles of responsive web design, some of which leverage CSS3 media queries.

- Adding custom Web fonts to your pages with `@font-face`.

- Using CSS3 effects such as opacity, background alpha transparency, gradients, rounded corners, drop shadows, shadows inside elements, text shadows, and multiple background images.

- Building forms to solicit input from your visitors, including using some of the new form input types in HTML5.

- Including media in your pages with the HTML5 `audio` and `video` elements.

And more.

These topics are complemented by many dozens of code samples that show you how to implement the features based on best practices in the industry.

What this book *won't* teach you

Alas, even after adding so many pages since the previous edition, there is so much to talk about when it comes to HTML and CSS that we had to leave out some topics.

With a couple of exceptions, we stuck to omitting items that you would have fewer occasions to use, are still subject to change, lack widespread browser support, require JavaScript knowledge, or are advanced subjects.

Some of the topics not covered include:

- The HTML5 `details`, `summary`, `menu`, `command`, and `keygen` elements.

- The HTML5 `canvas` element, which allows you to draw graphics (and even create games) with JavaScript.

- The HTML5 APIs and other advanced features that require JavaScript knowledge or are otherwise not directly related to the new semantic HTML5 elements.

- CSS sprites. This technique involves combining more than one image into a single image, which is very helpful in minimizing the number of assets your pages need to load. See www.bruceontheloose.com/sprites/ for more information.

- CSS image replacement. These techniques are often paired with CSS sprites. See www.bruceontheloose.com/ir/ for more information.

- CSS3 transforms, animations, and transitions.

- CSS3's new layout modules.

How This Book Works

Nearly every section of the book contains practical code examples that demonstrate real-world use (A and B). Typically, they are coupled with screen shots that show the results of the code when you view the Web page in a browser C.

Most of the screen shots are of the latest version of Firefox that was available at the time. However, this doesn't imply a recommendation of Firefox over any other browser. The code samples will look very similar in any of the latest versions of Chrome, Internet Explorer, Opera, or Safari. As you will learn in Chapter 20, you should test your pages in a wide range of browsers before putting them on the Web, because there's no telling what browsers your visitors will use.

The code and screen shots are accompanied by descriptions of the HTML elements or CSS properties in question, both to give the samples context and to increase your understanding of them.

In many cases, you may find that the descriptions and code samples are enough for you to start using the HTML and CSS features. But if you need explicit guidance on how to use them, step-by-step instructions are always provided.

Finally, most sections contain tips that relay additional usage information, best practices, references to related parts of the book, links to relevant resources, and more.

A You'll find a snippet of HTML code on many pages, with the pertinent sections highlighted. An ellipsis (...) represents additional code or content that was omitted for brevity. Often, the omitted portion is shown in a different code figure.

```
...
<body>
<header role="banner">
    ...
        <nav role="navigation">
            <ul class="nav">
                <li><a href="/" class="current">home</a></li>
                <li><a href="/about/">about</a></li>
                <li><a href="/resources/">resources</a></li>
                <li><a href="/archives/">archives</a></li>
            </ul>
        </nav>
    ...
</header>

...

</body>
</html>
```

B If CSS code is relevant to the example, it is shown in its own box, with the pertinent sections highlighted.

```
/* Site Navigation */
.nav li {
    float: left;
    font-size: .75em; /* makes the
    → bullets smaller */
}

.nav li a {
    font-size: 1.5em;
}

.nav li:first-child {
    list-style: none;
    padding-left: 0;
}
```

C Screen shots of one or more browsers demonstrate how the code affects the page.

Conventions used in this book

The book uses the following conventions:

- The word *HTML* is all encompassing, representing the language in general. *HTML5* is used when referring to that specific version of HTML, such as when discussing a feature that is new in HTML5 and doesn't exist in previous versions of HTML. The same approach applies to usage of the terms *CSS* (general) and *CSS3* (specific to CSS3).

- Text or code that is a placeholder for a value you would create yourself is italicized. Most placeholders appear in the step-by-step instructions. For example, "Or type **#rrggbb**, where **rrggbb** is the color's hexadecimal representation."

- Code that you should actually type or that represents HTML or CSS code appears in `this font`.

- An arrow (→) in a code figure indicates a continuation of the previous line—the line has been wrapped to fit in the book's column **B**. The arrow is not part of the code itself, so it's not something you would type. Instead, type the line continuously, as if it had not wrapped to another line.

- The first occurrence of a word is italicized when it is defined.

- *IE* is often used as a popular abbreviation of *Internet Explorer*. For instance, IE9 is synonymous with Internet Explorer 9.

- Whenever a plus sign (+) follows a browser version number, it means the version listed plus subsequent versions. For instance, Firefox 8+ refers to Firefox 8.0 and all versions after it.

Companion Web Site

The book's site, at www.bruceontheloose
.com/htmlcss/, contains the table of
contents, every complete code example
featured in the book (plus some additional
ones that wouldn't fit), links to resources
cited in the book (as well as additional
ones), information about references used
during writing, a list of errata, and more.

The site also includes reference sections
(Appendixes A and B) that we didn't have
room to include in the book. These are
handy for quickly looking up HTML elements and attributes or CSS properties and
values. (They also contain some information not covered in the book.)

You can find the code examples at www
.bruceontheloose.com/htmlcss/examples/.
You can browse them from there or download them to your computer—all the HTML
and CSS files are yours for the taking.

In some cases, I've included additional
comments in the code to explain more
about what it does or how to use it. A
handful of the code samples in the book
are truncated for space considerations, but
the complete versions are on the book's
Web site. Please feel free to use the code
as you please, modifying it as needed for
your own projects.

The URLs for some of the key pages on the
book's site follow:

- Home page: www.bruceontheloose
  .com/htmlcss/

- Code samples: www.bruceontheloose
  .com/htmlcss/examples/

- Appendix A: HTML Reference:
  www.bruceontheloose.com/ref/html/

- Appendix B: CSS Properties and Values:
  www.bruceontheloose.com/ref/css/

I hope you find the site helpful.

Web Page Building Blocks

While Web pages have become increasingly complex, their underlying structure remains remarkably simple. The first thing you should know is that it's impossible to create a Web page without HTML. As you will learn, HTML houses your content and describes its meaning. In turn, Web browsers render your HTML-encased content for users.

A Web page is primarily made up of three components:

- *Text content*: The bare text that appears on the page to inform visitors about your business, family vacation, products, or whatever the focus of your page may be.

- *References to other files*: These load items such as images, audio, video, and SVG files, and they link to other HTML pages and assets, as well as to style sheets (which control your page's layout) and JavaScript files (which add behavior to your page).

- *Markup*: The HTML elements that describe your text content and make the references work. (The *m* in HTML stands for *markup*.)

It's important to note that each of these components in a Web page is made up exclusively of text. This means that pages are saved in text-only format and can be viewed on practically any browser on any platform, whether desktop, mobile, tablet, or otherwise. It guarantees the universality of the Web. A page may look different when viewed on one device versus another, but that's OK. The important thing as a first step is to make content accessible to all users, and HTML affords that.

In addition to the three components that a Web page is primarily made up of, a page also includes HTML that provides information about the page itself, most of which your users don't see explicitly and that is primarily intended for browsers and search engines. This can include information about the content's primary language (English, French, and so on), character encoding (typically UTF-8), and more.

This chapter will walk you through a basic HTML page, discuss some best practices, and explain each of the three important components.

Note: As mentioned in the introduction, I use *HTML* to refer to the language in general. For those instances in which I'm highlighting special characteristics unique to a version of the language, I will use the individual name. For example, "*HTML5* introduces several new elements and redefines or eliminates others that previously existed in *HTML 4* and *XHTML 1.0*." For more details, please consult "How This Book Works" in the introduction.

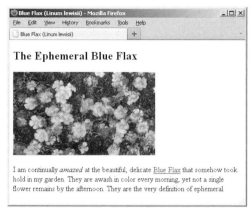

A A typical default rendering of the page. Although this shows the page in Firefox, the page displays similarly in other browsers.

A Basic HTML Page

Let's take a look at a basic HTML page to give you context for what's to follow in this chapter and beyond. Figure **A** illustrates how a desktop browser typically renders the HTML code in **B**. You'll learn some of the basics about the code **B**, but don't worry if you don't understand it all right now. This is just to give you a taste of HTML. You have the rest of the book to learn more about it.

You can probably guess some of what's going on in the code, especially in the **body** section. First let's look at the part before the **body**.

B Here is the code for a basic HTML page. I've highlighted the HTML portions so you can distinguish them from the page's text content. As demonstrated in **A**, the HTML surrounding the text content doesn't appear when you view the page in a browser. But, as you will learn, the markup is essential because it describes the content's meaning. Note, too, that each line happens to be separated with a carriage return. This isn't mandatory and does not impact the page's rendering.

```
<!DOCTYPE html>
<html lang="en">
<head>
    <meta charset="utf-8" />
    <title>Blue Flax (Linum lewisii)</title>
</head>
<body>
    <article>
        <h1>The Ephemeral Blue Flax</h1>

        <img src="blueflax.jpg" width="300" height="175" alt="Blue Flax (Linum lewisii)" />

        <p>I am continually <em>amazed</em> at the beautiful, delicate <a href="http://
        en.wikipedia.org/wiki/Linum_lewisii" rel="external" title="Learn more about Blue
        Flax">Blue Flax</a> that somehow took hold in my garden. They are awash in color every
        morning, yet not a single flower remains by the afternoon. They are the very definition
        of ephemeral.</p>
    </article>
</body>
</html>
```

Everything above the `<body>` start tag is the instructional information for browsers and search engines mentioned earlier Ⓒ. Each page begins with the DOCTYPE declaration, which tells the browser the HTML version of the page.

You should always use HTML5's DOCTYPE, which is `<!DOCTYPE html>`. The case of the text doesn't matter, but it's more common to use DOCTYPE in all uppercase. Regardless, always include the DOCTYPE in your pages. (See the sidebar "HTML5's Improved DOCTYPE" in Chapter 3 for more information.)

The bits that start at `<!DOCTYPE html>` and continue through `</head>` are invisible to users with one exception: the text between `<title>` and `</title>`—Blue Flax (Linum lewisii)—appears as the title at the very top of the browser window and on a browser tab Ⓑ. Additionally, it's typically the default name of a browser bookmark or favorite and is valuable information for search engines. Chapter 3 explains what the other parts of the top segment of a page do.

Ⓒ The `title` element text is the only part of the top area of an HTML document that the user sees. The rest is information about the page for browsers and search engines.

```
<!DOCTYPE html>
<html lang="en">
<head>
    <meta charset="utf-8" />
    <title>The Ephemeral Blue Flax
    → (Linum lewisii)</title>
</head>
```

D A page's content exists between the start and end tags of the **body** element. The document ends at **</html>**.

```
<!DOCTYPE html>
<html lang="en">
. . . [document head] . . .
<body>
    <article>
        <h1>The Ephemeral Blue Flax</h1>

        <img src="blueflax.jpg" width="300"
        → height="175" alt="Blue Flax (Linum
        → lewisii)" />

        <p>I am continually <em>amazed</em>
        → at the beautiful, delicate
        → <a href="http://en.wikipedia.org/
        → wiki/Linum_lewisii" rel="external"
        → title="Learn more about Blue Flax">
        → Blue Flax</a> that somehow took
        → hold in my garden. They are awash
        → in color every morning, yet not a
        → single flower remains by the
        → afternoon. They are the very
        → definition of ephemeral.</p>
    </article>
</body>
</html>
```

Meanwhile, your page's content—that is, what *is* visible to users—goes between **<body>** and **</body>**. Finally, the **</html>** end tag signals the end of the page **D**.

The code's indentation has absolutely no bearing on whether the code is valid HTML. It also doesn't affect how the content displays in the browser (the **pre** element, which you'll learn about in Chapter 4, is the one exception). However, it's customary to indent code that's nested in a parent element to make it easier to glean the hierarchy of elements as you read through the code. You'll learn more about parents and children later in this chapter. You'll also learn in greater detail about the default browser rendering.

First, let's discuss what it means to write semantic HTML and why it is a cornerstone of an effective Web site.

Semantic HTML: Markup with Meaning

HTML is a clever system of including information about the content in a text document. This information, called markup, describes the *meaning* of the content, that is, the *semantics*. You've already seen a few examples in our basic HTML page, such as the **p** element that marks up paragraph content.

HTML does *not* define how the content should appear in a browser; that's the role of CSS (Cascading Style Sheets). HTML5 stresses this distinction more than any prior version of HTML. It's at the core of the language.

You might be wondering why, if that's the case, some text in the basic HTML page **Ⓐ** looks larger than other text, or is bold or italicized **Ⓑ**.

Great question. The reason is that every Web browser has a built-in CSS file (a *style sheet*) that dictates how each HTML element displays by default, unless you create your own that overwrites it. The default presentation varies slightly from browser to browser, but on the whole it is fairly consistent. More importantly, the content's underlying structure and meaning as defined by your HTML remain the same.

Ⓐ The content of our basic page plus a second paragraph added at the end. The HTML elements don't dictate how the content should appear, just what they mean. Instead, each browser's built-in style sheet dictates how the content displays by default **Ⓑ**.

```
...
<body>
    <article>
        <h1>The Ephemeral Blue Flax</h1>

        <img src="blueflax.jpg" width="300"
        → height="175" alt="Blue Flax (Linum
        → lewisii)" />

        <p>I am continually <em>amazed</em>
        → at the beautiful, delicate
        → <a href="http://en.wikipedia.org/
        → wiki/Linum_lewisii" rel="external"
        → title="Learn more about Blue Flax">
        → Blue Flax</a> that somehow took
        → hold in my garden. They are awash
        → in color every morning, yet not a
        → single flower remains by the
        → afternoon. They are the very
        → definition of ephemeral.</p>

        <p><small>&copy; Blue Flax Society.
        → </small></p>
    </article>
</body>
</html>
```

The Ephemeral Blue Flax

I am continually *amazed* at the beautiful, delicate Blue Flax that somehow took hold in my garden. They are awash in color every morning, yet not a single flower remains by the afternoon. They are the very definition of ephemeral.

© Blue Flax Society

B A browser's default style sheet renders headings (**h1**–**h6** elements) differently than normal text, italicizes **em** text, and colors and underlines links. Additionally, some elements begin on their own line (**h1** and **p**, for example), and others display within surrounding content (like **a** and **em**). This example includes a second paragraph (the copyright notice) to make it clear that each paragraph occupies its own line. It's simple to overwrite any or all of these presentation rules with your own style sheets.

Block-level, Inline, and HTML5

As you can see, some HTML elements (for example, the `article`, **h1**, and **p**) display on their own line like a paragraph does in a book, while others (for example, the **a** and **em**) render in the same line as other content **B**. Again, this is a function of the browser's default style rules, not the HTML elements themselves. Allow me to elaborate. Before HTML5, most elements were categorized as either *block-level* (the ones that displayed on their own line) or *inline* (the ones that displayed within a line of text). HTML5 does away with these terms because they associate elements with presentation, which you've learned isn't HTML's role.

Instead, generally speaking, elements that had previously been dubbed inline are categorized in HTML5 as *phrasing content*— that is, elements and their contained text that primarily appear within a paragraph. (Chapter 4 focuses almost exclusively on phrasing content. See the full list at http://dev.w3.org/html5/spec-author-view/content-models.html#phrasing-content-0.)

The old block-level elements also now fall into new HTML5 categories that focus on their semantics. Many of these elements account for the main structural blocks and headings of your content (dig into Chapter 3 to learn more about sectioning content and heading content elements).

With all that said, browsers haven't changed the default display rules for these elements, nor should they. After all, you wouldn't want, say, the two paragraphs (the **p** elements) running into each other, or the **em** text ("amazed") to break the sentence by appearing on its own line (**em** is the element you use for adding emphasis).

So usually headings, paragraphs, and structural elements like **article** display on their own line, and phrasing content displays on the same line as surrounding content. And even though HTML5 no longer uses the terms block-level and inline, it helps to know what they mean. It's common for tutorials to use them since they were entrenched in HTML vernacular before HTML5. I might use them occasionally in the book to quickly convey whether an element occupies its own line or shares a line by default.

We'll cover CSS in detail in later chapters, but for now know that a style sheet, like an HTML page, is just text, so you can create one with the same text editor as your HTML.

HTML5's Focus on Semantics

HTML5 emphasizes HTML semantics, leaving all visual styling to CSS. That wasn't always the case with earlier versions of HTML.

A proper means to style pages didn't exist in the Web's nascent years; HTML was already a few years old by the time CSS1 was formally introduced in December of 1996. To fill that gap in the meantime, HTML included a handful of presentational elements whose purpose was to allow basic styling of text, such as making it bold, italicized, or a different size than surrounding text.

Those elements served their purpose for the time, but they rightfully fell out of favor as best practices evolved for Web development. Central to that thinking was—and still very much is—the notion that HTML is for describing the content's meaning only, not its display.

The presentational HTML elements broke this best practice. As such, HTML 4 deprecated their use, recommending authors use CSS to style text and other page elements instead.

HTML5 goes further; it eliminates some presentational elements and redefines others so they carry only semantic value instead of dictating presentation.

The **small** element is one such example. Initially, it was intended to make text smaller than regular text. However, in HTML5 **small** represents fine print, such as a legal disclaimer. You can use CSS to make it the largest text on the page if you'd like, but that won't change the meaning of your **small** content.

Meanwhile, **small**'s old counterpart, the **big** element, doesn't exist in HTML5. There are other examples, too, which you'll learn about as you progress through the book.

HTML5 also defines new elements, such as **header**, **footer**, **nav**, **article**, **section**, and many more that enrich the semantics of your content. You'll learn about those later as well.

However, whether you use an HTML element that's existed since the dawn of the language or one that's new in HTML5, your goal should be the same: Choose the elements that best describe the meaning of your content without regard for their presentation.

C The **body** of our basic page, which contains the **article**, **h1**, **img**, **p**, **em**, and **a** elements to describe the content's meaning. All the content is nested in the **article**.

```
<body>
    <article>
        <h1>The Ephemeral Blue Flax</h1>

        <img src="blueflax.jpg" width="300"
          height="175" alt="Blue Flax (Linum
          lewisii)" />

        <p>I am continually <em>amazed</em>
          at the beautiful, delicate
          <a href="http://en.wikipedia.org/
          wiki/Linum_lewisii" rel="external"
          title="Learn more about Blue Flax">
          Blue Flax</a> that somehow took
          hold in my garden. They are awash
          in color every morning, yet
          not a single flower remains by
          the afternoon. They are the very
          definition of ephemeral.</p>
    </article>
</body>
```

D Headings are critical elements in defining a page's outline. They make a page more accessible to users of screen readers, and search engines use them to determine the focus of a page.

```
<h1>The Ephemeral Blue Flax</h1>
```

E It's easy to add an image to a page with **img**. As defined by the **alt** attribute, "Blue Flax (Linum lewisii)" displays if our image doesn't.

```
<img src="blueflax.jpg" width="300"
  height="175" alt="Blue Flax (Linum lewisii)"
  />
```

The Semantics of Our Basic HTML Page

Now that you know HTML's role, let's look a little deeper at the thought process behind marking up sample content. As you'll see, there's no magic to writing semantic HTML. It's mostly common sense once you're familiar with the elements at your disposal. Let's revisit the **body** of our basic page for a taste of some of the most frequently used HTML elements **C**.

All the content is contained in an **article** element **C**. In short, **article** defines a distinct piece of content. The **article** element is the appropriate choice to surround the content for our basic page, but not necessarily for every page you'll write. You'll learn more about when to use **article** in Chapter 3.

Next is a heading **D**. HTML provides you six heading levels, **h1**–**h6**, with **h1** being the most important. An **h2** is a subheading of an **h1**, an **h3** is a subheading of an **h2**, and so on, just like when you type a document with various headings in a word processor.

Every HTML page should have an **h1** (or more, depending on your content), so marking up our heading with **h1** was the obvious choice. The heading elements **h1**–**h6** are covered more in Chapter 3.

Next, you have an image **E**. The **img** element is the primary choice for displaying an image, so again, there was no debate about which element was appropriate. The **alt** attribute provides text that displays if the image doesn't load or if the page is viewed in a text-only browser. You'll learn more about images in Chapter 5.

The paragraph is marked up with—surprise—the **p** element **F**. Just as in printed materials, a paragraph can contain a single sentence or several sentences. If our page needed another paragraph, you'd simply add another **p** element after the first one.

There are two elements nested within our paragraph that define the meaning of bits of text: **em** and **a** **F**. These are examples of the numerous phrasing content elements that HTML5 provides, the majority of which improve the semantics of paragraph text. As mentioned, those, along with **p**, are discussed in Chapter 4.

The **em** element means "stress emphasis." In the case of our page, it emphasizes the amazement the flowers induced **F**. Remember that because HTML describes the meaning of content, **em** dictates semantic, not visual, emphasis even though it's common to render **em** text in italics.

Finally, the basic page defines a link to another page with the **a** element ("anchor"), which is the most powerful element in all of HTML because it makes the Web, the Web: It links one page to another page or resource, and links one part of a page to another part of a page (either the same page or a different one). In the example, it signifies that the text "Blue Flax" is a link to a page on Wikipedia **G**.

F The **p** element may contain other elements that define the semantics of phrases within a paragraph. The **em** and **a** elements are two examples.

```
<p>I am continually <em>amazed</em> at
  the beautiful, delicate <a href="http://
  en.wikipedia.org/wiki/Linum_lewisii"
  rel="external" title="Learn more about
  Blue Flax">Blue Flax</a> that somehow
  took hold in my garden. They are awash in
  color every morning, yet not a single
  flower remains by the afternoon. They are
  the very definition of ephemeral.</p>
```

G This **a** element defines a link to the Wikipedia page about Blue Flax. The optional **rel** attribute adds to the semantics by indicating that the link points to another site. The link works without it, though. The optional **title** attribute enhances the semantics of the **a** by providing information about the linked page. It appears in the browser when a user hovers over the link.

```
<a href="http://en.wikipedia.org/wiki/Linum_
  lewisii" rel="external" title="Learn more
  about Blue Flax">Blue Flax</a>
```

Pretty easy, right? Once you've learned more about the HTML elements available to you, choosing the right ones for your content is usually a straightforward task. Occasionally, you'll come across a piece of content that reasonably could be marked up in more than one way, and that's OK. There isn't always a right and wrong way, just most of the time.

Lastly, HTML5 doesn't try to provide an element for every type of content imaginable, because the language would become ungainly. Instead, it takes a practical, real-world stance, defining elements that cover the vast majority of cases.

Part of HTML's beauty is that it's simple for anyone to learn the basics, build some pages, and grow their knowledge from there. So, although there are approximately 100 HTML elements, don't let that number scare you. There's a core handful you'll find yourself using time and again, while the remaining ones are reserved for less common cases. You've already learned the basics of several common elements, so you're well on your way.

Why Semantics Matter

Now that you know the importance of semantic HTML and have seen it in action, you need to know the reasons *why* it's important.

Here are some of the most important reasons (this isn't an exhaustive list), some of which we've touched on already:

- Improved accessibility and interoperability (content is available to assistive technologies for visitors with disabilities, and to browsers on desktop, mobile, tablet, and other devices alike)
- Improved search engine optimization (SEO)
- (Typically) lighter code and faster pages
- Easier code maintenance and styling

If you aren't familiar with *accessibility*, it's the practice of making your content available to all users, regardless of their capabilities (see www.w3.org/standards/webdesign/accessibility). Tim Berners-Lee, inventor of the Web, famously said, "The power of the Web is in its universality. Access by everyone regardless of disability is an essential aspect."

Any device with a browser is capable of displaying HTML, since it's just text. The means by which a user accesses content can vary, however. For instance, sighted users view the content, whereas a visually impaired user may increase the page or font size or use a screen reader, software that reads content aloud to them (one example of assistive technology). In some cases, screen readers announce the type of HTML element surrounding content in order to give the user context for what's to follow. For example, the user may be told that a list has been encountered before the individual list items are read aloud. Similarly, users are told when a link is encountered so they can decide whether to follow it.

Screen reader users can navigate a page in a variety of ways, such as jumping from one heading to the next via a keyboard command. This allows them to glean the key topics of a page and listen in more detail to the ones that interest them rather than having to listen to the entire page sequentially.

So you can see why good semantics make a marked difference to users with disabilities.

SEO—that is, your page's ranking in search engine results—can improve, because search engines put an emphasis on the portions of your content that are marked up in a particular way. For instance, the headings tell the search engine spider the primary topics of your page, helping the search engine determine how to index your page's content.

As you progress through the book, you'll learn why good semantics can make your code more efficient and easier to maintain and style.

Markup: Elements, Attributes, and Values

Now that you've seen some HTML, let's take a closer look at what constitutes markup.

HTML has three principal markup components: *elements*, *attributes*, and *values*. You've seen examples of each in our basic page.

Elements

Elements are like little labels that describe the different parts of a Web page: "This is a heading, that thing over there is a paragraph, and that group of links is navigation." We discussed a few elements in the previous section. Some elements have one or more attributes, which further describe the purpose and content (if any) of the element.

Elements can contain text and other elements, or they can be empty. A non-empty element consists of a *start tag* (the element's name and attributes, if any, enclosed in less-than and greater-than signs), the content, and an *end tag* (a forward slash followed by the element's name, again enclosed in less-than and greater-than signs) Ⓐ.

An *empty element* (also called a *void element*) looks like a combination start and end tag, with an initial less-than sign, the element's name followed by any attributes it may have, an optional space, an optional forward slash, and the final greater-than sign, which is required Ⓑ.

The space and forward slash before the end of an empty element are optional in HTML5. It's probably fair to say that those of us who previously coded in XHTML, which requires the forward slash to close an empty element, tend to use it in HTML5 too, though certainly others have dropped it. I include it in my code, but if you choose to omit it from yours, the page will behave

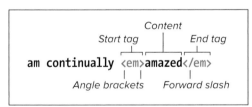

Ⓐ Here is a typical HTML element. The *start tag* and *end tag* surround the text the element describes. In this case, the word "amazed" is emphasized, thanks to the **em** element. It's customary to type your element tags in lowercase.

```
<img src="blueflax.jpg" width="300" height="175" alt="Blue Flax (Linum lewisii)" />
```
A space and forward slash

Ⓑ Empty elements, like **img** shown here, do not surround any text content (the **alt** attribute text is part of the element, not surrounded by it). They have a single tag which serves both to open and close the element. The space and forward slash at the end are optional in HTML5, but it's common to include them. However, the **>** that completes the element is required.

exactly the same. Whichever way you go, I recommend doing it consistently.

It's customary to type your element names in all lowercase, although HTML5 isn't picky here either, allowing uppercase letters instead. However, it's rare to find someone nowadays who codes in uppercase, so unless the rebel in you just can't resist, I don't recommend it. It's looked upon as a dated practice.

Attributes and Values

Attributes contain information about the content in the document, as opposed to being content itself (**C** and **D**). In HTML5, an attribute's value may optionally be enclosed in quotation marks, but it's customary to include them, so I recommend you always do so. And just as with element names, I recommend you type your attribute names in lowercase.

Although you'll find details about acceptable values for most attributes in this book, let me give you an idea of the kinds of values you'll run into as you progress.

Some attributes can accept any value, others are more limited. Perhaps the most common are those that accept enumerated or predefined values. In other words, you must select a value from a standard list of choices **E**. Be sure to write enumerated values in all lowercase letters.

---

for *is an attribute of* **label**

`<label for="email">Email Address</label>`

The value of the **for** *attribute*

C Here is a **label** element (which associates a text label with a form field) with a simple attribute-value pair. Attributes are always located inside an element's start tag. It's customary to enclose them in quotation marks.

---

href *is an attribute of* **a**   **rel** *is also an attribute of* **a**

Value for **href**   *Value for* **rel**

`<a href="http://en.wikipedia.org/wiki/Linum_lewisii" rel="external"`
`title="Learn more about Blue Flax">Blue Flax</a>`

Value for **title**

title *is an attribute of* **a**

D Some elements, like **a** shown here, can take one or more attributes, each with its own value. The order is not important. Separate each attribute-value pair from the next with a space.

`<link rel="stylesheet" media="screen" href="blueflax.css" />`

Predefined value

E Some attributes only accept specific values. For example, the **media** attribute in the **link** element can be set to **all**, **screen**, or **print**, among others, but you can't just make up a value for it like you can with the **title** attribute.

Many attributes require a number for their value, particularly those describing size and length. A numeric value never includes units, just the number. Where units are applicable, as in the width and height of an image or video, they are understood to be pixels.

Some attributes, like **href** and **src**, reference other files and thus must contain values in the form of a URL, or Uniform Resource Locator, a file's unique address on the Web. You'll learn more about URLs in the "URLs" section of this chapter.

Parents and Children

If one element contains another, it is considered to be the parent of the enclosed, or child, element. Any elements contained in the child element are considered descendants of the outer, parent element **F**. You can actually create a family tree of a Web page that shows the hierarchical relationships between each element on the page and that uniquely identifies each element.

This underlying, family tree-like structure is a key feature of HTML code. It facilitates both styling elements (which you'll begin learning about in Chapter 7) and applying JavaScript behavior to them.

It's important to note that when elements contain other elements, each element must be properly nested, that is, fully contained within its parent. Whenever you use an end tag, it should correspond to the last unclosed start tag. In other words, first open element 1, then open element 2, then close element 2, and then close element 1 **G**.

```
<article>
    <h1>The Ephemeral Blue Flax</h1>
    <img src="blueflax.jpg"... />
    <p>... continually <em>amazed</em> ... delicate <a ...>Blue Flax</a> ...</p>
</article>
```

F The **article** element is parent to the **h1**, **img**, and **p** elements. Conversely, the **h1**, **img**, and **p** elements are children (and descendants) of the **article**. The **p** element is parent to both the **em** and **a** elements. The **em** and **a** are children of the **p** and also descendants (but not children) of the **article**. In turn, **article** is their ancestor.

Correct (no overlapping lines)

```
<p>... continually <em>amazed</em> ...</p>
<p>... continually <em>amazed ...</p></em>
```

Incorrect (the sets of tags cross over each other)

G Elements must be properly nested. If you open **p** and then **em**, you must close **em** before you close **p**.

A Web Page's Text Content

The text contained within elements is perhaps a Web page's most basic ingredient. If you've ever used a word processor, you've typed some text. Text in an HTML page, however, has some important differences.

First, when a browser renders HTML it collapses extra spaces or tabs into a single space and either converts returns and line feeds into a single space or ignores them altogether (Ⓐ and Ⓑ).

Next, HTML used to be restricted to ASCII characters—basically the letters of the English language, numerals, and a few of the most common symbols. Accented characters (common to many languages of Western Europe) and many everyday symbols had to be created with special character references like **é** (for é) or **©** (for ©). See a full list at www.eliza bethcastro.com/html/extras/entities.html.

Unicode mitigates a lot of issues with special characters. It's standard practice to encode pages in UTF-8, as in the basic page Ⓒ, and save HTML files with the same encoding (see "Saving Your Web Page" in Chapter 2). I recommend you do the same.

Because Unicode is a superset of ASCII—it's everything ASCII is, and a lot more—Unicode-encoded documents are compatible with existing browsers and editors, except particularly old ones. Browsers that don't understand Unicode will interpret the ASCII portion of the document properly, while browsers that do understand Unicode will display the non-ASCII portion as well. Even so, it's still common to use character references at times, such as for the copyright symbol since it's easy to both remember and type **©** Ⓐ.

Ⓐ A page's text content (highlighted) is mostly anything besides the markup. In this example, note that each sentence is separated by at least one carriage return, and some words are separated by several spaces (just to emphasize the point about collapsing returns and spaces). Also, it includes a special character reference (**©**) for the copyright symbol to ensure that it is properly displayed no matter the encoding in which you save this document.

```
<p>I am continually <em>amazed</em> at the
→ beautiful,    delicate Blue Flax that
→ somehow took hold in my garden.

They are awash in        color every
→ morning, yet not a single flower
→ remains by the afternoon.



They are the very definition of
→ ephemeral.</p>
<p>&copy; Blue Flax Society.</p>
```

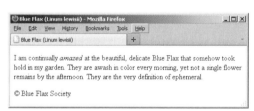

Ⓑ Note that when you view the document with a browser, the extra returns and spaces are ignored and the character reference is replaced by the corresponding symbol (©).

Ⓒ Specify your document's character encoding directly after the **head** start tag. The **charset** attribute sets the encoding type.

```
<!DOCTYPE html>
<html lang="en">
<head>
    <meta charset="utf-8" />
    <title>Blue Flax (Linum lewisii)</title>
</head>
<body>
...
</body>
</html>
```

A In our basic HTML document, there is a reference to an image file called `blueflax.jpg`, which the browser will request, load, and display when it loads the rest of the page. The page also includes a link to another page about Blue Flax.

```
...
<article>
    <h1>The Ephemeral Blue Flax</h1>

    <img src="blueflax.jpg" width="300"
    → height="175" alt="Blue Flax (Linum
    → lewisii)" />

    <p>I am continually <em>amazed</em> at
    → the beautiful, delicate <a href=
    → "http://en.wikipedia.org/wiki/Linum_
    → lewisii" rel="external" title="Learn
    → more about the Blue Flax">Blue Flax
    → </a> that somehow took hold in my
    → garden. They are awash in color every
    → morning, yet not a single flower
    → remains by the afternoon. They are the
    → very definition of ephemeral.</p>
</article>
...
```

B Images and other non-text content are referenced from a Web page, and the browser displays them together with the text.

Links, Images, and Other Non-Text Content

Of course, part of what makes the Web so vibrant are the links from one page to another, and the images, videos, music, animations, and more. Instead of actually enclosing the external files, such as videos, in the HTML file, these files are saved independently and are simply referenced from within the page **A**. Since the reference is nothing more than text, the HTML file remains nearly universally accessible.

Browsers can handle links and images (except in text-only browsers) without skipping a beat **B**. However, they can't necessarily handle every other kind of file. If you reference a file that your visitor's browser doesn't understand, the browser will often try to find a plugin or helper application—some appropriate program on the visitor's computer—that is capable of opening that kind of file.

You can also give browsers extra information about how to render content with a plugin if it requires it, or how to download the plugin if the visitor doesn't already have it on their computer.

All this business about downloading and installing plugins disrupts a user's experience on your site, assuming they stick around. Plugins can also introduce performance problems because they aren't a native part of the browser.

Flash, for instance, has been the most widespread plugin for years. No doubt you've watched an online video played through Flash at some point and experienced your computer slow down or the occasional browser crash (or both).

HTML5 attempts to mitigate many of these issues by introducing native media playback in the browser via the **audio** and **video** elements. Unfortunately, there's been debate among the browser vendors about which media formats to support, so you can't always do away with plugins altogether yet. But it's a start.

You'll learn more about images in Chapter 5, and go over plugins, HTML5's media elements, and more in Chapter 17.

File Names

Like any other text document, a Web page has a file name that identifies itself to you, your visitors, and your visitors' Web browsers. There are a few tips to keep in mind when assigning file names to your Web pages that will help you organize your files, make it easier for your visitors to find and access your pages, ensure that their browsers view the pages correctly, and improve SEO (Ⓐ and Ⓑ).

Use Lowercase File Names

Since the file name you choose for your Web page determines what your visitors will have to type in order to get to your page, you can save your visitors from inadvertent typos (and headaches) by using only lowercase letters in your file names. It's also a big help when you create links between your pages yourself. If all your file names have only small letters, it's just one less thing you'll have to worry about.

Separate Words with a Dash

Never include spaces between words in your file names. Instead, use a dash, for example, `company-history.html` and `my-favorite-movies.html`. You'll come across the occasional site that uses underscores ("_") instead, but they aren't recommended, because dashes are preferred by search engines.

Use the Proper Extension

The principal way a browser knows that it should read a text document as a Web page is by looking at its extension. Although `.htm` also works, `.html` is customary, so I recommend you use that as your extension. If the page has some other extension, such as `.txt`, the browser will treat it as text and show all your nice code to the visitor.

> **TIP** Be aware that neither Mac OS nor Windows always reveals a document's real extension. Change your folder options, if necessary, so you can see extensions.

File name, in all lowercase letters *Extension*

`buckminster-fuller.html`

Separate each word with a dash

File names with capital letters are a pain to type and to communicate

`Buckminster_Fuller.html`

Underscores are not as good for search engine optimization as dashes

Ⓐ Remember to use all lowercase letters for your file names, separate words with a dash, and add the .html extension. Mixing upper- and lowercase letters makes it harder for your visitors to type the proper address and find your page.

Correct approach

`http://www.yoursite.com/notable-architects/20th-century/buckminster-fuller.html`

`http://www.yoursite.com/NotableArchitects/20th_CENTURY/Buckminster_Fuller.html`

Incorrect approach

Ⓑ Use all lowercase letters and dashes for your directories and folders as well. The key is consistency. If you don't use uppercase letters, your visitors (and you) don't have to waste time wondering "Now, was that a capital B or a small one?"

URLs

Uniform Resource Locator, or URL, is a fancy name for address. It contains information about where a file is and what a browser should do with it. Each file on the Internet has a unique URL.

The first part of the URL is called the *scheme*. It tells the browser how to deal with the file that it is about to open. The most common scheme you will see is HTTP, or Hypertext Transfer Protocol. It is used to access Web pages **A**.

The second part of the URL is the name of the server where the file is located, followed by the path that leads to the file, and the file's name itself. Sometimes, a URL omits a file name and ends with a path, which may or may not include a trailing forward slash **B**. In this case, the URL refers to the default file in the last directory in the path, typically called **index.html**.

Other common schemes are **https**, for secure Web pages; **ftp** (File Transfer Protocol), for downloading files **C**; **mailto**, for sending email **D**; and **file**, for accessing files on a local hard disk or local file sharing networks (you won't have occasion to use the **file** scheme very often, if at all) **E**.

A scheme is generally followed by a colon and two forward slashes. **mailto** and **news** are exceptions; these take only a colon.

Notice that the **file** scheme is followed by a colon and three slashes. That's because the host, which in other schemes goes between the second and third slashes, is assumed to be the local computer. Always type schemes in lowercase letters.

Of these schemes, you will use **http** and **mailto** most frequently. The others are for specialized cases.

Scheme Server name Path File name

"http://www.site.com/tofu/index.html"

A Your basic URL contains a scheme, server name, path, and file name.

Trailing forward slash

"http://www.site.com/tofu/"

B A URL with a trailing forward slash and no file name points to the default file in the last directory named (in this case, the **tofu** directory). The most common default file name is **index.html**. So, this URL and the one from the previous example point to the same page.

Scheme Server name Path File name

"ftp://ftp.site.com/pub/proposal.pdf"

C When the user clicks this URL, the browser will begin an FTP transfer of the file **proposal.pdf**.

Scheme Email address

"mailto:somename@somedomain.com"

D A URL for an email address includes the **mailto** scheme followed by a colon but no forward slashes, and then the email address itself.

Scheme Drive letter Path and file name

"file:///c|/path/home.htm"

Vertical bar

E To reference a file on a local Windows machine, use the **file** scheme. For Macintosh, use **file:///Harddisk/path/filename**. No vertical bar is required. (This sometimes works for Windows as well.)

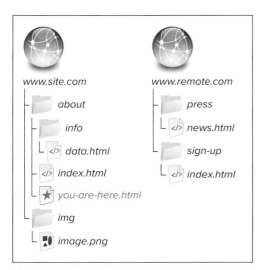

F The document that contains the URLs (**you-are-here.html** in this case) is the reference point for relative URLs. In other words, relative URLs are relative to that file's location on the server. Absolute URLs will work no matter where they are located, because they always contain the full URL to a resource.

Absolute URLs

URLs can be either absolute or relative. An *absolute URL* shows the entire path to the file, including the scheme, the server name, the complete path, and the file name itself **F**. An absolute URL is analogous to a complete street address, including name, street and number, city, state, zip code, and country. No matter where a letter is sent from, the post office will be able to find the recipient. In terms of URLs, this means that the location of the absolute URL itself has no bearing on the location of the actual file referenced—whether it is in a Web page on your server or another server, an absolute URL to a particular file will look exactly the same.

When you're referencing a file from someone else's server, you'll always use an absolute URL. You'll also need to use absolute URLs for FTP sites or, generally, any kind of URL that doesn't use an HTTP protocol.

Table 1.1 describes how you would access various files from **you-are-here.html**—both those on the same site (site.com) as the page and on another site (remote.com)—as a way of illustrating the difference between relative and absolute URLs.

TABLE 1.1 Absolute URLs vs. Relative URLs

File name	Absolute URL (can be used anywhere)	Relative URL (only works in you-are-here.html)
index.html	http://www.site.com/about/index.html	index.html
data.html	http://www.site.com/about/info/data.html	/info/data.html
image.png	http://www.site.com/img/image.png	../img/image.png
news.html	http://www.remote.com/press/news.html	(none: use absolute)
index.html	http://www.remote.com/sign-up/index.html	(none: use absolute)

Relative URLs

To give you directions to my neighbor's house, instead of giving her complete address I might just say, "it's three doors down on the right." This is a relative address—where it points to depends on where the information originates. With the same information in a different city, you'd never find my neighbor.

In the same way, a relative URL describes the location of the desired file with reference to the location of the file that contains the URL reference itself. So, you might have the URL say something like "link to the xyz page that's in the same directory as this page."

The relative URL for a file that is in the same directory as the current page (that is, the one containing the URL in question) is simply the file name and extension **G**. You create the URL for a file in a subdirectory of the current directory by typing the name of the subdirectory followed by a forward slash and then the name and extension of the desired file **H**.

To reference a file in a directory at a higher level of the file hierarchy, use two periods and a forward slash **I**. You can combine and repeat the two periods and forward slash to reference any file on the same server or drive as the current file.

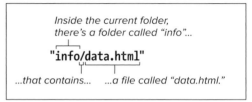

Inside the current folder,
there's a file called "index.html"...

`"index.html"`

G The relative URL to link to a file in the same folder (see **F**). Only the file's name and extension are required in the URL, rather than preceding those with `http://www.site.com/about/` (the folder in which both files live).

Inside the current folder,
there's a folder called "info"...

`"info/data.html"`

...that contains...   *...a file called "data.html."*

H To reference a file (`data.html`, in this example) that is within a folder inside the current folder (see **F**), add the sub-folder's name and a forward slash in front of the file name.

The folder that contains the current folder...

...contains...   *...a folder called "img"*

`"../img/image.png"`

...that contains...   *...a file called "image.png"...*

I This file, as you can see in **F**, is in a folder (*img*) that sits alongside the current folder (*about*) in the site's root directory. In that case, you use two periods and a forward slash to go up a level, and then note the subdirectory, followed by a forward slash, followed by the file name. (In normal practice, you'd choose a more descriptive image file name than `image.png`, which is deliberately generic for the example.)

Alternatively, if your files are on a Web server, you can avoid cumbersome file paths such as **`../../img/family/vacation.jpg`** by first jumping straight to your site's root and then drilling down from there to the targeted file. A single forward slash at the beginning achieves this, so the *root relative* URL in this case would be **`/img/family/vacation.jpg`** (assuming the `img` folder sits in the site's root folder, which is customary). Again, this only works on a Web server, like at the hosting provider that serves your site or one you're running locally on your machine (Apache is the most popular choice for that).

If you aren't developing your site locally on a server, then generally you'll want to use relative URLs (except when pointing to files on someone else's server, of course). They'll make it easy to move your pages from a local system to a server. As long as the relative position of each file remains constant, you won't have to change any of the paths, so the links will work correctly.

Key Takeaways

The basics of HTML and some key best practices provide the foundation for building effective Web sites. Let's revisit the key takeaways:

- A Web page is primarily made up of three components: text content, references to other files, and markup.

- HTML markup is composed of elements, attributes, and values.

- It's customary to write your HTML in all lowercase (DOCTYPE is an exception), surround your attribute values with quotes, and close empty elements with a space and a forward slash (/).

- Always begin your HTML documents with the DOCTYPE declaration:

  `<!DOCTYPE html>`

- A page's content goes in the **body** element. Instructions primarily intended for the browser and search engines are before that, mostly in the **head**.

- Mark up your content with semantic HTML and without regard for how it should appear in a browser.

- Semantic HTML improves accessibility and can make your site more efficient, and easier to maintain and style.

- CSS controls the presentation of HTML content.

- Each browser's own style sheet dictates the default presentation of HTML. You can overwrite these rules with your own CSS.

- Create file and folder names in all lowercase, and separate words with a dash instead of a space or underscore.

Next you'll learn about how to work with Web page files.

Working with Web Page Files

Before you start writing HTML elements and attributes, it's important to know how to create the files in which you'll use such code. In this chapter, you'll learn how to create, edit, and save Web page files. I'll also touch on some planning and organizational considerations.

If you can't stand waiting any longer and already know how to create the actual files, skip ahead to Chapter 3 where I begin to explain the HTML code itself.

In This Chapter

Planning Your Site

Although you can just jump in and start writing Web pages right away, it's a good idea to first think about and plan your site **A**. That way, you'll give yourself direction, and you'll need to do less reorganizing later.

To plan your site:

- Figure out why you're creating this site. What do you want to convey?

- Think about your audience. How can you tailor your content to appeal to this audience?

- How many pages will it need? What sort of structure would you like it to have? Do you want visitors to go through your site in a particular sequence, or do you want to make it easy for them to explore in any direction?

- Sketch out your site on paper.

- Devise a simple, consistent naming convention for your pages, images, and other external files (see "File Names" in Chapter 1).

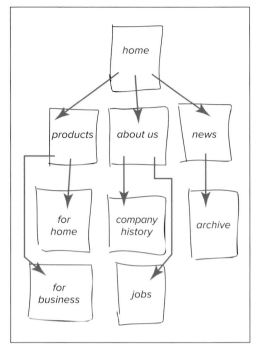

A Sketching out your site and thinking about what it might contain can help you decide what sort of structure it needs.

TIP Don't overdo the planning phase of your site. At some point, you've got to dig in and start writing content and code.

TIP If you're not very familiar with the Web, do some surfing first to get an idea of the possibilities. You might start with the sites of some of your competitors.

TIP It's common, but not required, to map your site's folder structure to how it's organized on paper **A**. See "Organizing Files."

TIP See Erin Kissane's article "A Checklist for Content Work" (www.alistapart.com/articles/a-checklist-for-content-work/) for ideas about how you might approach crafting your site's content. It's a taste of her book, which elaborates on the subject of content strategy.

TIP Jason Beaird's *The Principles of Beautiful Web Design* (SitePoint, 2010) may interest you if you're a non-designer or novice designer looking for guidance on how to design an attractive, effective site.

Creating a New Web Page

You don't need any special tools to create a Web page. You can use any text editor, even Notepad (and ©), which is included with Windows, or TextWrangler (Ⓐ and Ⓑ), which is a free download for OS X (www.barebones.com/products/textwrangler). (Macs include an editor called TextEdit, but it has a bug in some versions of OS X that makes it to difficult to work with HTML files.)

To create a new Web page:

1. Open any text editor.
2. Choose File > New to create a new, blank document Ⓐ.
3. Create the HTML content as explained in the rest of this book, starting with Chapter 3.
4. Be sure to save your file as directed in "Saving Your Web Page."

Ⓐ Open your text editor. Type your HTML in the blank document that appears, or choose File > New. The exact menu option may vary slightly. If you're using TextWrangler (Mac), it's File > New > Text Document, as shown (top). The other image is Notepad (Windows) (bottom).

Ⓑ On a Mac, you can use TextWrangler to write the HTML code for your page. See the tips for a list of Mac editors with more robust features for writing code.

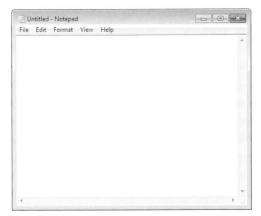

Ⓒ This is Notepad, the most basic program Windows users can use to create HTML pages. Several others are available (see the tips).

TIP There are various text editors for OS X and Windows that are specifically tailored for coding HTML (and CSS). They have code hinting and code completion features to help you code more accurately and quickly, they highlight code to make it easier to distinguish between HTML elements and the text content you've written within them, and they have assorted other helpful features; Notepad doesn't have any of them. Some free HTML editors are available, but the others are usually worth the investment and often include a free trial version you can test before making a purchase.

TIP Some popular editors for OS X are BBEdit (www.barebones.com/products/bbedit/), Coda (www.panic.com/coda/), Espresso (http://macrabbit.com/espresso/), Sublime Text (www.sublimetext.com), and TextMate (http://macromates.com). (TextWrangler is commonly thought of as "BBEdit Lite".) TextMate is the most popular of these, though it has seen the competition encroach on its user base. Sublime Text is also available on Windows, as are E Text Editor (www.e-texteditor.com), Notepad++ (http://notepad-plus-plus.org), and many others. Search online for "HTML editor" to find more.

TIP If you use an editor such as one mentioned in the previous tip, the process is similar for creating a new page. And to edit an existing page, just choose File > Open from your text editor of choice and open the file (see "Editing Web Pages"). Use the rest of this book to add your own HTML and CSS to create the page you want.

TIP Don't use word processors, like Microsoft Word, to code your HTML pages. They may add unnecessary or invalid code to your files.

Saving Your Web Page

You create Web pages with a text editor, but they are meant to be viewed with multiple browsers on multiple platforms. To be accessible to all of these different programs, you save Web pages in a universal "text only" format—without any of the proprietary formatting that a word processor might apply.

So that browsers (and servers) recognize Web pages and know to interpret the markup they contain, Web page files have the .html or .htm extension in their file names; this also distinguishes these files from plain text files that are not Web pages. Although both work, it's customary to use the .html extension, so I recommend you use it for your files.

Because of that extension, a Web page's icon matches the system's default browser—not the editor with which the file was written . Indeed, when you double-click a Web page file, it is opened in a browser, not a text editor. This may be great for testing a page in a browser, but it adds an extra step to editing Web pages (see "Editing Web Pages").

To summarize, when you save your Web page, you must save it in text-only format with either the .html or.htm extension.

Sales.xlsx
Microsoft Office Excel Worksh...
9 KB

webpage.html
HTML File
1 KB

Ⓐ An Excel worksheet has the .xlsx extension and is identified with the Excel icon (top). If you double-click it, it is displayed in Excel. A Web page file, no matter the text editor you create it with, has the .html or .htm extension and is identified with the default browser's icon (Firefox, in this case). If you double-click it, it is displayed in your default browser (not in the text editor).

B Choose File > Save As from your text editor.

C In Notepad, give your file a name with the .html or .htm extension, choose Text Documents from the "Save as type" drop-down menu, make sure Encoding is set to UTF-8 (see the last tip), and click Save. The options may be different (but similar) in another text editor.

D In TextWrangler, give your file a name and choose a location to save it. TextWrangler defaults to UTF-8 (which is what you'll want, except in special cases), but you can make a different choice from the Encoding drop-down menu (see the last tip). Click Save to save the file.

To save your Web page:

1. Once you've created your Web page, choose File > Save As from your text editor **B**.

2. In the dialog that appears, choose Plain Text or Text Document (or however your program words it) for the format.

3. Give the document the .html (prefer-ably) or .htm extension. (This is very important!)

4. Choose the folder in which to save the Web page.

5. Click Save (**C** and **D**).

TIP It doesn't matter whether you use .html or .htm, though .html is recommended because it's the common choice. Whichever you use, be consistent, because using the same extension will make it easier to remember your URLs later.

continues on next page

TIP Some text editors on Windows may add their default extension to your file name, even if you've already specified .html or .htm. (Note that this shouldn't be a problem with most editors designed specifically for editing HTML pages.) Your file, now named `webpage.html.txt`, won't be properly viewed in a browser. To make matters worse, Windows often hides extensions so that the problem is not completely obvious, especially to the uninitiated. There are two solutions. The first is to enclose your file name in double quotes when you save your document the first time. This should keep the extra extension from being added. Next, you can tell Windows to display file extensions **E**, so you can see the offending one and remove it from your file name.

TIP When you choose a text-only format, your file is usually saved with your system's default character encoding. If you want to create Web pages in another encoding (perhaps to include special symbols or text in other languages), you'll have to use a text editor that lets you choose the encoding. Typically, UTF-8 is the best encoding choice. If your editor has an option to save files encoded as "UTF-8, no BOM," "UTF-8, without BOM," or something similar, choose that. Otherwise, choose UTF-8 **F**. In some cases, an editor's UTF-8 mode doesn't include the BOM even if it doesn't explicitly note that fact in its encoding menu. (See http://en.wikipedia.org/wiki/Byte_order_mark if you're curious about BOM's meaning. Be prepared to be enthralled!)

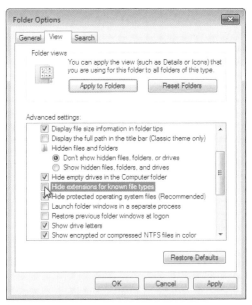

E From Windows Explorer, choose either Organize > Folder and search options or Tools > Folder Options (depending on your version of Windows) to view this dialog. It may look different depending on your version of Windows. Click the View tab and scroll down until you see "Hide extensions for known file types." Make sure it is deselected if you want to be able to see a file's extension (like .html) on the desktop.

F Many text editors let you choose the encoding for your file, so that you can save symbols and characters from different languages in the same document. UTF-8 is the recommended encoding in most instances. Choose the UTF-8 no BOM option if it's available in your editor. Otherwise, choose UTF-8. Some editors (like TextWrangler, shown here) default to it.

Save As: index.html

A Save the file as `index.html` in order to designate the file as the default page that should be opened in that directory.

B When the visitor types the path to the directory but omits the file name itself, the file with the default name is used. I typed http://bruceontheloose.com/htmlcss/examples/antoni-gaudi/ in this example. If I had typed http://bruceontheloose.com/htmlcss/examples/antoni-gaudi/index.html instead, the same page would have loaded.

Specifying a Default Page or Homepage

Most Web servers have a system for recognizing a default page in each folder, based on the name of the file. In almost all cases, `index.html` is recognized as the default page **A**, though servers typically will then look for file names like `index.htm` and `default.htm` if `index.html` doesn't exist. If your visitors type a URL with a directory but don't specify a file name, the default file is used **B**.

The default page (typically `index.html`) that you create at the top level of your Web directory (often called the *root*) is your site's homepage. This is the page that will appear when your visitors type your domain with no additional path information: www.*yourdomain*.com.

Similarly, you can create a default page for any and every directory on your site. For instance, the landing page (that is, the main page) for a `/products/` or `/about-us/` directory in your site would also be called `index.html`, but it would exist in its specific folder. (A directory is just a folder, like the ones you see on your computer's drive.) Visitors typically access these sections of your site from your homepage or via main navigation that exists on every page.

continues on next page

To specify a homepage for your site or a landing page for a directory within it:

Save your file as `index.html` (see "Saving Your Web Page") in the desired folder. (If `index.html` doesn't work as the default page on your site's server when you upload it per Chapter 21, consult your Web hosting provider.)

TIP If you don't have a default page in each directory, some servers may show a list of the directory's contents (which you may or may not want to reveal to your visitors). To keep those prying eyes out, create a default page for every directory on your site that contains HTML pages. Alternatively, you can change the server setting so the list of files is hidden (you can also show it if it's already hidden). Hiding the list is advisable for folders that contain assets, such as your images, media files, style sheets, and JavaScript files. Ask your Web hosting provider for instructions on how to do this.

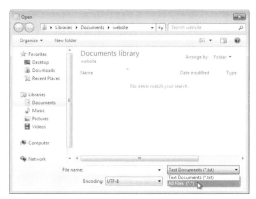

A Some text editors in Windows, like Notepad, can't automatically see HTML files. Choose All Files (or a similar option) if necessary to view files with any extension.

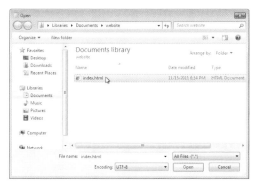

B Once files with any extension are displayed, you can choose the desired HTML file and click Open.

C In Windows, you can also right-click the document's icon or file name and then choose Edit or Open With in the pop-up menu that appears. On a Mac, right-click the icon, select Open With in the pop-up menu, and then choose the desired text editor.

Editing Web Pages

Because Web pages are most often viewed with a Web browser, when you double-click them on the desktop the default browser cheerily opens up and displays them. If you want to edit the Web page, you'll have to manually open it in your text editor.

To edit Web pages:

1. Open your text editor.

2. Choose File > Open.

3. Navigate to the directory that contains the desired file.

4. If you don't see your file listed, choose the All Files (or similar description) option (**A** and **B**). The name and location may vary slightly from program to program and platform to platform.

5. Click Open. Your file is ready to edit.

TIP Once you've made changes to an already saved document, you can usually simply choose File > **Save to save the changes, without having to worry about the format (as described in "Saving Your Web Page").**

Organizing Files

Before you have too many files, it's a good idea to figure out where you're going to put them. It's customary (but not required) to create a folder for each main section within your site, allowing you to group related HTML pages together.

To organize your files:

1. Create a central folder or directory to hold all the material that will be available on your Web site. On the Mac, choose File > New Folder in the Finder . In Windows, from the desktop (or within a folder of your choosing), right-click and choose New > Folder . Give the folder a name.

2. Create sub-folders in a way that reflects the organization of your Web site ( and). For instance, you may decide to create a separate folder for each section of your site, along with individual sub-folders within those as necessary.

3. It is common to create a top-level folder for your site's images and optionally add sub-folders to help you organize your images by section or other criteria. Another approach is to create a top-level folder named **Assets** (or something similar) and put your images folder in *that*, along with folders for other assets, such as video, style sheets, and so on. (You'll learn about style sheets beginning with Chapter 7.)

> **TIP** Use short, descriptive names for your files and folders, preferably separating words in a name with a dash (*not* a space). Use all lowercase letters so that your URLs are easier to type and thus your pages are easier to reach. For more details on how to create good file names, consult "File Names" in Chapter 1.

Ⓐ On a Mac, choose New Folder and then give the folder a name. Create a separate folder for each section of your site.

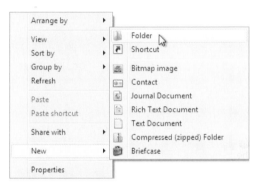

Ⓑ In Windows, from the desktop or Windows Explorer, right-click and choose New > Folder.

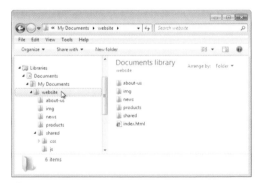

Ⓒ You can divide the folder into sub-folders if needed.

A From the desired browser (this is Firefox), choose File > Open File. In Internet Explorer, it's called File > Open.

B Choose the file that you want to open, and click the Open button.

C The page appears in the browser. Check it over carefully to see if it's coming out the way you planned.

Viewing Your Page in a Browser

Once you've created a page, you'll want to see what it looks like in a browser. In fact, since you don't know which browser your visitors will be using—and browsers don't always render pages exactly the same way—it's recommended to look at the page in several browsers.

To view your page in a browser:

1. Open a browser.

2. Choose File > Open, > Open File, or > Open Page (just not Open Location), depending on the browser **A**.

3. In the new dialog that appears, navigate to the folder on your computer that contains the desired Web page, select the page, and click Open **B**. The page is displayed in the browser **C** just as it will appear when you actually publish it on your Web server (see Chapter 21). These steps may vary slightly in different browsers.

TIP You can (usually) also double-click a Web page's icon to view it in a browser. Or, if you already have a browser open, you can drag the file icon or file name and drop it in the browser window. That's often the easiest way to view a page in a browser once you get the hang of it.

continues on next page

TIP Some modern browsers don't have a menu option equivalent to File > Open for opening a page. Try the drag-and-drop method described in the previous tip instead.

TIP If your Web page does not appear in the Open dialog, make sure that you have saved it as text-only and given it the .html or .htm extension (see "Saving Your Web Page").

TIP You don't have to close the document in the text editor before you view it with a browser, but you do have to save it. If you make a change to the page in your text editor after you've opened it in a browser, save the file again and use the browser's reload button to refresh the page. (You could follow the steps you used to view the page in the browser initially, but that would take longer.)

TIP Your visitors won't be able to view your Web site until you publish it to your Web server (see Chapter 21).

A All desktop browsers have a menu command that lets you view a page's HTML code. The name varies from View Source to Page Source (in Firefox, shown) to similar names. (In Chrome, it's Tools > View page source.)

B Most browsers will also let you right-click the page and then choose the View Source command (whatever it's called) from the menu that appears. Chrome is shown. This is often the easiest way to view source, because it can be hard to find the option in the main menu or sub-menu.

C Modern browsers display the code in their own tab or window (as shown), whereas older browsers may show it in a specified text editor. Colors distinguish page content from HTML elements, attributes, and attribute values. This is called *syntax highlighting*. The line numbers on the left are *not* part of the HTML code, and not all browsers show them in their View Source modes. They are just an indicator that Chrome includes in its View Source window.

The Inspiration of Others

One of the easiest ways to expand your HTML fluency is by looking at how other page developers and designers have created *their* pages. Luckily, HTML code is easy to view and learn from. However, text content, graphics, sounds, video, style sheets, and other external files may be copyrighted. As a general rule, use other's pages for inspiration for your HTML, and then create your own content.

To view other designers' HTML code with View Source:

1. Open a Web page with any browser.

2. Choose View Source (or the appropriate choice for a particular browser) (**A** and **B**). The HTML code will be displayed **C**.

3. If desired, save the file for further study.

To view other designers' HTML code with developer tools:

Another way to view a page's source is with a browser's developer tools. The tools are different for each browser vendor, but they all have some features that overlap.

These tools show a more interactive view of the source code. You can inspect the HTML and CSS for specific parts of a page, edit it in the browser, and see the changes reflected in the page immediately. And you can use them on any site, not just your own. The changes are temporary—they don't write over the actual HTML and CSS files the page loaded. This is valuable for learning, because you can see how a particular effect was achieved or fiddle with

the code to see what happens with no fear of damaging anything.

See the "Browser Developer Tools" sidebar in Chapter 20 for information about the browser developer tools for both modern and older browsers.

TIP **There's no rule about who gets to put a site on the Web. That's what's so great about it—it's an open medium with a relatively low barrier to entry. You can be a novice, an expert, or anywhere in between. Keep this in mind when you review the code from other sites. If some of the code looks fishy, don't assume its author knows better than you just because their site is on the Web. There are plenty of sites that serve as great examples of coding best practices, and there are plenty of others that are, shall we say, less than ideal. So keep a critical eye, and check this book and other resources when in doubt about the appropriateness of a particular technique.**

TIP **You can also save the source code by copying it from the View Source window and pasting it into your text editor. Then you can save the file.**

TIP **You can also save the source code and typically many of its assets (such as images) by selecting File > Save As (or File > Save Page As) in most browsers. However, the browser may rewrite portions of the code when saving the page, so it won't be exactly the same as if you'd saved it using the previous tip.**

TIP **For viewing the CSS in a Web page, see "The Inspiration of Others: CSS" in Chapter 8.**

3

Basic HTML Structure

This chapter covers the HTML elements you need to establish the foundation and structure of your documents. That is, the outline and primary semantic containers for your content.

You'll learn about:

- Starting a Web page
- The HTML5 document outline
- The **h1–h6**, **hgroup**, **header**, **nav**, **article**, **section**, **aside**, **footer**, and **div** elements (most of which are new in HTML5)
- How ARIA **role** attributes can improve your page's accessibility
- Applying a **class** or **id** to elements
- Applying the **title** attribute to elements
- Adding comments to your code

In This Chapter

Creating a clear and consistent structure not only sets up a good semantic foundation for your page, but also makes it that much easier to apply styles to your document with Cascading Style Sheets (CSS) (coverage begins in Chapter 7).

If you haven't done so already, I strongly suggest you read Chapter 1 before continuing. It shows a simple HTML page and explains some of the basic concepts. Since that is your first glimpse at a Web page, I'll repeat some (but not all) of the information here and assume you're familiar with the rest so you can build on those ideas.

Also, if you've read my book *The HTML Pocket Guide*, some of this material will be familiar to you.

Ⓐ Here's the foundation of every HTML page. The indentation doesn't matter, but the structure is crucial. In this example, the default language (per the **lang** attribute) is set to **en** for English. The character encoding is set to UTF-8.

```
<!DOCTYPE html>
<html lang="en">
<head>
    <meta charset="UTF-8" />
    <title></title>
</head>
<body>


</body>
</html>
```

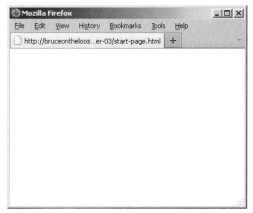

Ⓑ The minimal HTML foundation code as viewed in Firefox. As you can see, there's nothing to see! However, you'll start adding content soon enough.

Starting Your Web Page

At its most basic level, each of your HTML documents should contain the following components, as shown in Ⓐ:

- The DOCTYPE
- The **html** element (with the **lang** attribute, which is optional but recommended)
- The **head** element
- The character encoding in a **meta** element
- The **title** element (you'll add its content in a bit)
- The **body** element

This is the HTML equivalent of a blank sheet of paper, since it doesn't have any content in the **body** Ⓑ.

So, before you add any content or other information, you need to set up the foundation of your page:

To start an HTML5 page:

1. Type **<!DOCTYPE html>** to declare your page as an HTML5 document. (See the "HTML5's Improved DOCTYPE" sidebar for information relative to previous versions of HTML.)

2. Type **<html lang="*language-code*">** to begin the actual HTML portion of your document, where *language-code* is the language code that matches the default language of your page's content. For instance, **<html lang="es">** for English or **<html lang="fr">** for French. See www.bruceontheloose.com/references/language-codes.html for a list of available language codes.

continues on next page

3. Type **`<head>`** to begin the document head of your page.

4. Type **`<meta charset="UTF-8" />`** to declare the character encoding of your document as UTF-8. If you prefer, you may also type it as **`utf-8`** in your HTML. Also, the space and forward slash are optional, so **`<meta charset="UTF-8">`** works just the same. (Character encodings besides UTF-8 are valid too, but UTF-8 is the most versatile, so it's rare that you'd need to deviate.)

5. Type **`<title></title>`**. This will contain your page's title. You'll add title text in the "Creating a Title" section.

6. Type **`</head>`** to end the document head of your page.

7. Type **`<body>`** to start the body of your page. This is where your content will go (eventually).

8. Leave a few blank lines for creating your page content, which you'll do throughout the rest of this book.

9. Type **`</body>`** to end the body.

10. Type **`</html>`** to end your page.

That's a pretty healthy number of steps, but since all your pages will start that way, you could use a single HTML page as the template from which to begin every page, saving yourself some typing. In fact, most code editors allow you to specify the starter code for each new page, making it even easier. If you don't find a Settings or Preferences menu in your editor, search its Help section.

A page's two sections: head and body

Just as a quick recap of what you learned in Chapter 1, HTML pages are divided into two sections: the **head** and the **body** Ⓐ. The DOCTYPE, which starts each page, is a preamble of sorts.

The document **head** is where you define the title of your page, include information about your page for search engines like Google, load style sheets, and occasionally load JavaScript files (though, for performance reasons, it's preferable most of the time to load JavaScript right before the end **`</body>`** tag at the bottom of your page). You'll see examples of these as you progress through the book. Except for the **title**, which you'll cover more in just a bit, the content of the **head** is not visible to users when they visit your page.

The **body** element encloses your page's content, including text, images, forms, audio, video, and other interactive content. In other words, the stuff your visitors see. There are several chapters dedicated to HTML's content-related elements, some of which you'll get an early look at in this chapter.

TIP The HTML5 DOCTYPE makes sure browsers render in a reliable mode and tells the HTML validators to judge your code against HTML5's allowed elements and syntax. HTML validators are discussed in Chapter 20.

TIP HTML5's DOCTYPE isn't case sensitive. For instance, some choose to type it as `<!doctype html>`, but it's probably more common to use `<!DOCTYPE html>` **A**.

TIP The `html` element, which follows the DOCTYPE, must enclose all other elements in your page **A**.

TIP Be sure your code editor is configured to save files as UTF-8 to match the character encoding specified in the code by `<meta charset="UTF-8" />` **A**. (Or if you've specified a different `charset`, save your files in that.) Not all editors will save your pages as UTF-8 by default, but most do allow you to choose the encoding from a menu or in a panel (see "Saving your Web Pages" in Chapter 2). Without the UTF-8 setting in place, you may occasionally see funny characters in your content instead of an intended letter such as an accented i or an n with a tilde (~).

TIP You don't have to indent the code that is nested in the `head` element **A**. However, the benefit of doing so is that you can see at a glance where the `head` begins, what's in it, and where it ends. It's not unusual for the `head` to become very long in some pages.

HTML5's Improved DOCTYPE

Oh, how much simpler it is to start your Web page now that HTML5 is here. HTML5's DOCTYPE is refreshingly short, especially when compared to the DOCTYPEs of yore.

In the days of HTML 4 and XHTML 1.0, there were several DOCTYPEs from which to choose, each signifying both the version of HTML and whether it was in Transitional or Strict mode. You invariably had to copy them from somewhere else because they were too convoluted to remember.

For instance, here's the DOCTYPE for XHTML Strict documents.

```
<!DOCTYPE html PUBLIC "-//W3C//DTD XHTML 1.0 Transitional//EN" "http://www.w3.org/
→ TR/xhtml1/DTD/xhtml1-strict.dtd">
```

Gobbledygook.

Luckily, all browsers—both old and new—understand HTML5's DOCTYPE, so you can stick with it for all your pages and forget the other ones ever existed. (The only time they might be relevant is if you inherit an older site and the owner doesn't permit you to change the DOCTYPE to the HTML5 version.)

Creating a Title

The HTML foundation code in the previous section had `<title></title>` as a placeholder until it was time to discuss **title** further. Now's the time!

Each HTML page must have a **title** element. A title should be short, descriptive, and unique to each page 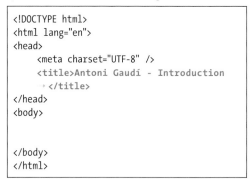. In most browsers, the title appears in the title bar of the window (Chrome is one exception) 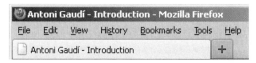. It also appears on the page's tab in browsers that support tabbed browsing—in other words, all the major browsers released in the past several years. The title also shows in your visitors' browser history lists and bookmarks .

Perhaps even more importantly, the title is used by search engines like Google, Bing, and Yahoo! both to get a sense of your page's content and typically as the link that appears in their search results .

In short, make your **title** unique for each page to improve search engine results and make your visitors' experience better.

C The title also appears in your visitor's History pane (shown), Favorites list, and Bookmarks list.

A The **title** element must be placed in the **head** section. Place it after the **meta** element that specifies the character encoding.

```
<!DOCTYPE html>
<html lang="en">
<head>
    <meta charset="UTF-8" />
    <title>Antoni Gaudí - Introduction
     '</title>
</head>
<body>


</body>
</html>
```

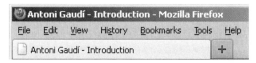

B In most browsers, like Firefox, the title of a Web page is displayed both in the title bar of the window and on the tab. However, Chrome (bottom) displays the title on the tab only.

D Perhaps most importantly, the title is typically used as the linked text pointing to your page in search results from Google and others. It's also an important factor for determining a page's relevance in search results. Here you see a title and partial body copy showing up in Google.

A Deeper Look at Page Titles

Many developers—even well-intentioned, fairly experienced ones—give little consideration to the **title** element. They'll simply input the name of their site and then copy it across all HTML pages. Or even worse, they'll leave the **title** text that their code editor may insert by default. If one of your goals is to drive traffic to your site, you'd be doing yourself and your potential readers a huge disservice by following suit.

Search engines have different algorithms that determine a page's rank and how its content is indexed. Universally, though, **title** plays a key role. Search engines may look to the **title** for an indication of what a page is about, and index a page's content in search of related text. An effective **title** focuses on a handful of key words that are central to a page's content.

As a best practice, choose **title** text that briefly summarizes a document's content to benefit both screen reader users and your search engine rankings. Secondarily, and optionally, indicate your site's name in the **title**. It's common to see a site's name at the beginning of the **title**, but it's better to put the unique, page-specific **title** text at the beginning instead.

I recommend you get your **title**'s core message into the first 60 characters, including spaces, because search engines often cut them off in their results at around that number (as a baseline). Browsers display a varying number of characters, but no more than 60, in the title bar at the top of the browser before cutting off the text. Browser tabs cut off the title even sooner because there's less real estate.

To create a title:

1. Place the cursor between `<title>` and `</title>` in the document **head**.

2. Enter the title of your Web page.

TIP The `title` element is required.

TIP A title cannot contain any formatting, HTML, images, or links to other pages.

TIP Some code editors pre-populate the `title` with default text when you start a new page unless you've instructed it to use specific starter code as described in "Starting Your Web Page." So be on the lookout for that, and be sure to replace any default text with a `title` of your own making.

TIP If your `title` contains special characters like accents or some symbols, you'll have to either make them part of your encoding (which typically won't be an issue if you're using UTF-8) or write them with references (see the list of available character entity references at www.elizabethcastro.com/html/extras/entities.html). Also, don't forget to set your code editor to save your pages with the proper encoding, such as UTF-8, so the special characters are saved properly (see "Saving Your Web Pages" in Chapter 2).

Creating Headings

HTML provides six heading levels for establishing the hierarchy of information in your pages. Mark up each heading with one of the **h1**–**h6** elements, where **h1** is a top-level heading, **h2** is a subheading of an **h1**, **h3** is a subheading of an **h2**, and so on. Headings are among the most important HTML elements in any page, as you will learn.

Think of the **h1**–**h6** headings as similar to headings within a non-HTML document you might write, like a sales report, term paper, product manual, news article—you get the idea. When you write those types of documents, you identify each major section of content with a heading and any number of subheadings (and *sub-subheadings*, and so on), as appropriate. Collectively, those headings represent the document's outline. The same is true for your Web pages **A**. I discuss this in greater depth in the next section, "Understanding the HTML5's Document Outline."

To organize your Web page with headings:

1. In the **body** section of your HTML document, type **<h*n*>**, where *n* is a number from 1 to 6, depending on the level of importance of the heading that you want to create. **h1** is the most important, and **h6** is the least important.

2. Type the contents of the header.

3. Type **</h*n*>** where *n* is the same number used in step 1.

A Use headings to define your document structure, just like an outline. Here, "La Casa Milà" and "La Sagrada Família"—marked up as **h2** elements—are subheadings of the top-level heading, "Antoni Gaudí," because it's an **h1**. (The **lang="es"** portion indicates that the content is in Spanish; it doesn't affect the outline.) If "La Sagrada Família" were an **h3** instead, then it would be a subheading of "La Casa Milà" (and a sub-subheading of "Antoni Gaudí"). The blank line between each heading is entirely optional and has no bearing on the content's display. If I were coding the rest of the page right now, the related content (paragraphs, images, video, and so on) would follow each heading. You'll see examples of this on subsequent pages.

```
<!DOCTYPE html>
<html lang="en">
<head>
     <meta charset="UTF-8" />
     <title>Antoni Gaudí - Introduction
     </title>
</head>
<body>

<h1>Antoni Gaudí</h1>

<h2 lang="es">La Casa Milà</h2>

<h2 lang="es">La Sagrada Família</h2>

</body>
</html>
```

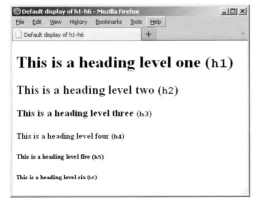

B While all headings display in boldface by default, **h1** is in a larger font than **h2**, which is larger than **h3**, and so on. But as you know, the appearance isn't relevant when deciding which heading level to use. You can change the presentation with CSS.

TIP Your h1–h6 headings are especially important because of their impact on defining your page's outline. By default, browsers display headings progressively smaller moving from h1 to h6 B. But don't forget to choose your heading levels solely based on what hierarchy is appropriate for your content, not on how big or small you want the text to appear. This makes your page stronger semantically, which in turn improves both SEO and accessibility. You can style the headings as you please with a particular font, size, color, and more. For details about achieving this with CSS, consult Chapter 10.

TIP Search engines weigh your headings heavily, particularly the likes of h1 (which is not to say load your page up with h1s; search engines are wise to that). Meanwhile, screen reader users often navigate a page by headings via the keyboard, because it allows them to quickly assess a page's content and find what most interests them without having to listen through the whole page. All the more reason to have a logical headings hierarchy.

TIP Use the heading levels consistently throughout your site for a better user experience.

TIP You may add an id to a heading if you want to create a link directly to it (see "Creating Anchors" in Chapter 6).

TIP As a side note, in A I used the lang attribute on each h2 to indicate that its contents are in a different language (Spanish, represented by the language code es) than the page's default (English) as declared by `<html lang="en">`.

Understanding HTML5's Document Outline

In the previous section, you learned that the headings elements, **h1**–**h6**, contribute to your HTML page's outline. You're going to dig under the hood more in this section to learn how a handful of elements unique to HTML5 also affect the outline.

One syntactical note before you continue. In the discussion and pages to follow, I'll often use "section" as a generic term to mean a distinct part of a page, as opposed to the `section` element (which you'll learn about) specifically. When I *am* referring to the `section` element, the word will be styled like code just like it is in this sentence.

OK, carrying on.

So, you know that each HTML document has an underlying outline, which is like a table of contents, as defined by the heading elements. Now, the outline isn't something that displays in your page explicitly—though browsers may one day provide a means to see it—but as with all semantics, it's meaningful to the likes of search engines and screen readers, which use the outline to glean the structure of your page and provide the information to users.

```
...
<body>
    <h1>Product User Guide</h1>
    <h2>Setting it Up</h2>
    <h2>Basic Features</h2>
    <h3>Video Playback</h3>
    <h2>Advanced Features</h2>
</body>
</html>
```

B Version 2 document outline (same outline as Version 1, but with more meaningful markup)

```
...
<body>
    <h1>Product User Guide</h1>
    <section>
        <h1>Setting it Up</h1>
    </section>

    <section>
        <h1>Basic Features</h1>
        <section> <!-- nested, so it's a
      ↪ subsection of its parent -->
            <h1>Video Playback</h1>
        </section>
    </section>

    <section>
        <h1>Advanced Features</h1>
    </section>
</body>
</html>
```

In the versions of HTML and XHTML that preceded HTML5, the **h1**–**h6** heading elements were all you had to structure the outline. HTML5, on the other hand, includes four *sectioning content* elements—**article**, **aside**, **nav**, and **section**—that demarcate distinct sections within a document and define the scope of the **h1**–**h6** (as well as **header** and **footer**) elements within them.

This means that each sectioning element has its own **h1**–**h6** hierarchy, which is a big shift from previous versions of the language. Also, not only is more than one **h1** in a page OK, it's generally recommended by the HTML5 spec (however, hold that thought; pretty soon I'm going to explain why you should limit your **h1**s).

All of this affects the outline. Let's compare two equivalent outlines to see how this works. For both, imagine that each heading is followed by a series of paragraphs and other content representing the section's information.

The first outline, which is perfectly valid HTML5 and will be familiar to those of you with HTML and XHTML experience, uses heading elements only A.

The second version B uses both headings and HTML5's **section** elements, including one nested **section**. (Note: The code indentation is unimportant and doesn't affect the outline, but it does make it clear to you which elements are contained in others.)

Earlier, I mentioned that browsers don't yet expose the outline to you. However, you can check it with Geoffrey Sneddon's HTML 5 Outliner (http://gsnedders.html5.org/outliner/), a simple but great tool that presents a visual representation of your document's outline. Using it to generate outlines for Versions 1 and 2 (Ⓐ and Ⓑ) shows that even though their **h1**–**h6** heading levels are different, both result in this outline:

1. Product User Guide
    1. Setting it Up
    2. Basic Features
        1. Video Playback
    3. Advanced Features

As you can see, each **section** element in Version 2 Ⓑ becomes a subsection of its nearest **h1**–**h6** or sectioning content ancestor (which is also **section**, in this case). The same behavior is true of all four HTML5 sectioning content elements I mentioned earlier (**article**, **aside**, **nav**, and **section**), even when they're mixed together.

By comparison, if Version 2 Ⓑ had no **sections**—let's call it Version 3 Ⓒ—its outline would be very different.

Namely, each heading would be at the same importance level, **h1**, meaning that there wouldn't be *any* subheadings (or sub-subheadings):

1. Product User Guide
2. Setting it Up
3. Basic Features
4. Video Playback
5. Advanced Features

Ⓒ Version 3 document outline (not the same outline as Versions 1 and 2)

```
...
<body>
    <h1>Product User Guide</h1>
    <h1>Setting it Up</h1>
    <h1>Basic Features</h1>
    <h1>Video Playback</h1>
    <h1>Advanced Features</h1>
</body>
</html>
```

D Sample outline with explicit semantics

```
...
<body>
    <article>
        <h1>Product User Guide</h1>
        <section>
            <h1>Setting it Up</h1>
        </section>

        <section>
            <h1>Basic Features</h1>
            <section>
                <h1>Video Playback</h1>
            </section>
        </section>

        <section>
            <h1>Advanced Features</h1>
        </section>
    </article>
</body>
</html>
```

Of the outlines with the same meaning (that is, Versions 1 and 2), both are valid HTML5, but the second is preferable because the **section** elements are more explicit semantically. In practice, you could wrap one **article** element around all of Version 2's content, since that's even more appropriate in this context (though the resulting outline is slightly different). Figure **D** shows an example.

Don't forget, too, that each heading would be followed by its related text, images, and other content, which you'll learn about as you progress. But for now, I've left all of that out so you can focus on learning about headings and outlines.

Doing what you can in today's ecosystem

But, wait! There's another adjustment you should make to the code. Remember when I said to "hold that thought; pretty soon I'm going to explain why you should limit your **h1**s"? While it is true that each sectioning content element (**article**, **aside**, **nav**, and **section**) *may* begin its heading hierarchy with **h1**, it isn't mandatory. In fact, for the foreseeable future, you're better off starting each with an **h2** or lower if they are to represent a subheading of an already existing **h1** for a related chunk of content.

Here's why.

There are a lot of moving parts in the ever-evolving world of the Web. New specifications like HTML5 change daily until they are final (which takes years, and hasn't yet happened for HTML5). New browser versions are released. New versions of screen readers and other assistive technologies are developed and released. None of this happens in perfect synchronicity.

Instead, each browser tends to add capabilities incrementally (mostly a very good thing), and not necessarily the same ones as their competitors (not so good), and certainly not on the same schedule as their competitors. The same goes for screen readers. So, although modern browsers support a lot of HTML5's features, none at the time of this writing exposes HTML5's document outline to screen readers, and screen readers don't expose it to users.

In short, this means that screen readers and other assistive technologies don't yet distinguish between an **h1** that's directly in **body**, and an **h1** that sits inside an **article**, **aside**, **nav**, or **section**. They are all top-level **h1**s from their perspective. Bruce Lawson, noted Web evangelist for Opera, was the first person I'm aware of to point this out (www.brucelawson.co.uk/2009/ headings-in-html-5-and-accessibility/; be aware that some other information at this URL is outdated because specs have changed since. See, too, his more recent *Introducing HTML5*, which he wrote with Remy Sharp).

Meanwhile, screen reader users don't have the luxury to wait for the Web to catch up with their needs. They will continue to leverage headings both to get an overview of a page's content and to navigate pages as they regularly have. A meaningful hierarchy of headings makes this easier and makes for a better experience for them on your site.

E Version 4 (the recommended approach to headings out of all four versions)

```
...
<body>
<article>
    <h1>Product User Guide</h1>
    <section>
        <h2>Setting it Up</h2>
    </section>

    <section>
        <h2>Basic Features</h2>
        <section>
            <h3>Video Playback</h3>
        </section>
    </section>

    <section>
        <h2>Advanced Features</h2>
    </section>
</article>
</body>
</html>
```

So until the ecosystem catches up a bit, you and your users are better off if you use headings that indicate the hierarchy explicitly with **h1–h6**, just as you would if sectioning elements weren't present. Lawson and others in the field recommend this approach, me included.

Let's see how to do it **E**.

What used to be **h1**s in the first level of **section** elements are now **h2**s, and the Video Playback heading that is in a **section** nested in another **section** is now an **h3** instead of an **h1**. The document outline hasn't changed, only the heading levels.

This example only demonstrates **h1–h3**, but use **h4–h6** as well in your pages if your content demands it. For instance, a subheading of Video Playback would be an **h4** (with or without a parent sectioning element, as you see fit), and so on.

And remember, this recommendation holds true for all sectioning elements—**article**, **aside**, **nav**, and **section**—not just the ones shown in the example.

Wrapping it up

I suggest re-reading this discussion about HTML5's document outline if any of it didn't quite sink in. It's not nearly as involved as it might seem. I highly recommend you create a variety of test pages and compare the results in the HTML5 Outliner to get a better feel for how the outline algorithm works. Use the Outliner during your project work, too, to ensure your structure is as intended. First, be sure you validate your HTML5 pages at either http://validator.nu/ or http://validator.w3.org/ to check for any coding errors (see "Validating Your Code" in Chapter 20).

TIP Please don't get the impression that you always must use an `article`, or that a `section` must always (and can only) be nested in an `article`. The example we discussed was just one way to use these elements, and, in fact, that same content could be marked up a few different ways and would still be valid HTML5. I explain `article` and `section` more later in this chapter, and as you'll see, they have a few applications, depending on your content.

How HTML5's Outline Algorithm Helps with Syndicated Content

If you've been following along so far, you've seen that—by virtue of being sectioning content and the rules of HTML5's outline algorithm—each **article**, **aside**, **nav**, and **section** has its own outline that may begin with **h1** and continue through **h6**.

Besides allowing a lot of flexibility with your document's headings, this has one not-so-obvious benefit: It allows your content to appear on other pages, even other *sites*, without wreaking havoc on the parent document's outline. And *its* outline remains intact, too.

Nowadays, content is shared between sites more than ever. You have news aggregation sites, blogs with RSS feeds, Twitter feeds, and so on. As you'll learn in "Creating an Article," the **article** element represents a self-contained composition that *could* be syndicated (not must be, just that it would be appropriate to do so).

Imagine that the following **article** from one site is displayed on another site:

```
...
<h2>News from around the Web</h2>

<article>
    <h1>Local Teen Prefers Vinyl over Digital</h1>

    <p>A local teen has replaced all her digital tracks with vinyl. "It's
    ⇢ groovy," she said, on the record.</p>

    <h2>Hooked after First Album</h2>
    ...
</article>
...
```

Checking the code with the HTML5 Outliner, you see this:

1. News from around the Web
    1. Local Teen Prefers Vinyl over Digital
        1. Hooked after First Album

So, even though the Local Teen heading is a higher rank (**h1**) than the **h2** it sits under, it's a subheading of the **h2** because it's contained in an **article** under that heading. And the Hooked **h2** is a sub-subheading of the News **h2**, not on equal standing.

The News heading could be an **h3**, an **h4**, or *any* heading level, and the outline would be exactly the same. The same is true for Local Teen and Hooked, as long as Local Teen has the higher-ranked heading.

Grouping Headings

Sometimes a heading has multiple consecutive levels, such as with headline subheadings, alternative titles, or tag lines. Grouping them in an **hgroup** element indicates they are related 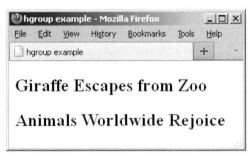. Each **hgroup** may contain only two or more **h1–h6** headings; no other elements are allowed.

Only the first instance of the highest-ranked heading in an **hgroup** appears in the document outline (see "Understanding HTML5's Document Outline"). So that could be another deciding factor for you when choosing to use **hgroup**. To be clear, though, all headings in an **hgroup** display in the browser ⓑ.

Ⓐ Two related headings are grouped together. In this example, the **h2** is a subheading of the article's **h1** headline. Because it's marked up with the highest-ranking heading, only "Giraffe Escapes from Zoo" appears in the document outline, but both display in the browser, as expected ⓑ. Similarly, if a second **h1** appeared after it in the **hgroup**, it would be omitted from the outline just like the **h2**. Also, since the **h2** doesn't appear in the outline, the next heading in the article could be **h2** (rather than **h3**) and be understood to be a direct subheading of the **h1**, "Giraffe Escapes from Zoo."

```
...
<body>

<article>
    <hgroup>
        <h1>Giraffe Escapes from Zoo</h1>
        <h2>Animals Worldwide Rejoice</h2>
    </hgroup>

    <p>... [article content] ...</p>
</article>

</body>
</html>
```

ⓑ Both headings display in the browser just like they would if they hadn't been contained in an **hgroup**.

To group two or more headings:

1. Type `<hgroup>`.

2. Type `<hn>`, where *n* is a number from 1 to 6, depending on the level of importance of the heading that you want to create.

3. Type the contents of the header.

4. Type `</hn>` where *n* is the same number used in step 2.

5. Repeat steps 2 through 4 for as many headings as you want to be part of the **hgroup**. Typically, the heading level for each subsequent heading would increment by one (for example, from **h1** to **h2**, and so on).

6. Type `</hgroup>`.

TIP Don't use `hgroup` around just one heading. It's intended for at least two.

TIP As mentioned, only the first instance of the highest-ranking heading in an `hgroup` appears in the document outline. The order of the headings is irrelevant. So if your `hgroup` had an h3 followed by an h2, the h2 would be in the outline. Typically, you'll order headings by priority level, though, so a lower-ranked one (like h3) wouldn't precede a higher-ranked one (like h2). You might encounter the occasional exception.

Common Page Constructs

No doubt you've visited dozens of sites arranged like the one shown in . Stripping away the content, you can see that there are four main components: a masthead with navigation, an article in the main content area, a sidebar with tangential information, and a footer B.

Now, you can't style a page like this A or arrange it as shown (A and B) without CSS. You'll start learning CSS in Chapter 7, see how to format text and add colors beginning in Chapter 10, and do a multi-column layout in Chapter 11.

However, the semantics that apply to these common page constructs are pretty similar no matter the layout. You'll explore them for most of the remaining pages of this chapter. Working from the top of the page down, you'll see how to use the **header**, **nav**, **article**, **section**, **aside**, and **footer** elements to define the structure of your pages, and then how to use **div** as a generic container for additional styling and other purposes. Except for **div**, none of these elements existed until HTML5. You've already caught a glimpse of some of them in previous code examples and discussions.

As you learn about these elements, don't get too attached to where they display in the sample layouts, and instead focus on their semantic meaning.

In the ensuing pages, you'll also get an early look at some other elements, such as **ul** (unordered list) and **a** (for links). Those will be properly explained in later chapters.

A A common layout with main navigation along the top, main content on the left, a sidebar on the right, and the footer at the bottom. CSS is required to make the page look like this.

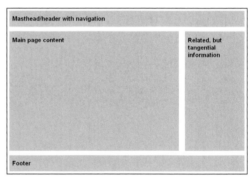

B The types of information commonly found in a page. This is just one type of arrangement, though a common one.

A This **header** represents the header for the whole page. It contains a list of links in a **nav** element to indicate it's a primary set of navigation on the page. See **C** for an example of applying the optional **role="banner"** to a page-level **header** for accessibility purposes. (See "Marking Navigation" for the **role** value that's specific to the **nav** element.)

```
...
<body>
<header>
    <nav>
        <ul>
            <li><a href="#gaudi">Barcelona's
            ⇢ Architect</a></li>
            <li lang="es"><a href="#sagrada-
            ⇢ familia">La Sagrada Família</a>
            ⇢ </li>
            <li><a href="#park-guell">Park
            ⇢ Guell</a></li>
        </ul>
    </nav>
</header>
</body>
</html>
```

B The page-level header containing the navigation.

Creating a Header

If a section of your page has a group of introductory or navigational content, mark it up with the **header** element.

A page can have any number of **header** elements, and their meaning can vary depending on their context. For instance, a **header** at or near the top of a page may represent the header (sometimes called a masthead) for the whole page **A**. Often-times the page header includes the site's logo, the main navigation **B**, other global links, and even a search box. Undoubtedly, this is the **header** element's most common use, but don't mistake it for its only one.

A **header** would also be appropriate for marking up a group of introductory or navigational content deeper within a page. One example is a section's table of contents **C** (on the next page).

The **header** element is one of the four sectioning content elements I mentioned in "Understanding HTML5's Document Outline." This means that any **h1–h6** heading inside a **header** is considered within the context of the **header**—not the page at large—as far as the document outline is concerned. So, a **header** often includes its section's heading (an **h1–h6** or **hgroup**), but this isn't mandatory. For example, you see headings in **C** but not in **A**.

To create a header:

1. Place the cursor within the element for which you want to create a header.

2. Type **<header>**.

3. Type the contents of the header, which can include a variety of content types marked up with their respective HTML elements (most of which you'll learn

C This page has two **header**s: one serving as the whole page's header and another as the header for the Frequently Asked Questions parent **article** element. Note that the first one doesn't have any **h1–h6** headings, but the second one does. See the last tip in this section for information about the optional **role** attribute shown on the first **header**.

```
...
<body>
<header role="banner">
    ... [site logo, navigation, etc.] ...
</header>

<article>
    <header>
        <h1>Frequently Asked Questions</h1>
        <nav>
            <ul>
                <li><a href="#answer1">What is your return policy?</a><li>
                <li><a href="#answer2">How do I find a location?</a><li>
                ...
            </ul>
        </nav>
    </header>

    <!-- the header links point to these -->
    <article id="answer1">
        <h2>What is your return policy?</h2>
        <p> ... [answer] ... </p>
    </article>

    <article id="answer2">
        <h2>How do I find a location?</h2>
        <p> ... [answer] ... </p>
    </article>
    ...
</article> <!-- end parent article -->

</body>
</html>
```

about in the rest of the book). For instance, a **header** might contain **h1–h6** headings, a logo or series of logos, navigation, a search box, and more.

4. Type **</header>**.

TIP Don't use header unnecessarily. If all you have is an h1–h6 or an hgroup and no companion content worthy of grouping with it, there's no need to wrap it in a header in most cases.

TIP A header is not interchangeable with a heading, as in the h1–h6 elements (see "Creating Headings"). Each has its own semantic purpose.

TIP You may not nest a footer element or another header within a header, nor may you nest a header within a footer or address element.

TIP A header doesn't always have to contain a nav element as the examples do (A and C), but in most cases, it likely will if the header contains navigational links. In the case of C, nav is appropriate around the list of Frequently Asked Questions links, since it's a major navigation group within the page, as discussed in "Marking Navigation."

TIP See "Creating Generic Containers" to learn about how header has replaced one of the div element's roles from its pre-HTML5 days.

TIP See "Improving Accessibility with ARIA" to learn how you may use role="banner" with header.

Marking Navigation

Earlier versions of HTML didn't have an element that explicitly represents a section of major navigation links, but HTML5 does: the **nav** element. Links in a **nav** may point to content within the page Ⓐ, to other pages or resources, or both. Whatever the case may be, use **nav** only for your document's most important groups of links, not all of them.

If you looked closely at the code in the previous section, you got a look at the **nav** element in action. I've carried that code sample over to this page, while highlighting **nav** Ⓐ. The **nav** element doesn't impose any default formatting on its contents Ⓑ.

Ⓐ These links (the **a** elements) represent an important set of navigation, so I've nested them in a **nav** element. Typically, you'll mark up a list of links with the **ul** element (unordered list) unless your links are breadcrumb links. In that case, use an **ol** (ordered list). See Chapter 15 for more information about lists. The **role** attribute is not required, but can improve accessibility. See the last tip in this section for information about applying **role="navigation"** to **nav**.

```
...
<body>
<header>
    <nav role="navigation">
        <ul>
            <li><a href="#gaudi">Barcelona's
              Architect</a></li>
            <li lang="es"><a href="#sagrada-
              familia">La Sagrada Família</a>
              </li>
            <li><a href="#park-guell">Park
              Guell</a></li>
        </ul>
    </nav>
</header>
</body>
</html>
```

B Our navigation looks rather plain by default. The bullets are not a product of the **nav** element, which has no default styling other than starting on its own line. The bullets display because each link is in an **li** element (a list item). With CSS, you can turn off the bullets or show different ones, as well as lay out the links horizontally, change their color, make them look like buttons, and more. You'll begin learning about CSS in Chapter 7.

To designate a group of links as important navigation:

1. Type `<nav>`.

2. Type your list of links structured as a **ul** (unordered list) unless the order of the links is significant (like breadcrumb navigation), in which case you should structure them as an **ol** (ordered list). (See Chapters 6 and 15 to learn about links and lists, respectively.)

3. Type `</nav>`.

TIP If you have some experience with HTML or XHTML, you're probably accustomed to structuring your links in a ul or ol element, as appropriate. In HTML5, nav doesn't replace that best practice; continue to use those elements, and simply wrap a nav around them **A**.

TIP Although screen readers on the whole are still catching up with the new semantics in HTML5, the nav element could help them identify your page's important navigation and allow users to jump to them via the keyboard. This makes your page more accessible, improving your visitors' experience.

TIP The HTML5 spec recommends not wrapping ancillary page footer links like "Terms of Use" and "Privacy Policy" in a nav, which makes sense. Sometimes, though, your page footer reiterates the top-level global navigation or includes other important links like "Store Locator" and "Careers." In most cases, I recommend putting those types of footer links in a nav.

TIP HTML5 doesn't allow nesting a nav within an `address` element.

TIP See "Improving Accessibility with ARIA" to learn how to use `role="navigation"` with nav **A**.

A Deeper Look at nav

As I mentioned earlier, just because you have a group of links in your page doesn't mean it should be contained in a **nav**.

The following sample news page includes four lists of links, only two of which are considered major enough to warrant being wrapped in a **nav**. (As you'll see, I've abbreviated portions of the code.)

```
...
<body>
    <header>
        <!-- site logo could go here -->
        <!-- site global navigation -->

        <nav>
            <ul> ... </ul>
        </nav>
    </header>

    <div id="main">
        <h1>Arts &amp; Entertainment</h1>
        <article>
            <h1>Gallery Opening Features the Inspired, Inspiring</h1>
            <p>... [story content] ... </p>

            <aside>
                <h1>Other Stories</h1>

                <!-- not wrapped in nav -->
                <ul> ... [story links] ... </ul>
            </aside>
        </article>
    </div>
```

A Deeper Look at nav *(continued)*

```
<aside id="sidebar">
    <nav><!-- secondary navigation -->
        <ul>
            <li><a href="/arts/movies/">Movies</a></li>
            <li><a href="/arts/music/">Music</a></li>

            ...
        </ul>
    </nav>
</aside>


<footer>
    <!-- Ancillary links not wrapped in nav. -->
    <ul> ... </ul>
</footer>
</body>
</html>
```

The secondary navigation in the **aside** (see "Specifying an Aside") allows the user to navigate to other pages in the Arts & Entertainment directory, so it constitutes a major navigational section of the page. However, the Other Stories **aside** with links does not.

So how do you decide when a group of links deserves a **nav**? Ultimately, it's a judgment call based on your content organization. At a minimum, mark up your site's global navigation (that is, what allows users to jump to sections of the site) with **nav**. Often, but not always, that particular **nav** appears within a page-level **header** element (see "Creating a Header").

Creating an Article

Another of the elements that's new thanks to HTML5 is **article** Ⓐ. You've seen some examples of it in play already. Now let's learn more about what makes it tick.

Based on its name, you'd rightly guess that you can use **article** to contain content like a newspaper article. However, it isn't limited to that. In HTML5, "article" is more akin to "item."

Here's how HTML5 defines it:

> The **article** element represents a self-contained composition in a document, page, application, or site and is, in principle, independently distributable or reusable, e.g., in syndication. This could be a forum post, a magazine or newspaper article, a blog entry, a user-submitted comment, an interactive widget or gadget, or any other independent item of content.

Other **article** examples could include a movie or music review, a case study, a product description, and more. You might have been surprised to learn that it also can be an interactive widget or gadget, but those too are independent, redistributable items of content.

Ⓐ I've abbreviated the article contents and the **nav** code from the previous section to keep it simple. You can see the complete version of the page code on the book site at www.bruceontheloose .com/htmlcss/examples/. Although this example includes paragraphs and images only, an **article** can contain a variety of content types, such as video, figures, lists, and more.

```
...
<body>
<header>
    <nav role="navigation">
        ... [ul with links] ...
    </nav>
</header>
<article>
    <h1 id="gaudi">Barcelona's Architect</h1>

    <p>Antoni Gaudí's incredible buildings
    → bring millions of tourists to
    → Barcelona each year.</p>

    <p>Gaudí's non-conformity, already
    → visible in his teenage years, coupled
    → with his quiet but firm devotion to
    → the church, made a unique foundation
    → for his thoughts and ideas. His
    → search for simplicity, based on his
    → careful observations of nature, are
    → quite apparent in his work, from the
    → <a href="#park-guell">Park Guell</a>
    → and its incredible sculptures and
    → mosaics, to the Church of the <a href=
    → "#sagrada-familia">Sacred Family</a>
    → and its organic, bulbous towers.</p>

    <h2 id="sagrada-familia" lang="es">La
    → Sagrada Família</h2>

    ... [image and paragraphs] ...

    <h2 id="park-guell">Park Guell</h2>

    ... [image and paragraphs] ...
</article>

</body>
</html>
```

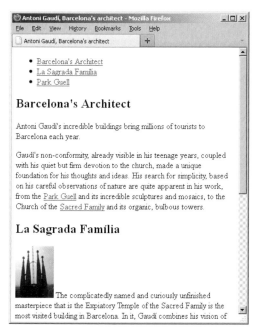

B Now the page has **header**, **nav**, and **article** elements, as well as their contents. The **article** headings may be a different size by default depending on the browser. You can standardize their look across browsers with CSS (see Chapter 10).

To create an article:

1. Type **<article>**.

2. Type the article's contents, which could include any number of elements, such as paragraphs, lists, audio, video, images, figures, and more.

3. Type **</article>**.

TIP As you learned in "Understanding HTML5's Document Outline," **article** is one of the four sectioning content elements along with **header**, **section**, and **aside**.

TIP You can nest an **article** inside another one as long as the inner **article** is related to the **article** on the whole. You can't nest an **article** inside an **address** element, though.

TIP A page may contain several **article** elements (or none at all). For example, a blog's homepage typically includes a few of the most recent postings; each could be its own **article**.

TIP It isn't mandatory that an **article** have one or more **section** elements. It's perfectly valid to let the h1–h6 elements within an **article** stand on their own, though by defining **sections** you're making the **article**'s semantics more explicit. And each **section** can have its own hierarchy of heading levels, as discussed in "Understanding HTML5's Document Outline."

TIP The **article** and **section** elements are easily (and rightfully) confused with one another, which is why I quoted directly from HTML5's definitions; I didn't want you learning about them through a filter. I discuss **section** and choosing between the two in "Defining a Section."

TIP See "Improving Accessibility with ARIA" to learn how you may use role="main" with **article** under a certain circumstance. It would be appropriate to include it on the **article** in Ⓐ because it's the container for the page's main content, but I omitted it to avoid giving the impression that role="main" is right for all **article** elements.

More article Examples

The previous example (A) is just one way to use **article**. Let's take a look at some more possibilities.

Example 1 (basic article):

```
<article>

    <h1>The Diversity of Papua New Guinea</h1>

    <p>Papua New Guinea is home to more than 800 tribes and languages ...</p>

    ... [rest of story content] ...


    <footer> <!-- the article's footer, not the page's -->

        <p>Leandra Allen is a freelance journalist who earned her degree in
        → anthropology from the University of Copenhagen.</p>

        <address>

        You may reach her at <a href="mailto:leandra@therunningwriter.com">
        → leandra@therunningwriter.com</a>.

        </address>

    </footer>

</article>
```

Note the use of the **footer** and **address** elements (see discussions about them in this chapter and Chapter 4, respectively). Here, **address** applies only to its parent **article** (the one shown), not to the page or any **article**s nested within that **article**, such as the reader comments in Example 2.

Example 2 demonstrates nested **article** elements in the form of user-submitted comments to the parent **article**, just like you see in the comments section of blogs or news sites. It also shows one use for the **section** element (see "Defining a Section") and the **time** element, covered in Chapter 4.

More article Examples *(continued)*

Example 2 (nested articles):

```
<article>

    <h1>The Diversity of Papua New Guinea</h1>

    ... [parent article content] ...


    <footer>
        ... [parent article footer] ...
    </footer>


    <section>

        <h2>Reader Comments</h2>

        <article>

            <footer>travelgal wrote on <time datetime="2011-11-17"
            ⇥ pubdate>November 17, 2011</time>:</footer>

            <p>Great article! I've always been curious about Papua New
            ⇥ Guinea.</p>

        </article>

        <article>

            ... [next reader comment] ...

        </article>

    </section>

</article>
```

These are just a couple of more common ways to leverage **article** and its companion elements.

Defining a Section

The **article** element has a less semantically specific cousin, **section**, which is another of the elements unique to HTML5.

In part, HTML5 defines **section** as follows:

> The section element represents a generic section of a document or application. A section, in this context, is a thematic grouping of content, typically with a heading Ⓐ.

> Examples of sections would be chapters, the various tabbed pages in a tabbed dialog box, or the numbered sections of a thesis. A Web site's homepage could be split into sections for an introduction, news items, and contact information.

The **article** and **section** elements are pretty similar. If you aren't quite sure how to differentiate the two, see the sidebar "How Do you Decide between **article** and **section**?"

To define a section:

1. Type **<section>**.

2. Type the section's contents, which could include any number of elements, such as paragraphs, lists, audio, video, images, figures, and more.

3. Type **</section>**.

Ⓐ The code is the same as before except I've wrapped a **section** around each of the two sections of the **article** that follows the introduction. I've simplified the code again for brevity.

```
...
<body>
<header>
    <nav role="navigation">
        ... [ul with links] ...
    </nav>
</header>

<article>
    <h1 id="gaudi">Barcelona's Architect</h1>

    <p>Antoni Gaudí's incredible buildings
    → bring millions of tourists to
    → Barcelona each year.</p>

    ... [another introductory paragraph] ...

    <section>
        <h2 id="sagrada-familia" lang="es">La
        → Sagrada Família</h2>

        <p><img src="img/towers.jpg"
        → width="75" height="100" alt=
        → "Sagrada Família Towers" /> The
        → complicatedly named and curiously
        → unfinished masterpiece that is
        → the Expiatory Temple of the
        → Sacred Family is the most visited
        → building in Barcelona. In it, Gaudí
        → combines his vision of nature and
        → architecture with his devotion
        → to his faith. The Sagrada Família
        → attracts even the non-religious to
        → its doors in large part due to its
        → tragic story and its still
        → unfinished state, of which the
        → everpresent scaffolding and cranes
        → are permanent reminders.</p>
    </section>

    <section>
        <h2 id="park-guell">Park Guell</h2>

        ... [another image and paragraphs] ...
    </section>
</article>
</body>
</html>
```

B Now the page has **header**, **nav**, **article**, and **section** elements, as well as their contents. The default rendering is the same as before you added the **section** elements.

TIP As you learned in "Understanding HTML5's Document Outline," `section` is one of the four sectioning content elements along with **nav**, `article`, and `aside`.

TIP By default, you may not see a difference when viewing a page with `sections` (or `articles`, for that matter), but what's important is that you strengthen the semantics of your document by using them **B**. Of course, you can style `section` and `article` elements however you like with CSS.

TIP Keep in mind that `section` is not a generic container like **div**, because `section` conveys meaning and **div** has absolutely no semantic meaning (see "Creating Generic Containers").

TIP There are several examples throughout this chapter to help you get a sense of how to use both `article` and `section` (in a variety of ways).

TIP See "Improving Accessibility with ARIA" to learn how you may use `role="main"` with `section` under a certain circumstance.

How Do You Decide between `article` and `section`?

I deliberately quoted HTML5's definitions of **section** and **article** (see "Creating an Article") to help you understand the distinction, because it is subtle at times. Think of them this way. Is your content an independent piece of content or a widget that would be appropriate for syndication? If yes, use **article**. (Otherwise, in most cases use **section**, though see "Creating Generic Containers" to learn about when to use **div** instead.) It doesn't mean you *have* to syndicate or otherwise distribute **article** content, just that the content is fit for it.

If you're still thinking **article** and **section** seem pretty similar at times, don't worry, you're not alone. Even seasoned developers apply these two elements differently at times.

As mentioned in Chapter 1, there isn't always a right choice and wrong choice when it comes to marking up your content, just most of the time. The other times come down to personal decisions about which HTML elements you feel best describe your content.

So, do give careful thought when deciding between **article** and **section**, but don't wring your hands worrying about whether you get them exactly right every time. Sometimes it's a little subjective, and in any case, your page will continue to work. Plus, no one's going to come knocking at your door in the middle of the night.

Well, *I* might, but that's just because it's dark and scary outside.

An Example of section without article

So far you've seen examples of **section** nested in an **article** Ⓐ. That's just one use of the element.

In the following slightly modified example from the HTML5 spec, you see **section** used without **article**. (You also get an early glimpse of ordered lists in action. Learn more about the **ol** and other list elements in Chapter 15.)

```
...
<body>
    <h1>Graduation Program</h1>

    <section>
        <h2>Ceremony</h2>
        <ol>
            <li>Opening Procession</li>
            <li>Speech by Valedictorian</li>
            <li>Speech by Class President</li>
            <li>Presentation of Diplomas</li>
            <li>Closing Speech by Headmaster</li>
        </ol>
    </section>

    <section>
        <h2>Graduates (alphabetical)</h2>
        <ol>
            <li>Molly Carpenter</li>
            <li>Anastasia Luccio</li>
            <li>Ebenezar McCoy</li>
            <li>Karrin Murphy</li>
            <li>Thomas Raith</li>
            <li>Susan Rodriguez</li>
        </ol>
    </section>
</body>
</html>
```

Specifying an Aside

Sometimes you have a section of content that is tangentially related to the main content on your page but that could stand on its own Ⓐ. How would you indicate that semantically?

Ⓐ This **aside**, featuring information about Barcelona's architectural wonders, is tangentially related to the Antoni Gaudí content that's the focus of the page, but it could also stand on its own. I could have nested it within the **article** since they are related, but I decided to put it after the **article** in order to treat it visually later like a sidebar Ⓒ. The **role="complementary"** on the **aside** is optional, but can improve accessibility. See the last tip for more information.

```
...
<body>

<header>
    <nav role="navigation">
        ... [ul with links] ...
    </nav>
</header>

<article>
    <h1 id="gaudi">Barcelona's Architect</h1>
    ... [introductory paragraphs] ...

    <section>
        <h2 id="sagrada-familia" lang="es">La Sagrada Família</h2>
         ... [image and paragraph] ...
    </section>

    <section>
        <h2 id="park-guell">Park Guell</h2>
        ... [another image and paragraphs] ...
    </section>
</article>

<aside role="complementary">
    <h1>Architectural Wonders of Barcelona</h1>

    <p>Barcelona is home to many architectural wonders in addition to Gaudí's work. Some of them
      include:</p>
    <ul>
        <li lang="es">Arc de Triomf</li>
        <li>The cathedral <span lang="es">(La Seu)</span></li>
        <li lang="es">Gran Teatre del Liceu</li>
        <li lang="es">Pavilion Mies van der Rohe</li>
        <li lang="es">Santa Maria del Mar</li>
    </ul>

    <p>Credit: <a href="http://www.barcelona.de/en/barcelona-architecture-buildings.html"
      rel="external"><cite>Barcelona.de</cite></a>.</p>
</aside>

</body>
</html>
```

Until HTML5, there was no way to do this explicitly. Now, you have the **aside** element  **B**.

It's common to think of an **aside** as a sidebar **C**, but you can place an **aside** element in a variety of places in your page, depending on the context. It may be a box (conceptually or literally) within the main content itself, in the same column but not nested in the main content, or in (or as) a secondary column like a sidebar. Examples of **aside** include a pull quote, a sidebar, a box of links to related articles on a news site, advertising, groups of **nav** elements (for instance, a blog roll), a Twitter feed, and a list of related products on a commerce site.

B The **aside** appears below the article because it follows it in the HTML itself **A**. As you can see, browsers don't apply any special formatting to an **aside** by default (except starting them on their own line). However, you have complete control over its appearance with CSS **C**.

C When you apply CSS to the finished page, you can make the **aside** (which begins with "Architectural Wonders of Barcelona") appear alongside the main content instead of below it. So in this case, you've treated the **aside** like a sidebar. (You'll learn how to do a two-column CSS layout in Chapter 11.)

To specify an aside:

1. Type **<aside>**.

2. Type the **aside**'s content, which could include any number of elements, such as paragraphs, lists, audio, video, images, figures, and more.

3. Type **</aside>**.

TIP Although one way **aside** is used is to mark up content in a sidebar **C**, the **aside** element itself doesn't affect the layout of the page **B**.

TIP If you use one or more **asides** in or as a sidebar, place the sidebar content after your page's main content in the HTML **A**. It's better for SEO and accessibility purposes to place the most important content first. You can change the order in which they display in the browser with CSS.

TIP Use the **figure** element (see Chapter 4), not **aside**, to mark up figures that are related to your content, such as a chart, a graph, or an inset photo with a caption.

TIP HTML5 disallows nesting an **aside** inside an **address** element.

TIP See "Improving Accessibility with ARIA" to learn how you may use **role="complementary"** with **aside**.

Other aside Examples

As mentioned, **aside** can appear in the same column as your main content, nested within your main content, or in a sidebar.

Example 1 shows an **aside** nested within its related content.

Example 1 (nested in main content):

```
...
<body>
<article>
    <h1>The Diversity of Papua New Guinea</h1>
    ... [article content] ...
    <aside>
        <h1>Papua New Guinea Quick Facts</h1>
        <ul>
            <li>The country has 38 of the 43 known birds of paradise</li>
            <li>Though quite tropical in some regions, others occasionally
            → experience snowfall.</li>
            ...
        </ul>
    </aside>
    ... [more article content] ...
</article>
</body>
</html>
```

That same **article** might include a pull quote from the article text. That, too, would be in an **aside**. Or it could have a "Related Stories" **aside** containing a list of links to other essays about the country or surrounding region (Indonesia, Australia, and so on). Alternatively, that **aside** could be in a different page column instead of nested in the **article**.

You've already seen one example of an **aside** in a sidebar (Ⓐ and Ⓒ). Now, let's consider an example of a design portfolio or set of case studies, in which each HTML page focuses on a single project and you provide links (nested in a **nav**) to the other project pages in an adjacent column (as controlled by CSS, not simply by virtue of arranging the code as shown in Example 2).

Other aside Examples *(continued)*

Example 2 (aside not nested in main content and containing a nav):

```
...
<body>
<!-- main content on the page -->
<article>
    <h1>... [name of project] ...</h1>
    <figure>... [project photo] ...</figure>
    <p>... [project write-up] ...</p>
</article>

<!-- this aside is not nested in the article -->
<aside>
    <h1>Other Projects</h1>
    <nav>
        <ul>
            <li><a href="habitat-for-humanity.html">Habitat for Humanity
            → brochure</a></li>
            <li><a href="royal-philharmonic.html">Royal Philharmonic Orchestra
            → site</a></li>

            ...
        </ul>
    </nav>
</aside>
</body>
</html>
```

It would be perfectly fine to nest this particular **aside** in the project **article** too, since they are related.

Creating a Footer

When you think of a footer, you probably think of a page footer. HTML5's **footer** element is appropriate for that, but like **header**, you can also use it elsewhere.

The **footer** element represents a footer for the nearest **article**, **aside**, **blockquote**, **body**, **details**, **fieldset**, **figure**, **nav**, **section**, or **td** element in which it is nested. It's the footer for the *whole* page only when its nearest ancestor is the **body** (Ⓐ and Ⓑ). And if a **footer** wraps *all* the content in its section (an **article**, for example), it represents the likes of an appendix, index, long colophon, or long license agreement, depending on its content.

Ⓐ This **footer** represents the footer for the whole page, since its nearest ancestor is the **body** element. Our page now has **header**, **nav**, **article**, **section**, **aside**, and **footer** elements. Not every page requires them all, but they do represent the primary page constructs available in HTML.

```
...
<body>
<header>
    <nav role="navigation">
        ... [ul with links] ...
    </nav>
</header>

<article>
    <h1 id="gaudi">Barcelona's Architect</h1>
    ... [introductory paragraphs] ...

    <section>
        <h2 id="sagrada-familia" lang="es">La
        → Sagrada Família</h2>
        ... [image and paragraph] ...
    </section>

    <section>
        <h2 id="park-guell">Park Guell</h2>
        ... [another image and paragraphs] ...
    </section>
</article>

<aside role="complementary">
    <h1>Architectural Wonders of Barcelona
    → </h1>
    ... [rest of aside] ...
</aside>

<footer>
    <p><small>&copy; Copyright 2011</small>
    → </p>
</footer>

</body>
</html>
```

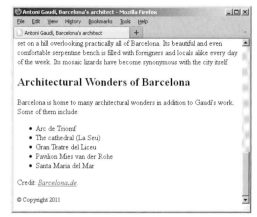

B The **footer** element itself doesn't impose any formatting on the text by default. Here, the copyright notice is smaller than normal text because it's nested in a **small** element to represent legal print semantically (see Chapter 4). Like everything else, you can change the font size with CSS.

To create a footer:

1. Place the cursor within the element for which you want to create a footer.

2. Type **<footer>**.

3. Type the contents of the footer.

4. Type **</footer>**.

TIP A **footer** typically includes information about its section, such as links to related documents, copyright information, its author, and similar items. See Examples 1 and 2 in the "Other **footer** Examples" sidebar.

TIP A **footer** doesn't need to be at the end of its containing element, though usually it is.

TIP It's invalid to nest a **header** or another **footer** within a **footer**. Also, you can't nest a **footer** within a **header** or **address** element.

TIP See "Creating Generic Containers" to learn how **footer** has replaced one of the **div** element's roles from its pre-HTML5 days.

TIP See "Improving Accessibility with ARIA" to learn how you may use **role="contentinfo"** with **footer** in a certain circumstance. It would be appropriate to include it on the **footer** in **A** because it represents the footer for the whole page, but I omitted it to avoid giving the impression that **role="contentinfo"** is right for all **footer** elements. See "Other **footer** Examples" for an example that both shows the distinction and uses the role properly.

Other footer Examples

You saw one small example of a footer for the whole page (Ⓐ and Ⓑ). Here is another page footer, but with more content.

Example 1 (as page footer):

```
...
<body>
... [page header and content] ...


<!-- this is a page footer because body is its nearest ancestor -->
<footer role="contentinfo">
    <p><small>&copy; Copyright 2011 The Corporation, Inc.</small></p>


    <ul>
        <li><a href="terms-of-use.html">Terms of Use</a></li>
        <li><a href="privacy-policy.html">Privacy Policy</a></li>
    </ul>
</footer>
</body>
</html>
```

The next example demonstrates a **footer** in the context of a page section (in this case an **article**), and a second **footer** for the whole page. (See "More **article** Examples" for an explanation of the **address** element's scope here.)

Example 2 (as a footer for a page section and the whole page):

```
...
<body>
...
<article>
    <h1>... [article header] ...</h1>
    <p>... [article content] ...</p>
```

Other footer Examples *(continued)*

```html
<!-- the article footer -->
<footer>
    <p>Leandra Allen is a freelance journalist who earned her degree
    → in anthropology from the University of Copenhagen.</p>
    <address>
    You may reach her at <a href="mailto: leandra@therunningwriter.
    → com">leandra@therunningwriter.com</a>.
    </address>
</footer>
</article>


<!-- the page footer -->
<footer id="footer-page" role="contentinfo">
    ... [copyright, terms of use, privacy policy] ...
</footer>
</body>
</html>
```

The **id="footer-page"** (you can specify any valid **id**) on the page footer is optional and is just to differentiate it from the other **footer** for styling control. Note that only the page **footer** is given the optional **role="contentinfo"**. See "Improving Accessibility with ARIA" to learn more about this role.

Creating Generic Containers

Sometimes you need to wrap a container around a segment of content because you want to apply some styling with CSS or maybe an effect with JavaScript. Your page just wouldn't be the same without it **A**. But, when you assess the content, you determine that using the likes of **article**, **section**, **aside**, **nav**, or other elements wouldn't be appropriate semantically. What you really need is a generic container, one without any semantic meaning at all. That container is the **div** element (think of a "division") **B**. With a **div** in place, you can apply the desired style **C** or JavaScript effect to it. Be sure to read the sidebar to learn more about when to use **div** in your pages.

A I achieved this design without any **div** elements in the page. But by adding a **div** around all the page's content **B**, I now have a generic container to which I can apply some more styles (see the results in **C**).

B Now a **div** surrounds all the content. The page's semantics are unchanged, but now I have a generic container I can hook some styles onto with CSS **C**.

```
...
<body>

<div>
    <header>
        <nav role="navigation">
            ... [ul with links] ...
        </nav>
    </header>

    <article>
        <h1 id="gaudi">Barcelona's Architect
         </h1>
        ... [introductory paragraphs] ...

        <section>
            ... [heading, image and
             paragraph] ...
        </section>

        <section>
            ... [heading, another image, and
             paragraphs] ...
        </section>
    </article>

    <aside role="complementary">
        <h1>Architectural Wonders of
         Barcelona</h1>
        ... [rest of aside] ...
    </aside>

    <footer>
        ... [copyright] ...
    </footer>
</div>

</body>
</html>
```

C A `div` element doesn't have any of its own styling by default except that it starts on a new line **D**. However, you can apply styles to `div` to implement your designs. Here, I added the light blue background and a box shadow to the `div`. That allowed me to change the **body** element's background to purple so the content pops. I also added a thin border to the **aside**. You can see how I achieved this in the page's HTML and CSS (www. bruceontheloose.com/htmlcss/examples/).

D The same page with no CSS applied to the `div`, the headings, the paragraphs, or any other element. As you can see, the `div` doesn't make anything look fancy on its own.

To create a generic container:

1. Type `<div>`.

2. Create the contents of the container, which could include any number of elements.

3. At the end of the container, type `</div>`.

TIP Like `header`, `footer`, `article`, `section`, `aside`, `nav`, `h1–h6`, `p`, and many others, `div` automatically displays on a new line by default.

TIP `div` is also helpful when implementing certain interactions or effects with JavaScript. For instance, displaying a photo or dialog box in a semi-transparent overlay that covers the page (the overlay is typically a `div`).

TIP For all of my stressing the point that HTML describes the meaning of your content, `div` isn't the only element that has no semantic value. The `span` element is `div`'s counterpart. Whereas `div` is a semantic-less container for blocks of content, `span` (written as `<span>content goes here</span>`) is one for phrases, like within a `p` element for paragraphs. See more about `span` in Chapter 4.

TIP See "Improving Accessibility with ARIA" to learn how you may use landmark roles with `div`.

Some History about `div` and When to Use It in HTML5

Of the structural elements featured in this chapter, **div** is the only one besides **h1–h6** that pre-dates HTML5. Until HTML5, **div** was the de facto choice for surrounding chunks of content such as a page's header, footer, main content, insets, and sidebars so you could style them with CSS. But **div** had no semantic meaning then, and it still doesn't today.

That's why HTML5 introduced **header**, **footer**, **article**, **section**, **aside**, and **nav**. These types of building blocks were so prevalent on Web pages that they deserved their own elements *with* meaning. **div** doesn't go away in HTML5, you'll just have fewer occasions to use it than in the past.

Let's look at a couple of common instances in which **div** is the right choice.

You've seen one already: to wrap a whole page with a container for styling purposes (B and C).

How did I get the two-column layout with **div**? I applied some CSS to the **article** element to make it display as column one and to the **aside** element to make it display as column two. (See Chapter 7 to start learning CSS, and see Chapter 11 for layouts with CSS.)

Much (if not most) of the time, however, each of your columns has more than one section of content. For instance, maybe you want another **article** (or **section**, or **aside**, and so on) in the main content area below the first **article**. And maybe you want an additional **aside** in the second column, say, with a list of links to other sites about Gaudí. Or perhaps you'd like yet another type of element in that column.

You'd need to group together the content you want to represent each column in a **div** E and then style that **div** accordingly. (If you were thinking **section** would be an option instead, it isn't intended as a generic container for styling.) I've provided a diagram F to help you visualize the relationship between the code E and a potential CSS layout. Keep in mind that it's just one layout possibility for this HTML; CSS is quite powerful.

So, it's very common to have a **div** around each group of content that you want to style as a column (of course, you can do more than two). In terms of what goes *in* them, well that can vary wildly, based on what content you want in your pages. Don't forget that, as your primary semantic containers for sections of content, **article**, **section**, **aside**, and **nav** can go nearly anywhere. As can **header** and **footer**, as you learned in this chapter. Don't read too much into the fact that the example (E and F) shows only **article**s in the main content area and **aside**s in the sidebar.

To be sure, though, **div** should be your last resort as a container because it has no semantic value. Most of the time it'll be right to use the likes of **header**, **footer**, **article**, **section**, **aside**, and possibly **nav** instead. However, *don't* use one of those just to avoid **div** if it's not semantically appropriate to do so. **div** has its place, you just want to limit its use.

Having said that, there is a valid situation in which it is fine to use **div** for all (or most, it's up to you) containers in a page instead of the new HTML 5 elements. See "Styling HTML5 Elements in Older Browsers" in Chapter 11 for more information.

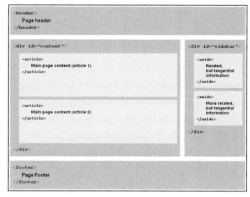

E This page has the **div** that contains the whole page, plus two new ones. One **div** with **id="content"** groups the main content so it can be styled as column one. Another **div** with **id="sidebar"** surrounds the content you want to display as column two. Then you can use the **id** in your CSS to target each specific **div** for styling.

```
...
<body>

<!-- Start page container -->
<div id="container">
      <header>
        ...
      </header>

      <!-- Column One when CSS applied -->
      <div id="content">
          <article>
            ...
          </article>

          <article>
            ...
          </article>

          ... [more sections as desired] ...
      </div>
      <!-- end column one -->

      <!-- Column Two when CSS applied -->
      <div id="sidebar">
          <aside>
            ...
          </aside>

          <aside>
            ...
          </aside>

          ... [more sections as desired] ...
      </div>
      <!-- end column two -->

      <footer>
        ...
      </footer>
</div>
<!-- end page container -->

</body>
</html>
```

F This diagram illustrates how the code in **E** could map to a CSS layout conceptually. It's a very common arrangement, but just one of many possibilities CSS affords you with the same HTML. Be sure to see the next section, "Improving Accessibility with ARIA," to learn how to enhance the semantics and accessibility of your pages even more.

Improving Accessibility with ARIA

As you learned in the section "Why Semantics Matter" in Chapter 1, accessibility improves simply by marking up your content with the HTML that best describes it. So if you're already doing that, you're doing great. In this section, I'll tell you how adding a few simple attributes to your HTML can help your visitors even more.

WAI-ARIA (Web Accessibility Initiative's Accessible Rich Internet Applications), or ARIA for short, is a specification that declares itself "a bridging technology." That is, it fills semantic gaps with attributes until languages like HTML provide their own equivalent semantics.

For instance, what HTML markup would you use to let a screen reader know how to jump to (or past) the main content of your page? Or to a search box? As you'll learn, there is some overlap between ARIA and HTML5 (which has also tried to fill some of the gaps), but not even HTML5 has solutions for those two. ARIA's *landmark roles* do; they identify a set of page regions partly for this purpose: **application**, **banner**, **complementary**, **contentinfo**, **form**, **main**, **navigation**, and **search**.

Where there is overlap between landmark roles and HTML5 elements, screen reader support currently is further along for ARIA. So you can continue to create HTML as you always would, and add ARIA roles to enhance the accessibility of your pages.

In Ⓐ, I've added ARIA landmark roles and a **nav** element to the example from "Creating Generic Containers." Although I placed a **complementary** role on each **aside** element, it would be just

Ⓐ The example from "Creating Generic Containers" with the addition of a **nav** element and five different landmark roles.

```
...
<body>

<!-- Start page container -->
<div id="container">
    <header role="banner">
        ...
        <nav role="navigation">
            ... [ul with links] ...
        </nav>
    </header>

    <!-- Column One when CSS applied -->
    <div id="content" role="main">
        <article>
            ...
        </article>

        <article>
            ...
        </article>

        ... [more sections as desired] ...
    </div>
    <!-- end column one -->

    <!-- Column Two when CSS applied -->
    <div id="sidebar">
        <aside role="complementary">
            ...
        </aside>

        <aside role="complementary">
            ...
        </aside>

        ... [more sections as desired] ...
    </div>
    <!-- end column two -->

    <footer role="contentinfo">
        ...
    </footer>
</div>
<!-- end page container -->

</body>
</html>
```

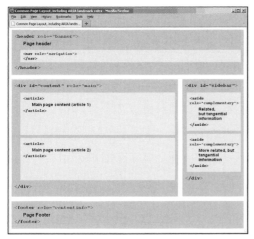

B This is the layout diagram from "Creating Generic Containers," but now it includes the ARIA roles. As noted, the sidebar **div** could have `role="complementary"` instead of the `aside` elements.

as valid to code `<div id="sidebar" role="complementary">`, marking the entire sidebar instead. Before doing so in your pages, be sure all of your **div** content qualifies as **complementary** content.

Below are some of the landmark role definitions found in the ARIA spec, followed by my recommended usage. They are demonstrated in **A** and in a diagram **B** similar to the one from "Creating Generic Containers."

■ `role="banner"`

A region that contains mostly site-oriented content, rather than page-specific content.

Site-oriented content typically includes things such as the logo or identity of the site sponsor, and a site-specific search tool. A banner usually appears at the top of the page and typically spans the full width.

Usage: Add it to your page-level masthead (typically a **header** element), and use it only once on each page.

■ `role="navigation"`

A collection of navigational elements (usually links) for navigating the document or related documents.

Usage: This mirrors HTML5's **nav** element, so add it to each **nav** element, or if one isn't present, add it to the container around your links. You can use this **role** more than once on each page.

■ `role="main"`

The main content of a document.

Usage: Add it to the container of your main section of content. Often this will be a **div** element, but it could be an **article** or **section**, too. Except in rare circumstances, your page should have only one area marked with **main**.

- `role="complementary"`

  A supporting section of the document, designed to be complementary to the main content … but that remains meaningful when separated from the main content.

  The complementary role indicates that the contained content is relevant to the main content.

  Usage: This mirrors HTML5's **aside** element, so add it to an **aside** or **div** that contains all complementary content. You can include more than one **complementary** role in each page.

- `role="contentinfo"`

  A large perceivable region that contains information about the parent document.

  Examples of information included in this region of the page are copyrights and links to privacy statements.

  Usage: Add it once on a page to your page-level footer (typically a **footer** element).

In summary, it's generally a good idea to add ARIA landmark roles to your HTML. I've included them in some other examples throughout the book, as well as on the book site. To be clear, your pages will work without them, but including them can improve the experience for some users. You may find the screen reader test results listed in the tips helpful in deciding whether to use them yourself (support is solid outside of the screen reader Window-Eyes 7.5).

TIP The `form` role is redundant semantically with the `form` element, `search` marks a search `form` (BBC, Yahoo!, and Google use this as well as some other landmark roles in some cases), and `application` is for advanced use.

TIP Landmark roles are just one of many features of the ARIA spec (www.w3.org/TR/wai-aria/). You may also be interested in this implementation guide: www.w3.org/WAI/PF/aria-practices/.

TIP Accessibility advocates Steve Faulkner and Jason Kiss posted separate tests of screen reader landmark role support at www.html5accessibility.com/tests/landmarks.html and www.accessibleculture.org/research/html5-aria-2011/, respectively. See Faulkner's related discussions at www.paciellogroup.com/blog/2011/11/latest-aria-landmark-support-data/ and at www.paciellogroup.com/blog/2011/07/html5-accessibility-chops-aria-landmark-support/.

TIP NVDA (Windows, free download at www.nvda-project.org/), VoiceOver (free as part of Mac OSX and iOS 4+), and JAWS (Windows, free trial available at www.freedomscientific.com/) are among the most advanced screen readers available. I can't recommend strongly enough that you try at least one of these to better appreciate how your semantic HTML choices influence the screen reader user experience. Better yet, test your pages in a screen reader as part of your normal development process.

TIP You can use ARIA role attributes in your CSS selectors. In fact, by using the proper landmark roles, you could omit the `id="content"` and `id="sidebar"` attributes from code sample Ⓐ. See Chapter 11 for details.

Naming Elements with a Class or ID

Although it isn't required, you can give your HTML elements a unique identifier, assign them a particular class (or classes), or both. After doing so, you can apply styles to all elements with a given `id` or `class` name. That's certainly their most popular use, but not their only one (see the tips in this section).

To name an element with a unique id:

Within the start tag of the element, type `id="name"`, where *name* uniquely identifies the element Ⓐ. *name* can be almost anything, as long as it doesn't start with a number or contain any spaces.

To assign an element a class:

Within the start tag of the element, type `class="name"`, where *name* is the identifying name of the class Ⓐ. If you want to assign more than one class, separate each one with a space, as in `class="name anothername"`. (You may assign more than two class names.)

> **TIP** Each `id` in an HTML document must be unique. In other words, no two elements in the same page can be named with the same `id`, and each element may have only one `id`. The same `id` can appear on multiple pages and doesn't have to be assigned to the same element each time, though it is customary to do so.

> **TIP** Conversely, a particular `class` name can be assigned to any number of elements in a page, and an element may have more than one `class`.

continues on page 94

The `class` Attribute and Microformats

There's a common misperception that the `class` attribute was created solely for applying CSS to groups of elements. That's not the case. It was also designed to enrich HTML's semantics without adding more elements to the markup language.

Microformats do just that. They use agreed-upon `class` names to identify a piece of HTML as, say, an event or calendar entry (the `hCalendar` microformat); to identify people, organizations, and companies (`hCard`); or to describe the relationship between people (XFN). Those are just a few of the many microformats defined today, and more are always in the works.

Applications, search bots, and other software can read and make use of the microformats in your HTML. For example, Operator, a Firefox add-on, exposes the microformats in any given page.

You can learn more about implementing microformats at http://microformats.org.

Ⓐ Add a unique **id** attribute to an element in order to identify it for later formatting, links, or JavaScript behavior. Add a **class** attribute to one or more elements to be able to format them all in one fell swoop. For example, the **architect** and **project** classes could be applied to content about other architects for consistent formatting. The links in the **nav** point to the **id**s on the **h1** and **h2**s (see Chapter 6 for more information about links). The other **id**s are for formatting. See "Creating Generic Containers" for more information about **id**s, as well as another example that uses them. The **id** and **class** attributes don't affect an element's appearance unless CSS references them.

```
...
<body>

<div id="container">
    <header>
        <nav role="navigation">
            <ul id="toc">
                <li><a href="#gaudi">Barcelona's Architect</a></li>
                <li><a href="#sagrada-familia" lang="es">La Sagrada Família</a></li>
                <li><a href="#park-guell">Park Guell</a></li>
            </ul>
        </nav>
    </header>

    <article class="architect" role="main">
        <h1 id="gaudi">Barcelona's Architect</h1>

        <p>Antoni Gaudí's incredible buildings bring millions of tourists to Barcelona each year.</p>
        ...

        <section class="project">
            <h2 id="sagrada-familia" lang="es">La Sagrada Família</h2>
            ...
        </section>

        <section class="project">
            <h2 id="park-guell">Park Guell</h2>
            ...
        </section>
    </article>
    ...
</div>
</body>
</html>
```

TIP The `class` and `id` attributes may be added to any HTML element. An element may have both an `id` and any number of `classes`.

TIP For information about applying styles to an element with a particular `id` or `class`, consult "Selecting Elements by Class or ID" in Chapter 9.

TIP Choose meaningful (that is, semantic) names for your `ids` and `classes`, regardless of how you intend to use them. For instance, if you use a `class` for styling, avoid names that describe the presentation, like `class="red"` —that's a cardinal sin (get it, red, cardinal?). In all seriousness, `class="red"` is a poor choice because you might decide next week to change your site's color scheme to blue. Changing the color assigned to a `class` in CSS is incredibly simple, but then your HTML would have a `class` called red that really renders in a different color. Changing all the `class` names in your HTML usually isn't trivial.

TIP When choosing between applying a `class` or an `id` to an element for styling pur-poses, generally it's preferable to use a `class` because you can reuse its associated styles on other elements with the same `class`. How-ever, certainly there will be times you want to direct your styles to one element (and possibly any of its descendants) via its `id`.

TIP The `id` attribute automatically turns the element into a named anchor, to which you can direct a link. For more details, see "Creat-ing Anchors" in Chapter 6.

TIP You can use the `class` attribute to imple-ment microformats (see the sidebar for more details).

TIP You can use JavaScript to access both the `id` and `class` attributes to apply behavior to particular elements.

A You can add titles to any elements you wish, though it's most common to use them on links.

```
...
<body>
    <header role="banner">
        <nav role="navigation">
            <ul id="toc" title="Table of
            Contents">
                <li><a href="#gaudi" title=
                → "Learn about Antoni
                → Gaudí">Barcelona's
                → Architect</a></li>
                <li><a href="#sagrada-familia"
                → lang="es">La Sagrada Família
                → </a></li>
                <li><a href="#park-guell">Park
                → Guell</a></li>
            </ul>
        </nav>
    </header>

    ...
</body>
</html>
```

B When your visitors point at the labeled element, the title will appear. If you were pointing at the Barcelona's Architect link, you'd see "Learn about Antoni Gaudí," since it has its own **title** attribute.

Adding the Title Attribute to Elements

You can use the **title** attribute—not to be confused with the **title** *element*—to add a tool tip label to practically any part of your Web site (**A** and **B**). They aren't just for tool tips, though. Screen readers may read title text to users, improving accessibility.

To add a title to elements in a webpage:

In the HTML element for the item you want to label with a title, add **title="*label*"**, where **label** is the brief descriptive text that should appear in the tool tip when a visitor points at the element or that will be read aloud by a screen reader.

TIP Old versions of Internet Explorer (IE7 and earlier) also make tool tips out of the **alt** attribute used in **img** elements (see Chapter 5). However, if both the **title** and **alt** attributes are present in an **img** element, the tool tip is set to the contents of the **title** attribute, not the **alt** attribute.

Adding Comments

You can add comments to your HTML documents to note where sections begin or end, to comment to yourself (or future editors) the purpose of a particular piece of code, to prevent content from displaying, and more Ⓐ. These comments only appear when the document is opened with a text editor or via a browser's View Source option. They are invisible to visitors in the browser otherwise Ⓑ.

Ⓐ This sample includes four comments. Two combine to mark the beginning and end of the article. Another "comments out" the first paragraph so it won't be displayed in the page (if you want the paragraph to be removed long-term, it would be best to delete it from the HTML). The last comment is a reminder to add more content before putting the page on the live site. Just be sure to remove any temporary comments like "to dos" before making your page live, in case visitors view your code. "Creating Generic Containers" has more sample comments.

```
...
<body>

    ...

    <!-- ==== START ARTICLE ==== -->
    <article class="architect">
        <h1 id="gaudi">Barcelona's Architect</h1>

    <!-- This paragraph doesn't display because it's commented out.
        <p>Antoni Gaudí's incredible buildings bring millions of tourists to Barcelona each
        → year.</p>
    -->

        <p>Gaudí's non-conformity, already visible in his teenage years, coupled with his quiet
        → but firm devotion to the church, made a unique foundation for his thoughts and ideas. His
        → search for simplicity ...</p>

        <section class="project">
            <h2 id="sagrada-familia" lang="es">La Sagrada Família</h2>
            ...
        </section>

        <section class="project">
            <h2 id="park-guell">Park Guell</h2>
            ...
        </section>
    </article>
    <!-- end article -->

    <!--
TO DO: Add another article here about other famous buildings before making page live.
    -->

    ...
</body>
</html>
```

B Comments are invisible (though they readily appear when the source code is displayed). Similarly, if you wrap a comment around some of your content, it won't display **A**. Here, the first paragraph in the code doesn't show.

To add a comment to your HTML page:

1. In your HTML document, where you wish to insert a comment, type `<!--`.

2. Type the comments.

3. Type `-->` to complete the commented text.

TIP A good use for comments is to remind yourself (or future editors) to include, remove, or update certain sections **A**.

TIP Another use for comments is to note a revision number.

TIP It's common to comment the beginning and end of major sections of code to make it easier for you or fellow coders to modify later (pages can get long). I like to use a different, more prominent format for a starting comment than for one signifying the end of a block so my eye can easily distinguish between the two points as I scan the code **A**.

TIP You should view your commented page with a browser before publishing. This will help you avoid displaying your (possibly) private comments to the public because you accidentally formatted a comment wrong.

TIP Beware, however, of comments that are too private. While invisible when visiting your page normally in the browser, they can be seen via a browser's View Source feature or if the user saves the page as HTML code (source).

TIP Comments may not be nested within other comments.

TIP The syntax shown is for HTML comments only. CSS and JavaScript have a different commenting syntax. CSS and JavaScript both use `/* Comment goes here */` for a comment covering one or more lines, while JavaScript also has `// Comment goes here` for single-line comments.

Text

Unless a site is heavy on videos or photo galleries, most content on Web pages is text. This chapter explains which HTML semantics are appropriate for different types of text, especially (but not solely) for text within a sentence or phrase.

For example, the **em** element is specifically designed for indicating emphasized text, and the **cite** element's purpose is to cite works of art, movies, books, and more.

Browsers typically style many text elements differently than normal text. For instance, both the **em** and **cite** elements are italicized. Another element, **code**, which is specifically designed for formatting lines of code from a script or program, displays in a monospace font by default.

How content will look is irrelevant when deciding how to mark it up. So, you shouldn't use **em** or **cite** just because you want to italicize text. That's the job of CSS.

Instead, focus on choosing HTML elements that describe the content. If by default a browser styles it as you would yourself with CSS, that's just a bonus. If not, just override the default formatting with your own CSS.

Starting a New Paragraph

HTML does not recognize the returns or other extra white space that you enter in your text editor. To start a new paragraph in your Web page, you use the **p** element (Ⓐ and Ⓑ).

To begin a new paragraph:

1. Type `<p>`.
2. Type the contents of the new paragraph.
3. Type `</p>` to end the paragraph.

Ⓐ Not surprisingly, **p** is one of the most frequently used HTML elements.

```
...
<body>

<article>
    <h1>Antoni Gaudí</h1>
    <p>Many tourists are drawn to
     ·Barcelona to see Antoni Gaudí's
     →incredible architecture.</p>

    <p>Barcelona celebrated the 150th
     →anniversary of Gaudí's birth in
     ·2002.</p>

    <h2>La Casa Milà</h2>
    <p>Gaudí's work was essentially useful.
     ·<span lang="es">La Casa Milà</span> is
     ·an apartment building and real people
     ·live there.</p>

    <h2>La Sagrada Família</h2>
    <p>The complicatedly named and curiously
     →unfinished Expiatory Temple of the
     ·Sacred Family is the most visited
     ·building in Barcelona.</p>
</article>

</body>
</html>
```

B Here you see the typical default rendering of paragraphs. As with all content elements, you have full control over the formatting with CSS.

TIP You can use styles to format paragraphs with a particular font, size, or color (and more). For details, consult Chapter 10.

TIP To control the amount of space between lines, consult "Setting the Line Height" in Chapter 10. To control the amount of space after a paragraph, consult "Setting the Margins around an Element" or "Adding Padding around an Element," both of which are in Chapter 11.

TIP You can justify paragraph text or align it to the left, right, or center with CSS (see "Aligning Text" in Chapter 10).

Adding Author Contact Information

You might think the **address** element is for marking up a postal address, but it isn't (except for one circumstance; see the tips). In fact, there isn't an HTML element explicitly designed for that purpose.

Instead, **address** defines the contact information for the author, people, or organization relevant to an HTML page (usually appearing at the end of the page, if at all) or part of a page, such as within a report or a news article (Ⓐ and Ⓑ).

To provide the author's contact information:

1. If you want to provide author contact information for an **article**, place the cursor within that **article**. Alternatively, place the cursor within the **body** (or, more commonly, the page-level **footer**) if you want to provide author contact information for the page at large.

2. Type **<address>**.

3. Type the author's email address, a link to a page with contact information, and so on.

4. Type **</address>**.

Ⓐ This page has two **address** elements: one for the **article**'s author and the other in a page-level **footer** for the people who maintain the whole page. Note that the **address** for the **article** contains contact information only. Although the background information about Tracey Wong is also in the **article**'s **footer**, it's outside the **address** element.

```
...
<body>

<article>
      <h1>Museum Opens on the Waterfront</h1>
      <p>The new art museum not only introduces
      → a range of contemporary works to the
      → city, it's part of larger development
      → effort on the waterfront.</p>
      ... [rest of story content] ...

      <!-- the article's footer with address
      → information for the article -->
      <footer>
            <p>Tracey Wong has written for <cite>
            → The Paper of Papers</cite> since
            → receiving her MFA in art history
            three years ago.</p>
            <address>
            Email her at <a href="mailto:
            → traceyw@thepaperofpapers.com">
            → traceyw@thepaperofpapers.com
            → </a>.
            </address>
      </footer>
</article>

<!-- the page's footer with address
→ information for the whole page -->
<footer>
      <p><small>&copy; 2011 The Paper of
      → Papers, Inc.</small></p>

      <address>
      Have a question or comment about the
      → site? <a href="site-feedback.html">
      → Contact our Web team</a>.
      </address>
</footer>

</body>
</html>
```

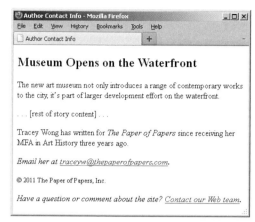

B The **address** element renders in italics by default.

TIP Most of the time, contact information takes the form of the author's email address or a link to a page with more contact information. The contact information could very well be the author's postal address, in which case marking it up with `address` would be valid. But if you're creating the Contact Us page for your business and want to include your office locations, it would be incorrect to code those with `address`.

TIP `address` pertains to the nearest `article` element ancestor, or to the page's body if `address` isn't nested within an `article`. It's customary to place `address` in a `footer` element when noting author contact information for the page at large **A**.

TIP An `address` in an `article` provides contact information for the author of that `article` **A**, not for any `articles` nested within that `article`, such as user comments.

TIP `address` may contain author contact information only, not anything else such as the document or `article`'s last modified date **A**. Additionally, HTML5 forbids nesting any of the following elements inside `address`: h1–h6, article, address, aside, footer, header, hgroup, nav, and section.

TIP See Chapter 3 to learn more about the `article` and `footer` elements.

Creating a Figure

As you well know, it's a common convention in the print world to associate figures with text. A figure may be a chart, a graph, a photo, an illustration, a code segment, and so on. You've seen these at play in newspapers, magazines, reports, and more. Why, this very book has figures on most pages.

Prior to HTML5, there wasn't an element designed for this purpose, so developers cobbled together solutions on their own, often involving the less-than-ideal, non-semantic **div** element. HTML5 changes that with **figure** and **figcaption**. By definition, a **figure** is a self-contained piece of content (with an optional caption) that is referred to by the main content of your document (Ⓐ and Ⓑ). The optional **figcaption** is a **figure**'s caption or legend and may appear either at the beginning or at the end of a **figure**'s content Ⓐ.

To create a figure and figure caption:

1. Type **<figure>**.

2. Optionally, type **<figcaption>** to begin the figure's caption.

3. Type the caption text.

4. Type **</figcaption>** if you created a caption in steps 2 and 3.

5. Create your figure by adding code for images, videos, data tables, and so on.

6. If you didn't include a **figcaption** before your **figure**'s content, optionally follow steps 2–4 to add one after the content.

7. Type **</figure>**.

Ⓐ This **figure** has a chart image, though more than one image or other types of content (such as a data table or video) are allowed as well. The **figcaption** element isn't required, but it must be the first or last element in a **figure** if you do include it. A **figure** doesn't have a default styling aside from starting on its own line in modern browsers Ⓑ.

```
...
<body>

<article>
    <h1>2011 Revenue by Industry</h1>
    ... [report content] ...

    <figure>
       <figcaption>Figure 3: 2011 Revenue
       → by Industry</figcaption>

       <img src="chart-revenue.png"
       → width="180" height="143" alt=
       → "Revenue chart: Clothing 42%,
       → Toys 36%, Food 22%" />
    </figure>

    <p>As Figure 3 illustrates, ... </p>

    ... [more report content] ...
</article>

</body>
</html>
```

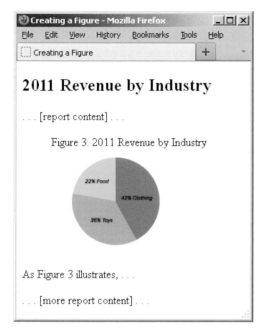

B The **figure** with the chart and caption appears within the **article** text. It would be simple to style the **figure** with CSS so, for example, it has a border and so the article text wraps around it.

TIP Typically, `figure` is part of the content that refers to it **A**, but it could also live elsewhere on the page or on another page, such as in an appendix.

TIP The `figure` element may include multiple pieces of content. For instance, **A** could include two charts: one for revenue and another for profits. Keep in mind, though, that regardless of how much content a `figure` has, only one `figcaption` is allowed.

TIP Don't use `figure` simply as a means to embed all instances of self-contained content within text. Oftentimes, the `aside` element may be appropriate instead (see "Specifying an Aside" in Chapter 3).

TIP The `figure` element is known as a sectioning root in HTML5, which means it can have h1–h6 headings (and thus, its own outline), but they don't contribute to the document outline. This is very different than sectioning *content*. Please see "Understanding HTML5's Document Outline" in Chapter 3.

TIP You can't use the optional `figcaption` element unless it's in a `figure` with other content.

TIP `figcaption` text doesn't have to begin with "Figure 3" or "Exhibit B." It could just as well be a brief description of the content, like a photo caption.

TIP If you include a `figcaption`, it must be either the first or last element of the `figure`.

Specifying Time

You can mark up a precise time or calendar date with the **time** element. This element is new in HTML5. (See the sidebar "Understanding the **datetime** Format" for more specifics about the calendar date system.)

One of the most common uses of **time** is to indicate the publication date of an **article** element. To do so, include the **pubdate** attribute. The **time** element with **pubdate** represents the publication date of the nearest ancestor **article** element . You could also time-stamp an **article**'s reader-submitted comments with **time**, **datetime**, and **pubdate**, assuming each comment is wrapped in an **article** element that is nested in the **article** to which the comment relates (see Example 2 of the sidebar in "Creating an Article" in Chapter 3).

You can represent time with the **time** element in a variety of ways (Ⓐ and Ⓒ). The optional text content inside **time** (that is, **<time>text</time>**) appears on the screen as a human-readable version (Ⓑ and Ⓓ) of the optional, machine-readable **datetime** value.

Ⓐ As is proper, the **datetime** attribute and the **time** element's text reflect the same date, though they can be written differently than one another (see Ⓒ for more examples). This **time** element represents the date the article was published, because the **pubdate** attribute is included.

```
...
<body>

<article>
    <header>
        <h1>Cheetah and Gazelle Make Fast
        → Friends</h1>
        <p><time datetime="2011-10-15"
        → pubdate="pubdate">October 15,
        → 2011</time></p>
    </header>

    ... [article content] ...
</article>

</body>
</html>
```

Ⓑ The **article**'s publication date appears underneath its heading. The text content version of the **time** element displays, not the **datetime** value.

C The **time** element can be utilized several ways. The simplest form (the first example) lacks a **datetime** attribute. But it *does* provide the date and times in the valid format as required when **datetime** is omitted. The top three examples contain time and/or date with text inside **time**, which will display on the screen **D**. I suggest you always include this human-readable form of the time, since, currently, browsers won't display a value otherwise **B**.

```
...
<body>

<p>The train arrives at <time>08:45</time>
→ and <time>16:20</time> on
→ <time>2012-04-10</time>.</p>

<p>We began our descent from the peak of
→ Everest on <time datetime="1952-06-12T11:
→ 05:00">June 12, 1952 at 11:05 a.m.
→ </time></p>

<p>They made their dinner reservation
→ for <time datetime="2011-09-20T18:
→ 30:00">tonight at 6:30</time>.</p>

<p>The record release party is on <time
→ datetime="2011-12-09"></time>.</p>

</body>
</html>
```

D The first three paragraphs show a time. The last does not (see the last tip).

To specify a precise time, calendar date, or both:

1. Type **<time** to begin a **time** element.

2. If desired, type **datetime="*time*"** where *time* is represented in the approved format (see the "Understanding the **datetime** Format" sidebar).

3. If the time represents the publication date of an **article** or the whole page, type either **pubdate="pubdate"** or **pubdate**.

4. Type **>** to complete the start tag.

5. If you want the time to display in the browser, type text that reflects the time, the date, or both (see the first tip about the allowed text format).

6. Type **</time>**.

TIP If you omit the **datetime** attribute, the text content must conform to the valid date or time format. In other words, the first example in **C** could not be coded as <p>The train arrives at <time>8:45 a.m.</time> and <time>4:20 p.m.</time> on <time>October 4th, 2012</time>.</p>. However, when you do include **datetime**, you're free to represent the date or time in the text content as you wish, as seen in the second and third examples of **C**.

TIP Don't use **time** to mark up imprecise dates or times, such as "the mid-1900s," "just after midnight," "the latter part of the Renaissance," or "early last week."

TIP Always include a text version of the time and date inside the **time** element if you want it to show in your page. If it's missing, browsers are supposed to display text that is based on **datetime**'s value, but support is lacking greatly at the time of this writing **D**.

continues on page 109

Understanding the `datetime` Format

The **time** element's time is based on a 24-hour clock with an optional time-zone offset from UTC (Coordinated Universal Time). The **datetime** attribute provides the date and time in a machine-readable format, which I've simplified for this initial example:

YYYY-MM-DDThh:mm:ss

For example (local time):

2011-11-03T17:19:10

This means "November 3, 2011, at 10 seconds after 5:19 p.m. local time." **T** separates the date (**YYYY-MM-DD**) and time (**hh:mm:ss**), and if you include a time, the seconds are optional. (You may also provide time with milliseconds in the format of **hh:mm.sss**. Note the period before the milliseconds.)

If you'd like, you can represent your time in a global context instead. Add a **Z** at the end, and the time zone is UTC.

For example (global time in UTC):

2011-11-03T17:19:10Z

Or, you can specify a time-zone offset from UTC by omitting **Z** and preceding the offset with – (minus) or + (plus).

For example (global time with offset from UTC):

2011-11-03T17:19:10-03:30

This means "November 3, 2011, at 10 seconds after 5:19 p.m. Newfoundland standard time (it's minus three and a half hours from UTC)." A list of time zones by UTC offsets is available at http://en.wikipedia.org/wiki/List_of_time_zones_by_UTC_offset.

If you do include **datetime**, it doesn't require the full complement of information I just described, as the examples in ⓒ show. Technically speaking, dates in the **time** element are based on the proleptic Gregorian calendar (as you may know, the Gregorian calendar is the internationally accepted civil calendar system in common use today). As such, HTML5 recommends you don't use it for pre-Gregorian dates (chances are this won't be an issue for your content, but just so you know about it). There has been a lot of discussion about this limitation, but it's a complicated topic. Read http://dev.w3.org/html5/spec-author-view/the-time-element.html for more information and examples, or www.quirksmode.org/blog/archives/2009/04/making_time_saf.html for an extensive explanation of some of the issues.

TIP If you use `time` with `pubdate` to indicate an `article`'s publication date, it's common but not mandatory to place it in either a `header` or `footer` element of the `article` element. Regardless, be sure it's nested somewhere within the relevant `article`.

TIP If a `time` element with the `pubdate` attribute doesn't have an `article` element as an ancestor, it represents the publication date and time of the whole page.

TIP You can specify `pubdate` as either

`<time pubdate></time>`

or `<time pubdate="pubdate"></time>`.

However, if you include it, either `datetime` or a text content version of the time is required Ⓐ.

TIP The `datetime` attribute's machine-readable format (see the "Understanding the `datetime` Format" sidebar) allows for syncing dates and times between Web applications. As of this writing, no browser displays the `datetime` value (Ⓑ and Ⓓ).

TIP You may not nest a `time` element inside another one.

Marking Important and Emphasized Text

The **strong** element denotes important text, while **em** conveys emphasis. You can use them individually or together as your content requires (Ⓐ and Ⓑ).

To mark important text:

1. Type **<strong>**.

2. Type the text that you want to mark as important.

3. Type **</strong>**.

To emphasize text:

1. Type **<em>**.

2. Type the text that you want to emphasize.

3. Type **</em>**.

> **TIP** Do not use the **b** and **i** elements as replacements for **strong** and **em**, respectively. Although they may look similar in a browser, their meanings are very different (see the sidebar "The **b** and **i** Elements: Redefined in HTML5").

> **TIP** You may nest **strong** text inside a phrase that is also marked with **strong**. If you do, the importance of **strong** text increases each time it's a child of another **strong**. The same is true of the level of emphasis for **em** text nested in another **em**. For example, "due by November 17th" is marked as more important semantically than the other **strong** text in this sentence: **<p><strong>Remember that entries are** <strong>due by November 17th</strong>**.</strong></p>**.

> **TIP** You can style any text as bold or italic with CSS, as well as override the browser's default styling of elements like **strong** and **em** Ⓑ. For details, consult "Creating Italics" and "Applying Bold Formatting" in Chapter 10.

Ⓐ The first sentence has both **strong** and **em**, while the second has **em** only. If **<em>under any circumstances</em>** were marked up instead as **<strong>under any circumstances</strong>**, it would have greater importance than the text contained in the surrounding **strong**.

```
...
<body>

<p><strong>Warning: Do not approach the
 zombies <em>under any circumstances</em>.
 </strong> They may <em>look</em>
 friendly, but that's just because they want
 to eat your arm.</p>

</body>
</html>
```

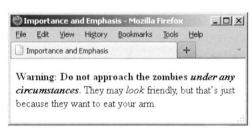

Ⓑ Browsers typically display **strong** text in boldface and **em** text in italics. If **em** is a child of a **strong** element (see the first sentence in Ⓐ), its text will be both italicized and bold.

The b and i Elements: Redefined in HTML5

HTML5 focuses on semantics, not on an element's presentation. The **b** and **i** elements are hold-overs from the earliest days of HTML, when they were used to make text bold or italic (CSS didn't exist yet). They rightly fell out of favor in HTML 4 and XHTML 1 because of their presentational nature. Coders were encouraged to use **strong** instead of **b**, and **em** instead of **i**. It turns out, though, that **em** and **strong** are not always semantically appropriate. HTML5 addresses this by redefining **b** and **i**.

Some typographic conventions in traditional publishing fall through the cracks of available HTML semantics. Among them are italicizing certain scientific names (for example, "The *Ulmus americana* is the Massachusetts state tree."), named vehicles (for example, the "We rode the *Orient Express*."), and foreign (to English) language phrases (for example, "The couple exhibited a *joie de vivre* that was infectious."). These terms aren't italicized for emphasis, just stylized per convention.

Rather than create several new semantic elements (and further muddy the waters) to address cases like these, HTML5 takes a practical stance by trying to make do with what is available: **em** for all levels of emphasis, **strong** for importance, and **b** and **i** for the through-the-cracks cases.

The notion is that although **b** and **i** don't carry explicit semantic meaning, the reader will recognize that a difference is implied because they differ from the surrounding text. And you're still free to change their appearance from bold and italics with CSS. HTML5 emphasizes that you use **b** and **i** only as a last resort when another element (such as **strong**, **em**, **cite**, and others) won't do.

The b Element in Brief

HTML5 redefines the **b** element this way:

> The **b** element represents a span of text to which attention is being drawn for utilitarian purposes without conveying any extra importance and with no implication of an alternate voice or mood, such as key words in a document abstract, product names in a review, actionable words in interactive text-driven software, or an article lede.

For example:

```
<p>The <b>XR-5</b>, also dubbed the <b>Extreme Robot 5</b>, is the best robot we've ever
→ tested.</p>
```

The **b** element renders as bold by default.

The i Element in Brief

HTML5 redefines the **i** element this way:

> The **i** element represents a span of text in an alternate voice or mood, or otherwise offset from the normal prose in a manner indicating a different quality of text, such as a taxonomic designation, a technical term, an idiomatic phrase from another language, a thought, or a ship name in Western texts.

Here are some examples:

```
<p>The <i lang="la">Ulmus americana</i> is the Massachusetts state tree.</p>
<p>The <i>Orient Express</i> began service in 1883.<p>
<p>The couple exhibited a <i lang="fr">joie de vivre</i> that was infectious.<p>
```

The **i** element displays in italics by default.

Indicating a Citation or Reference

Use the **cite** element for a citation or reference to a source. Examples include the title of a play, script, or book; the name of a song, movie, photo, or sculpture; a concert or musical tour; a specification; a newspaper or legal paper; and more (Ⓐ and Ⓑ).

To cite a reference:

1. Type **<cite>**.

2. Type the reference's name.

3. Type **</cite>**.

> **TIP** For instances in which you are quoting from the cited source, use the **blockquote** or **q** elements, as appropriate, to mark up the quoted text (see "Quoting Text"). To be clear, **cite** is only for the source, not what you are quoting from it.

Ⓐ The **cite** element is appropriate for marking up the titles of works of art, music, movies, and books.

```
...

<p>He listened to <cite>Abbey Road</cite>
→ while watching <cite>A Hard Day's Night
→ </cite> and reading <cite>The Beatles
→ Anthology</cite>.

<p>When he went to The Louvre, he learned
→ that <cite>Mona Lisa</cite> is also known
→ as <cite lang="it">La Gioconda</cite>.</p>

...
```

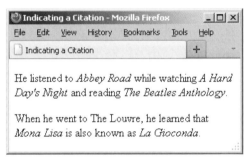

Ⓑ The **cite** element renders in italics by default.

HTML5 and Using the **cite** Element for Names

Amid a good amount of disagreement from the development community, HTML5 explicitly declares that using **cite** for a reference to a person's name is invalid, even though previous versions of HTML allowed it and many developers and designers used it that way.

The HTML 4 spec provides the following example (I've changed the element names from uppercase to lowercase):

```
As <cite>Harry S. Truman</cite> said,
<q lang="en-us">The buck stops here.</q>
```

In addition to instances like that, sites have often used **cite** for the name of visitors who leave comments in blog postings and articles (the default WordPress theme does too).

Many developers have made it clear that they intend to continue to use **cite** on names associated with quotes in their HTML5 pages because HTML5 doesn't provide an alternative they deem acceptable (namely, the **span** and **b** elements). Jeremy Keith made the case vociferously in http://24ways.org/2009/incite-a-riot/.

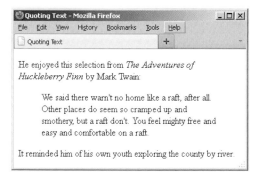

(A) A **blockquote** can be as short or as long as you need. Optionally, include the **cite** attribute—not to be confused with the **cite** element shown in the first paragraph—to provide the location of the quoted text. However, browsers don't display the **cite** attribute's information **(B)**. (See the second tip for a related recommendation.)

```
...
<body>

<p>He enjoyed this selection from <cite>The
  Adventures of Huckleberry Finn</cite> by
  Mark Twain:</p>

<blockquote cite="http://www.marktwain
  books.edu/the-adventures-of-huckleberry
  -finn/">
    <p>We said there warn't no home like a
      raft, after all. Other places do seem
      so cramped up and smothery, but a
      raft don't. You feel mighty free and
      easy and comfortable on a raft.</p>
</blockquote>

<p>It reminded him of his own youth exploring
  the county by river.</p>

</body>
</html>
```

(B) Browsers typically indent **blockquote** text by default. Historically, browsers haven't displayed the **cite** attribute's value (see the second tip for a related recommendation). The **cite** element, on the other hand, is supported by all browsers and typically renders in italics, as shown. All of these defaults can be overridden with CSS.

Quoting Text

There are two special elements for marking text quoted from a source. The **blockquote** element represents a quote (generally a longer one, but not necessarily) that stands alone **(A)** and renders on its own line by default **(B)**. Meanwhile, the **q** element is for short quotes, like those within a sentence **(C)** (on the next page).

Browsers are supposed to enclose **q** element text in language-specific quotation marks automatically, but Internet Explorer didn't support this until IE8. Some browsers have issues with nested quotes, too. Be sure to read the tips to learn about alternatives to using the **q** element.

To quote a block of text:

1. Type **<blockquote** to begin a block quote.

2. If desired, type **cite="*url*"**, where ***url*** is the address of the source of the quote.

3. Type **>** to complete the start tag.

4. Type the text you wish to quote, surrounding it with paragraphs and other elements as appropriate.

5. Type **</blockquote>**.

To quote a short phrase:

1. Type **<q** to begin quoting a word or phrase.

2. If desired, type **cite="*url*"**, where *url* is the address of the source of the quote.

3. If the quote's language is different than the page's default language (as specified by the **lang** attribute on the **html** element), type **lang="*xx*"**, where *xx* is the two-letter code for the language the quote will be in. This code is *supposed* to determine the type of quote marks that will be used ("" for English, «» for many European languages, and so on), though browser support for this rendering can vary.

4. Type **>** to complete the start tag.

5. Type the text that should be quoted.

6. Type **</q>**.

TIP Although it's allowed, avoid placing text directly between the start and end blockquote tags. Instead, enclose it in p or other semantically appropriate elements within the blockquote.

TIP You can use the optional cite attribute on blockquote and q to provide a URL to the source you are quoting. Unfortunately, browsers traditionally haven't presented the cite URL to users **B**, so it's not the most useful of attributes on its own. Consequently, if you do include cite, I recommend you repeat the URL in a link (the a element) in your content, allowing visitors to access it. Less effectively, you could expose cite's value via JavaScript.

C Add the **lang** attribute to the **q** element if the quoted text is in a different language than the page's default (as specified by the **lang** attribute on the **html** element).

```
...
<body>

<p>And then she said, <q>Have you read
→ Barbara Kingsolver's <cite>High Tide in
→ Tucson</cite>? It's inspiring.</q></p>

<p>She tried again, this time in French:
→ <q lang="fr">Avez-vous lu le livre
→ <cite>High Tide in Tucson</cite> de
→ Kingsolver? C'est inspirational.</q></p>

</body>
</html>
```

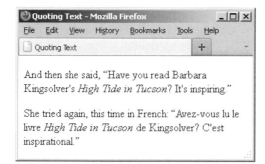

 Browsers are supposed to add curly double quotes around **q** elements (and curly single quotes around nested **q** elements) automatically. As shown here, Firefox does, but not all browsers do (for example, older versions of Internet Explorer).

TIP The **blockquote** element is known as a sectioning root in HTML5, which means it can have **h1–h6** headings (and thus, its own outline), but they don't contribute to the document outline. This is very different than sectioning *content*. Please see "Understanding HTML5's Document Outline" in Chapter 3.

TIP The **q** element is invalid for a quote that extends beyond one paragraph.

TIP Be sure you don't use **q** simply because you want quotation marks around a word or phrase. For instance, `<p>Every time I hear the word <q>soy</q>, I jump for joy.</p>` is improper because "soy" isn't a quote from a source.

TIP You can nest **blockquote** and **q** elements. For example, `<p>The short story began, <q>When she was a child, she would say, <q>Howdy, stranger!</q> to everyone she passed.</q></p>`. Nested **q** elements should automatically have the appropriate quotation marks—in English the outer quotes should be double and the inner ones should be single—but browser support varies. Since outer and inner quotations are treated differently in languages, add the **lang** attribute to **q** as needed (and).

TIP Because of cross-browser issues with **q** , many (probably the majority of) coders choose to simply type the proper quotation marks or use character entities instead of the **q** element. In his in-depth article "Quoting and citing with `<blockquote>`, `<q>`, `<cite>`, and the **cite** attribute" at HTML5 Doctor, Oli Studholme discusses this and more, such as a series of options for styling quotation marks with the **q** element and related browser support information (http://html5doctor.com/blockquote-q-cite/).

Highlighting Text

We've all used a highlighter pen at some point or another. Maybe it was when studying for an exam or going through a contract. Whatever the case, you used the highlighter to mark key words or phrases that were relevant to a task.

HTML5 replicates this with the new **mark** element. Think of **mark** like a semantic version of a highlighter pen. In other words, what's important is that you're noting certain words; how they appear is irrelevant. Style its text with CSS as you please (or not at all), but use **mark** only when it's pertinent to do so.

No matter when you use **mark**, it's to draw the reader's attention to a particular text segment. Here are some use cases for it:

- To highlight a search term when it appears in a search results page or an article. When people talk about **mark**, this is the most common context. Suppose you used a site's search feature to look for "solar panels." The search results or each resulting article could use **<mark>solar panels</mark>** to highlight the term throughout the text.

- To call attention to part of a quote that wasn't highlighted by the author in its original form (**A** and **B**).

- To draw attention to a code fragment (**C** and **D**).

A Although **mark** may see its most widespread use in search results, here's another valid use of it. The phrase "15 minutes" was not highlighted in the instructions on the packaging. Instead, the author of this HTML used **mark** to call out the phrase as part of the story. Default browser rendering of **mark** text varies **B**.

```
...
<body>

<p>So, I went back and read the instructions
  myself to see what I'd done wrong. They
  said:</p>

<blockquote>
    <p>Remove the tray from the box. Pierce
      the overwrap several times with a
      fork and cook on High for <mark>15
      minutes</mark>, rotating it half way
      through.</p>
</blockquote>

<p>I thought he'd told me <em>fifty</em>. No
  wonder it exploded in my microwave.</p>

</body>
</html>
```

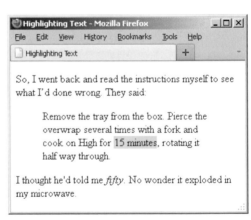

B Browsers with native support of the **mark** element display a yellow background behind the text by default. Older browsers don't, but you can tell them to do so with a simple rule in your style sheet (see the tips).

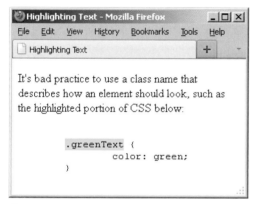

C This example uses **mark** to draw attention to a segment of code.

```
...
<body>

<p>It's bad practice to use a class name that
→ describes how an element should look, such
→ as the highlighted portion of CSS below:
<pre>
    <code>
    <mark>.greenText</mark> {
        color: green;
    }
    </code>
</pre>

</body>
</html>
```

D This code noted with **mark** is called out.

To highlight text:

1. Type **<mark>**.

2. Type the word or words to which you want to call attention.

3. Type **</mark>**.

TIP The **mark** element is not the same as either **em** (which represents emphasis) or **strong** (which represents importance). Both are covered in this chapter as well.

TIP Since **mark** is new in HTML5, older browsers don't render a background color by default **B** and **D**. You can instruct them to do so by adding **mark { background-color: yellow; }** to your style sheet.

TIP Be sure not to use **mark** simply to give text a background color or other visual treatment. If all you're looking for is a means to style text and there's no proper semantic HTML element with which to wrap it, use the **span** element (covered in this chapter) and style it with CSS.

Explaining Abbreviations

Abbreviations abound, whether as Jr., M.D., or even good ol' HTML. You can use the **abbr** element to mark up abbreviations and explain their meaning (Ⓐ through Ⓒ). You don't have to wrap every abbreviation in **abbr**, only when you think it would be helpful for visitors to be given the expanded meaning.

To explain abbreviations:

1. Type **<abbr**.

2. Optionally, next type **title="*expansion*"**, where *expansion* is the words that represent the abbreviation.

3. Type **>**.

4. Then type the abbreviation itself.

5. Finally, finish up with **</abbr>**.

6. Optionally, type a space and **(*expansion*)**, where *expansion* is the words that represent the abbreviation.

Ⓐ Use the optional **title** attribute to provide the expanded version of an abbreviation. Alternatively, and arguably preferably, you could place the expansion in parentheses after the abbreviation. Or mix and match. Most people will be familiar with words like *laser* and *scuba*, so marking them up with **abbr** and providing titles isn't really necessary, but I've done it here for demonstration purposes.

```
...
<body>

<p>The <abbr title="National Football
→ League">NFL</abbr> promised a <abbr
→ title="light amplification by
→ stimulated emission of radiation">
→ laser</abbr> show at 9 p.m. after every
→ night game.</p>

<p>But, that's nothing compared to what
→ <abbr>MLB</abbr> (Major League
→ Baseball) did. They gave out free
→ <abbr title="self-contained underwater
→ breathing apparatus">scuba</abbr> gear
→ during rain delays.</p>

</body>
</html>
```

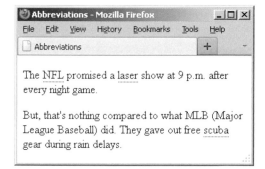

B When abbreviations have a **title** attribute, Firefox and Opera draw attention to them with a dotted underline. (You can instruct other browsers to do the same with CSS; see the tips.) In all browsers except IE6, when your visitors hover on an **abbr**, the contents of the element's **title** are shown in a tool tip.

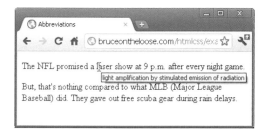

C Chrome and some other browsers display the title of abbreviations as a tool tip, but they don't display the abbreviation itself any differently unless you apply some CSS yourself.

TIP It's common practice to include an abbreviation's expansion (by way of a **title** or a parenthetical) only the first time it appears on a page **A**.

TIP A parenthetical abbreviation expansion is the most explicit way to describe an abbreviation, making it available to the widest set of visitors **A**. For instance, users on touch screen devices like smartphones and tablets may not be able to hover on an **abbr** element to see a **title** tool tip. So if you provide an expansion, consider putting it in parentheses whenever possible.

TIP If you use an abbreviation in its plural form, make the expansion plural as well.

TIP As a visual cue to sighted users, browsers like Firefox and Opera display **abbr** with a dotted bottom border if it has a **title** **B**. If you'd like to replicate that effect in all browsers (except IE6), add the following to your style sheet: `abbr[title] { border-bottom: 1px dotted #000; }`. Browsers provide the **title** attribute's contents as a tool tip **C** regardless of whether the **abbr** is styled with a border.

TIP If you don't see the dotted bottom border on your **abbr** in Internet Explorer 7, try adjusting the parent element's CSS `line-height` property (see Chapter 10).

TIP IE6 doesn't support **abbr**, so you won't see a border or a tool tip, just the text. If you really want to style **abbr** in IE6, you could put `document.createElement('abbr');` in a JavaScript file targeted for IE6 before your CSS. I say skip that and let IE6 be an outlier in this case. (See Chapter 11 to learn more about `document.createElement` as it pertains to styling elements that are new in HTML5 in IE8 and lower.)

TIP HTML had an `acronym` element before HTML5, but developers and designers often were confused by the difference between an abbreviation and an acronym, so HTML5 eliminated the `acronym` element in favor of `abbr` for all instances.

Defining a Term

The **dfn** element marks the one place in your document that you define a term. Subsequent uses of the term are not marked. You wrap **dfn** only around the term you're defining, not around the definition 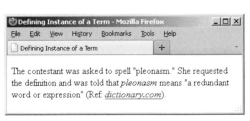.

It's important where you place the **dfn** in relation to its definition. HTML5 states, "The paragraph, description list group, or section that is the nearest ancestor of the **dfn** element must also contain the definition(s) for the term given by the **dfn** element." This means that the **dfn** and its definition should be in proximity to each other. This is the case in both Ⓐ and the example given in the third tip; the **dfn** and its definition are in the same paragraph.

To mark the defining instance of a term:

1. Type **<dfn>**.

2. Type the term you wish to define.

3. Type **</dfn>**.

> **TIP** You can also use dfn in a definition list (the dl element). See Chapter 15.

> **TIP** If you want to direct users to the defining instance of a term, you can add an id to the dfn and link to it from other points in the site.

> **TIP** dfn may also enclose another phrasing element like abbr, when appropriate. For example, <p>A <dfn><abbr title= "Junior">Jr.</abbr></dfn> is a son with the same full name as his father.</p>.

> **TIP** HTML5 says that if you use the optional title attribute on a dfn, it should have the same value as the dfn term. As in the previous tip, if you nest a single abbr in dfn and the dfn has no text node of its own, the optional title should be on the abbr only.

Ⓐ Note that although pleonasm appears twice in the example, **dfn** marks the second one only, because that's when I defined the term (that is, it's the defining instance). Similarly, if I were to use pleonasm subsequently in the document, I wouldn't wrap it in **dfn** because I've already defined it. By default, browsers style **dfn** text differently than normal text Ⓑ. Also, you don't have to use the **cite** element each time you use **dfn**, just when you reference a source.

```
...
<body>

<p>The contestant was asked to spell
→"pleonasm." She requested the definition
→and was told that <dfn>pleonasm</dfn>
→means "a redundant word or expression"
→(Ref: <cite><a href=" http://dictionary.
→reference.com/browse/pleonasm" rel=
→"external">dictionary.com</a></cite>).</p>

</body>
</html>
```

Defining Instance of a Term - Mozilla Firefox
File Edit View History Bookmarks Tools Help
Defining Instance of a Term   +

The contestant was asked to spell "pleonasm." She requested the definition and was told that *pleonasm* means "a redundant word or expression" (Ref: *dictionary.com*).

Ⓑ The **dfn** element renders in italics by default in some browsers (Firefox, in this case), just like **cite**, but not in Webkit-based browsers such as Safari and Chrome. You can make them consistent by adding **dfn { font-style: italic; }** to your style sheet (see Chapters 8 and 10).

A One use of the **sup** element is to indicate footnotes. I placed the footnotes in a **footer** within the **article** rather than on the page at large because they are associated. I also linked each footnote number within the text to its footnote in the footer so visitors can access them more easily. Note, too, that the **title** attribute on the links provides another cue.

```
...
<body>

<article>
    <h1>Famous Catalans</h1>
    <p>When I was in the sixth grade, I
    → played the cello. There was a
    → teacher at school who always used
    → to ask me if I knew who "Pablo
    → Casals" was. I didn't at the time
    → (although I had met Rostropovich once
    → at a concert). Actually, Pablo Casals'
    → real name was <i>Pau</i> Casals, Pau
    → being the Catalan equivalent of Pablo
    → <a href="#footnote-1" title="Read
    → footnote"><sup>1</sup></a>.</p>

    <p>In addition to being an amazing
    → cellist, Pau Casals is remembered in
    → this country for his empassioned
    → speech against nuclear proliferation
    → at the United Nations <a href=
    → "#footnote-2" title="Read
    → footnote"><sup>2</sup></a> which
    → he began by saying "I am a Catalan.
    → Catalonia is an oppressed nation."</p>

    <footer>
        <p><sup>1</sup>It means Paul in
        → English.</p>
        <p><sup>2</sup>In 1963, I believe.</p>
    </footer>
</article>

</body>
</html>
```

Creating Superscripts and Subscripts

Letters or numbers that are raised or lowered slightly relative to the main body text are called superscripts and subscripts, respectively **A**. HTML includes elements for defining both kinds of text. Common uses for superscripts include marking trademark symbols, exponents, and footnotes **B**. Subscripts are common in chemical notation.

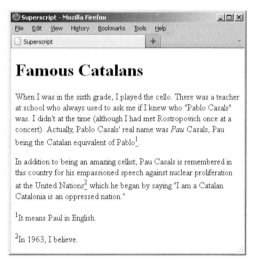

B Unfortunately, the **sub** and **sup** elements spoil the line spacing. Notice that there is more space between lines 4 and 5 of the first paragraph and lines 2 and 3 of the second than between the other lines. A little CSS comes to the rescue, though; see the sidebar "Fixing the Spacing between Lines when Using **sub** or **sup**" to learn how to fix this. You could also change the treatment of linked superscripts so that an underline doesn't appear so far from the superscripted text.

To create superscripts or subscripts:

1. Type `<sub>` to create a subscript or `<sup>` to create a superscript.

2. Type the characters or symbols that represent the subscript or superscript.

3. Type `</sub>` or `</sup>`, depending on what you used in step 1, to complete the element.

TIP Most browsers automatically reduce the font size of sub- or superscripted text by a few points.

TIP Superscripts are the ideal way to mark up certain foreign language abbreviations like M[lle] for *Mademoiselle* in French or 3[a] for tercera in Spanish, or numerics like 2nd and 5th.

TIP One proper use of subscripts is for writing out chemical molecules like H_2O. For example, `<p>I'm parched. Could I please have a glass of H<sub>2</sub>O?</p>`.

TIP Super- and subscripted characters gently spoil the even spacing between lines **B**. See the sidebar for a solution.

Fixing the Spacing between Lines when Using sub or sup

The **sub** and **sup** elements tend to throw off the line height between lines of text Ⓑ. Fortunately, you can set it straight with a bit of CSS.

The following code comes from Nicolas Gallagher and Jonathan Neal's excellent **normalize.css** (http://necolas.github.com/normalize.css/). They didn't invent the method that follows; they borrowed it from https://gist.github.com/413930 and removed the code comments. The second GitHub link includes a full explanation of what this CSS does, so I encourage you to give it a look. I also recommend checking out **normalize.css**, which you can use on your own projects. It helps you achieve a consistent baseline for rendering across browsers and is documented thoroughly (see "Resetting or Normalizing Default Styles" in Chapter 11).

```
/*
 * Prevents sub and sup affecting line-height in all browsers
 * gist.github.com/413930
 */
sub,
sup {
    font-size: 75%;
    line-height: 0;
    position: relative;
    vertical-align: baseline;
}

sup {
    top: -0.5em;
}

sub {
    bottom: -0.25em;
}
```

You may need to adjust this CSS a bit to level out the line heights, depending on your content's font size, but this should give you a very good start at the least. You'll learn about creating style sheets and how to add this CSS to your site in Chapter 8.

Noting Edits and Inaccurate Text

Sometimes you may want to indicate content edits that have occurred since the previous version of your page, or mark up text that is no longer accurate or relevant. There are two elements for noting edits: the **ins** element represents content that has been added, and the **del** element marks content that has been removed (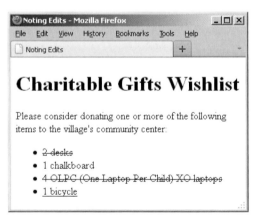**A** through **D**). You may use them together or individually.

Meanwhile, the **s** element notes content that is no longer accurate or relevant (it's not for edits) (**E** and **F**).

To mark an edit involving newly inserted text:

1. Type **<ins>**.
2. Type the new content.
3. Type **</ins>**.

To mark an edit involving deleted text:

1. Place the cursor before the text or element you wish to mark as deleted.
2. Type **<del>**.
3. Place the cursor after the text or element you wish to mark as deleted.
4. Type **</del>**.

A One item (the bicycle) has been added to this gift list since it was previously published, and purchased items have been removed, as noted by the **del** elements. You are not required to use **del** each time you use **ins**, or vice versa. Browsers differentiate the contents of each element visually by default **B**.

```
...
<body>

<h1>Charitable Gifts Wishlist</h1>

<p>Please consider donating one or more
→ of the following items to the village's
→ community center:</p>

<ul>
    <li><del>2 desks</del></li>
    <li>1 chalkboard</li>
    <li><del>4 <abbr>OLPC</abbr> (One
    → Laptop Per Child) XO laptops
    → </del></li>
    <li><ins>1 bicycle</ins></li>
</ul>

</body>
</html>
```

B Browsers typically display a line through deleted text and underline inserted text. You can change these treatments with CSS.

C Both **del** and **ins** are rare in that they can surround both phrasing ("inline" in pre-HTML5 parlance) content and blocks of content, as shown here. However, default browser rendering varies **D**.

```
...
<body>

<h1>Charitable Gifts Wishlist</h1>

<del>
    <p>Please consider donating one or more of the following items to the village's community
       center:</p>
</del>

<ins>
    <p>Please note that all gifts have been purchased.</p>
    <p>Thank you <em>so much</em> for your generous donations!</p>
</ins>

<del>
    <ul>
        <li><del>2 desks</del></li>
        <li>1 chalkboard</li>
        <li><del>4 <abbr>OLPC</abbr> (One Laptop Per Child) XO laptops</del></li>
        <li><ins>1 bicycle</ins></li>
    </ul>
</del>

</body>
</html>
```

D Most browsers, like Chrome (left), display **del** and **ins** wrapped around blocks of content by default as expected. That is, they reflect that entire pieces of content have been deleted or inserted. As of this writing, Firefox does not; it only renders the lines for **del** and **ins** text phrases within other elements. See the "Getting **del** and **ins** to Display Consistently" sidebar to learn how to rectify this.

To mark text that is no longer accurate or relevant:

1. Place the cursor before the text you wish to mark as no longer accurate or relevant.

2. Type **<s>**.

3. Place the cursor after the text you wish to mark.

4. Type **</s>**.

TIP Both del and ins support two attributes: cite and datetime. The cite attribute (not the same as the cite element) is for providing a URL to a source that explains why an edit was made. For example, **<ins cite="http://www.movienews.com/ticket-demand-high.html">2 p.m. (this show just added!)</ins>**. Use the datetime attribute to indicate the time of the edit. (See "Specifying Time" to learn about datetime's acceptable format.) Browsers don't display the values you assign to either of these attributes, so their use isn't widespread, but feel free to include them to add context to your content. The values could be extracted with JavaScript or a program that parses through your page.

E This example shows an ordered list (the **ol** element) of show times. The time slots for which ticket availability is no longer relevant have been marked with the **s** element. You can use **s** around any phrases, not just text within list items (**li** elements), but not around a whole paragraph or other "block-level" element like you can with **del** and **ins**.

```
...
<body>

<h1>Today's Showtimes</h1>

<p>Tickets are available for the following
→ times today:</p>

<ol>
    <li><ins>2 p.m. (this show just added!)
    → </ins></li>
    <li><s>5 p.m.</s> SOLD OUT</li>
    <li><s>8:30 p.m.</s> SOLD OUT</li>
</ol>

</body>
</html>
```

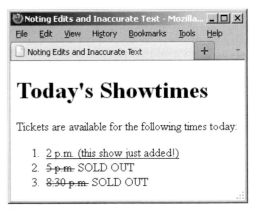

F The **s** element renders as a strikethrough by default in browsers.

Getting `del` and `ins` to Display Consistently

Browsers render content in a block-level `del` and `ins` inconsistently. Most display a strikethrough for `del` and an underline for `ins` on all nested content as expected, but at the least, Firefox does not ⑩.

You can rectify this with the following explicit CSS rules (the * means that every element inside `del` and `ins` gets the treatment):

```
del * {
    text-decoration:
    →line-through;
}

ins * {
    text-decoration: underline;
}
```

Please consult Chapter 8 if you aren't sure how to add this CSS to a style sheet.

TIP Use `del` and `ins` anytime you want to inform your visitors of your content's evolution. For instance, you'll often see them used in a Web development or design tutorial to indicate information learned since it was initially posted, while maintaining the copy as it originally stood for completeness. The same is true of blogs, news sites, and so on.

TIP Text marked with the `ins` element is generally underlined ⑧. Since links are often underlined as well (if not in your site, then in many others), this may be confusing to visitors. You may want to use styles to change how inserted passages (or links) are displayed (see Chapter 10).

TIP Text marked with the `del` element is generally struck out ⑧. Why not just erase it and be done with it? It depends on the context of your content. Striking it out makes it easy for sighted users to know what has changed. (Also, screen readers could announce the content as having been removed, but their support for doing so has been lacking historically.)

TIP Only use `del`, `ins`, and `s` for their semantic value. If you wish to underline or strike out text purely for cosmetic reasons, you can do so with CSS (see "Decorating Text" in Chapter 10).

TIP HTML5 notes that "The `s` element is not appropriate when indicating document edits; to mark a span of text as having been removed from a document, use the `del` element." You may find the distinction a little subtle at times. It's up to you to decide which is the appropriate semantic choice for your content.

Marking Up Code

If your content contains code samples, file names, or program names, the **code** element is for you (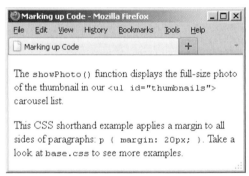**A** and **B**). To show a standalone block of code (outside of a sentence), wrap the **code** element with a **pre** element to maintain its formatting (see "Using Preformatted Text" for an example).

To mark up code or a file name:

1. Type **<code>**.

2. Type the code or file name.

3. Type **</code>**.

> **TIP** You can change the default mono-spaced font applied to code **B** with CSS (see Chapter 10).

A The **code** element indicates that the text is code or a file name. It also renders as a monospaced font by default **B**. If your code needs to display **<** or **>** signs, use the **<** and **>** character entities instead, respectively. Here, the second instance of **code** demonstrates this. If you did use **<** and **>**, the browser would treat your code as an HTML element, not text.

```
...
<body>

<p>The <code>showPhoto()</code> function
  displays the full-size photo of the
  thumbnail in our <code>&lt;ul id=
  "thumbnail"&gt;</code> carousel list.</p>

<p>This CSS shorthand example applies a
  margin to all sides of paragraphs:
  <code>p { margin: 20px; }</code>. Take
  a look at <code>base.css</code> to see
  more examples.</p>

</body>
</html>
```

The showPhoto() function displays the full-size photo of the thumbnail in our <ul id="thumbnails"> carousel list.

This CSS shorthand example applies a margin to all sides of paragraphs: p { margin: 20px; }. Take a look at base.css to see more examples.

B The **code** element's text even looks like code because of the monospaced default font.

Other Computer and Related Elements: kbd, samp, and var

The **kbd**, **samp**, and **var** elements see infrequent use, but you may have occasion to take advantage of them in your content. I'll explain each briefly.

The kbd Element

Use **kbd** to mark up user input instructions.

```
<p>To log into the demo:</p>
<ol>
    <li>Type <kbd>tryDemo</kbd> in the User Name field</li>
    <li><kbd>TAB</kbd> to the Password field and type <kbd>demoPass</kbd></li>
    <li>Hit <kbd>RETURN</kbd> or <kbd>ENTER</kbd></li>
</ol>
```

Like **code**, **kbd** renders as a monospaced font by default.

The samp Element

The **samp** element indicates sample output from a program or system.

```
<p>Once the payment went through, the site returned a message reading,
 → <samp>Thanks for your order!</samp></p>
```

samp also renders as a monospaced font by default.

The var Element

The **var** element represents a variable or placeholder value.

```
<p>Einstein is best known for <var>E</var>=<var>m</var><var>c</var><sup>2</sup>.
 → </p>
```

var can also be a placeholder value in content, like a Mad Libs sheet in which you'd put
 → `<var>adjective</var>`, `<var>verb</var>`, and so on.

var renders in italics by default.

Note that you can use the **math** and other **MathML** elements in your HTML5 pages for advanced math-related markup. See http://dev.w3.org/html5/spec-author-view/mathml.html for more information.

Using Preformatted Text

Usually, browsers collapse all extra returns and spaces and automatically break lines according to the size of the window. Preformatted text lets you maintain and display the original line breaks and spacing that you've inserted in the text. It is ideal for computer code examples 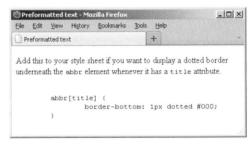, though you can also use it for text (hello, ASCII art!).

To use preformatted text:

1. Type **<pre>**.
2. Type or copy the text that you wish to display as is, with all the necessary spaces, returns, and line breaks. Unless it is code, do not mark up the text with any HTML, such as **p** elements.
3. Type **</pre>**.

Ⓐ The **pre** element is ideal for text that contains important spaces and line breaks, like the bit of CSS code shown here. Note, too, the use of the **code** element to mark up pieces of code or code-related text outside of **pre** (see "Marking Up Code" for more details).

```
...
<body>

<p>Add this to your style sheet if you want
   to display a dotted border underneath the
   <code>abbr</code> element whenever it has
   a <code>title</code> attribute.</p>

<pre>
    <code>
    abbr[title] {
        border-bottom: 1px dotted #000;
    }
    </code>
</pre>

</body>
</html>
```

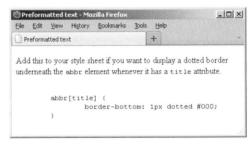

Ⓑ Notice that the indentation and line breaks are maintained in the **pre** content.

Presentation Considerations with pre

Be aware that browsers typically disable automatic word wrapping of content inside a **pre**, so if it's too wide, it might affect your layout or force a horizontal scrollbar. The following CSS rule enables wrapping within **pre** in many browsers, but not in Internet Explorer 7 and below.

```
pre {
    white-space: pre-wrap;
}
```

On a related note, in most cases I don't recommend you use the **white-space: pre;** CSS declaration on an element such as **div** as a substitute for **pre**, because the whitespace can be crucial to the semantics of the enclosed content, especially code, and only **pre** always preserves it. (Also, if the user has disabled CSS in his or her browser, the formatting will be lost.)

Please see CSS coverage beginning in Chapter 7. Text formatting, in particular, is discussed in Chapter 10.

TIP Preformatted text is typically displayed with a monospaced font like Courier or Courier New **B**. You can use CSS to change the font, if you like (see Chapter 10).

TIP If what you want to display—such as a code sample in a tutorial—contains HTML elements, you'll have to substitute each < and > around the element name with their appropriate character entities, < and > respectively (see "Marking Up Code" for an example). Otherwise the browser may try to display those elements. Be sure to validate your pages to see if you've nested HTML elements in **pre** when you shouldn't have (see "Validating Your Code" in Chapter 20).

TIP The **pre** element isn't a shortcut for avoiding marking up your content with proper semantics and styling its presentation with CSS. For instance, if you want to post a news article you wrote in a word processor, don't simply copy and paste it into a **pre** because you like the spacing the way it is. Instead, wrap your content in p (and other relevant text elements) and write CSS to control the layout as desired.

TIP **pre**, like a paragraph, always displays on a new line by default **B**.

Specifying Fine Print

According to HTML5, **small** represents side comments such as fine print, which "typically features disclaimers, caveats, legal restrictions, or copyrights. Small print is also sometimes used for attribution or for satisfying licensing requirements." **small** is intended for brief portions of inline text, not for text spanning multiple paragraphs or other elements (Ⓐ and Ⓑ).

To specify fine print:

1. Type **<small>**.

2. Type the text that represents a legal disclaimer, note, attribution, and so on.

3. Type **</small>**.

TIP Be sure to use **small** only because it fits your content, not because you want to reduce the text size, as happens in some browsers Ⓑ. You can always adjust the size with CSS (even making it larger if you'd like). See "Setting the Font Size" in Chapter 10 for more information.

TIP **small** is a common choice for marking up your page's copyright notice (Ⓐ and Ⓑ). It's meant for short phrases like that, so don't wrap it around long legal notices, such as your Terms of Use or Privacy Policy pages. Those should be marked up with paragraphs and other semantics, as necessary.

Ⓐ The **small** element denotes brief legal notices in both instances shown. The second one is a copyright notice contained in a page-level **footer**, a common convention.

```
...
<body>

<p>Order now to receive free shipping.
→ <small>(Some restrictions may apply.)
→ </small></p>

...

<footer>
    <p><small>&copy; 2011 The Super
    → Store. All Rights Reserved.
    → </small></p>
</footer>

</body>
</html>
```

Ⓑ The **small** element may render smaller than normal text in some browsers, but the visual size is immaterial to whether you should mark up your content with it.

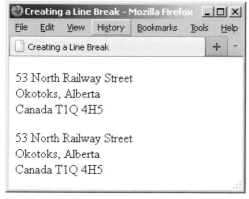

A The same address appears twice, but I coded them a little differently for demonstration purposes. Remember that the returns in your code are always ignored, so both paragraphs display the same way **B**. Also, you can code **br** as either `<br />` or `<br>` in HTML5.

```
...
<body>

<p>53 North Railway Street<br />
Okotoks, Alberta<br />
Canada T1Q 4H5</p>

<p>53 North Railway Street <br />Okotoks,
→ Alberta <br />Canada T1Q 4H5</p>

</body>
</html>
```

B Each **br** element forces the subsequent content to a new line.

Creating a Line Break

Browsers automatically wrap text according to the width of the block or window that contains content. It's best to let content flow like this in most cases, but sometimes you'll want to force a line break manually. You achieve this with the **br** element.

To be sure, using **br** is a last resort tactic because it mixes presentation with your HTML instead of leaving all display control to your CSS. For instance, never use **br** to simulate spacing between paragraphs. Instead, mark up the two paragraphs with **p** elements and define the spacing between the two with the CSS **margin** property.

So, when might **br** be OK? Well, the **br** element is suitable for creating line breaks in poems, in a street address (**A** and **B**), and occasionally in other short lines of text that should appear one after another.

To insert a line break:

Type `<br />` (or `<br>`) where the line break should occur. There is no separate end **br** tag because it's what's known as an *empty* (or *void*) *element*; it lacks content.

TIP Typing **br** as either `<br />` or `<br>` is perfectly valid in HTML5.

TIP Styles can help you control the space between lines in a paragraph (see "Setting the Line Height" in Chapter 10) and between the paragraphs themselves (see "Setting the Margins around an Element" in Chapter 11).

TIP The hCard microformat (http://microformats.org/wiki/hcard) is "for representing people, companies, organizations, and places" in a semantic manner that's human- and machine-readable. You could use it to represent a street address instead of the provided example **A**.

Creating Spans

The **span** element, like **div**, has absolutely no semantic meaning. The difference is that **span** is appropriate around a word or phrase only, whereas **div** is for blocks of content (see "Creating Generic Containers" in Chapter 3).

span is useful when you want to apply any of the following to a snippet of content for which HTML doesn't provide an appropriate semantic element:

- Attributes, like **class**, **dir**, **id**, **lang**, **title**, and more (Ⓐ and Ⓑ)
- Styling with CSS
- Behavior with JavaScript

Because **span** has no semantic meaning, use it as a last resort when no other element will do.

Ⓐ In this case, I want to specify the language of a portion of text, but there isn't an HTML element whose semantics are a fit for "La Casa Milà" in the context of a sentence. The **h1** that contains "La Casa Milà" before the paragraph is appropriate semantically because the text is the heading for the content that follows. So for the heading, I simply added the **lang** attribute to the **h1** rather than wrap a **span** around the heading text unnecessarily for that purpose.

```
...
<body>

<h1 lang="es">La Casa Milà</h1>

<p>Gaudí's work was essentially useful.
 <span lang="es">La Casa Milà</span> is
 an apartment building and <em>real people
 </em> live there.</p>

</body>
</html>
```

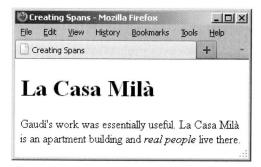

La Casa Milà

Gaudí's work was essentially useful. La Casa Milà is an apartment building and *real people* live there.

B The **span** element has no default styling.

To add spans:

1. Type **<span**.

2. If desired, type **id="*name*"**, where *name* uniquely identifies the spanned content.

3. If desired, type **class="*name*"**, where *name* is the name of the class that the spanned content belongs to.

4. If desired, type other attributes (such as **dir**, **lang**, or **title**) and their values.

5. Type **>** to complete the start **span** tag.

6. Create the content you wish to contain in the **span**.

7. Type **</span>**.

TIP A span doesn't have default formatting **B**, but just as with other HTML elements, you can apply your own with CSS (see Chapters 10 and 11).

TIP You may apply both a **class** and **id** attribute to the same **span** element, although it's more common to apply one or the other, if at all. The principal difference is that **class** is for a group of elements, whereas **id** is for identifying individual, unique elements on a page.

TIP Microformats often use **span** to attach semantic class names to content as a way of filling the gaps where HTML doesn't provide a suitable semantic element. You can learn more about them at http://microformats.org.

Other Elements

This section covers other elements that you can include within your text, but which typically have fewer occasions to be used or have limited browser support (or both).

The u element

Like **b**, *i*, **s**, and `small`, the **u** element has been redefined in HTML5 to disassociate it from its past as a non-semantic, presentational element. In those days, the **u** element was for underlining text. Now, it's for unarticulated annotations. HTML5 defines it thus:

> The **u** element represents a span of text with an unarticulated, though explicitly rendered, non-textual annotation, such as labeling the text as being a proper name in Chinese text (a Chinese proper name mark), or labeling the text as being misspelt.

Here is an example of how you could use **u** to note misspelled words:

```
<p>When they <u class="spelling">
→ recieved</u> the package, they put
→ it with <u class="spelling">there
→ </u> other ones with the intention
→ of opening them all later.</p>
```

The **class** is entirely optional, and its value (which can be whatever you'd like) doesn't render with the content to explicitly indicate a spelling error. But, you could use it to style misspelled words differently (though **u** still renders as underlined text by default). Or, you could add a `title` attribute with a note such as "[sic]," a convention in some languages to indicate a misspelling.

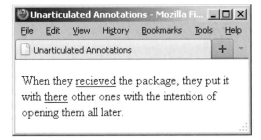

A Like links, **u** elements are underlined by default, which can cause confusion unless you change one or both with CSS.

Use **u** only when an element like **cite**, **em**, or **mark** doesn't fit your desired semantics. Also, it's best to change its styling if **u** text will be confused with linked text, which is also underlined by default **A**.

The **wbr** element

HTML5 introduces a cousin of **br** called **wbr**. It represents "a line break opportunity." Use it in between words or letters in a long, unbroken phrase (or, say, a URL) to indicate where it could wrap if necessary to fit the text in the available space in a readable fashion. So, unlike **br**, **wbr** doesn't force a wrap, it just lets the browser know where it *can* force a line break if needed.

Here are a couple of examples:

```
<p>They liked to say,
"FriendlyFleasandFireFlies<wbr />
→ FriendlyFleasandFireFlies<wbr />
→ FriendlyFleasandFireFlies<wbr />
→" as fast as they could over and
→ over.</p>
```

```
<p>His favorite site is this<wbr
/>is<wbr />a<wbr />really<wbr
/>really<wbr />longurl.com.</p>
```

You can type **wbr** as either **<wbr />** or **<wbr>**. As you might have guessed, you won't find many occasions to use **wbr**. Additionally, browser support is inconsistent as of this writing. Although **wbr** works in current versions of Chrome and Firefox, Internet Explorer and Opera simply ignore it.

The `ruby`, `rp`, and `rt` elements

A *ruby annotation* is a convention in East Asian languages, such as Chinese and Japanese, typically used to show the pronunciation of lesser-known characters. These small annotative characters appear either above or to the right of the characters they annotate. They are often called simply *ruby* or *rubi*, and the Japanese ruby characters are known as *furigana*.

The **ruby** element, as well as its **rt** and **rp** child elements, is HTML5's mechanism for adding them to your content. **rt** specifies the ruby characters that annotate the base characters. The optional **rp** element allows you to display parentheses around the ruby text in browsers that don't support **ruby**.

The following example demonstrates this structure with English placeholder copy to help you understand the arrangement of information both in the code and in a supporting browser **B**. The area for ruby text is highlighted:

B A supporting browser will display the ruby text above the base (or possibly on the side), without parentheses.

C Now, the ruby markup for "Beijing" as seen in a supporting browser.

```
<ruby>
    base <rp>(</rp><rt>ruby chars
    </rt><rp>)</rp>
    base <rp>(</rp><rt>ruby chars
    </rt><rp>)</rp>
</ruby>
```

Now, a real-world example with the two Chinese base characters for "Beijing," and their accompanying ruby characters **C**:

```
<ruby>
    北 <rp>(</rp><rt>ㄅㄟˇ</rt><rp>)
    </rp>
    京 <rp>(</rp><rt>ㄐㄧㄥ</rt><rp>)
    </rp>
</ruby>
```

北(ㄅㄟˇ) 京(ㄐㄧㄥ)

D A browser that supports ruby ignores the `rp` parentheses and just presents the `rt` content **B** and **C**. However, a browser that doesn't support ruby displays the `rt` content in parentheses, as seen here.

You can see how important the parentheses are for browsers that don't support `ruby` **D**. Without them, the base and ruby text would run together, clouding the message.

TIP At the time of this writing, only Safari 5+, Chrome 11+, and all versions of Internet Explorer have basic `ruby` support (all the more reason to use `rp` in your markup). The HTML Ruby Firefox add-on (https://addons.mozilla .org/en-US/firefox/addon/6812) provides support for Firefox in the meantime.

TIP You can learn more about ruby characters at http://en.wikipedia.org/wiki/ Ruby_character.

The `bdi` and `bdo` elements

If your HTML pages ever mix left-to-right characters (like Latin characters in most languages) and right-to-left characters (like characters in Arabic or Hebrew), the **bdi** and **bdo** elements may be of interest.

But, first, a little backstory. The base directionality of your content defaults to left-to-right unless you set the `dir` attribute on the `html` element to `rtl`. For instance, `<html dir="rtl" lang="he">` specifies the base directionality of your content is right-to-left and the base language is Hebrew.

Just as I've done with `lang` in several examples throughout the book, you may also set `dir` on elements within the page when the content deviates from the page's base setting. So, if the base were set to English (`<html lang="en">`) and you wanted to include a paragraph in Hebrew, you'd mark it up as `<p dir="rtl" lang="he">...</p>`.

With those settings in place, the content will display in the desired directionality most of the time; Unicode's bidirectional ("bidi") algorithm takes care of figuring it out.

The **bdo** ("bidirectional override") element is for those occasions when the algorithm *doesn't* display the content as intended and you need to override it. Typically, that's the case when the content in the HTML source is in visual order instead of logical order.

Visual order is just what it sounds like—the HTML source code content is in the same order in which you want it displayed. *Logical order* is the opposite for a right-to-left language like Hebrew; the first character going right to left is typed first, then the second character (in other words, the one to the left of it), and so on.

In line with best practices, Unicode expects bidirectional text in logical order. So, if it's visual instead, the algorithm will still reverse the characters, displaying them opposite of what is intended. If you aren't able to change the text in the HTML source to logical order (for instance, maybe it's coming from a database or a feed), your only recourse is to wrap it in a **bdo**.

To use **bdo**, you must include the `dir` attribute and set it to either `ltr` (left-to-right) or `rtl` (right-to-left) to specify the direction you want. Continuing our earlier example of a Hebrew paragraph within an otherwise English page, you would type, `<p lang="he"><bdo dir="rtl">...</bdo></p>`. **bdo** is appropriate for phrases or sentences within a paragraph. You wouldn't wrap it around several paragraphs.

The **bdi** element, new in HTML5, is for cases when the content's directionality is unknown. You don't have to include the **dir** attribute because it's set to auto by default. HTML5 provides the following example, which I've modified slightly:

This element is especially useful when embedding user-generated content with an unknown directionality.

In this example, usernames are shown along with the number of posts that the user has submitted. If the **bdi** element were not used, the username of the Arabic user would end up confusing the text (the bidirectional algorithm would put the colon and the number "3" next to the word "User" rather than next to the word "posts").

```
<ul>

    <li>User <bdi>jcranmer</bdi>:
    → 12 posts.</li>

    <li>User <bdi>hober</bdi>:
    → 5 posts.</li>

    <li>User <bdi>ناي إ</bdi>:
    → 3 posts.</li>

</ul>
```

TIP If you want to learn more on the subject of incorporating right-to-left languages, I recommend reading the W3C's article "Creating HTML Pages in Arabic, Hebrew, and Other Right-to-Left Scripts" (www.w3.org/International/tutorials/bidi-xhtml/).

The meter element

The **meter** element is another that is new thanks to HTML5. You can use it to indicate a fractional value or a measurement within a known range. Or, in plain language, it's the type of gauge you use for the likes of voting results (for example, "30% Smith, 37% Garcia, 33% Clark"), the number of tickets sold (for example, "811 out of 850"), numerical test grades, and disk usage.

HTML5 suggests browsers could render a **meter** not unlike a thermometer on its side—a horizontal bar with the measured value colored differently than the maximum value (unless they're the same, of course). Chrome, one of the few browsers that supports **meter** so far, does just that . For non-supporting browsers, you can style **meter** to some extent with CSS or enhance it further with JavaScript.

Although it's not required, it's best to include text inside **meter** that reflects the current measurement for non-supporting browsers to display ❶.

Here are some **meter** examples (as seen in ❶ and ❶):

```
<p>Project completion status: <meter
→ value="0.80">80% completed</meter>
→ </p>
```

```
<p>Car brake pad wear: <meter low=
→ "0.25" high="0.75" optimum="0"
→ value="0.21">21% worn</meter></p>
```

```
<p>Miles walked during half-marathon:
→ <meter min="0" max="13.1" value="4.5"
→ title="Miles">4.5</meter></p>
```

meter doesn't have defined units of measure, but you can use the **title** attribute to specify text of your choosing, as in the last example. Chrome displays it as a tooltip ❶.

❶ A browser like Chrome that supports **meter** displays the gauge automatically, coloring it in based on the attribute values. It doesn't display the text in between **<meter>** and **</meter>**.

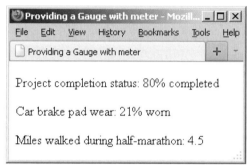

❶ Most browsers, like Firefox, don't support **meter**, so instead of a colored bar, they display the text content inside the **meter** element. You can change the look with CSS.

TIP `meter` supports several attributes. The `value` attribute is the only one that's required. `min` and `max` default to 0 and 1.0, respectively, if omitted. The `low`, `high`, and `optimum` attributes work together to split the range into low, medium, and high segments. `optimum` indicates the optimum position within the range, such as "0 brake pad wear" in one of the examples. Set `optimum` in between if neither a low nor a high value is optimal.

TIP At the time of this writing, `meter` is supported only by Chrome 11+ and Opera 11+. This partially explains why you don't yet see it in the wild too much. Feel free to use it, but just understand that most browsers will render the `meter` text rather than the visual gauge by default **F**.

TIP The style of the gauge that each supporting browser displays may vary.

TIP Some people have experimented with styling `meter` CSS for both supporting and non-supporting browsers. Search online for "style HTML5 meter with CSS" to see some of the results (note that some use JavaScript).

TIP `meter` is not for marking up general measurements, such as height, weight, distance, or circumference, that have no known range. For example, you cannot do this: `<p>I walked <meter value="4.5">4.5</meter> miles yesterday.</p>`.

TIP Be sure not to mix up your uses of the `meter` and `progress` elements.

The progress element

The **progress** element is yet another of the new elements in HTML5. You use it for a progress bar, like the kind you might see in a Web application to indicate progress while it is saving or loading a large amount of data.

As with **meter**, supporting browsers automatically display a progress bar based on the values of the attributes . And again like **meter**, it's usually best to include text (for example, "0% saved," as shown in the example) inside **progress** to reflect the current progress for older browsers to display , even though it's not required.

Here's an example:

```
<p>Please wait while we save your
  data. Current progress: <progress
  max="100" value="0">0% saved
  </progress></p>
```

A full discussion of **progress** is beyond the scope of this book since typically you would dynamically update both the **value** attribute and the inner text with JavaScript as the task progresses (for example, to indicate that it's 37% completed). The visual results are the same whether you do that with JavaScript or hard-code it in the HTML, that is, **<progress max="100" value="37">37% saved</progress>** . Of course, non-supporting browsers would display it similarly to .

G A browser like Chrome that supports **progress** displays the progress bar automatically, coloring it in based on the value. It doesn't display the text in between **<progress>** and **</progress>**. The **value** attribute is set to **0** in this example, so the whole bar is the same color.

H Firefox doesn't support **progress**, so instead of a colored bar, it displays the text content inside the element. You can change the look with CSS.

I The **progress** bar in Chrome when the **value** attribute is set to **37** programmatically with JavaScript (or directly in the HTML), assuming **max="100"**.

TIP The `progress` element supports three attributes, all of which are optional: `max`, `value`, and `form`. The `max` attribute specifies the total amount of work for the task and must be greater than 0. `value` is the amount completed relative to the task. Assign the `form` attribute to the `id` of a `form` element on the page if you want to associate the `progress` element with a `form` it isn't nested within.

TIP Here's a small taste of how to modify a `progress` element with JavaScript. Let's assume the bar had been coded with an `id` of your choosing, like this:

```
<progress max="100" value="0"
 id="progressBar">0% saved</progress>
```

JavaScript such as the following would give you access to the element:

```
var bar = document.getElementById
 ('progressBar');
```

Then you could get or set the value via `bar.value` as needed. For example, `bar.value = 37;` would set it.

TIP The `progress` element has pretty solid support among modern browsers as of this writing: Chrome 11+, Firefox 6+, Internet Explorer 10 (available only as a Platform Preview at the time of this writing), and Opera 11+. Safari doesn't support it.

TIP The style of the `progress` bar that each supporting browser displays may vary, though you can style it yourself to some extent with CSS.

5

Images

Creating images for the Web is a bit different from creating images for output on paper. Although the basic characteristics of Web images and printable images are the same, six main factors distinguish them: format, color, size/resolution, speed, transparency, and animation. This chapter will discuss the important aspects of each of these six factors and will explain how to use that knowledge to create the most effective images for your Web site.

Once you've created your images, we'll go on to insert them on your Web page.

In This Chapter

About Images for the Web

Let's look at the six factors you should keep in mind as you create Web images.

Format

People who print images on paper don't have to worry about what their readers will use to look at the images. You do. The Web is accessed every day by millions of Macs, Windows-based PCs, phones, tablets, and other kinds of devices. The graphics you use in your Web page should be in a format that each of these operating systems can recognize. Presently, the three most widely used formats on the Web are GIF, PNG, and JPEG. Current browsers can view all three image formats.

You want to choose a format that gives you the best quality with the smallest file size.

The JPEG format is good for color photographs because it handles large amounts of color and it compresses well, so your file sizes will be small . It is a lossy format, so you lose some of the image's original information when you save it as a JPEG, but usually this is a worthy compromise, because your pages load quickly. We'll talk more about this in the "Speed" section.

The PNG and GIF formats are often used when you're saving files like logos with large amounts of solid colors and patterns or when you need transparency. The PNG and GIF formats compress areas of continuous colors or repetitive patterns better than the JPEG format does. PNG is often the better choice, because it has a better compression algorithm for smaller file sizes and it has superior transparency support (alpha transparency) .

Ⓐ Full-color photographs should be saved in the JPEG or PNG-24 format.

Ⓑ Logotypes and other computer-generated images or images with few colors are compressed efficiently with ZIP and thus are often saved in PNG-8 format.

C This image is 2048 pixels wide. In Photoshop, it has an output resolution of 256 ppi and only measures 6 x 8 inches. Here in Firefox, its resolution is determined by the visitor's monitor—about 72 ppi—which means the picture is 28 inches wide!

At a Tibetan Buddhist monastery in northern India, monks beautifully created a walkway of stones.

D This image is 500 pixels wide, which is about half the width of a browser window that is 1024 pixels wide.

Color

Most computer monitors can display millions of colors, but this wasn't always the case. Some image formats have a limited color palette. GIF and PNG-8 images can have only 256 colors, which is often fine for logos and icons.

Photographs and complex illustrations should be saved in the JPEG or PNG-24 format, because they accommodate more colors in a single image.

Size and resolution

Digital images are measured in pixels. A 3-megapixel digital camera can take pictures that are 2048 pixels wide by 1536 pixels high. How big is that? It depends. If you print the image to a printer at 256 ppi (pixels per inch), it will measure 8 by 6 inches. But if you're using that page on the Web, the image's size will depend on the resolution of your visitor's monitor, which is more likely to be around 86 ppi (and might be as low as 72 or as high as 100 or so), and thus the image could display as big as 28 x 21 inches (about 75 x 54 cm). Too big C.

Perhaps a better way to think of image size is with respect to the average Web page. Since monitors with a resolution of 1024 pixels wide by 768 pixels high were the standard for so long, Web page designers got used to keeping their pages around 960 pixels wide, so that viewers could see the entire contents of the page without scrolling horizontally.

While it's true that there are more and more people who have bigger monitors (these days, more than 85 percent are larger than 1024 x 768), it doesn't necessarily follow that folks will fill up those bigger monitors with a single browser window. Aside from having other programs to consult (or even other browser

windows), it's cumbersome to read text in a browser that's too wide. Still, designers have tended to widen their designs and use flexible-width designs that expand and contract with a visitor's browser window.

Also, the use of smartphones and tablets is rapidly increasing, so you should always consider screen size and limited download speeds.

Note that resolution can mean one of two quite distinct concepts: the actual number of pixels on a monitor or in an image (say, 640 x 480) and the number of pixels in an inch of that monitor or image (say, 72 or 86 ppi). Regardless, the higher the resolution, the more pixels. On paper, pixels can add details *or* size. Onscreen, more pixels *always* translates to a bigger image.

Speed

Another difference between Web images and printed images is that your visitors have to wait for Web images to download. (Imagine waiting for pictures to appear in your morning paper!)

How can you keep download time to a minimum? The easiest way is to use small images. The larger an image's file size, the longer it takes to appear before your visitors' eyes.

The second way to speed up download time is by compressing the image. JPEG is great at dramatically reducing an image's file size, but JPEG has two main disadvantages. First, its compression information takes up a lot of space and is simply not worth it for very small images. Second, it is lossy compression—permanently eliminating details in order to save space. Uncompressing the image will not restore the lost data. If you plan to edit the image in the future, you should save a copy in an uncompressed format (for example, PSD or

TIFF) and only save it as a JPEG after you have made your final edits.

PNG and GIF are lossless formats, so they can compress your images without losing quality. Images that have large areas of a single color, like logos, rendered text, and illustrations, are best for this. PNG compresses better than GIF.

Transparency

Transparency is important for two reasons. First, you can use it to create complex layouts by making one image move behind another. Second, you can take advantage of transparency to give an image a non-rectangular outline, adding visual interest to your pages. Both PNG and GIF allow transparency; JPEG does not.

In the GIF format, a pixel can be transparent or not. PNG supports alpha transparency, a method of supporting both partial and full transparency. This means that images with complex transparent backgrounds often look better as a PNG than as a GIF, because the edges appear smooth instead of jagged.

Animation

One thing you won't be seeing on paper any time soon is moving images. On the Web, they're everywhere. Animated images can be saved as GIFs but not as JPEGs or PNGs.

Animation inside an image is becoming increasingly rare. Animation is generally created using Flash, CSS Animations, and JavaScript. In recent years, the use of Flash for animations on the Web has declined because of iOS's lack of support for Flash and the increasing capability of JavaScript and CSS.

Getting Images

So how do you get an image that you can use for your Web page? There are several ways. You can buy or download ready-made images, digitize photographs or hand-drawn images with a scanner, use a digital camera, or draw images from scratch in an image editing program like Adobe Photoshop. Once you've got them in your computer, you can adapt them for use on the Web.

To get images:

- You can use Google to find images on the Web by clicking the Images link above the Search box and entering criteria as usual. See the "Creative Commons Licenses" sidebar for more information on copyrights for those images.

- Generally, even free images found on the Web are restricted in one form or another (see the "Creative Commons Licenses" sidebar). Images you buy can usually be used for any purpose (except reselling the images themselves). Read any disclaimers or licenses carefully.

- Many companies sell stock photography and images for a very reasonable price. They often have several versions of each image for different purposes and resolutions.

- Scanners and digital cameras are popular and effective ways to create your own images.

Creative Commons Licenses

Creative Commons (www.creativecommons.org) is a non-profit organization that has developed a system of copyright templates that let artists share their work in specified ways without giving up all rights over their work. Web site designers, musicians, and photographers are some of the many artists who use Creative Commons licenses to get their work out in the marketplace without fear that it will be used in a way they don't agree with.

Flickr, the popular photo-sharing Web application (www.flickr.com), asks its users to designate a Creative Commons license for each photo they upload. Flickr then lets visitors search for photos according to the licenses assigned to them. It can be a great place to find photos for your Web site.

You can also use Google to restrict searches based on usage rights. (Click Advanced Search and then choose the desired option from the Usage Rights drop-down menu.)

Choosing an Image Editor

There are many, many different software programs that you can use to create and save images for the Web. Most modern image editors have special tools for creating Web images, which take into account the factors discussed earlier in this chapter.

The industry standard is no doubt Photoshop, along with its cousin, Abobe Fireworks (www.adobe.com). Fireworks is a very powerful program in its own right. Both are available for Macintosh and Windows. I have used these two programs to illustrate a few techniques in this chapter.

Let me stress, however, that the basic strategies for optimizing images for the Web are the same regardless of the software you choose. The command names may be slightly different, and there may be more or fewer steps, but the ideas remain the same.

There are many alternatives to Photoshop, including Paint.NET (for Windows, www.getpaint.net) and Acorn or Pixelmator (for the Mac, www.pixelmator.com). Also, online editors such as Photoshop.com and Aviary.com are becoming more and more capable. Feel free to use whatever program you're most comfortable with.

Saving Your Images

Now that you have your images created, it's time to save them. This process is a balancing act between the visual quality of the image and its file size.

You can use trial versions of Photoshop and Fireworks if you don't have the software installed on your computer.

Adobe Photoshop

Photoshop offers the Save for Web & Devices command on the File menu. It lets you visually compare the original image with up to three versions that you can optimize while keeping an eye on any resulting savings in file size and download time.

To use Photoshop's Save for Web & Devices command:

1. Open Photoshop and create your image. Or open an existing image, and prepare it for publishing by cropping, sizing, and editing it.

2. Choose File > Save for Web & Devices. The Save For Web & Devices dialog appears.

3. Click the 2-Up tab to see one optimized version, or click the 4-Up tab to see three.

4. Click an optimized version, if necessary.

5. Choose the desired format.

   In general, images that have been created on a computer, including logos, banners, line art, text, and any graphic with large areas of a single color and sharp detail, should be saved in PNG-8 or GIF format 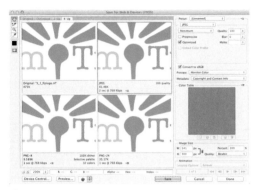.

   Images with continuous tones, like photographs, should be saved in either JPEG or PNG-24 format 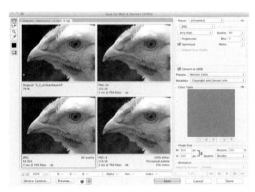.

A The Save for Web & Devices dialog, which shows the original image (upper left) and three possible compressed versions. This image has a lot of flat color, as well as text, that should be kept sharp. Note that the PNG-8 format (lower left) compresses the image the best, to just under 10K. PNG-24, with more colors available, is 35K. JPEG at high quality is huge. If you adjust the JPEG to medium quality (not shown), it's still big and ugly.

B The JPEG (lower left) offers good image quality with the smallest file size (63K). The PNG-8 compression leaves banding in the photograph (lower right), and the file size (114K) is almost twice the size of the JPEG. The PNG-24 (upper right) offers a high-quality image but at a much larger file size (322K).

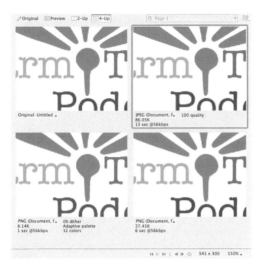

C Notice that the PNG-8 image (lower left) has a slightly smaller file size than its Photoshop counterpart. The other two formats, JPEG (upper right) and PNG-24 (lower right), are larger.

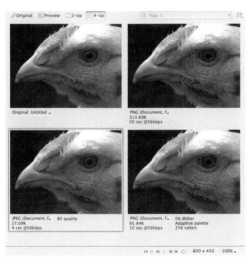

D Fireworks optimizes this image significantly better, with smaller file sizes for JPEG (lower left), PNG-8 (lower right), and PNG-24 (upper right). The JPEG and PNG-8 file sizes are half of Photoshop!

6. Adjust the additional settings that appear until you get the smallest file possible with an acceptable quality.

7. Click Save. Choose a directory, and name the new file. It will automatically carry the extension of the selected format (and thus normally will not replace the original image).

Adobe Fireworks

Photoshop is designed for a variety of uses, whereas Fireworks is designed for creating images for the Web (**C** and **D**). It used to optimize PNGs with smaller file sizes than Photoshop, but the gap has closed. Fireworks offers an extra export option for higher-quality PNGs: the PNG-32 format.

TIP Remember that your main objective is to get the smallest file size possible while maintaining acceptable image quality.

TIP Images should be created in RGB, not CMYK (which is for print).

TIP If you're not sure which format to choose, compare two optimizations and see which format compresses better.

TIP PNG-24 is a powerful lossless format that can be used for both computer-generated and "natural" color images. It is often better than PNG-8 but not quite as good as JPEG.

TIP If you have an image with both types of content, you can slice it into chunks, compress them separately, and reassemble them with CSS; or just use a single format and let it do its best.

TIP The Save for Web & Devices command creates a new image and leaves the original image intact—unless you save the new image with the same name and extension, and in the same folder, as the old.

TIP Only an image's visible layers are saved in the optimized version.

Inserting Images on a Page

You can place all kinds of images on your Web page, from logos to photographs. Images placed as described here appear automatically when the visitor jumps to your page, as long as the browser is set up to view them.

To insert an image on a page:

1. Place the cursor in the HTML code where you want the image to appear.

2. Type **<img src="*image.url*"**, where *image.url* indicates the location of the image file on the server.

3. Type a space and then the final **/>**.

> **TIP** Images must be uploaded to the server before visitors will be able to see them.

> **TIP** Don't expect your visitors to wait very long for your page to load and view. Test it (keeping in mind that you may have a faster connection than your visitors). If you can't wait, they won't either. One alternative is to create miniatures of large images and let visitors choose to view the larger images through a link.

> **TIP** There is a deprecated `border` attribute (`border="n"`, where *n* is the width in pixels) that adds or eliminates a border around images, especially the automatic border that appears around images used in links. Better yet, you can use styles to control this and all other aspects of images.

A The URL for this image, since it contains only the file name and no path, indicates that the image is located in the same folder as this Web page.

```
...
<body>

<h2>Barcelona's Market</h2>

<img src="cornermarket.jpg" />

<p>This first picture shows one of the
→ fruit stands in the Mercat de la Boquería,
→ the central market that is just off the
→ Rambles. It's an incredible place, full
→ of every kind of fruit, meat, fish, or
→ whatever you might happen to need. It
→ took me a long time to get up the nerve
→ to actually take a picture there. You
→ might say I'm kind of a chicken, but
→ since I lived there, it was just sort
→ of strange. Do you take pictures of your
→ supermarket?</p>

</body>
</html>
```

B Images are aligned to the left side of the page to match the alignment of the text. You can change the alignment or wrap text around an image by using CSS properties such as **float** (see "Making Elements Float" in Chapter 11).

Ⓐ While the alternate text can theoretically be as long as you like, most browsers don't automatically wrap long lines. Therefore, it's a good idea to keep it under 50 characters or so.

```
...
<body>

<h2>Barcelona's Market</h2>

<img src="cornermarket.jpg" alt="Fruit Stand
  in Market" />

<p>This first picture shows one of the
  fruit stands in the Mercat de la Boquería,
  the central market that is just off the
  Rambles. It's an incredible place, full
  of every kind of fruit, meat, fish, or
  whatever you might happen to need. It
  took me a long time to get up the nerve
  to actually take a picture there. You
  might say I'm kind of a chicken, but
  since I lived there, it was just sort
  of strange. Do you take pictures of your
  supermarket?</p>

</body>
</html>
```

Ⓑ In Internet Explorer, the alternate text appears next to a small box with a red x. In other browsers, the text appears alone.

Offering Alternate Text

While images are great on a big screen with a fast connection, they can be less useful—and downright problematic—on handhelds, on phones, with slow connections, or for the blind. You can add descriptive text that will appear if the image, for whatever reason, does not appear. That same text will also be read by screen readers.

To offer alternate text when images don't appear:

1. Within the **img** tag, after the **src** attribute and value, type **alt="**.

2. Type the text that should appear if, for some reason, the image itself does not (Ⓐ and Ⓑ).

3. Type **"**.

TIP The **alt** attribute is required for all **img** elements in HTML5.

TIP Screen readers such as JAWS can read the alternate text out loud so that blind or visually impaired visitors can get an idea of what the image is about.

TIP If the image is not relevant to nonvisual users, the W3C suggests you use **alt=""**. Images with a caption or nearby text that accurately describes the image can have blank **alt** text.

Specifying Image Size

Sometimes when you load a Web page, you see the text first, and then when the images load a few moments later, the text jumps around to accommodate them. This happens because the size of the image is not specified in the HTML.

When a browser gets to the HTML code for an image, it must load the image to see how big it is and how much space must be reserved for it. If you specify the image's dimensions, the browser will reserve the space and can fill in the text around the image as the image loads, so that your lay-out will remain stable as your page loads.

You can use either your browser or your image editing program to get the exact dimensions of your image.

Browsers will also stretch or shrink an image to fit the size you've specified in your HTML (or CSS). You can use this to your advantage if you want to use the same image file in different contexts, but be careful to update your code if you edit the image file and change its dimensions.

To find the size of your image with your browser:

1. Right-click the image. A contextual pop-up menu appears **Ⓐ**.

2. Choose Properties or View Image Info (depending on your browser) **Ⓐ**. A box appears that shows the dimensions of your image in pixels **Ⓑ**.

Ⓐ Right-click the image in the browser to make the contextual pop-up menu appear. The browser will offer a way to inspect the image, show its properties, or get the dimensions.

Type:	JPEG Image
Size:	Unknown (not cached)
Dimensions:	300px × 399px
Associated Text:	Fruit Stand in Market

Ⓑ A box appears (its appearance varies depending on the browser you're using) that shows the size of the image in pixels.

Ⓒ In Photoshop, click the document info bar at the bottom of a document window to see the image's properties. (If the document info bar doesn't show, make the window a little wider.)

D If you specify the exact height and width in pixels, the browser won't have to spend time doing it and will display the image more quickly.

```
...
<body>

<h2>Barcelona's Market</h2>

<img src="cornermarket2.jpg" alt="Fruit Stamd
  in Market" width="300" height="399" />

<p>This first picture shows one of the
  fruit stands in the Mercat de la Boquería,
  the central market that is just off the
  Rambles. It's an incredible place, full
  of every kind of fruit, meat, fish, or
  whatever you might happen to need. It
  took me a long time to get up the nerve
  to actually take a picture there. You
  might say I'm kind of a chicken, but
  since I lived there, it was just sort
  of strange. Do you take pictures of your
  supermarket?</p>

</body>
</html>
```

E If you open an image directly in a browser (this is Firefox for Windows), its dimensions are displayed in the title bar.

To find the size of your image with Photoshop:

1. Open the image in Photoshop.

2. Make the document window wide enough so that the document info bar is visible in the lower-left border of the window.

3. Click the document info bar. A small box appears with information about the image, including its size **C**.

To specify the size of your image in HTML:

1. Determine the size of your image using one of the techniques described in "To find the size of your image with your browser" or "To find the size of your image with Photoshop."

2. Within the **img** tag, after the **src** attribute, type **width="x" height="y"**, using the values you found in step 1 to specify the values for **x** and **y** (the width and height of your image) in pixels.

TIP The **width** and **height** attributes don't necessarily have to reflect the actual size of the image.

TIP If you have several images that are the same size, you can set their height and width all at the same time with styles.

TIP You can also find the size of an image in a browser by opening the image in its own window. The size is shown in the title bar **E**.

TIP In Photoshop or Fireworks, you can select the entire image and then view the Info panel for the image's dimensions.

Scaling Images with the Browser

You can change the display size of an image just by specifying a new height and width in pixels (**Ⓐ** through **Ⓒ**). It is best, however, to display images at their original size.

The methods browsers use to scale images aren't as advanced as those of Photoshop or other image editors, so test the results.

To reduce load time, you can scale up your image by adjusting the height and width in HTML or CSS. But be careful—if you enlarge the image too much, it might look grainy and ugly.

To scale an image with the browser:

1. Type `<img src="`*`image.url`*`"`, where *image.url* is the location on the server of the image.

2. Type `width="`*`x`*`" height="`*`y`*`"` where *x* and *y* are the desired width and height, respectively, in pixels, of your image.

3. Add any other image attributes as desired, and then type the final `/>`.

TIP You can also use a percentage value in step 2, with respect to the browser window (not to the original image size).

TIP Using the `width` and `height` attributes is a quick and dirty way to change how the image displays on a Web page. However, since the file itself is not changed, the visitor always gets cheated. Reduced images take longer to view than images that are really that size; enlarged images appear grainy. A better solution is to use your image editor to change the size of the image.

TIP You can set just the width or just the height and have the browser adjust the other value proportionally.

Ⓐ At its original size of 440 by 341 pixels, the image is way too big on the page.

Ⓑ Adjust the `height` and `width` attributes, and be sure to keep the aspect ratio the same. In this case, we divided both the `height` and `width` by two.

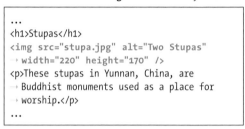

```
...
<h1>Stupas</h1>
<img src="stupa.jpg" alt="Two Stupas"
→ width="220" height="170" />
<p>These stupas in Yunnan, China, are
→ Buddhist monuments used as a place for
→ worship.</p>
...
```

Ⓒ The image appears at half its original size. It's important to note, however, that it takes the same time to load as before. After all, it's the same file.

Scaling Images with an Image Editor

A The original photograph, snapped with my digital camera's default settings, measured 2048 by 1536 pixels, which (besides being big enough for almost four browsers) weighed in at a whopping 211.3K when compressed as a high-quality JPEG.

B Type the new width, 400 pixels, in the W field, and click Apply. The reduced image will fit properly on the page and will take only 1 second to download at 768Kbps (or less with a faster connection).

Most images are too big for a Web page. While an image destined for print might measure 1800 pixels across (to print at 300 dpi and be six inches wide), images for Web pages should rarely be wider than 600 pixels, and often more like 200.

When you need images to be larger, find a larger original image and scale it down with an image editor. When that is not an option, scaling an image up with an image editor looks better than using the browser. But it will increase the image's file size and your page's load time.

To scale an image with Photoshop:

1. In the lower-right portion of the Save For Web & Devices window, click the W (Width) box or the H (Height) box in the Image Size section **A**.

2. Enter a new width or height in pixels, or a percentage, and then press the Tab key for the image to resize **B**.

3. You can continue to adjust the size up or down until you're satisfied. The image is not resampled until you press Save.

TIP You can also change the size of an image before you Save for Web & Devices by using the Image Size command under the Image menu item. Remember that the Resolution box is irrelevant (it refers to the output resolution, which is determined on the Web not by you or Photoshop, but rather by the visitor's monitor). Instead, base the size on the number of pixels in the image. You will have to select the Resample Image box to get it to change the image's size (as opposed to its output resolution).

TIP Another great way to reduce the size of an image is to crop out unwanted areas.

Adding Icons for Your Web Site

The small icon (associated with a Web site) that you see in address bars, tabs, and bookmarks is known as a *favicon*, which is short for favorites icon.

Apple asks for larger icons for the home screens of their devices (iPhone, iPod touch, and iPad); they recommend the size be 114 pixels x 114 pixels. Don't worry about adding the fancy rounded corners, drop shadow, and reflective shine; the device's operating system will do that for you. The Android operating system supports these icons too.

To add an icon for your Web site:

1. Create a 16 pixel by 16 pixel image, and save it in the ICO format . You can also save it in the PNG and GIF formats.

2. Create a 114 pixel by 114 pixel image for touch devices, and save in the PNG format.

3. In the **head** section of your HTML5 document, type **<link rel="shortcut icon" href="*favicon.ico*" />**, where *favicon.ico* is the name and location of your icon on your server. If your image is a PNG, type **<link rel="icon" type="image/png" href="favicon.png" />**. If your image is a GIF, type **<link rel="icon" type="image/gif" href="favicon.gif" />**.

4. In the **head** section of your HTML5 document, type **<link rel="apple-touch-icon" href="*/apple-touch-icon.png*" />**, where *apple-touch-icon.png* is the name and location of your icon on your server.

A Favicons, in real life, are small. They measure a measly 16 x 16 pixels.

B Most browsers will display your favicon without this **link** element if you name the files **favicon.ico** and **apple-touch-icon.png** and place them at the root of your site.

```
...
<head>
    <meta charset="utf-8" />
    <title>Farm Training Podcasts</title>
    <link rel="shortcut icon"
     → href="/favicon.ico" />
    <link rel="apple-touch-icon"
     → href="/apple-touch-icon.png" />
    ...
</head>
...
```

C The favicon is typically used in the address bar, in Favorites and Bookmarks menus, and in tabs. Because the browser often displays your icon over gray or other colors, you may want to make your icon's background transparent.

D The `apple-touch-icon` is used when you add your Web site to the home screen of iOS devices from Safari.

TIP Favicons should generally be saved in the ICO format (**B** and **C**). There is a useful Photoshop plugin for creating ICO-format icons that is made by Telegraphics (www.telegraphics.com.au/sw/).

TIP You can also create favicons in the **PNG** and **GIF** formats. Be sure to use the proper **MIME** type for `type`.

TIP Internet Explorer originally required the `favicon.ico` file to be placed in the root directory of your Web site. This is no longer the case, though browsers will still look there if the `link` element is not present.

6

Links

Links are the lifeblood of the Web. Without them, every page would just exist on its own, completely disconnected from all the others.

In This Chapter

The Anatomy of a Link

A link has two main parts: a destination and a label. The first part, the *destination*, is arguably the most important. You use it to specify what will happen when the visitor triggers the link. You can create links that go to another page, jump within a page, show an image, download files, send an email message, and more. The most common links, however, connect to other Web pages 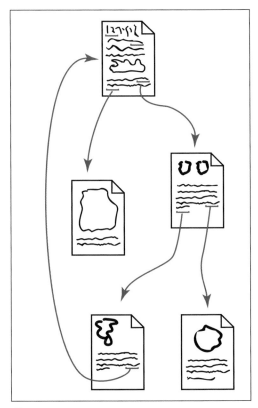, and sometimes to specific locations on other Web pages, called *anchors*. Destinations are defined by writing a URL (see Chapter 1) and are generally only visible to the visitor in the browser's status bar (on desktop browsers).

The second part of the link is the *label*, the part the visitor sees in a browser or hears in a screen reader and then activates to reach the destination. It can be text, an image, or both. Browsers typically show label text as underlined and in blue by default. It's easy to change this with CSS.

Note that it's common for people to say that a user *clicks* a link, a reflection of the ubiquity of the mouse as a means to navigate Web pages. Whenever possible, however, I avoid this term in favor of words like *trigger* and *activate*, to recognize the diverse ways in which users interact with links. For instance, users with touchscreen devices (such as most smartphones and tablets) tap on links, while other mobile users may activate links via a trackball. Meanwhile, some users navigate pages with the keyboard, whether out of preference or necessity; they may have a physical impairment that makes it difficult or impossible to use a mouse, digital pen, or similar device. These users typically tab to links (using the Tab key to move forward, and Shift-Tab to move backward) and then trigger them with the Enter or Return key.

A Some of your pages may have links to many other pages. Other pages may have only one link. And still others may have no links at all.

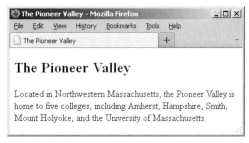

A Since there is only a file name (and no path) referenced in the **href** attribute, the file **pioneer-valley.html** must be in the same directory as this Web page that contains the link. Otherwise, the browser won't be able to find **pioneer-valley.html** when the user activates the link.

```
...
<body>

<article>
    <h1>Cookie and Woody</h1>

    <img src="img/cookiefora.jpg" width="143"
  → height="131" alt="Cookie" />

    <img src="img/woodygran.jpg" width="202"
  → height="131" alt="Woody" />

    <p>Generally considered the sweetest
  → and yet most independent cats in the
  → <a href="pioneer-valley.html">
  → Pioneer Valley</a>, Cookie and Woody
  → are consistently underestimated by
  → their humble humans.</p>
</article>

</body>
</html>
```

B When a visitor points at a link (displayed in most browsers as blue, underlined text by default), the destination URL is shown in the status bar. You can change the default styling with CSS. If a user activates a link...

Creating a Link to Another Web Page

If you have more than one Web page, you will probably want to create links from one page to the next (**A** through **D**) and back again. You can also link to pages on other sites, whether they are your own or the creation of others (**F** through **H**).

To create a link to another Web page:

1. Type **<a href="*page.html*">**, where *page.html* is the URL of the destination Web page.

2. Type the label text, that is, the text that is highlighted by default **B** and that when activated will take the user to the page referenced in step 1. Alternatively (or in addition to label text), add an **img** element as the label. (See **A** in "Creating Other Kinds of Links" as well as "Linking Thumbnail Images" in that section.)

3. Type **</a>** to complete the definition of the link.

C ...the page associated with that destination URL is displayed in the user's browser.

HTML5's Block-Level Links

HTML5 allows wrapping a link around nearly any kind of element or group of elements **D**. Examples include paragraphs, lists, entire articles and sections—pretty much anything except interactive content such as other links, **audio**, **video**, form elements, **iframes**, and so on. Testing your pages in an HTML validator (see "Validating Your Code" in Chapter 20) will reveal when you've wrapped a link around an element that isn't allowed.

These *block-level links*, as they are called unofficially, are a big departure from previous versions of HTML, which only allowed linking text, images, and what were known as *inline* elements. That is, the elements that mark up phrases of text, like **em**, **strong**, **cite**, and the like (these are categorized as *phrasing content* in HTML5).

The funny thing is that although block-level links were disallowed in the previous HTML specifications, browsers supported them anyway. This means you can use them now, and they'll work in both older and modern browsers. However, use them with care (**D** and **E**).

There are some accessibility concerns to consider, particularly pertaining to how different screen readers treat block-level links. These two articles, by accessibility experts Derek Featherstone and Steve Faulkner, respectively, discuss the issues in more depth: http://simplyaccessible.com/article/html5-block-links/ and www.paciellogroup.com/blog/2011/06/html5-accessibility-chops-block-links/. They advise putting the most pertinent content at the beginning of a link and not putting too much content in one link. As Featherstone notes, the accessibility issues are likely temporary as screen readers and browsers catch up with supporting block-level links officially.

D This type of link is invalid in prior versions of HTML, but HTML5 allows it.

```
...
<body>

<a href="giraffe-escapes.html">
    <hgroup>
        <h1>Giraffe Escapes from Zoo</h1>
        <h2>Animals worldwide rejoice</h2>
    </hgroup>
</a>

...
</body>
</html>
```

E Don't go overboard. Avoid doing what is shown here, which is to wrap a link around a large chunk of content. Although the link will work and it's valid HTML5, a screen reader may read all the content more than once, and even that much content *once* is more link information than a visitor typically wants to hear. It's better to narrow the focus of your link to the most relevant content.

```
...
<body>

<a href="pioneer-valley.html">
    <article>
        <h1>Cookie and Woody</h1>

        <img src="img/cookiefora.jpg" width=
        → "143" height="131" alt="Cookie" />

        <img src="img/woodygran.jpg" width=
        → "202" height="131" alt="Woody" />

        <p>Generally considered the sweetest
        → and yet most independent cats
        → in the Pioneer Valley, Cookie
        → and Woody are consistently
        → underestimated by their humble
        → humans.</p>
    </article>
</a>

...
</body>
</html>
```

F If you're creating links to someone else's Web site, you'll have to use an absolute URL, with the `http://`, server, full path, and file name. The `rel` and `title` attributes are optional, but I recommend using `rel="external"` to indicate that a link points to a different site. (See Chapter 4 to learn about the `cite` element.)

```
...
<body>

<article>
    <h1>The Glory of Cats</h1>

    <p><a href="http://en.wikipedia.org/
    ↪ wiki/Cat" rel="external" title="Cat
    ↪ entry on Wikipedia">Cats</a> are
    ↪ wonderful companions. Whether it's a
    ↪ bottle cap, long string, or your legs,
    ↪ they always find something to chase
    ↪ around.</p>

    <p>In fact, cats are so great they even
    ↪ have <a href="http://www.catsthe
    ↪ musical.com/" rel="external"
    ↪ title="Official site of Andrew
    ↪ Lloyd Webber's musical">their own
    ↪ musical</a>. It was inspired by T.S.
    ↪ Eliot's <cite>Old Possum's Book of
    ↪ Practical Cats</cite>.</p>
</article>

</body>
</html>
```

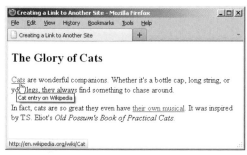

G Just as with a link to a page within your site, when a visitor points at a link (displayed in blue, underlined text, by default) to another site, the destination URL is shown in the status area and the `title` text, if specified, displays near the link. If the visitor activates a link…

Generally speaking, you'll want to stick with the simpler, traditional style of link shown in the first example **A**, but know that smartly crafted block-level links are available to you as well.

TIP `href` stands for hypertext reference.

TIP You can change the default styling of the label text (see Chapter 10) or even use an image as a label (see "Creating Other Kinds of Links" in this chapter).

TIP As a general rule, use relative URLs for links to Web pages on your site, and absolute URLs for links to Web pages on other sites. For more details, consult "URLs" in Chapter 1.

TIP A link to a page at another site might look like this: `<a href="http://www.site.com/ directory/page.html" rel="external"> Label text</a>` (**F** through **H**). The `rel` attribute is optional, since the link works the same without it. It describes the relationship between the page containing the link and the page to which you're linking. It's yet another way of improving the semantics of your HTML. Search engines may leverage the information, too. An ever-evolving list of `rel` values is maintained at http://microformats.org/wiki/ existing-rel-values.

H …the page associated with that destination URL is displayed in the visitor's browser.

TIP Specify the path but omit the file name to link to the default file for a directory, which is typically index.html: `www.site.com/directory/`. Omit the path as well to link to a site's default (home) page: `www.site.com`.

TIP Use all lowercase letters for your URLs unless you're pointing to a page or directory name that has uppercase letters. (For your own sites, name all folders and files in lowercase and match your link URLs accordingly.)

TIP Don't make the link's label too long. If the label is part of a sentence, keep only the key words within the link definition, with the rest of the sentence before and after the less-than and greater-than signs of the a element.

TIP Whatever you do, avoid using "Click here" as a label. This type of linked text is unfortunately all too common on the Web, and it's bad for usability, for accessibility, and for you as a site owner. When users quickly scan links on a page (whether visually or via a screen reader), "click here" lacks context ("Click here? Why?"). There's little incentive to activate the link, and it relies on the visitor reading the link's surrounding text in hopes that it will explain the link's purpose. Understandably, your visitor is probably more likely to skip it. Also, as mentioned at the beginning of this chapter, the word "click" doesn't apply to how all users trigger links. Instead, identify the link by using the key words that already exist in your text. For example, "Learn about our sale" instead of "Click here to learn about our sale."

TIP Be sure each page on your site contains navigation to the key sections of your site, including the home page. This allows visitors to browse your site freely, whether they came to your site directly or via a link from another site. You never know where visitors will enter your site. It might be via a link that "deep links" to one of your inner pages, so you'll typically want to allow them to access the rest of the site from there.

TIP To create a link to a particular place on a page, use an anchor (see "Creating Anchors" in this chapter).

TIP As noted in this chapter's introduction, you may navigate through a page with the keyboard. Each time you press Tab, the focus shifts to the next link, form control, or image map as it appears *in the HTML code*, which is not necessarily the same as where it appears onscreen, because a page's CSS layout may be different. HTML's `tabindex` attribute allows you to change the tabbing sequence, but I discourage you from using it, because it's an unnecessary, dated practice in most instances. (There are certain cases where it's helpful, but usually it's when you're enhancing an interaction with JavaScript, a bit of an advanced topic.) Instead, give care to marking up your content so the tabbing sequence is logical. Test this by tabbing through your own pages to see how you like it as a user, and adjust the HTML accordingly.

The `target` Attribute

It's possible to make a link open in a new window or tab (depending on the browser), but it's considered bad practice, so I recommend that you don't do it. There are a few arguments against it.

Primarily, it should be the user's decision to open a link in a different window or tab, not yours or mine as HTML developers. Otherwise, we're dictating the browsing behavior on our users' behalf.

There are usability and accessibility concerns as well. Less experienced users may be confused when they activate a link and don't see the results display in their current window. Using a browser isn't straightforward for everyone; I've shown browser tabs to people of various ages who previously had no idea that they could have more than one page open at a time. Similarly, users of assistive devices such as screen readers will have to negotiate their way over to that new window or tab, assuming it's even clear which one loaded the new content.

If all this hasn't convinced you to avoid loading links in other windows and tabs, or your boss or client won't listen to your reasoned argument against it, here's how to do it: type **`target="`*`window`*`"`** in your link definition, where ***`window`*** is the name of the window (of your own choosing) where the corresponding page should be displayed.

For instance, **`<a href="some-page.html" target="doodad">Some page</a>`** opens **`some-page`**
`.html` in a new window or tab named doodad.

If you target several links to the same window (that is, using the same name), the links will all open in that same window. Or, if you always want a link to open in a different window or tab (even if you activated the same link more than once), use HTML's predefined name, **`_blank`**, as in **`target="_blank"`**.

But remember, you didn't read any of that here.

There is one other use for **`target`**, which is to open a link in an **`iframe`**. You code the **`target`** the same way, except its value should match the **`id`** of the **`iframe`**. You'll rarely have occasion to use this, especially since **`iframe`**s are generally discouraged (sometimes they have their place, though). Learn more about the **`iframe`** element at https://developer.mozilla.org/en/HTML/Element/iframe.

Although image maps aren't covered here, you should know that they allow you to add a link to one or more regions of a single image. You define the shape of each linked area as a rectangle, circle, or polygon. Less experienced coders often misuse them to create image-based navigation, rather than using preferred techniques such as HTML text styled with CSS (or with an image-replacement technique when CSS alone isn't enough). The heyday of image maps was years and years ago before these techniques were prevalent (or even possible). You rarely see image maps in practice now, but there is the occasional legitimate use case—for example, an image of a country, in which you want to define links to various regions, provinces, or states. You can learn more about image maps by searching online for "HTML image maps."

Creating Anchors

Generally, activating a link brings the user to the *top* of the corresponding Web page. If you want to have the user jump to a specific section of the Web page, create an *anchor* and reference that anchor in the link Ⓐ.

Ⓐ Each link `href` value that begins with `#` anchors to the element with the corresponding `id` (sans the `#`). For instance, `<a href="#rising-action">Rising Action</a>` anchors to `<h2 id="rising-action">Rising Action</h2>`. You may apply an `id` to any element as long as any given `id` exists in a page only once (see "Naming Elements with a class or id" in Chapter 3). This example also gives you an early look at an unordered list (`ul`), by far the most frequently used list type on the Web. (Lists are covered extensively in Chapter 15.)

```
...
<body>

<h1>Frankie and Johnny</h1>

<header>
    <h2>Table of Contents</h2>
    <nav>
        <ul>
            <li><a href="#intro">Introduction</a></li>
            <li><a href="#main-characters">Description of the Main Characters</a></li>
            <li><a href="#rising-action">Rising Action</a></li>
        </ul>
    </nav>
</header>

<article>
    <h2 id="intro">Introduction</h2>
    <p>This is the intro. If I could think of enough things to write about, it could span a few
    → pages, giving all the introductory information that an introduction should introduce.</p>

    <h2 id="main-characters">Description of the Main Characters</h2>
    <p>Frankie and Johnny are the main characters. She's jealous, and seems to have a reason to be.
    → He's a sleaze, and will pay the price.</p>

    <h2 id="rising-action">Rising Action</h2>
    <p>This is where everything starts happening. Johnny goes out, without Frankie, without even
    → tellin' her where he's going. She's not crazy about it, but she lets him go. A while later,
    → she gets thirsty and decides to go down to the corner bar for some beer. Chatting with the
    → bartender, she learns that Johnny has been there with no other than Nellie Bly. Furious, she
    → catches the crosstown bus to find him.</p>
</article>

</body>
</html>
```

B The first example **A** was kept simple by design, just to demonstrate basic anchoring. However, you could go a step further with the semantics by wrapping each answer in a **section** element, placing the **id**s on those instead of the headings. This denotes them as sections of the parent **article**. And yet another way (not shown) to mark up this content would be to treat each of the answers as its own **article** by removing the parent **article** and replacing each **section** with an **article**. It just depends on how you want to describe your content's meaning (do you think of the answers as one article of content or as individual articles?).

```
...
<header>
    <h2>Table of Contents</h2>
    <nav>
        <ul>
            <li><a href="#intro">
            → Introduction</a></li>
            ...
        </ul>
    </nav>
</header>

<article>
    <section id="intro">
        <h2>Introduction</h2>
        <p>This is the intro...</p>
    </section>

    <section id="main-characters">
        <h2>Description of the Main
        → Characters</h2>
        ...
    </section>

    <section id="rising-action">
        <h2>Rising Action</h2>
        ...
    </section>
</article>

</body>
</html>
```

To create an anchor:

1. Place the cursor in the start tag of the element that you wish the user to jump to.

2. Type **id="*anchor-name*"**, where ***anchor-name*** is the text you will use internally to identify that section of the Web page. Be sure there is a space between the element's name and the **id**, for example, **<h2 id="rising">**.

TIP Give your anchor **id**s meaningful names to increase the semantic richness of your HTML document. In other words, avoid generic **id**s like **anchor1** and **item5**.

TIP Spaces are not allowed in **id**s. Separate multi-word **id** values with a dash instead.

TIP In some cases, you may want to include a link below each section of content to anchor back to the table of contents (you're probably accustomed to seeing these as "Back to top" links). However, if your page has several long sections, you may want to consider splitting it into multiple pages instead.

Linking to a Specific Anchor

Once you have created an anchor via an `id`, you can define a link so when a user triggers it, the page jumps directly to the section of the document that contains the anchor (Ⓐ and Ⓑ), rather than to the top of the document.

To create a link to an anchor:

1. Type `<a href="#anchor-name">`, where *anchor-name* is the value of the destination's `id` attribute (see step 2 of "To create an anchor").

2. Type the label text, that is, the text that is highlighted (usually blue and underlined by default) and that when activated will take the user to the section referenced in step 1.

3. Type `</a>` to complete the definition of the link.

TIP If the anchor is in a separate document, use `<a href="`*page.html#anchor-name*`">` to reference the section. (There should be no space between the URL and the #.) If the anchor is on a page on a different server, you'll have to type `<a href="`*http://www.site .com/path/page.html#anchor-name*`">` (with no spaces).

TIP Although you obviously can't add anchors to other people's pages, you can take advantage of the ones that they have already created. View the source code of their documents to see which anchors correspond to which sections. (For help viewing source code, consult "The Inspiration of Others" in Chapter 2.)

TIP If the anchor is at the bottom of the page, it may not display at the top of the window, but rather toward the middle.

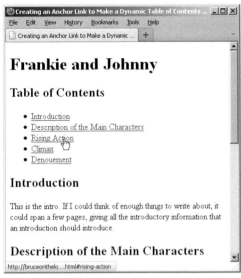

Ⓐ When the visitor points at a link that refers to an anchor, the URL and the anchor name appear in the status bar (in the lower-left corner of the window) on desktop browsers.

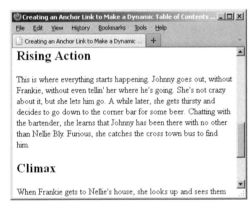

Ⓑ Once the visitor activates the link, the particular part of the page that the anchor references is displayed at the top of the browser window.

Creating Other Kinds of Links

You are not limited to creating links to other Web pages. You can create a link to any URL—RSS feeds, files that you want visitors to be able to download, email addresses, and more (A).

(A) You can create links to all different kinds of URLs. This page includes five links, but the two around the images may not be obvious in all browsers (B). (This example also frequently uses the **abbr** element to mark up abbreviations, as well as the **code** element, which, not surprisingly, designates content that is code. Both are covered in Chapter 4.)

```
...
<body>

<h1>Other Types of Links</h1>

<p>There are lots of different kinds of links that you can create on a Web page. More precisely,
→ there are a lot of different files you can link to on your Web page.</p>

<p>You can create links directly to <a href="img/blueflax.jpg">a photo</a> or even make links out
→ of photos.</p>

<p>For example, here are Cookie and Woody again, except this time they are linked to other pages.
→ <a href="cookie.html" title="All about Cookie"><img src="img/cookiefora.jpg" width="143"
→ height="131" alt="Cookie" /></a> <a href="woody.html" title="All about Woody"><img src="img/
→ woodygran.jpg" width="202" height="131" alt="Woody" /></a></p>

<p>You can link directly to <a href="http://www.sarahsnotecards.com/catalunyalive/segadors.mov"
→ rel="external">a video</a> file, too, though it's usually better to link to a page with the
→ video embedded in it, such as with the <abbr title="Hypertext Markup Language revision 5">HTML5
→ </abbr> <code>video</code> element.</p>

<p>Although you can make a link to <a href="mailto:someone@somedomain.com">someone's email
→ addresss</a> with the <code>mailto:</code> protocol, I don't recommend it, since spambots pick
→ those up and then bombard them with spam. It's too bad, because they are so convenient. If you
→ activate the link, it opens your email program. It's probably better to offer your email address
→ in a descriptive way, like &quot;someone at somedomain,&quot; although that isn't always foolproof
→ either.</p>

<body>
</html>
```

To create other kinds of links:

1. Type **<a href="**.

2. Type the URL.

   For a link to any file on the Web, including images, ZIP files, programs, PDFs, Excel spreadsheets, or whatever, type **http://www.site.com/path/file.ext**, where **www.site.com** is the name of the server and **path/file.ext** is the path to the desired file, including its extension.

3. Type **">**.

4. Type the label for the link, that is, the text that will be underlined and highlighted by default and that when activated will take the visitor to the URL referenced in step 2. Alternatively (or in addition to label text), add an **img** element as the label. (See 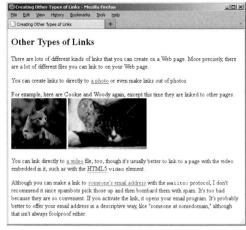 and "Linking Thumbnail Images.")

5. Type **</a>**.

B No matter where a link goes, it looks pretty much the same by default in browsers unless you wrap it around a photo (some browsers show a border around the image, and some don't). Notice that I've tried to create labels that flow with the body of the text, instead of using "click me."

Linking Thumbnail Images

No doubt you've visited a photo gallery page that shows several thumbnails (miniature versions of your images) linked to larger versions. This allows you to see a lot of photos at a glance before choosing which ones to view full size.

Implementing a basic version of this would be similar to the example code that links the Cookie and Woody images to other pages Ⓐ. Each of those pages could contain a full-size photo. (Advanced approaches beyond the capabilities of HTML alone could allow for a single, dynamic page.)

Be careful not to go crazy with the number of thumbnails on any given page. They may be small, but each thumbnail is a separate request to the Web server, and those add up, slowing down your page. There's no set rule on how many is appropriate. It partially depends on the number and size of other assets your page loads, as well as your intended audience. For instance, mobile devices typically load assets more slowly.

So, if you have a lot of thumbnails, consider splitting them up into more than one page. Generally, about 20–30 thumbnails per page could be reasonable, again, taking into consideration the factors I noted. You may want to test your pages to determine what works best.

Lastly, I recommend marking up your list of thumbnails with an unordered list (`ul`), covered in Chapter 15.

TIP If you create a link to a file that a browser doesn't know how to handle (an Excel file, for example), the browser will either try to open a helper program to view the file or try to download it to the visitor's drive.

TIP Although you can link to PDFs and other non-HTML documents (Word, Excel, and so on), try to avoid it whenever possible. Instead, link to an HTML page that contains the information. PDFs can take a long time to load, and some browsers and systems (particularly older ones) can get sluggish while trying to display them. For those times when a PDF is your only option, make it clear to users that the link points to a PDF rather than to another HTML page so they won't be surprised (users don't appreciate being tricked into time-consuming downloads). That advice goes for other non-HTML documents, too. You can message this simply by putting the file type and size in parentheses; showing an icon helps as well. Here's an example (without an icon): `<a href="q2-sales-report.pdf">Q2 Sales Report` `(PDF, 725kb)``</a>`. You may want to include a `title` attribute (such as `title="Opens a PDF"`) on the link, too, especially if you put the parenthetical note outside the link.

TIP It's a good idea to compress large files and groups of files that you want visitors to download. For instance, a set of Photoshop templates saved as PSD files. Search online for "ZIP and RAR" to find tools for both creating and opening file archives using these popular compression formats.

TIP If you want to "create links to content on the iTunes Store, the App Store, the iBookstore, and the Mac App Store" (per the URL that follows), you can use Apple's Link Maker (http://itunes.apple.com/linkmaker) to generate the URL to include in your HTML. If you are an affiliate (www.apple.com/itunes/affiliates/), Apple pays you a commission on items people buy through your links.

CSS Building Blocks

Whereas HTML defines your content's meaning and gives your Web pages their basic structure, CSS (Cascading Style Sheets) defines the appearance.

A style sheet is simply a text file that contains one or more rules that determine—through properties and values—how certain elements in your Web page should be displayed. There are CSS properties for controlling basic formatting such as font size and color, layout properties such as positioning and float, and print controls such as deciding where page breaks should appear when visitors print a page. CSS also has a number of dynamic properties that allow items to appear and disappear and that are useful for creating drop-down lists and other interactive components.

In This Chapter

CSS2 is the version that is best supported across browsers both new and old, so this book will cover it extensively. CSS3, which is still evolving as a specification, builds upon CSS2 to provide features that designers and developers have long been clamoring for. The great news is that modern browsers have implemented several CSS3 components already, so you're able to start using them today. You'll learn some of the most useful features with the best support.

The wonderful thing about CSS is that it can be created outside of a Web page and then applied to all the pages on your site at once. It is flexible, powerful, and efficient and can save you lots of time and bandwidth.

To get the full benefit of CSS, your Web pages must be marked up well and consistently according to the recommendations in the HTML chapters.

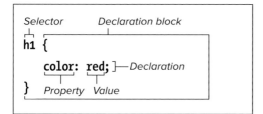

A A style rule is made up of a selector (which indicates which elements will be formatted) and a declaration block (which describes the formatting that should be executed). Each declaration within the block is a property/value pair separated by a colon and ending with a semicolon. A left curly brace begins a declaration block, and a right curly brace ends it.

```
h1 {
    background: yellow;
    color: red;
}
```
Two declarations, each with a property and a value

B The order of declarations doesn't matter unless the same property is defined twice. In this example, **color: red** could be before **background: yellow** and have the same effect. Note the extra spacing and indenting (optional, but recommended) to keep everything readable.

Constructing a Style Rule

Each style rule in a style sheet has two main parts: the *selector*, which determines which elements are affected, and the *declaration block*, made up of one or more property/value pairs (each constitutes a *declaration*), which specifies just what should be done (**A** and **B**).

To construct a style rule:

1. Type *selector*, where *selector* identifies the element or elements you wish to format. You'll learn how to create all sorts of selectors in Chapter 9.

2. Type { (an opening curly bracket) to begin the declaration block.

3. Type *property*: *value*;, where *property* is the name of the CSS property that describes the sort of formatting you'd like to apply and *value* is one of a list of allowable options for that property. Descriptions of CSS properties and values begin in Chapter 8.

4. Repeat step 3 as needed. Typically, you'll enter each **property: value** (a declaration) on its own line.

5. Type } to complete the declaration block and the style rule.

TIP You may add extra spaces, tabs, or returns in a style rule to keep the style sheet readable **B**. The format in the example is perhaps the most common among coders.

TIP Although each property/value pair should be separated from the next by a semicolon, you may omit the semicolon that follows the last pair in the list. But I recommend you always include it, since it's a best practice to do so.

TIP Missing (or duplicate) semicolons can cause the browser to ignore the style rule.

Adding Comments to Style Rules

It's a good idea to add comments to your CSS to note the primary sections of your style sheets or simply to explain something about a particular rule or declaration. Comments help not only you but also others who are viewing your code. For your own sake, you'll be happy that you left yourself comments if you revisit the code some months after having initially worked on it.

To add comments to style rules:

1. In your style sheet, type **/*** to begin your comment.

2. Type the comment.

3. Type ***/** to signal the end of the comment.

TIP Comments may include returns and thus span several lines Ⓐ.

TIP You may not put comments inside other comments. In other words, comments may not include */.

TIP You may start comments on their own line Ⓐ, inside a declaration block Ⓑ, or after a rule Ⓑ.

Ⓐ Comments can be long or short, though they tend to be short. Use them as you see fit to describe the purpose of a style rule or a group of related rules. Comments go a long way toward making your style sheet easier to maintain.

```
/* This is a CSS comment. It can be one
→ line long or span several lines. This
→ one is longer than most. Regardless, a
→ CSS comment never displays in the
→ browser with your site's HTML content.
→ The next one is more in line with a
→ comment's typical use. */

/* Set default rendering of certain HTML5
→ elements for older browsers. */

article, aside, details, figcaption, figure,
→ footer, header, hgroup, menu, nav, section {
    display: block;
}
```

Ⓑ You can also insert comments within the declaration block or after a rule.

```
/* Add rounded corners in supporting browsers */
.box {
    -webkit-border-radius: 12px; /* Safari 3-4 */
    -moz-border-radius: 12px; /* Firefox 3.6 and below */
    border-radius: 12px; /* modern browsers */
} /* One more comment for good measure! */
```

Ⓒ Comments make your life easier when managing style sheets. Simply comment primary sections of rules within your style sheets to keep them organized. I find that using a format like the one here (with all caps and an underline) makes it clear where each major grouping begins. This treatment clearly distinguishes them from other comments, such as the ones in Ⓐ and Ⓑ.

```
/* GLOBAL NAVIGATION
----------------------------- */
... rules for global nav ...


/* MAIN CONTENT
----------------------------- */
... rules for main content ...


/* SIGN-UP FORM
----------------------------- */
... rules for sign-up form ...


/* PAGE FOOTER
----------------------------- */
... rules for page footer ...
```

Ⓓ You can "comment out" a declaration that you don't want to affect the page. Here, all images will get a four-pixel solid red border but not a right margin treatment, because `margin-right: 12px;` is inside a comment. A comment can go around an entire rule too, as long as there aren't any comments inside the comment.

```
img {
    border: 4px solid red;
    /* margin-right: 12px; */
}
```

TIP **Comments are extremely helpful as an organizational tool. Style sheets can quickly get long, so organizing them is critical to making your CSS easy to evolve and maintain. It's common practice to group related rules together and precede each with a descriptive comment Ⓒ.**

TIP **However you format your comments Ⓒ, I recommend you decide on a convention and use it consistently, especially if you're working with a team.**

TIP **You can put comments around or within style rules to hide them from the browser Ⓓ. This is a good way to test a style sheet without permanently removing the commented portion until (and if) you are ready to do so. It's a helpful debugging tool; comment out something you think might be causing a problem, refresh the page in the browser, and see if the problem is fixed.**

TIP **Although these examples are heavy on comments for demonstration purposes, don't feel the need to comment everything. You'll probably find your style sheets harder to read if they have too many comments. You'll probably find that a good mix entails organizational comments coupled with descriptive ones as needed. Find the balance that works for you and the others on your team.**

The Cascade: When Rules Collide

Styles come from many sources. As you learned in Chapter 1, every browser has its own default styles. But you can apply your own styles to override or complement those in three ways: You can load one or more from an external file (the recommended method) **Ⓐ**, insert them at the top of an HTML document, or apply them to a specific HTML element right in the code (though this is to be avoided whenever possible). See the next chapter for specifics about each method.

Also, some browsers let your visitors create and apply their own style sheets to any pages they visit—including yours. Finally, some styles are passed down from parent element to child.

Ⓐ This is the style sheet for the HTML document in **Ⓑ**. Don't worry too much about the details right now, but do notice that there is a rule for **p** elements, but not for **h1**, **em**, or **small** elements.

```
p {
    color: #36c;
    font-family: "Trebuchet MS",
    → "Helvetica", sans-serif;
    font-weight: bold;
}

img {
    float: left;
    margin-right: 10px;
}
```

Ⓑ The **em** and **small** elements are contained within the **p** element and thus are children of **p**. However, the **h1** is not, so it isn't blue like the other text **Ⓒ**.

```
...
<body>

<h1>The Ephemeral Blue Flax</h1>

<img src="img/blueflax.jpg" width="300"
→ height="175" alt="Blue Flax (Linum
→ lewisii)" />

<p>I am continually <em>amazed</em> at the
→ beautiful, delicate Blue Flax that somehow
→ took hold in my garden. They are awash in
→ color every morning, yet not a single
→ flower remains by the afternoon. They are
→ the very definition of ephemeral.</p>

<p><small>&copy; by Blue Flax Society.
→ </small></p>

</body>
</html>
```

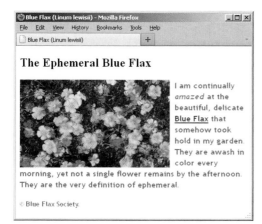

The Ephemeral Blue Flax

I am continually *amazed* at the beautiful, delicate **Blue Flax** that somehow took hold in my garden. They are awash in color every morning, yet not a single flower remains by the afternoon. They are the very definition of ephemeral.

Blue Flax Society.

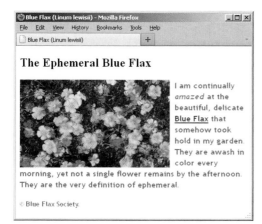 In the absence of a rule specified explicitly for the **em** and **small** elements in , they inherit their font, weight, and color from their parent, the **p** element. The italics come from the browser's default styling of **em**. The size of the legal notice marked up with **small** (that is, legal "fine print") is reduced for the same reason. The **h1** does not have its own style and is not a child of **p**, so it displays entirely in accordance with the browser default.

What happens, you might ask, when there is more than one style rule that applies to a given element? CSS uses the principle of the cascade to take into account such important characteristics as *inheritance*, *specificity*, and *location* in order to determine which of a group of conflicting rules should win out.

Let's start with inheritance. Many CSS properties not only affect the elements defined by the selector but are also *inherited* by the descendants of those elements (through). For example, suppose you make all your **h1** elements blue with a red border. It so happens that the **color** property is inherited, but the **border** property is not. Thus, any elements contained within the **h1** elements will also be blue, but they will not have their own red border. You'll learn which properties are inherited in the individual section describing each property (and in Appendix B on the book's site). You can also use a value of **inherit** with most properties to force inheritance (see the next section, "A Property's Value").

While inheritance determines what happens if no style rule is applied to an element, *specificity* is the key when more than one rule is applied (**D** through **F**). The law of specificity states that the more specific the selector, the stronger the rule. Makes sense, right? So if one rule states that all **h1** elements should be blue but a second rule states that all **h1** elements with a **class** of **spanish** be red, the second rule will override the first for all those **h1** elements whose **class** is **spanish**, because **h1.spanish** is a more specific selector than simply **h1**.

Note that **id** attributes are considered the most specific (since they must be unique in a document), while the presence of a **class** attribute makes a selector more specific than a simple selector that has none. Indeed, a selector with more than one **class** is more specific than a selector with only one. Selectors with only element names come next on the specificity scale; inherited rules are considered to be the most general of all and are overruled by any other rule.

For the exact rules of calculating specificity, see Section 6.4.3 of the CSS specifications (www.w3.org/TR/CSS21/cascade.html#specificity).

D In this example, there are four rules of varying specificity. The first affects any **p** element, the second affects only those **p** elements with a **class** equal to **group**, and the third and fourth affect only the single **p** element with an **id** equal to **last**.

```
p {
    color: red;
}

p.group {
    color: blue;
}

p#last {
    color: green;
}

p#last {
    color: magenta;
}
```

E Three paragraphs: one generic one, one with just a **class**, and one with a **class** and an **id**.

```
...
<body>

<p>Here's a generic <code>p</code> element.
  It will be red.</p>

<p class="group">Here's a <code>p</code>
  element with a <code>class</code> of
  <code>group</code>. There are two rules
  that apply, but since the <code>p.group
  </code> rule is more specific, this
  paragraph will be blue.</p>

<p id="last" class="group">Here's a <code>
  p</code> element with an <code>id</code>
  of <code>intro</code>. There are four rules
  that could apply to this paragraph. The
  first two are overruled by the more
  specific last two. The position breaks
  the tie between the last two: the one
  that appears later wins, and thus this
  paragraph will be magenta.</p>

</body>
</html>
```

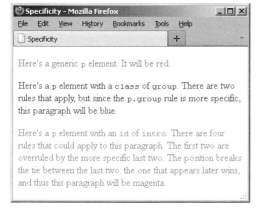

Here's a generic p element. It will be red.

Here's a p element with a class of group. There are two rules that apply, but since the p.group rule is more specific, this paragraph will be blue.

Here's a p element with an id of intro. There are four rules that could apply to this paragraph. The first two are overruled by the more specific last two. The position breaks the tie between the last two: the one that appears later wins, and thus this paragraph will be magenta.

F Since the third and fourth rules have the same specificity, their position becomes a factor—and thus the fourth rule wins out since it appears last.

Sometimes, specificity is not enough to determine a winner among competing rules. In that case, the *location* of the rule breaks the tie: Rules that appear later have more weight (**D** through **F**). For example, rules that are applied inline right in the HTML element (again, not recommended) are considered to appear after (and thus have more weight than) equally specific rules applied in either an external style sheet or one embedded at the top of the HTML document. For details, consult "The Importance of Location" in Chapter 8.

If that isn't enough, you can override the whole system by declaring that a particular rule should be more important than the others by adding **!important** at the end of the rule. (This also isn't recommended except in uncommon cases.)

In summary, in the absence of a rule, many styles are passed down from parent element to child. With two competing rules, the more specific the rule, the more weight or importance it has—regardless of its location. With two rules of equal specificity, the one that appears later in the style sheet wins.

If any of this sounds confusing, don't worry about it right now. Once you start playing with CSS and different selectors, I think you'll find that the cascade operates just as you'd expect it to in most cases.

A Property's Value

Each CSS property has different rules about what values it can accept. Some properties accept only one of a list of predefined values. Others accept numbers, integers, relative values, percentages, URLs, or colors. Some can accept more than one type of value. The acceptable values for each property are listed in the section describing that property (mostly in Chapters 10 and 11), but you'll learn the basic systems here.

Inherit

You can use the **inherit** value for any property when you want to explicitly specify that the value for that property be the same as that of the element's parent.

Predefined values

Most CSS properties have a few pre-defined values that can be used. For example, the **float** property can be set to **left**, **right**, or **none**. In contrast with HTML, you don't need to—and indeed *must not*—enclose predefined values in quotation marks Ⓐ.

Lengths and percentages

Many CSS properties take a length for their value. All length values must contain a quantity and a unit, with no spaces between them. For example, **3em** or **10px** Ⓑ. The only exception is **0**, which may be used with or without units.

A preset value

```
border: none;
```

Ⓐ Many CSS properties will only accept values from a predefined list. Type them exactly and do not enclose them in quotation marks.

A length

```
font-size: 24px;
```

Ⓑ Lengths must always explicitly state the unit. There should be no space between the unit and the measurement.

```
                A percentage
                     ┌┴┐
font-size: 80%;
```

C Percentages are generally relative to the parent element. So in this example, the font would be set to 80 percent of the parent's font size.

```
                 A number
                    ┌┴┐
line-height: 1.5;
```

D Don't confuse numbers and integers with length. A number or integer has no unit (like **px**). In this case, the value shown here is a factor that will be multiplied by the font size to get the line height.

There are length types that are relative to other values. An **em** is roughly equal to the element's font size, so **2em** would mean "twice the font size." (When the **em** is used to set the element's **font-size** property itself, its value is derived from the font size of the element's parent.) The **ex** should be equal to the font's x-height, that is, the height of a letter x in the font, but its support varies, so you aren't likely to use it.

Pixels (**px**) are not relative to other style rules. For instance, values in **px** aren't affected by the **font-size** setting, as **em**s are. A pixel on one type of device isn't necessarily the same size as on another. (See Peter-Paul Koch's detailed description at www.quirksmode.org/blog/archives/2010/04/a_pixel_is_not.html.)

There are also the largely self-explanatory absolute units, such as points (**pt**), which is a unit that should be reserved for print style sheets. (There are others, but there's little point in mentioning them, because they aren't used in practice.) In general, you should only use absolute lengths when the size of the output is known (as with **pt** and the printed page).

Percentage values—**65%**, for example—work much like **em**s, in that they are relative to some other value **C**.

Of all these, you will use ems, pixels, and percentages the most.

Bare numbers

A very few CSS properties accept a value in the form of a number without a unit, like **3**. The most common are **line-height** **D** and **z-index** (see "Setting the Line Height" in Chapter 10 and "Positioning Elements in 3D" in Chapter 11, respectively). (The others are mostly for print and aural style sheets and are not yet well supported.)

URLs

Some CSS properties allow you to specify the URL of another file, particularly images. In that case, use **url(*file.ext*)**, where *file.ext* is the path and file name of the desired asset **ⓔ**. Note that the specifications state that relative URLs should be relative *to the style sheet* and not to the HTML document.

While you may use quotation marks around the file name, they're not required. On the other hand, there should be no space between the word **url** and the opening parentheses. White space between the parenthesis and the address is allowed but not required (or customary).

For more information on writing the URLs themselves, consult "URLs" in Chapter 1.

CSS colors

You can specify colors for CSS properties in several ways. First, and easiest, the value can be one of the predefined color keywords. CSS3 specifies a basic list of 16 names **ⓕ** and adds 131 more to align with the 147 SVG 1.0 color keyword names. The full list is available at www.w3.org/TR/css3-color/#svg-color.

Of course, no one remembers any of those color names outside of the obvious ones anyway. Also, you typically grab the colors from tools like Adobe Photoshop, and they don't use the CSS color name. So in practice, it's more common to define your CSS colors with the hexadecimal format (the most common by far) or the RGB format. As you will learn, you can also specify a color with the HSL format, and the level of color transparency with RGBA and HSLA, all of which are new in CSS3.

A URL

`background:` `url(bg_flax.jpg);`

ⓔ URLs in CSS properties do not need to be enclosed in quotation marks.

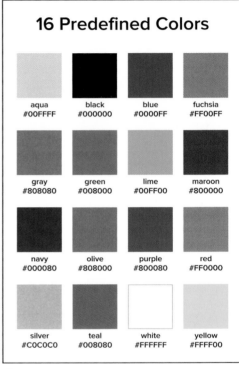

16 Predefined Colors

aqua #00FFFF	black #000000	blue #0000FF	fuchsia #FF00FF
gray #808080	green #008000	lime #00FF00	maroon #800000
navy #000080	olive #808000	purple #800080	red #FF0000
silver #C0C0C0	teal #008080	white #FFFFFF	yellow #FFFF00

ⓕ The most common way in CSS to define a color is by specifying, with hexadecimal numbers, the amounts of red, green, and blue that it contains.

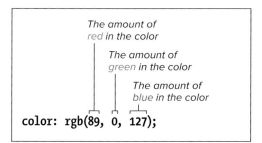

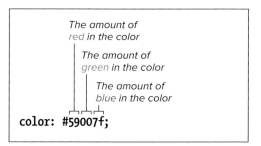

The amount of
red in the color

The amount of
green in the color

The amount of
blue in the color

color: rgb(89, 0, 127);

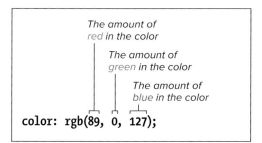

G Another way to express color in CSS is with RGB numeric values from 0–255. Define red first, followed by green, and then blue.

The amount of
red in the color

The amount of
green in the color

The amount of
blue in the color

color: #59007f;

H The most common way in CSS to define a color is by specifying, with hexadecimal numbers, the amounts of red, green, and blue that it contains.

RGB

You can construct your own color by specifying its amount of red, green, and blue (hence the name *RGB*). You can give the values of each of these contributing colors as a number from 0–255, a percentage, or a hexadecimal representation of the number. For example, if you wanted to create a dark purple, you might use 89 red, no green, and 127 blue. That color could be written **rgb(89, 0, 127)**, as shown in **G**.

Alternatively, you could represent each value as a percentage, though it is far less common to do so, likely because image editors like Photoshop tend to provide you numerical RGB values. But if you do want to use percentages, you could write the same color as **rgb(35%, 0%, 50%)**, since 89 is 35% of 255 and 127 is 50% of 255.

Hexadecimal

I've saved the most common method for last **H**. Convert those numerical values to hexadecimals, join them together, and prefix the value with a #, as in **#59007F**. (59 is the hexadecimal equivalent of 89, 00 is the hexadecimal equivalent of 0, and 7F is the hex equivalent of 127.) You can also write **7F** as **7f** (my preference, but plenty of developers and designers go the other way).

When a hexadecimal color is composed of three pairs of repeating digits, as in **#ff3344**, you may abbreviate the color to **#f34**. In fact, it's a best practice to do so, since there's no reason to make your code longer than it needs to be.

If you're scratching your head about hexadecimals, don't fret. Just as Photoshop and the like include tools for choosing colors and displaying their RGB values, so, too, do they for hex.

More color options in CSS3: RGBA, HSLA, and HSL

CSS3 introduces another way to specify colors—HSL—and the ability to set alpha transparency via RGBA and HSLA. (You can't indicate alpha transparency with hexadecimal notation.)

RGBA

RGBA is the same as RGB except the *A* stands for *alpha transparency*. You can specify the amount of transparency with a decimal from 0 to 1 after the red, green, and blue values. So, the syntax is the following:

property: rgba(red, green, blue,
→ alpha transparency);

The closer to 0 the alpha setting, the more transparent the color becomes. If it *is* 0, it's completely transparent, as if you hadn't set a color at all. Similarly, 1 is completely opaque, meaning it's not transparent at all. Here are some example declarations to illustrate the point:

```
/* no transparency, so the same as
→ rgb(89, 0, 127); */
background: rgba(89,0,127,1);
```

```
/* completely transparent */
background: rgba(89,0,127,0);
```

```
/* 25% transparent */
background: rgba(89,0,127,0.75);
```

```
/* 60% transparent */
background: rgba(89,0,127,0.4);
```

ⓘ This simple style sheet applies a repeating background image and default text color to the whole page, with slightly different background treatments for the **h1–h3** headings. Modern browsers display the result shown in Ⓙ. As you'll learn later, versions of Internet Explorer prior to IE9 don't support RGBA, so they ignore the declarations on the **h1** and **h2**.

```
/* Set repeating page background image and
→ default text color */
body {
    background: url(../img/blueflax.jpg);
    color: #ff0;
}

/* 25% transparent */
h1 {
    background: rgba(89,0,127,0.75);
}

/* 60% transparent */
h2 {
    background: rgba(89,0,127,0.4);
}

/* Solid background (not transparent) */
h3 {
    background: rgb(89,0,127);
}
```

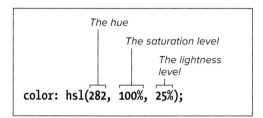 In this gaudy but effective example, you can see the page background image peeking through the background of the first two headings but not of the last one. The background color for all three is the same, but they look like three different shades of purple because of their different alpha transparency settings. (The text is yellow because the **color** property set on the **body** element cascades down to all text on a page unless it is overridden by a style rule for another element.)

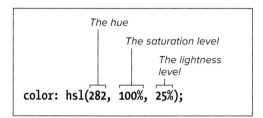 The breakdown of the HSL formatting.

Of course, in order to make those work, you'll need to include them in one or more rules . As shown, it's common to leverage alpha transparency on the background color of an element, because alpha transparency allows whatever is behind the element—an image, other colors, text, and so on—to peek through and blend with it . To be clear, though, you can also set alpha transparency on other color-based properties, such as **color**, **border**, **border-color**, **box-shadow**, and **text-shadow**, with varying degrees of browser support (you're in the clear with modern browsers).

As you can see, the RGB color *values* are the same in the code, but the colors themselves appear different in the browser because of their different levels of transparency .

HSL and HSLA

HSL and HSLA are the other new additions in CSS3. The latter is the alternative to RGBA for setting alpha transparency on a color. You specify the alpha the same way you do with RGBA. You'll see that in a second, but first take a look at how HSL works.

HSL stands for *hue*, *saturation*, and *lightness*, where hue is a number from 0–360, and both saturation and lightness are percentages from 0 to 100 . In CSS, the syntax is:

property: hsl(hue, saturation,
→lightness);

And, as you guessed it, the HSLA format is this:

property: `hsla(hue, saturation,`
`  lightness, alpha transparency);`

For instance, here's the same purple from the RGBA and RGB example ❶ expressed in HSLA and HSL instead:

```
/* 25% transparent */

h1 {

    background: hsla(282,100%,
      25%,0.75);

}
```

```
/* 60% transparent */

h2 {

    background: hsla(282,100%,
      25%,0.4);

}
```

```
/* Solid background (not
   transparent) */

h3 {

    background: hsl(282,100%,25%);

}
```

The result in modern browsers is the same as before ❿.

Think of the hue value as a degree on a circle, with 0 and 360 meeting at the top. This means that both 0 and 360 are the same color—red. (Don't confuse HSL with HSB or HSV. They are similar, but not the same.)

Not all image editors specify HSL out of the box (you can get a plugin for Photoshop). However, Mathis's *HSL Color Picker* is a great, free online tool that allows you to pick a color and get its HSL, hex, and RGB values, or you can type in values

How to Think in HSL

Learning HSL's logic takes some time, but once you get a feel for it you may find it easier to work with than other formats. In the "Why?" section of his *HSL Color Picker* site (http://hslpicker.com), Brandon Mathis provides a nice explanation of HSL. He writes:

> "Pick a hue from 0 to 360, and with saturation at 100 and luminosity at 50 you'll have the purest form of that color. Reduce the saturation and you move toward gray. Increasing the luminosity moves you toward white, decreasing it moves you toward black."

For example, here are some core colors as you move around the circle:

- Red is **hsl(0,100%,50%);**
- Yellow is **hsl(60,100%,50%);**
- Green is **hsl(120,100%,50%);**
- Cyan is **hsl(180,100%,50%);**
- Blue is **hsl(240,100%,50%);**
- Magenta is **hsl(300,100%,50%);**

(L) Modern browsers render the RGBA declaration because it comes after the default hexadecimal background setting (which it also understands, so the order is important). Meanwhile, versions of IE prior to IE9 ignore the RGBA setting because they don't understand it, so the hex background stands. You could use RGB (but not RGBA) instead of hex in the first line, but as noted, hex is the most common way to denote non-transparent colors.

```
/* The order of the background declarations
→ is important. Older versions of IE use the
→ first line, and modern browsers understand
→ both lines but apply the second because
→ it's last. */

h1 {
    background: #59007f;
    background: rgba(89,0,127,0.75);
}
```

(M) Look away before your eyes burn! This verbose mixture of code sandwiches declarations for pre-IE9 versions (highlighted) around the standard RGBA notation (not highlighted). As usual, the older versions of IE ignore what they don't understand. Similarly, modern browsers ignore the **-ms-filter**, **filter**, and **zoom** values since they don't understand them. The order of the declarations is essential to making this technique work.

```
/* If you're like me, you've already begun to
→ cry. Every declaration except the second
→ one is for older versions of IE to mimic
→ alpha transparency. */

h1 {
    background: transparent;
    background: rgba(89,0,127,0.75);

    /* IE8 */
    -ms-filter: "progid:DXImageTransform.
    → Microsoft.gradient(startColorstr=
    → #BF59007F,endColorstr=#BF59007F)";

    /* IE6 & 7 */
    filter: progid:DXImageTransform.
    → Microsoft.gradient(startColorstr=
    → #BF59007F,endColorstr=#BF59007F);

    zoom: 1;
}
```

for any of the formats to see the color change. Another such tool is located at www.workwithcolor.com/hsl-color-picker-01.htm. It shows the colors on a circle, which may help you get a better feel for HSL. (In contrast, *HSL Color Picker* shows them on a line.) You can find other color tools by searching online.

RGBA, HSL, and HSLA in Internet Explorer

Sadly, as is often the case with the latest developments in the standards world, no version of Internet Explorer prior to IE9 supports these features. Instead, they ignore any declaration they don't understand.

There is a workaround for pre-IE9 versions regarding RGBA and HSLA. But in terms of HSL, you'll want to stick with hexadecimal (or RGB) to specify your colors.

For RGBA and HSLA in pre-IE9 versions, you're left with three options (but only one at a time):

- Do nothing and let your page look fairly different in these versions.

- Provide a fallback color declaration for them, meaning they will display a solid color not a transparent one **(L)**.

- Mimic the alpha transparency by including declarations specifically for them, most of which are proprietary IE CSS; modern browsers will still use the standard CSS, though **(M)**.

This last option uses Internet Explorer's Gradient filter in conjunction with proprietary code that no other browser understands. That means modern browsers will ignore it and use the standard notation instead, which in this case is **background: rgba(89,0,127,0.75);** (it overrides the previous **background** value). Be aware that the declarations must be in the order shown for the transparency effect to apply

properly across browsers both modern and otherwise Ⓜ.

I won't bother to explain how IE's Gradient filter syntax works, since it's so convoluted you'll probably never write it by hand. I don't. Instead, another free online tool rescues you (you'll see more and more of these as you learn more about CSS3).

This one comes in the form of Michael Bester's *RGBa & HSLa CSS Generator for Internet Explorer* (http://kimili.com/journal/rgba-hsla-css-generator-for-internet-explorer). As he explains, you enter an RGBA or HSLA declaration, and the tool creates the equivalent CSS for pre-IE9. Then you copy and paste it into your style sheet. One important note: The code that the tool generates does *not* include the standard RGBA or HSLA declaration for modern browsers. So, you'll have to add that yourself *directly after* `background: transparent`, just as it is shown in the example Ⓜ. Alternatively (and often preferably), as Michael notes, you can place the pre-IE9 CSS in its own style sheet and load it inside what are known as *conditional comments*. (See http://reference.sitepoint.com/css/conditionalcomments for more information.)

TIP Internet Explorer's filters, such as the Gradient filter Ⓜ, can affect the browser's performance because they require extra processing power. You likely won't have any noticeable issues if a filter is applied to a reasonable number of elements on a page, but a delay can sometimes be seen beyond that. It can depend on what's on the rest of your page, too. So be mindful of this as you're building a page, and if you're seeing a slow-down in IE you may want to turn off the filter to see if that's the issue. IE filters can sometimes have other unexpected side effects, like adversely affecting the quality of text rendering. To clarify, these won't affect other browsers since they don't understand filters.

8

Working with Style Sheets

Before you start defining your style sheets, it's important to know how to create and use the files that will contain them. In this chapter, you'll learn how to create a style sheet file and then how to apply CSS to multiple Web pages (including a whole site), a single page, or an individual HTML element. You achieve these via three methods: external style sheets (the preferred choice), embedded style sheets, and inline styles (the least desirable).

You'll learn how to create the content of your style sheets in the chapters that follow.

In This Chapter

Creating an External Style Sheet

External style sheets are ideal for giving most or all of the pages on your Web site a consistent look. You can define all your styles in an external style sheet and then tell each page on your site to load the external sheet, thus ensuring that each will have the same settings. Although later you will learn about embedded and inline styles, adding CSS to your page from an external style sheet is a best practice, so I highly recommend you use this method (allowing for occasional exceptions).

To create an external style sheet:

1. Create a new text document in your text editor of choice 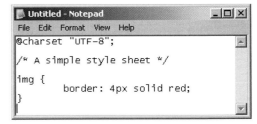.

2. Define the style rules for your Web pages as described beginning with Chapter 7. Also, include CSS comments as you see fit **A**.

3. Save the document in a text-only format in the desired directory. Any name will do, but give the document the extension **.css** to designate it as a Cascading Style Sheet **B**.

A Use any text editor you like to create a style sheet. This is Notepad (an older version). Most people use the same editor to create both HTML and CSS documents. The text between **/* */** is a CSS comment that neither affects your page's display nor appears in your page.

B Be sure to save the CSS file with the .css extension and in text-only format (as a Text Document or Plain Text or ASCII or whatever your text editor calls it).

TIP You can name your style sheets however you please. `base.css` and `global.css` are two popular names for the style sheet that contains the display rules intended for all or the majority of pages on a site. Site authors often create additional, section-specific CSS files to complement the base styles. For instance, if you're building a commerce site, `products.css` could contain the rules for your product-related pages. Regardless of the file names you choose, make sure they don't contain any spaces.

TIP External style sheets can be either linked to (as demonstrated in "Linking to External Style Sheets") or imported (via `@import`), but I don't recommend you import them. The `@import` directive negatively affects page download and rendering speed, particularly in Internet Explorer, as discussed by Steve Souders at www.stevesouders.com/blog/2009/04/09/dont-use-import/.

TIP The `@charset` declaration that begins the style sheet isn't always required, but there is no harm in always including it **A**. However, it *is* required if your style sheet will contain non-ASCII characters, which can be the case if you're using CSS-generated content (a somewhat advanced topic) or a Web font with a special character in its name. For this reason, you may choose to always include `@charset` so you won't have to worry about adding it later if your style sheet needs it. Just be sure it's on the very first line of your style sheet. However, *never* include `@charset` in embedded or inline styles (covered later in this chapter).

Linking to External Style Sheets

Now that you've created a style sheet Ⓐ, you need to load it into your HTML pages so the style rules are applied to the content. The best way to do so is to link to the style sheet Ⓑ.

To link an external style sheet:

1. Type `<link rel="stylesheet"` in the **head** section of each HTML page in which you wish to use the style sheet.

2. Type a space and then `href="url.css"`, where *url.css* is the name of your CSS style sheet (see previous section).

3. Type a space and the final `/>`. (Or, if you prefer, type no space and simply `>`; HTML5 allows both approaches, and they work exactly the same.)

TIP When you make a change to an external style sheet, all the pages that reference it are automatically updated as well (Ⓒ and Ⓓ). That is the awesome power of an external style sheet!

TIP Another benefit to an external style sheet is that once a browser has loaded it for one page, it typically doesn't need to retrieve it from the Web server for subsequent pages. The browser caches the file, which is to say it saves it on the user's computer and uses that version, which speeds up the load time of your pages. Don't worry, though; if later you make changes to your style sheet and upload it to your Web server, browsers will download your updated file rather than use the cached one (technically there are exceptions, but none you're likely to face often).

Ⓐ Here's the **base.css** external style sheet created earlier in the chapter (minus the "A simple style sheet" comment, which has no bearing on the HTML's display). Don't worry about the properties and values yet (they just mean "create a solid red border around all **img** elements").

```
@charset "UTF-8";

img {
    border: 4px solid red;
}
```

Ⓑ The **link** element goes inside the **head** section of your HTML document. Your page may contain more than one **link** element, but it's best to keep the total to a minimum so your page loads faster.

```
<!DOCTYPE html>
<html lang="en">
<head>
    <meta charset="UTF-8" />
    <title>El Palau de la Música</title>
    <link rel="stylesheet"
     → href="base.css" />
</head>
<body>
<article>
    <h1>El Palau de la Música</h1>

    <img src="img/palau250.jpg" width="250"
     → height="163" alt="El Palau de la
     → Música" />
    <img src="img/tickets.jpg" width="87"
     → height="163" alt="The Ticket Window" />

    <p>I love the <span lang="es">Palau de la
     → Música</span>. It is ornate and gaudy
     → and everything that was wonderful
     → about modernism. It's also the home
     → of the <span lang="es">Orfeó Català
     → </span>, where I learned the benefits
     → of Moscatell.</p>
</article>
</body>
</html>
```

El Palau de la Música

I love the Palau de la Música. It is ornate and gaudy and everything that was wonderful about modernism. It's also the home of the Orfeó Català, where I learned the benefits of Moscatell.

C The style rule (a solid red border that is four pixels thick) is applied to each **img** element.

Sunflowers

There are fields and fields of sunflowers, that turn with the passing of the sun.

D Other documents can link to the very same external style sheet to have the same styles applied.

TIP For simplicity's sake, the `link` example shown here assumes that the HTML page lives in the same directory as `base.css` **B**. However, in practice it is best to organize your style sheets in a sub-folder rather than mix them with your HTML pages. Popular style sheet folder names include `css` and `styles`, but you can name it whatever you like as long as you refer to it properly in the `link`'s `href` value. For example, if `base.css` is in a folder named `css` and your HTML is in the folder above it, the `link` element would read `<link rel="stylesheet" href="css/base.css" />`.

TIP URLs *in* an external style sheet are relative to the location of the style sheet file on the server, not to the HTML page's location. You'll see this in action when you learn about CSS background images in Chapter 10 ("Setting the Text's Background").

TIP An external style sheet's rules may be overridden by styles within an HTML document. The relative influence of styles applied in different ways is summarized in "The Importance of Location," later in this chapter.

TIP You can link to several style sheets at a time. In the event that a competing display rule appears in more than one file, the one in the later file takes precedence over the earlier ones.

TIP You can offer alternate versions of linked style sheets and let your visitors choose among them. See "Offering Alternate Style Sheets," later in this chapter.

TIP You can limit style sheets to a particular kind of output by setting the `media` attribute. For more details, see "Using Media-Specific Style Sheets," later in this chapter.

TIP Previous versions of HTML asked you to include `type="text/css"` in your `link` element definitions, but HTML5 doesn't require it, so you can omit it as I have in the code examples in this chapter.

Creating an Embedded Style Sheet

An embedded style sheet is the second way to apply CSS to a page. It lets you set the styles directly in the HTML document you want to affect (typically it goes in the **head**) **Ⓐ**. Because the styles are in that HTML file only, the CSS won't apply to other pages like a linked external style sheet does, and you won't get the same caching benefits either. As mentioned earlier, an external style sheet is the recommended approach for most cases, but it's important to understand your options for the times you'll need to deviate.

Ⓐ When embedding a style sheet, the `style` element and its enclosed style rules typically go in the **head** section of your document. The browser renders your page the same as if the styles were loaded from an external style sheet **Ⓑ**. Note that embedded style sheets should never have the `@charset` declaration at the beginning (or anywhere else, for that matter).

```
...
<head>
    <meta charset="UTF-8" />
    <title>El Palau de la Música</title>
    <style>
    img {
        border: 4px solid red;
    }
    </style>
</head>
<body>
...
    <img src="img/palau250.jpg" width="250"
    → height="163" alt="El Palau de la
    → Música" />
    <img src="img/tickets.jpg" width="87"
    → height="163" alt="The Ticket Window" />
...
</body>
</html>
```

El Palau de la Música

I love the Palau de la Música. It is ornate and gaudy and everything that was wonderful about modernism. It's also the home of the Orfeó Català, where I learned the benefits of Moscatell.

B The result is exactly the same as if you had linked to the styles in an external style sheet. The difference is that no other Web page can take advantage of the styles used on this page.

To create an embedded style sheet:

1. Type `<style>` in the **head** section of your HTML document.

2. Define as many style rules as desired (see "Constructing a Style Rule" in Chapter 7).

3. Type `</style>` to complete the embedded style sheet Ⓐ.

TIP Conflicting styles applied in an embedded style sheet override those in external style sheets if—and only if—the `style` element comes after the `link` element. For more details, see "The Importance of Location," later in this chapter.

TIP Embedded style sheets are the second-best way to add CSS to your page. (There are rare exceptions, such as very high-trafficked sites under certain conditions.) The recommended approach is to load external style sheets. For more information, see "Creating an External Style Sheet," earlier in this chapter.

TIP Though I *strongly* discourage you from doing so, you can also apply styles directly to individual HTML elements. For more details, see "Applying Inline Styles," later in this chapter.

TIP *Technically*, it is possible to embed a style sheet in a page's body too, though avoid it whenever possible. Mixing your HTML and CSS breaks a key best practice, which is to separate content (HTML), presentation (CSS), and behavior (JavaScript). From a practical standpoint, it's easier to maintain your CSS if it's in an external style sheet rather than embedded in your HTML (especially the body).

Applying Inline Styles

Inline styles are the third way to apply CSS to HTML. However, they are by far the least desirable option because they intertwine your content (HTML) and presentation (CSS), a cruel slap in the face to best practices **A**. An inline style affects only one element **B**, so you lose one of the key benefits an external style sheet provides: Write once and see everywhere. Imagine having to sift through a slew of HTML pages to make a simple font color change, and you can see why inline styles aren't intended for regular use.

However, an inline style can be helpful if you want to try something out quickly as a test before removing it from your HTML and placing it in your external style sheet (assuming you were happy with the test results), where it'll be easier to maintain moving forward.

A Rules applied inline affect only a single element; in this case, the first `img`.

```
...
<head>
     <meta charset="UTF-8" />
     <title>El Palau de la Música</title>
</head>
<body>
...
     <img src="palau250.jpg" width="250"
     → height="163" alt="El Palau de la
     → Música" style="border: 4px solid
     → red" />
     <img src="tickets.jpg" width="87"
     → height="163" alt="The Ticket Window" />
...
</body>
</html>
```

B Only the first image has a border. To repeat the effect shown in the rest of this chapter, you'd have to add `style="border: 4px solid red"` to every single `img` element individually. As you can see, inline styles are not particularly efficient and would be a headache to apply and update across a site.

To apply inline styles:

1. Type `style="` within the HTML element that you want to format. (Add it to the start tag of non-void elements.)

2. Create a style rule without curly brackets or a selector. The selector isn't necessary since you're placing it directly inside the desired element.

3. To create additional style definitions, type `;` (a semicolon) and repeat step 2.

4. Type the final quote mark `"`.

TIP Be careful not to confuse the equals sign with the colon. Since they both assign values, it's easy to interchange them without thinking.

TIP Don't forget to separate multiple property definitions with a semicolon.

TIP Don't forget to enclose your style definitions in straight quote marks.

TIP Styles applied inline take precedence over all other styles unless a conflicting style elsewhere is marked with `!important` (see "The Importance of Location" in this chapter).

TIP If you specify the font family in an inline style declaration, you'll have to enclose multi-word font names with single quotes in order to avoid conflict with the `style` element's double quotes. You can't use the same type of quotes in both places.

TIP Probably the most common use of inline styles is applying them to elements from JavaScript functions as part of making portions of a page dynamic. You may notice these generated inline styles when looking at the source of a page in, say, Firebug or Chrome's Developer Tools. In most cases, the JavaScript that applies those is separate from the HTML, so it still maintains the desired separation of content (HTML), presentation (CSS), and behavior (JavaScript).

The Importance of Location

It's not unusual for more than one style rule to apply to the same element, particularly on larger sites that require more effort to manage the CSS. As mentioned in "The Cascade: When Rules Collide" in Chapter 7, a style's location can break a tie in the contest between inheritance and specificity. The basic rule is that, with all else equal, the later the style appears, the more precedence or importance it has (🅐 through 🅓).

So, inline styles have the most precedence and will override any conflicting styles applied elsewhere.

In an embedded **style** element, any **@import** rules present will lose out to any individual style rules that also appear in the **style** element (since these must follow the **@import** rules, by definition).

The relationship between the embedded **style** element and any linked external style sheets depends on their relative positions. If the **link** element comes later in the HTML code, it overrides the **style** element. If it comes earlier, the **style** element (and any imported style sheets it contains) overrides the rules in the linked style sheet.

🅐 In this example, the **style** element comes last. Therefore, its rules will have precedence over the rules in the **base.css** style sheet (as long as the conflicting rules have the same inheritance and specificity factors).

```
...
<head>
    <title>El Palau de la Música</title>
    <link rel="stylesheet"
    ⇢ href="base.css" />
    <style>
    img {
        border-style: dashed;
    }
    </style>
</head>
...
```

🅑 The **style** element's dashed border wins out over the solid border from the linked **base.css**.

C Here, the linked style sheet comes last and has precedence over rules in the **style** element (all else being equal).

```
...
<head>
    <title>El Palau de la Música</title>
    <style>
    img {
        border-style: dashed;
    }
    </style>
    <link rel="stylesheet" href="base.css"
/>
</head>
...
```

D The solid border from the **base.css** style sheet wins out over the internal **style** element's dashed border.

External style sheets can also contain **@import** rules (though, as noted earlier, I advise not using them, for performance reasons). In that case, the imported rules are overridden by the other rules contained in the external style sheet (since, by definition, they must follow the **@import** rule). Their relationship with the document's other style sheets is determined by the position of the link to the external style sheet, as usual.

There is one exception to how the order of conflicting styles affects which one wins out. A style marked with **!important** always wins, whether it's first in the order, last, or somewhere in between. Here's an example: **p { margin-top: 1em !important; }**. Avoid using it, though. It makes your declarations too strong, and your CSS will get bogged down with longer rules if you need to override it.

The only thing that wins out over a declaration with **!important** is a *user* style sheet. Yes, you and I as visitors to sites can create our own style sheet for the browser, and it takes precedence. For example, we might always prefer to view certain font sizes or a level of contrast between the text and background colors. However, most users don't even know they can do this, so it's pretty uncommon.

Using Media-Specific Style Sheets

You can designate a style sheet to be used only for a particular output, perhaps only for printing or only for viewing onscreen in the browser. For example, you might create one general style sheet with features common to both the print and screen versions, and then create individual print and screen style sheets with properties to be used only for print or screen, respectively.

To designate media-specific style sheets:

1. Add media="*output*" to the **link** or **style** start tags, where *output* is one or more of the following: **print**, **screen**, or **all** (these are the most common types, though others exist) **Ⓐ**. Separate multiple values with commas.

2. Alternatively, use the **@media** at-rule in your style sheet **Ⓑ**. This method does not require specifying a media type in the **link** element.

Ⓐ Limit the style sheet to a particular output by adding the **media** attribute to the **link** element. In this example, **base.css** affects the page when viewed in the browser (due to **media="screen"**), while **print.css** affects how the page prints (due to **media="print"**).

```
...
<head>
    <meta charset="UTF-8" />
    <title>El Palau de la Música</title>
    <link rel="stylesheet" href="base.css"
    → media="screen" />
    <link rel="stylesheet" href="print.css"
    → media="print" />
</head>
<body>
...
    <img src="img/palau250.jpg" width="250"
    → height="163" alt="El Palau de la
    → Música" />
    <img src="img/tickets.jpg" width="87"
    → height="163" alt="The Ticket Window" />
...
</body>
</html>
```

B The `@media` at-rule in a style sheet is another way to target other media types (see Chapter 12). This example shows styles affecting all media types (including print) on top, and print-specific styles at the bottom. A Print Preview or printout of a page with this style sheet would show no images (`display: none` turns them off) and black, italicized paragraph text. The `font-style: italic` declaration applies to print mode too, since the print style sheet doesn't specify a different `font-style`.

```css
@charset "UTF-8";

/* Styles for all media */
img {
    border: 4px solid red;
}

p {
    color: green;
    font-style: italic;
}

/* Print Style Sheet */
@media print {
    img {
        display: none;
    }

    p {
        color: black;
    }
}
```

TIP The default value for the `media` attribute is `all`, so declaring `media="all"` is redundant. In other words, you can leave out the `media` attribute unless you need to be specific. Some coders prefer to be explicit by always including `media="all"`.

TIP There are nine possible output types: `all`, `aural`, `braille`, `handheld`, `print`, `projection`, `screen`, `tty`, and `tv`, with varying degrees of support (most have modest support). Practically speaking, the ones you will likely ever use are `screen` and `print` (and perhaps `all`); each has very wide support. On the other hand (so to speak), `handheld` never got much support from devices, so typically you'll use `screen` instead when designing for mobile (see Chapter 12). Opera's projection mode, Opera Show, supports the `projection` type, which is geared toward projectors and similar views.

TIP See Christian Krammer's article at www.smashingmagazine.com/2011/11/24/how-to-set-up-a-print-style-sheet/ to learn more about creating a print style sheet.

Offering Alternate Style Sheets

You can link to more than one style sheet Ⓐ and let visitors choose the styles they like best. The specifications allow for a base set of *persistent* styles Ⓑ that are applied regardless of the visitor's preference, a default or *preferred* set of additional styles Ⓒ that are applied if the visitor makes no choice, and one or more *alternate* style sheets Ⓓ that the visitor can choose Ⓔ, at which point the preferred set (though not the persistent set) is deactivated and ignored. Alternate style sheets allow you to provide different themes for your site.

To offer alternate style sheets:

1. To designate the style sheet that should be used as a base, regardless of the visitor's preferences, use the simple syntax described in "Linking to External Style Sheets," with no `title`.

2. To designate the style sheet that should be offered as a first choice, but that can be deactivated by another choice, add `title="label"` to the `link` element, where `label` identifies the preferred style sheet.

3. To designate a style sheet that should be offered as an alternate choice, use `rel="alternate stylesheet"` `title="label"` in the `link` element, where `label` identifies the alternate style sheet.

Ⓐ In order, I've defined the base or persistent style sheet, the preferred or automatic style sheet, and an alternative style sheet. Each style sheet needs its own `link` element.

```
...
<head>
      <meta charset="UTF-8" />
      <title>Palau de la Música</title>
      <link rel="stylesheet"
      → href="base.css" />
      <link rel="stylesheet" href=
      → "preferred.css" title="Dashed" />
      <link rel="alternate stylesheet"
      → href="alternate.css"
      → title="Dotted" />
</head>
...
```

Ⓑ As an example, this CSS file (**base.css**) will be the persistent style sheet and will be applied no matter what the visitor does.

```
img {
      border: 4px solid red;
}
```

Ⓒ This style sheet (**preferred.css**) will be the one loaded by default in addition to **base.css** when the visitor jumps to the page.

```
img {
      border-style: dashed;
}
```

Ⓓ The visitor will be able to load this alternate style sheet if they want. Its file name is **alternate.css**, though as is the case with the others, you can name it as you like.

```
img {
      border-style: dotted;
}
```

 When the page is loaded, it has a dashed border (the preferred value overrides the base value of solid, but the base color is maintained). If the visitor were to choose Dotted, the alternate style sheet would be used instead.

TIP You don't have to offer a preferred style sheet in order to provide an alternate style sheet. The example shown could have the `link` elements for `base.css` and `alternate.css` only. Similarly, it could link to `preferred.css` and `alternate.css` without specifying a persistent style sheet. You may also have more than one alternate style sheet.

TIP Firefox  and Opera offer an easy way to switch from one style sheet to another. However, there are JavaScript solutions for other browsers. Search online for "style sheet switcher" to find code you can use.

TIP Alternate style sheets were more common several years ago as a means to allow users to choose from one of several font sizes. Nowadays, browsers tend to make it easier to increase the font size without the assistance of an alternate style sheet, and many users are more aware of these features (page zoom being the primary one).

TIP You can also load style sheets just for printing your Web page. For details, see "Using Media-Specific Style Sheets" in this chapter.

The Inspiration of Others: CSS

In Chapter 2, you learned how to see the source code for a Web page. Viewing someone's CSS is not much more difficult.

To view other designers' CSS code:

1. First view the page's HTML code 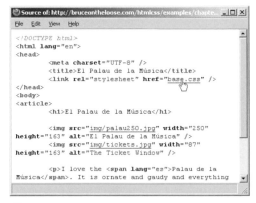 A. For more details on viewing HTML source code, see "The Inspiration of Others" in Chapter 2.

   If the CSS code is in an embedded style sheet, you'll be able to see it already.

2. If the CSS is in an external style sheet, locate the reference to it in the HTML and click the file name A. The style sheet displays in the browser window B. You can copy it from there and paste it into your text editor if you like.

> **TIP** As with HTML, use other designers' code for inspiration, then write your own style sheets. View their code with a careful eye, though. Just because it's on the Web doesn't mean it's always an example of the best way to code a particular effect, despite the author's best intentions.

> **TIP** Modern browsers allow you to click the style sheet name in the HTML source, as shown in the figures. To view a style sheet in an older browser, you may need to copy the URL shown in the `link` element, paste it in the address bar of your browser (replacing the HTML file name), and hit Enter. If the style sheet's URL is a relative address (see "URLs" in Chapter 1), you may have to reconstruct the style sheet's URL by combining the Web page's URL with the style sheet's relative URL.

> **TIP** The developer tools offered in modern browsers also allow quick access to viewing a page's CSS. They come bundled with most browsers, and there's an extension called Firebug for Firefox (see Chapter 20).

A View the source code for the HTML page that contains the style sheet you want to view, and click the style sheet file name.

B The style sheet displays in the browser window.

9

Defining Selectors

As you saw in "Constructing a Style Rule" in Chapter 7, there are two principal parts of a CSS style rule. The *selector* determines which elements the formatting will be applied to, and the *declarations* define just what formatting will be applied. In this chapter, you'll learn how to define CSS selectors.

While the simplest selectors let you format all the elements of a given type—say, all the **h1** headings—more complex selectors let you apply formatting rules to elements based on their class or id, context, state, and more.

Once you've defined the selectors, you can go on to create the declarations (with actual properties and values) in Chapters 10–14. Some more-specialized style properties are discussed throughout the rest of this book. Until then, you'll use the very simple and relatively obvious `{color: red;}` in the examples.

In This Chapter

Constructing Selectors

The selector determines which elements a style rule is applied to. For example, if you want to format all **p** elements with the Times font, 12 pixels high, you'd need to create a selector that identifies just the **p** elements while leaving the other elements in your code alone. If you want to format the first **p** in each section with a special indent, you'll need to create a slightly more complicated selector that identifies only those **p** elements that are the first element in their section of the page.

A selector can define up to five different criteria for choosing the elements that should be formatted:

- The type or name of the element **A**.
- The context in which the element is found **B**.
- The **class** or **id** of an element (**C** and **D**).
- The pseudo-class of an element or a pseudo-element **E** (I'll explain both of those, I promise).
- Whether or not an element has certain attributes and values **F**.

```
Name of desired element
  ┌┴┐
  h1 {
      color: red;
  }
```

A The simplest kind of selector is simply the name of the type of element that should be formatted—in this case, the **h1** element.

```
Context
  │      Name of desired element
  ┌┴┐    ┌┴┐
  h1  em {
      color: red;
  }
```

B This selector uses context. The style will only be applied to the **em** elements within **h1** elements. The **em** elements found elsewhere are not affected.

```
Class
┌┴┐
.very {
    color: red;
}

       ID
      ┌┴┐
#gaudi {
    color: red;
}
```

C The first selector chooses all elements that belong to the **very** class. In other words, any element with **class="very"** in its HTML start tag. The second selector chooses the one element with an **id** of **gaudi**, as specified by **id="gaudi"** in its HTML start tag. You'll recall that an **id** may appear once in each page, whereas a **class** may appear any number of times.

```
Name of desired element
    │   Class
    ┌┴┐ ┌─┴─┐
em.very {
    color: red;
}
```

```
Name of desired element
    │          ID
    ┌───┴──┐ ┌──┴──┐
article#gaudi {
    color: red;
}
```

Selectors can include any combination of these in order to pinpoint the desired elements. Mostly, you use one or two at a time. In addition, you can apply the same declarations to several selectors at once if you need to apply the same style rules to different groups of elements (see "Specifying Groups of Elements," later in this chapter).

The rest of this chapter explains exactly how to define selectors.

D You can be more specific by prefixing a **class** or **id** selector with the element name to target. In this case, the first selector chooses only the **em** elements with the **very** class rather than every element with the **very** class. Similarly, the second selector chooses the one **article** element with an **id** of **gaudi**. In general, don't use this approach unless you have to; the less specific selector in the previous example **C** is preferred.

```
Name
   │   Pseudo-class
   ┌┴┐ ┌───┴───┐
a:link {
    color: red;
}
```

E In this example, the selector chooses **a** elements that belong to the **link** pseudo-class (that is, the **a** elements that haven't yet been visited).

```
Name
   │   Attribute
   ┌┴┐ ┌──┴──┐
a[name] {
    color: red;
}
```

F You can use the square brackets to add information to a selector about the desired element's attributes, values, or both.

Selecting Elements by Name

Perhaps the most common criterion for choosing which elements to format is the element's name or type. For example, you might want to make all of the **h1** elements big and bold and format all of the **p** elements with a sans-serif font.

Ⓐ This HTML code has two **h2** elements. (In case you're wondering, the `lang` attribute indicates that the content is in a different language than the page's default language, which is specified on the `html` element that follows the DOCTYPE at the beginning of each page. In this case, `lang="es"` on each **h2** indicates that their content is in Spanish.)

```
<!DOCTYPE html>
<html lang="en">
<head>
...
</head>
<body>
...
<article class="about">
    <h1>Antoni Gaudí</h1>

    <p>Many tourists are drawn to Barcelona to see Antoni Gaudí's incredible architecture.</p>
    <p>Barcelona <a href="http://www.gaudi2002.bcn.es/english/" rel="external">celebrated the 150th
     ⇢ anniversary</a> of Gaudí's birth in 2002.</p>

    <section class="project">
       <h2 lang="es">La Casa Milà</h2>
       <p>Gaudí's work was essentially useful. <span lang="es">La Casa Milà</span> is an apartment
        ⇢ building and <em>real people</em> live there.</p>
    </section>

    <section class="project">
       <h2 lang="es">La Sagrada Família</h2>
       <p>The complicatedly named and curiously unfinished Expiatory Temple of the Sacred Family is
        ⇢ the <em>most visited</em> building in Barcelona.</p>
    </section>
</article>
...
```

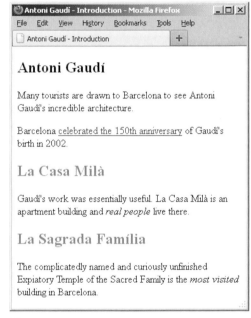

B This selector will choose all the **h2** elements in the document and make them red **C**.

```
h2 {
    color: red;
}
```

C All the **h2** elements are colored red.

To select elements to format based on their type:

Type *selector*, where *selector* is the name of the desired type of element, without any attributes **B**.

TIP Unless you specify otherwise (using the techniques in the rest of this chapter), all the elements of the specified type will be formatted, no matter where they appear in your document.

TIP Not all selectors need to specify an element's name. If you want to apply formatting to an entire class of elements, regardless of which type of elements have been identified with that class, you'd want to leave the name out of the selector. The next section explains how to do this.

TIP The wildcard, * (asterisk), matches any element name in your code. For example, `* { border: 2px solid green; }` gives every element a two-pixel, green, solid border!

TIP You can choose a group of element names for a selector by using the comma to separate them. For more details, consult "Specifying Groups of Elements," later in this chapter.

Selecting Elements by Class or ID

If you've labeled elements with a **class** Ⓐ or an **id** (see Chapter 3), you can use that criterion in a selector to apply formatting to only those elements that are so labeled Ⓑ.

Ⓐ There are two **article** elements with a **class** of **about**. A short paragraph without the **class** is in between them.

```
...
<article id="gaudi" class="about">
    <h1>Antoni Gaudí</h1>

    <p>Many tourists are drawn to Barcelona to see Antoni Gaudí's incredible architecture.</p>
    <p>Barcelona <a href="http://www.gaudi2002.bcn.es/english/" rel="external">celebrated the 150th
      ⸳ anniversary</a> of Gaudí's birth in 2002.</p>

    <section class="project">
        <h2 lang="es">La Casa Milà</h2>
        <p>Gaudi's work was essentially useful. <span lang="es">La Casa Milà</span> is an apartment
          ⸳ building and <em>real people</em> live there.</p>
    </section>

    ...
</article>

<p>This paragraph doesn't have <code>class="about"</code>, so it isn't red when the CSS is
  ⸳ applied.</p>

<article class="about">
    <h1>Lluís Domènech i Montaner</h1>

    <p>Lluís Domènech i Montaner was a contemporary of Gaudí.</p>
    ...
</article>
...
```

B This selector will choose the elements with a **class** equal to **about**. In this case, they're both **article** elements, but you could apply the classes to any elements. If you wanted to apply the style *only* when an **article** element has this class, you would write the selector as **article.about**. But that's more specific than you'll usually need to be.

```
.about {
    color: red;
}
```

C The **article** with the **about** class is displayed in red, but the **p** element at the end of the page is not. (In case you're wondering, the link is in blue because of the browser's default styles, but you can write your own rule to override it.)

To select elements to format based on their class:

1. Type **.** (a period).

2. With no intervening space, immediately type *classname*, where *classname* identifies the class to which you'd like to apply the styles.

To select elements to format based on their id:

1. Type **#** (a hash or pound sign).

2. With no intervening space, immediately type *id*, where *id* uniquely identifies the element to which you'd like to apply the styles.

TIP You can use **class** and **id** selectors alone or together with other selector criteria. For example, **.news { color: red; }** would affect all elements with the **news** class, while **h1.news { color: red; }** would affect only the **h1** elements with the **news** class. It's best to omit the element name from an **id** or **class** selector unless you have to target it specifically.

continues on next page

TIP Notice in Ⓐ and Ⓑ that I used a `class` name (about) that conveys the meaning of the content to which it's applied rather than calling it red. It's best to avoid creating a `class` name that describes how something looks, because you might change the styles later, like making the text green in this case. And `class`es add semantic value to your HTML like elements do.

TIP If the example in Ⓑ were written instead as #gaudi { color: red; }, only the text in the first `article` would be red, because it's the only one with id="gaudi". Each `id` must be unique, so you can't reuse that `id` on the `article` about Lluís Domènech i Montaner.

TIP For more information on assigning `class`es to elements in the HTML code, consult "Naming Elements with a Class or ID" in Chapter 3.

Class Selectors vs. ID Selectors

When deciding between **class** selectors and **id** selectors, I suggest using **class**es whenever possible, in large part because you can reuse them. Some advocate not using **id**s at all, an argument I understand, though ultimately the choice comes down to you as you develop your sites. It's a subject that can yield some pretty strong opinions on both sides. In any case, here are two of the issues that **id** selectors introduce:

- Their associated styles can't be reused on other elements (remember, an **id** may appear on only one element in a page). This can lead to repeating styles on other elements, rather than sharing them via a **class**.

- They are far more specific than **class** selectors. This means that if you ever need to override styling that was defined with an **id** selector, you'll need to write a CSS rule that's even more specific. A few of these might not be hard to manage, but once you're working on a site of a decent size, your CSS can get longer and more complicated than necessary.

Those two points probably will become more clear to you as you work with CSS more. (On the flip side, one reason some people like using **id**s is so they'll know at a glance if an element is unique.)

So, I recommend looking for opportunities to combine shared styles into one or more **class**es so you can reuse them, and to keep **id** selectors to a minimum if you do use them (see the sample page in Chapter 11 for an example of how you could do this). You may find your style sheets shorter and easier to manage.

A I've shortened the text to make the relationships between elements easier to see. Each indentation represents a generation. Note that in this snippet there are two second-generation **p** elements directly within the **article** with the **about** class, and one third-generation **p** element within the **project section**s (within the **article**). There's another third-generation **p** in the full code, not shown. The **h2** instances are also third generation.

```
...
<article class="about">
    <h1>Antoni Gaudí</h1>

    <p>Many tourists ... </p>
    <p>Barcelona ... </p>

    <section class="project">
        <h2 lang="es">La Casa Milà</h2>
        <p>Gaudí's work ... </p>
    </section>

    <section class="project">
        <h2 lang="es">La Sagrada Família</h2>
        ...
    </section>
</article>
...
```

B The space between **article.about** and **p** means that this selector will find any **p** element that is a descendant of **article**s with the **about** class, regardless of its generation. However, prefixing the **class** (or especially an **id**) with the element name is usually more specific than you need to be in practice. See the next example for less-specific selectors **C**.

```
article.about p {
    color: red;
}
```

Selecting Elements by Context

In CSS, you can pinpoint elements depending on their ancestors, their parent, or their siblings (see "Parents and Children" in Chapter 1) (**A** through **D**).

An *ancestor* is any element that contains the desired element (the *descendant*), regardless of the number of generations that separate them.

C There is often more than one way to craft your selectors to get the desired effect. It comes down to how specific you need to be. The selector in the first example here (**article p { }**) is less specific than both the one that follows it (**.about p { }**) and the one in **B**. The second example here combines a **class** selector with a descendant selector; you can combine with **id** selectors, too. You'll find yourself using these all the time rather than the more specific and verbose model in **B**.

```
/* Other ways to get the same effect
------------------------------------ */

/* Any p that is a descendant of any article.
 ⤷The least specific approach. */
article p {
    color: red;
}

/* Any p that is a descendant of any element
 ⤷with the about class. The second most
 ⤷specific of the three. */
.about p {
    color: red;
}
```

To select an element to format based on its ancestor:

1. Type *ancestor*, where *ancestor* is the selector for the element that contains the element you wish to format.

2. Type a space.

3. If necessary, repeat steps 1 and 2 for each successive generation of ancestors.

4. Type *descendant*, where *descendant* is the selector for the element you wish to format.

TIP A selector based on an element's ancestor had been known as a *descendant selector*, but CSS3 renamed it a *descendant combinator*. (Some people still say "selector.")

TIP Don't be thrown off by the `article .about` portion of the example B. Remember that it simply means "the `article` whose `class` is equal to `about`." So `article.about p` means "any `p` element that is contained in the `article` element whose `class` is equal to `about`." By comparison, the less-specific `.about p` means "any `p` element that is contained in *any* element whose `class` is equal to `about`" C. That's because `id` selectors in this context are more specific than element and `class` selectors.

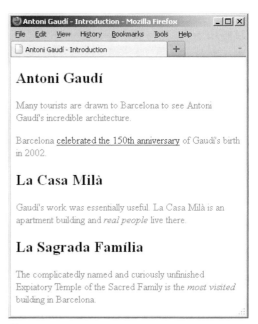

D All the **p** elements that are contained within the element with the **about** class are red even if they're also within other elements within the element with the **about** class. Each of the style rules in B and C yield the result shown here.

E This selector will only choose those **p** elements that are children (not grandchildren, great grandchildren, and so on) of **article** elements with the **about** class. In order to qualify, they may not be contained within any other element.

```
article.about > p {
    color: red;
}
```

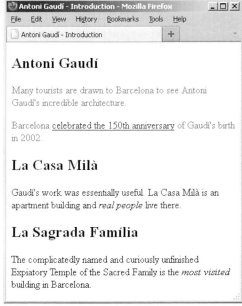

F Only the first two **p** elements are children of the **about** class **article**. The two other **p** elements are children of the **section** elements within the **article**. For the HTML code used in this example, see **A**.

The previous examples showed descendant combinators. CSS also has *child combinators*, which allow you to define a rule for an immediate descendant (in other words, a *child*) of a parent element. You may know them as *child selectors*, the pre-CSS3 terminology. A *parent* is an element that directly contains another element (a child), meaning they are only one generation away.

To select an element to format based on its parent:

1. Type *parent*, where *parent* is the selector for the element that directly contains the element you wish to format.

2. Type > (the greater than sign) **E**.

3. If necessary, repeat steps 1 and 2 for each successive generation of parents.

4. Type *child*, where *child* is the selector for the element you wish to format.

TIP Just as you saw with the descendant combinator, you can omit the element name before the **class**. In fact, I recommend it (unless you need the extra specificity to achieve the desired styling). For example, `.about > p { color: red; }` yields the same effect in this case. Or, to be even less specific, leave out the **class** entirely, as in `article > p { color: red; }`. Use these simpler forms whenever possible before resorting to more-specific ones. Some of the examples that follow in the rest of the chapter could be simplified in a similar manner. Now that you have a taste for how it's done, I won't call out these alternatives, but keep in mind that generally it is best to be *less* specific to keep your styles easier to reuse.

TIP You may also use **id** selectors in child combinators, though I recommend using less-specific selectors like element type or **class** whenever possible.

TIP Internet Explorer 6 doesn't support the child selector.

It's sometimes useful to be able to select only the *first* child of an element, as opposed to all the children of an element. Use the `:first-child` pseudo-class to achieve this (G through J).

To select an element to format that is the first child of its parent:

1. Optionally, type *parent*, where *parent* is the selector for the desired element's parent.

2. If you included a **parent** in step 1, type a space followed by **>** followed by another space.

3. Optionally, type the selector that represents the first child you want to style (for example, **p** or **.news**).

4. Type `:first-child` (just like that) I. (Note that you don't have to specify a parent in step 1. For instance, `p:first-child { font-weight: bold; }` would make any paragraph that is the first child of any element bold.)

G The `:first-child` pseudo-selector chooses only the first child of an element, *not* the first instance of an element that is a child. So, although you might be inclined to think the rule shown will make the first paragraph in the sample page red, it won't H, because the **h1** is the first child of the **article** that has the **about** class assigned to it. For the HTML code used in this example, see A.

```
/* You might think this will make the first
   paragraph red, but it won't! */

.about > p:first-child {
    color: red;
}
```

H The rule has no effect on the page, because there isn't a **p** element that's the first child of an element with the **about** class.

I This selector chooses only the **h1** element that is the first child of elements with **class="about"** assigned in the HTML. This rule *does* affect the display of our page **J**.

```
/* h1 is the first child, so this works. */

.about > h1:first-child {
    color: red;
}
```

J The **h1** element contained in the **article** is red because it's the first child of an element with the **about** class. If there were other **h1** elements inside the **article**, they wouldn't be red.

Continuing with the familial theme, *sibling* elements are elements of any kind that are children of the same parent. *Adjacent siblings* are elements that are next to each other directly, meaning no other sibling sits between them. In the following crude example, the **h1** and **p** are adjacent siblings, and the **p** and **h2** are adjacent siblings, but the **h1** and **h2** are not. However, they are all siblings (and children of the **body** element):

```
...
<body>
        <h1>...</h1>
        <p>...</p>
        <h2>...</h2>
</body>
</html>
```

The CSS *adjacent sibling combinator* allows you to target a sibling element that is preceded immediately by a sibling you specify. (See the last tip regarding the *general sibling combinator*, new in CSS3.)

To select an element to format based on an adjacent sibling:

1. Type *sibling*, where *sibling* is the selector for the element that directly precedes the desired element within the same parent element. (They don't have to be the same element type as long as they are directly next to each other, as explained previously.)

2. Type **+** (a plus sign).

3. If necessary, repeat steps 1 and 2 for each successive sibling.

4. Type *element*, where *element* is the selector for the element you wish to format .

TIP Also see "Parents and Children" in Chapter 1.

TIP The :first-child part of the selector is called a *pseudo-class*, because it identifies a group of elements without you (the designer or developer) having to mark them in the HTML code.

TIP Neither the :first-child nor adjacent sibling selectors are supported by IE 6.

TIP CSS3 introduces the *general sibling combinator*, which allows you to select a sibling that is not necessarily immediately preceded by another sibling. The only difference in syntax from an adjacent sibling combinator is that you use a ~ (tilde) instead of a + to separate the siblings. For instance, h1~h2 { color: red; } would make any h2 element red as long as it is preceded by a sibling h1 somewhere within the parent (it could be immediately adjacent, but it doesn't have to be).

K This adjacent sibling combinator chooses only those **p** elements that directly follow a sibling **p** element.

```
.about p+p {
    color: red;
}
```

L Only the **p** elements that *directly* follow a sibling **p** element are red. If there were a third, fourth, or more consecutive paragraphs, they too would be red. For example, an adjacent sibling combinator would be useful for indenting all paragraphs except the first.

A There's no telling which words will be affected by **first-line** until you view the page in the browser and see how the content flows. It's not determined by what line the words are on in the HTML itself.

```
<article class="about">
    <h1>Antoni Gaudí</h1>

    <p>Many tourists are drawn to Barcelona
    → to see Antoni Gaudí's incredible
    → architecture.</p>
    <p>Barcelona <a href="http://
    → www.gaudi2002.bcn.es/english/"
    → rel="external">celebrated the 150th
    → anniversary</a> of Gaudí's birth in
    → 2002.</p>

    <section class="project">
        <h2 lang="es">La Casa Milà</h2>
        <p>Gaudí's work was essentially
        → useful. <span lang="es">La Casa
        → Milà</span> is an apartment
        → building and <em>real people</em>
        → live there.</p>
    </section>

    <section class="project">
        <h2 lang="es">La Sagrada Família</h2>
        <p>The complicatedly named and
        → curiously unfinished Expiatory
        → Temple of the Sacred Family is the
        → <em>most visited</em> building in
        → Barcelona.</p>
    </section>
</article>
```

B Here the selector will choose the first line of each **p** element.

```
p:first-line {
    color: red;
}
```

Selecting Part of an Element

You can also select just the first letter or first line of an element and then apply formatting to that.

To select the first line of an element:

1. Type *element*, where *element* is the selector for the element whose first line you'd like to format.

2. Type **:first-line** to select the entire first line of the element referenced in step 1.

C Adjusting the width of the window changes the content of the first lines (and thus, what is formatted).

To select the first letter of an element:

1. Type *element*, where *element* is the selector for the element whose first line you'd like to format.

2. Type **:first-letter** to select the first letter of the element referenced in step 1.

TIP According to the CSS specifications, punctuation that precedes the first letter should be included in the selector. Modern browsers support this, but older versions of IE don't. Instead, they consider the punctuation itself as the first letter.

TIP Only certain CSS properties can be applied to :first-letter pseudo-elements: **font, color, background, text-decoration, vertical-align** (as long as the :first-letter is not floated), **text-transform, line-height, margin, padding, border, float,** and **clear.** You'll learn about all these in Chapters 10 and 11.

TIP You may combine the **:first-letter** or **:first-line** pseudo-elements with more-complicated selectors than those used in this example. For example, if you wanted to select just the first letter of each paragraph contained in the elements with the **project** class, your selector would be `.project p:first-letter`.

D Here the selector will choose just the first letter of each **p** element. For the corresponding HTML code, see **A**.

```
p:first-letter {
    color: red;
}
```

Antoni (

Many tourists are
Antoni Gaudí's ind

Barcelona celebra
Gaudí's birth in 2(

E The **first-letter** selector could conceivably be used to create drop caps (once you've learned more properties besides **color**).

Pseudo-Elements, Pseudo-Classes, and CSS3's `::first-line` and `::first-letter` Syntax

In CSS3, the syntax of `:first-line` is `::first-line` and `:first-letter` is `::first-letter`. Note the double colons instead of single colons.

The intent of this change was to distinguish the four pseudo-elements—`::first-line`, `::first-letter`, `::before`, `::after`—from pseudo-classes like `:first-child`, `:link`, `:hover`, and more.

A *pseudo-element* is one that doesn't exist as an element in the HTML. For instance, you don't mark up your first letter or first line of text with HTML that defines it as such. Instead, they are content that's part of another element, like the **p** elements in the example.

A *pseudo-class*, on the other hand, *does* apply to an HTML element. You saw that with `:first-child`, which selects the specified element that is the first child of its parent element.

The double-colon syntax of `::first-line` and `::first-letter` is preferred moving forward, and modern browsers support it. The original, single-colon syntax is deprecated, but browsers continue to support it for backward compatibility. However, no version of Internet Explorer prior to IE9 supports the double colon, so you may decide to continue using the single-colon syntax unless you serve different CSS to IE8 and below.

Selecting Links Based on Their State

CSS lets you apply formatting to links based on their current state; that is, whether the visitor is hovering their cursor on top of one, whether a link has been visited, or whatever. You achieve these with a series of pseudo-classes.

To select links to format based on their state:

1. Type **a** (since **a** is the name of the element for links).

2. Type **:** (a colon).

3. Type **link** to change the appearance of links that haven't yet been or aren't currently being activated or pointed at.

   Or type **visited** to change links that the visitor has already activated.

   Or type **focus** if the link is selected via the keyboard and is ready to be activated.

   Or type **hover** to change the appearance of links when pointed to.

   Or type **active** to change the appearance of links when activated.

Ⓐ You can't specify in the code what state a link will have; it's controlled by your visitors. Pseudo-classes allow you to access the state and change the display as you please.

```
...
    <p>Many tourists are drawn to Barcelona
    ↪ to see Antoni Gaudí's incredible
    ↪ architecture.</p>
    <p>Barcelona <http://www.gaudi2002.
    ↪ bcn.es/ english/">celebrated</a> the
    ↪ 150th anniversary of Gaudí's birth
    ↪ in 2002.</p>
...
```

Ⓑ Styles for links should always be defined in this order, to avoid overriding properties when a link is in more than one state (say, visited and hovered).

```
a:link {
    color: red;
}

a:visited {
    color: orange;
}

a:focus {
    color: purple;
}

a:hover {
    color: green;
}

a:active {
    color: blue;
}
```

architecture.

Barcelona celebrated t   **C** Links will be red
                          when new and not
La Casa Milà   visited.

architecture.

Barcelona celebrated t   **D** Once the link has
                          been visited, it turns
La Casa Milà   orange.

architecture.

Barcelona celebrated t   **E** If the link gets the
                          focus (such as with the
La Casa Milà   Tab key), it is purple.

architecture.

Barcelona celebrated t   **F** When the visitor
                          hovers over the link
                          with the pointer, it is
La Casa Milà   green.

architecture.

Barcelona celebrated t   **G** As the visitor
                          activates the link, it
La Casa Milà   turns blue.

TIP You may also apply the `:active` and `:hover` pseudo-classes to other elements. For instance, `p:hover { color: red; }` would change the color of each paragraph to red when you hover over it. (If you're keeping score, this works in Internet Explorer 7 and above, but not in IE6. Neither IE6 nor IE7 supports `:active` on elements besides a. All other browsers support both features.)

TIP Since a link can be in more than one state at a time (say, simultaneously active and hovered above) and later rules override earlier ones, it's important to define the rules in the following order: `link`, `visited`, `focus`, `hover`, `active` (LVFHA). One popular way to remember this is the mnemonic "Lord Vader's Former Handle Anakin." Some argue for ordering the rules LVHFA instead; it works too.

Selecting Elements Based on Attributes

You can also apply formatting to those elements that have a given attribute or attribute value.

To select elements to format based on their attributes:

1. Type *element*, where *element* is the selector for the element whose attributes are in question.

2. Type [*attribute*, where *attribute* is the name of the attribute that an element must have to be selected.

3. Type ="*value*" if you want to specify the *value* that the attribute's value must equal for its element to be selected.

   Or type ~="*value*" to specify an exact *value* that the attribute's value must contain (along with other content

Ⓐ For demonstration purposes, I've changed the **class** value on the second **section** element from **project** to **work**.

```
<article class="about">
    <h1>Antoni Gaudí</h1>

    <p>Many tourists are drawn to Barcelona to see Antoni Gaudí's incredible architecture.</p>
    <p>Barcelona <a href="http://www.gaudi2002.bcn.es/english/" rel="external">celebrated the 150th
    → anniversary</a> of Gaudí's birth in 2002.</p>

    <section class="project">
        <h2 lang="es">La Casa Milà</h2>
        <p>Gaudí's work was essentially useful. <span lang="es">La Casa Milà</span> is an apartment
        → building and <em>real people</em> live there.</p>
    </section>

    <section class="work">
        <h2 lang="es">La Sagrada Família</h2>
        <p>The complicatedly named and curiously unfinished Expiatory Temple of the Sacred Family is
        → the <em>most visited</em> building in Barcelona.</p>
    </section>
</article>
```

B The square brackets enclose the desired attribute and any desired value. In this case, the value is omitted in order to select any section with any **class** attribute.

```
section[class] {
    color: red;
}
```

C Every **section** element that contains a **class** attribute, regardless of the **class**'s value, is red.

space-separated values) for its element to be selected. It matches a complete word, not part of a word.

Or type **|="*value*"** (that was the pipe symbol, not a "1" or the letter "l") to specify that the attribute's value must be equal to *value* or begin with *value* (that is, what you typed followed by a hyphen) in order for its element to be selected. (This is most common when searching for elements containing the **lang** attribute.)

Or type **^="*value*"** to specify that the attribute's value must begin with *value* as either a full word or substring (new in CSS3; see the tip in this section).

Or type **$="*value*"** to specify that the attribute's value must end with *value* as either a full word or substring for its element to be selected (new in CSS3; see the tip in this section).

Or type ***="*value*"** to specify that the attribute's value must contain at least one instance of the *value* substring for its element to be selected. In other words, *value* doesn't need to be a complete word in the attribute's value (new in CSS3; see the tip in this section).

4. Type **]**.

TIP Selecting elements based on the attributes (and values) they contain is supported by all current major browsers (including IE as of version 7). IE7 and IE8 have a few quirks related to the three attribute selectors noted in step 3 as being new in CSS3. See http://reference.sitepoint.com/css/css3attributeselectors for more information.

More Attribute Selector Examples

Attribute selectors are pretty powerful. Here are a few more examples to demonstrate some of the diverse ways in which you can use them.

- This selects any **a** element with a **rel** attribute equal to **external** (it has to be an exact match).

```
a[rel="external"] {
    color: red;
}
```

- Imagine you have one **section** element with two classes, such as **<section** class="project barcelona">, and another that has one, **<section** class="barcelona">. The ~= syntax tests for a partial match of a complete word within a whitespace-separated list of words, making both elements red in this case.

```
section[class~="barcelona"] {
    color: red;
}

/* This would also match because this selector matches partial
→ strings (complete words not required). */
section[class*="barc"] {
    color: red;
}

/* This would NOT match because barc is not a full word in the
→ whitespace-separated list. */
section[class~="barc"] {
    color: red;
}
```

- This selects any **h2** with a **lang** attribute that begins with **es**. There are two instances of these in the HTML code example Ⓐ.

```
h2[lang|="es"] {
    color: red;
}
```

More Attribute Selector Examples *(continued)*

- By using the universal selector, this selects *any* element with a **lang** attribute that begins with **es**. There are three instances of these in the HTML code example Ⓐ.

  ```
  *[lang|="es"] {
      color: red;
  }
  ```

- Combining a couple of the methods, this selects any **a** element with both any **href** attribute and any **title** attribute containing the word **howdy**.

  ```
  a[href][title~="howdy"] {
      color: red;
  }
  ```

- As a less precise variation of the previous one, this selects any **a** element with both any **href** attribute and any **title** attribute containing **how** as a complete word or a substring (it matches if the title's value is **how**, **howdy**, **show**, and so on, regardless of where in the value **how** appears).

  ```
  a[href][title*="how"] {
      color: red;
  }
  ```

- This matches any **a** element with an **href** attribute value that begins with **http://**.

  ```
  a[href^="http://"] {
      color: orange;
  }
  ```

- This matches any **img** element with a **src** attribute value of exactly **logo.png**.

  ```
  img[src="logo.png"] {
      border: 1px solid green;
  }
  ```

- This is less specific than the previous one, matching any **img** element with a **src** attribute value that ends with **.png**.

  ```
  img[src$=".png"] {
      border: 1px solid green;
  }
  ```

That's by no means the limit of what you can do, but hopefully it inspires you to explore further.

Specifying Groups of Elements

It's often necessary to apply the same style rules to more than one element. You can either reiterate the rules for each element, or you can combine selectors and apply the rules in one fell swoop. Of course, the latter approach is more efficient and generally makes your style sheets easier to maintain.

To apply styles to groups of elements:

1. Type *selector1*, where *selector1* is the name of the first element that should be affected by the style rule.

2. Type **,** (a comma).

3. Type *selector2*, where *selector2* is the next tag that should be affected by the style rule.

4. Repeat steps 2 and 3 for each additional element.

Ⓐ The code contains one **h1** and two **h2** elements.

```
...
<article id="gaudi" class="about">
    <h1>Antoni Gaudí</h1>

    <p>Many tourists are drawn ...</p>
    <p>Barcelona ...</p>

    <section class="project">
        <h2 lang="es">La Casa Milà</h2>
        <p>Gaudí's work was ...</p>
    </section>

    <section class="project">
        <h2 lang="es">La Sagrada Família
        → </h2>
        <p>The complicatedly named ...</p>
    </section>
</article>
...
```

B You can list any number of individual selectors (whether they include element names, **id**s, or **class**es), as long as you separate each with a comma. Each selector doesn't have to be on its own line as shown, but many developers use this convention to make it easier to read. The benefit is more obvious when the selectors are longer.

```
h1,
h2 {
    color: red;
}
```

C The **h1** and **h2** elements are colored red with a single rule.

TIP Styling elements as a group is nothing more than a handy shortcut. The rule **h1, h2 { color: red; }** is precisely the same as the two rules

h1 { color: red; } and **h2 { color: red; }**.

TIP You can group any kind of selector, from the simplest (as shown in **B**) to the most complex. For example, you could use **h1, .project p:first-letter** to choose the level one headings and the first letter of the p elements in elements whose **class** is equal to **project**.

TIP It is sometimes useful to create a single style rule with the common styles that apply to several selectors and then create individual style rules with the styles they do not share. Remember that rules specified later override rules specified earlier in the style sheet (see "The Cascade: When Rules Collide" in Chapter 7).

Combining Selectors

The examples throughout the chapter have been simple to help you get a feel for various selector types. However, the real power lies in the fact that you can combine any of the techniques in order to pinpoint the elements that you're interested in formatting.

A bit of an extreme example is shown in 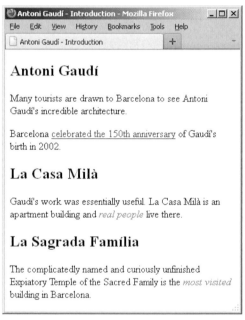 to demonstrate what's possible. Here are a few ways you could achieve the same results, moving from least specific to most specific:

```
em {
    color: red;
}
```

```
.project em {
    color: red;
}
```

```
.about .project em {
    color: red;
}
```

```
#gaudi em {
    color: red;
}
```

Ⓐ Here's a doozy for you. Moving right to left, it says "choose only the **em** elements that are found within **p** elements that are immediately adjacent siblings to **h2** elements that have a **lang** attribute whose value begins with **es** inside of any element with a **class** equal to **project**." Got that? You will rarely, if ever, have occasion to write something that complicated, but at least you know you can if necessary. Or if you just want to scare anyone reading your code.

```
.project h2[lang|="es"] + p em {
    color: red;
}
```

Ⓑ All that code Ⓐ just to turn the **em** elements red?!? If you're thinking it would be much better (and easier) to simply write something like `.about em { color: red; }`, you're absolutely right. Unless you need to be *highly* specific, in which case you can use the doozy.

More Selectors in CSS3

CSS3 adds a lot of new selectors to your toolbox. You saw some of them in this chapter. Most of the other new ones are pseudo-classes, some of which are fairly complex, but powerful as a result. You can find a table of all CSS3 selectors and full descriptions at www.w3.org/TR/css3-selectors/#selectors, brief descriptions and examples at www.w3.org/wiki/CSS/Selectors, and browser support at http://findmebyip.com/litmus. As you'll see, browser support is solid except in Internet Explorer, which didn't begin supporting most of the new CSS3 selectors (particularly the pseudo-classes and pseudo-elements) until IE9.

Each of these is typical of the kind of selectors you'll write day to day (though, as noted earlier, it's a good idea to minimize your use of **id** selectors). It doesn't require a lot of crazy selectors to implement most designs, no matter how intricate they may appear.

So, combine selectors when it makes sense to, but I recommend making your style rules only as specific as necessary. For instance, if you just want to target **em** elements inside elements with `class="project"`, go with `.project em { color: red; }`. Even though the **em** elements are nested inside **p** elements in the HTML, there's no point in writing `.project p em { color: red; }` unless there are **em** elements *outside of* paragraphs you want to leave alone. In short, start simple and get more specific as needed.

Selectors Recap

To recap, we focused on these selectors, any of which can be combined:

- Selecting elements by context
- Selecting elements by name
- Selecting elements by `class` or `id`
- Selecting with a pseudo-class or pseudo-element
- Selecting elements based on attributes

Formatting Text with Styles

With CSS, you can change the font, size, weight, slant, line height, foreground and background color, and spacing and alignment of text. You can decide whether it should be underlined or struck through, and you can convert it to all uppercase, all lowercase, or small caps. And you can apply those changes to an entire document or an entire site in just a handful of lines of code. In this chapter, you'll learn how.

In This Chapter

While many of the properties discussed in this chapter apply mostly to text, that doesn't mean they work only with text. Many of them work just fine on other types of content as well.

We'll continue with CSS layout in Chapter 11.

A Here is what the page looks like with no style sheet applied. (The default heading sizes in particular may be different across browsers.) You can find the HTML source code (and all subsequent CSS examples) in the Examples section of the book's site: www.bruceontheloose.com/htmlcss/examples/.

Ⓐ Because I specified Palatino Linotype on the **body** element, it cascades down to other elements. I overrode that setting for the **h1** and **h2** elements by setting their font to Arial Black. However, as you'll see, defining a single font at a time is not sufficient, because not all operating systems may support it. In the case of Palatino Linotype, it's common on Windows but might not be available on Mac OS or Linux systems.

```
body {
    font-family: "Palatino Linotype";
}

h1, h2 {
    font-family: "Arial Black";
}
```

Ⓑ On this Windows system, Palatino Linotype was installed and thus displays properly here. As you can see, the **body font-family** setting cascaded down to the **a** and **p** elements. The **h1** and **h2** elements would show it too, if we hadn't specified Arial Black for them.

Ⓒ Palatino Linotype does not come installed on some Mac systems. If you choose a font that is not installed on your visitor's system, their browser, as shown here, will use the default font instead (in this case, that is Times).

Choosing a Font Family

One of the most important choices you'll make for your Web site is the font for the body and headlines. As you'll learn, not every system supports the same fonts by default, so you should define alternate fonts as fallbacks. But first let's see how to define a single font family (Ⓐ and Ⓑ) and the ramifications of not providing the alternates Ⓒ.

To set the font family:

After the desired selector in your style sheet, type **font-family:** *name*, where *name* is your first choice of font.

TIP Surround multi-word font names with quotes (single or double).

TIP If your font names contain non-ASCII characters, you'll have to declare the encoding for your style sheet. Do so by adding **@charset "UTF-8";** on *the very first line* of your style sheet. In fact, there's no harm in including it in all your style sheets even if you don't need to right away. Doing so can help you avoid a problem later.

TIP While you can specify any font you want, your visitor will only see the fonts that they already have installed on their system. See the next section for more details.

TIP You can set the font family, font size, and line height all at once by using the general **font** property. See "Setting All Font Values at Once," later in this chapter.

TIP The **font-family** property is inherited.

Specifying Alternate Fonts

Although you can specify whichever font you want, your visitors will see that font only if they have it installed on their computer. So, it's best to use fonts that you can reasonably expect them to have. There is a small list of fonts that both Windows and Mac OS have by default (see the next sidebar for details).

Then there are the other cases to consider. If the font has different names on each system, you can specify both names, and each OS will use the one it has installed. Similarly, if the font you want only comes on one operating system, you can choose an alternate font for the other system. It may or may not match exactly, but the goal is to specify a font that's as close as possible. Finally, it's best to specify a generic standard font in case the systems don't support the others you listed A.

A The `font-family` property lets you include alternate fonts that the browser should use if the system does not have the first one installed. In this case, you can tell the browser to look for Palatino on systems that don't have Palatino Linotype installed C, and then fall back to a standard `serif` font if neither is installed. A list of fonts is known as a *font stack*. I added alternates for the headings as well.

```
body {
    font-family: "Palatino Linotype",
      ‣Palatino, serif;
}

h1,
h2 {
    font-family: "Arial Black", Arial,
      ‣sans-serif;
}
```

Default Fonts Shared by Mac OS and Windows

There is a very limited list of fonts to choose from that both Mac OS and Windows have by default: Arial, Arial Black, Comic Sans MS, Courier New, Georgia, Impact, Trebuchet MS, Times New Roman, and Verdana. Consequently, the vast majority of sites on the Web use one of these fonts (Arial is probably the most common). They might not render in exactly the same way in browsers on Mac OS and Windows, but you can be confident that they will display.

You also have options beyond these. Both Mac OS and Windows include more (but different) system fonts you can use in your font stacks. Search online for "font stacks" to see a range of font-family declarations that you can copy and paste into your style sheets to provide each visitor a similar font.

It's also possible to load a font that systems don't have by default, an approach that is becoming increasingly common. Learn how in Chapter 13.

B Systems that have Palatino Linotype installed will continue to use that font.

C Systems that don't have Palatino Linotype will use Palatino, as long as they have it (as most Mac systems do). If they don't have Palatino either, the browser will try the third choice. Virtually all systems include generic serif and sans-serif fonts. Note that the default line height is still different. You'll adjust this a bit later.

To specify alternate fonts:

1. Type **font-family:** *name*, where *name* is your first choice of font.

2. Type **, *name2***, where ***name2*** is your second font choice. Separate each choice with a comma and a space.

3. Repeat step 2 as desired, and finish your list of fonts with a generic font name (**serif**, **sans-serif**, **cursive**, **fantasy**, or **monospace**; whichever style is most appropriate based on your preferred font).

TIP You can specify fonts for different alphabets in the same **font-family** rule (such as Japanese and English) to format a chunk of text that contains different languages and writing systems.

TIP Systems typically have a font that maps to the following generic font names: serif, sans-serif, cursive, fantasy, and monospace—which is why it's standard practice to specify one at the end of your font stack in case all else fails. Of these, you'll use serif and sans-serif the most (by far), since they correspond to the most commonly used fonts.

Creating Italics

In traditional publishing, italics are often used to set off quotations, emphasized text, words that are foreign relative to a language (e.g., *de rigueur*), some scientific names (e.g., *Homo sapiens*), movie titles, and much more.

Browsers typically italicize some HTML elements (such as **cite**, **em**, and **i**) by default, so you don't need to italicize them in your CSS. As you learned in "Semantic HTML: Markup with Meaning" in Chapter 1, you use HTML to describe the meaning of content, not to make it look a certain way. Sometimes you'll want to make something italic, but it isn't appropriate to mark up the content with one of the elements that also happens to render italic text. The CSS **font-style** property allows you to do this to any element.

Just as an example, let's see how to do this to paragraphs Ⓐ. (We won't leave them this way because they'd be exceedingly difficult to read, so we'll omit the rule from subsequent examples.)

The italic version of a font often is created by a font designer from scratch, especially for serif fonts. It is not merely a slanted version of the normal text, but instead includes differences appropriate to the form. For example, Palatino Linotype has a true italic font face Ⓑ. The letter "a" in particular is clearly not just slanted to mimic italics. But a font may not have an italic version. If you set text in that font to **font-style: italic**, the browser may display a computer-simulated, faux italic that *does* simply slant the normal letters to mimic the style. However, the quality isn't the same.

Ⓐ In this example, I've made the paragraphs display in italics.

```
body {
    font-family: "Palatino Linotype",
    → Palatino, serif;
}

h1,
h2 {
    font-family: "Arial Black", Arial,
    → sans-serif;
}

p {
    font-style: italic;
}
```

B The paragraphs are italicized, but not the list items at the top or the headings.

Additionally, a font designer may create an oblique version of a font, which typically *is* the normal letters slanted, perhaps with some adjustments to spacing and the like, but with the same letters. You can set `font-style: oblique;`, though it's uncommon to do so. Faux italic may show in the absence of an oblique or italic version of the font.

To create italics:

1. Type `font-style:`.

2. After the colon (:), type `italic` for italic text, or `oblique` for oblique text. (You'll probably use `italic` 99 percent of the time. You might not notice a difference with `oblique` in all instances.)

To remove italics:

Type `font-style: normal`.

TIP One reason you might want to remove italics is to emphasize some text in a paragraph that has inherited italic formatting from a parent element. For more details about inheritance, consult "The Cascade: When Rules Collide" in Chapter 7.

TIP The `font-style` property is inherited.

Applying Bold Formatting

Bold formatting is probably the most common and effective way to make text stand out. For instance, browsers typically style the **h1**–**h6** headings in bold by default. Just as with italics, you may style any text in bold or turn it off. Style sheets give you a lot of flexibility with bold text, providing relative values. However, the fonts themselves don't always include different weights that map to the relative values, often making them look the same (when in doubt, just specify the weight as **bold**) (A and B).

To apply bold formatting:

1. Type **font-weight:**.

2. Type **bold** to give an average bold weight to the text. You'll likely use this value the vast majority of the time.

   Or type **bolder** or **lighter** to use a value relative to the current weight.

   Or type a multiple of **100** from **100** and **900**, where **400** represents normal or book weight and **700** represents bold. This approach is useful when you're working with fonts that have numerous weights available.

To remove bold formatting:

Type **font-weight: normal**.

Ⓐ Browsers add bold formatting to headings (like **h1** and **h2**) automatically. I applied a normal font weight to remove it from all **h2** elements so you could see the difference in the page. I've also added bold formatting to **em** text and new and hovered links Ⓑ. (Note that I've changed the headings' **font-family** from Arial Black to Arial just for the examples in this section. See the second-to-last tip.)

```
body {
    font-family: "Palatino Linotype",
    ⤷ Palatino, serif;
}

h1,
h2 {
    font-family: Arial, Helvetica,
    ⤷ sans-serif;}

h2 {
    font-weight: normal;
}

em,
a:link,
a:hover {
    font-weight: bold;
}
```

Ⓑ The **h1** heading is bold, and the **h2** has a normal weight. New links stand out, while visited ones are less obtrusive.

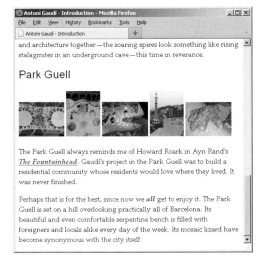

and architecture together—the soaring spires look something like rising stalagmites in an underground cave—this time in reverance.

Park Guell

The Park Guell always reminds me of Howard Roark in Ayn Rand's *The Fountainhead*. Gaudí's project in the Park Guell was to build a residential community whose residents would love where they lived. It was never finished.

Perhaps that is for the best, since now we *all* get to enjoy it. The Park Guell is set on a hill overlooking practically all of Barcelona. Its beautiful and even comfortable serpentine bench is filled with foreigners and locals alike every day of the week. Its mosaic lizard have become synonymous with the city itself.

C At the bottom of the page, you see a link ("The Fountainhead") and the word "all." Both are not only bold from our new style rule, but also italic because of the browser's default rendering of their containing elements. They are marked up with **cite** and **em**, respectively, to reflect their meaning. (You'll also notice that the "Park Guell" **h2** has a normal weight, not bold.)

TIP Since the way weights are defined varies from font to font, the predefined values may not be relative from font to font. They are designed to be relative within a given font family.

TIP If the font family has fewer than nine weights, or if they are concentrated on one end of the scale, some numeric values will correspond to the same font weight.

TIP For the reasons noted in the previous two tips, it's customary to assign bold simply with `font-weight: bold`, which will always work.

TIP What can you remove bold formatting from? Any element where it's been applied automatically (`strong`, h1–h6, and b come to mind) or where it's been inherited from a parent element (see "The Cascade: When Rules Collide" in Chapter 7).

TIP The rest of the examples in this chapter use Arial Black as the `font-family` for the h1 and h2 headings instead of the Arial setting shown in **A** through **C**. However, in those remaining examples, I've set `font-weight: normal;` on both h1 and h2, because Arial Black is already a bold font by nature. When you apply `font-weight: bold;` to Arial Black, the browser may display a faux bold styling in an attempt to make it look bolder. By setting `font-weight: normal;` to these Arial Black headings, I've returned them to the font's natural, very heavy state. See a related discussion of faux italics in "Creating Italics."

TIP The `font-weight` property is inherited.

Setting the Font Size

There are two basic ways to set the font size for the text in your Web page. You can mandate that a specific size be used 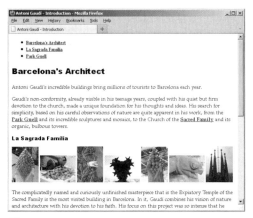, or you can have the size be relative to the element's parent font size ©.

Setting the size relative to the parent takes a little getting used to; you need to understand how the browser treats these units relative to their parents, and I'll explain that more in a minute.

But first, when you use this method it's best to establish a baseline on the **body** element, namely by declaring **body { font-size: 100%; }** ©. Most of the time, this sets the size to the equivalent of 16px, which is the default font size on most systems. As usual, that value cascades down to the other elements (remember, **font-size** is an inherited property) unless given their own **font-size**.

B The sizes I've specified are displayed in the browser. The links in the table of contents (top of the page), the headings, and the paragraphs all reflect the **font-size** additions to the style sheet.

A Here I use pixel values to have control over the initial size of the text (which I've decreased in size throughout, compared with most browsers' defaults). The paragraphs inherit the **font-size** set on **body**. You can see the results in **B**.

```
body {
    font-family: "Palatino Linotype",
Palatino, serif;
    font-size: 14px;
}

h1,
h2 {
    font-family: "Arial Black", Arial,
    ‣ sans-serif;
    font-weight: normal; /* removes faux
    ‣ bold from the already heavy Arial
    ‣ Black */
}

h1 {
    font-size: 22px;
}

h2 {
    font-size: 15px;
}

em,
a:link,
a:hover {
    font-weight: bold;
}

/* Table of Contents navigation */
.toc a {
    font-size: 12px;
}
```

C The **font-size: 100%** declaration on **body** sets a baseline from which the em font sizes are based. That **100%** translates to an equivalent default text size of 16 pixels on most systems. As such, this style sheet result will be equivalent to the one shown in **A**. The comment following each **font-size** value explains how it was calculated, showing the typical pixel equivalents.

```
body {
     font-family: "Palatino Linotype",
     → Palatino, serif;
     font-size: 100%; /* 16px */
}

h1,
h2 {
     font-family: "Arial Black", Arial,
     → sans-serif;
     font-weight: normal;
}

h1 {
     font-size: 1.375em; /* 22px / 16px */
}

h2 {
     font-size: .9375em; /* 15px / 16px */
}

p {
     font-size: .875em; /* 14px / 16px */
}

em,
a:link,
a:hover {
     font-weight: bold;
}

/* Table of Contents navigation */
.toc a {
     font-size: .75em; /* 12px / 16px */
}
```

So, how do you figure out what em values to specify? Well, 1em is equal to the default size, in this case 16px. From there you can determine the em (or percentage) values with just a tiny bit of division.

desired size / parent's size = value

For example, you want the **h1** to resemble 22px, and you already know the parent's size is 16px. So:

22 / 16 = 1.375

So by defining **h1 { font-size: 1.375em; }**, you're all set **C**. What this says is, "Make the **h1** text 1.375 times as large as its parent's text." Another way to write the rule would be **h1 { font-size: 137.5%; }**. However, aside from setting the base **font-size** on **body** with a percentage, it's more common to size type in ems than percentages.

Here's another one. You want the paragraphs to be 14px, and:

14 / 16 = .875

So, you set **p { font-size: .875em; } C**. (Alternatively, this could be **87.5%**.)

Let's discuss one more example, since this is where you can get tripped up. The first paragraph contains two links (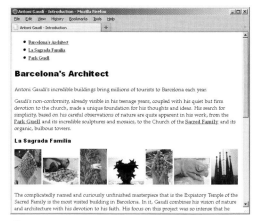 and). Suppose you want to make the links 16px while leaving the other paragraph text at the defined 14px. You might be inclined to set the link **font-size** to **1em**, thinking that 1em = 16px.

But, remember, these values are relative to their parent, and the parent in this case is the **p**, not **body**. And the paragraph size is 14px. So, in order to make the links 16px, you need to use an em value larger than 1em.

16 / 14 = 1.1428457

So, the slightly verbose **a { font-size: 1.1428457em; }** gives us the desired result.

One final point: Remember that a **body font-size** of **100%** maps to a default of 16px most of the time. One case in which that can deviate is if a user overrides the default in their browser settings; for instance, making it 20px if they're visually impaired. With **body** set to **100%**, your page respects this and sizes the rest of the text accordingly, er, *relatively*! That's the beauty of sizing your text with the likes of ems and percentages.

D On most systems with default settings, the em-based font sizes match those from the pixel-based version **B**.

E Part of the HTML, which has two **a** elements nested in their parent **p**.

```
...
<p>Gaudí's non-conformity, already visible in his teenage years, coupled with his quiet but firm
  devotion to the church, made a unique foundation for his thoughts and ideas. His search for
  simplicity, based on his careful observations of nature are quite apparent in his work, from the
  <a href="#park-guell">Park Guell</a> and its incredible sculptures and mosaics, to the Church
  of the <a href="#sagrada-familia">Sacred Family</a> and its organic, bulbous towers.</p>
...
```

To mandate a specific font size:

1. Type `font-size:`.

2. Type a specific size after the colon (:), such as **13px**.

   Or use a keyword to specify the size:

   xx-small, **x-small**, **small**, **medium**, **large**, **x-large**, or **xx-large**.

TIP See "A Property's Value" in Chapter 7 for details about units.

TIP There shouldn't be any spaces between the number and the unit.

TIP If you set the font size with pixels, visitors using Internet Explorer will not be able to make the text bigger or smaller with the browser's text size option. That's one argument for sizing your fonts with ems or percentages. Beginning with IE7, visitors can zoom the *entire* page in and out, which is an improvement over IE6, though it isn't the same as changing only the text size. If you're wondering about IE6's reach (since it doesn't have page zoom), it has seen a dramatic drop-off in overall use around the world in the past few years, so some designers and developers disregard it entirely (it's notoriously buggy too). However, it still has a large user base in some countries, particularly China and South Korea. You can check approximate worldwide numbers at www.ie6countdown.com/.

TIP Different browsers may interpret the keywords in different ways.

TIP Use points (`pt`) as the unit type only in print style sheets, not for the screen.

TIP Because of wildly varying screen resolutions, avoid setting `font-size` in cm, mm, and picas. They're rarely used in practice.

TIP The `font-size` property is inherited.

To set a size that depends on the parent element's size:

1. Type `font-size:`.

2. Type the relative value following the colon (:), such as **1.5em** or **150%**.

   Or use a relative keyword: `larger` or `smaller`. (These are less common to use than percentages, which are themselves less common than ems.)

TIP An em unit (not to be confused with the HTML em element) is equal to the size of the font. So one em equals 100%.

TIP The parent element's size may be set by the user or by you (the designer), may be inherited, or may come from the browser's defaults. As mentioned, on most current browsers the default size for the body element is 16 pixels.

TIP The child of an element with a relative size inherits the size, not the factor. So, the a elements in the p **E** inherit a size of 14 pixels **C**, not a relative value of .875em. The links display as 14px unless you override it.

TIP You can set font size together with other font values. See "Setting All Font Values at Once," later in this chapter.

TIP CSS3 introduces some new units. One of the most interesting ones is rem, short for root em. It's like em, but it sizes everything relative to the root, so you don't have to do the parent element font size division I described for ems. Browser support is strong in modern browsers. Internet Explorer didn't support it until version 9 (http://caniuse.com/#search=rem), so you'd have to provide a default value for earlier versions of IE. Jonathan Snook describes how to use rem and one possible strategy for addressing IE8 and below: http://snook.ca/archives/html_and_css/font-size-with-rem. (I recommend setting body to 100%, rather than 62.5% as he shows, and creating your rem sizes from there.)

TIP There's also an ex unit, which refers to the x-height of the parent element, but it is not widely supported.

A Assuming a default **body** element of 16 pixels, the font size of the **p** element will be .875em, or about 14 pixels. The line height will be 1.6 times those 14 pixels, or about 22.4 pixels.

```
body {
    font-family: "Palatino Linotype",
    → Palatino, serif;
    font-size: 100%;
}

h1,
h2 {
    font-family: "Arial Black", Arial,
    → sans-serif;
    font-weight: normal;
}

h1 {
    font-size: 1.375em;
}

h2 {
    font-size: .9375em;
}

p {
    font-size: .875em; /* 16px / 14px */
    line-height: 1.6;
}

...
```

B Spacing out lines with `line-height` can make them more attractive and easier to read.

Setting the Line Height

Line height refers to a paragraph's leading, which is the amount of space between each line in a paragraph. Using a large line height can sometimes make your body text easier to read. A small line height for headings with more than one line often makes them look more stylish.

To set the line height:

1. Type `line-height:`.

2. Type **n**, where **n** is a number that will be multiplied by the element's font size to obtain the desired line height. (This is the most common approach, just a number with no unit.)

   Or type **a**, where **a** is a value in ems, pixels, or points (use points only for print).

   Or type **p%**, where **p%** is a percentage of the font size.

TIP You can specify the line height together with the font family, size, weight, style, and variant, as described in the next section.

TIP If you use a number to determine the line height, this factor is inherited by all child items. So if a parent's font size is 16 pixels (or the equivalent in ems or such) and the line height is 1.5, the parent's line height will be 24 (16 × 1.5). If the child's font size is 10, its line height will be 15 (10 × 1.5).

TIP If you use a percentage or em value, only the resulting size (or "computed value") is inherited. So, given a parent at 16 pixels with a line height of 150%, the parent's line height will still be 24 pixels. However, all child elements will also inherit a line height of 24 pixels, regardless of their font size.

Setting All Font Values at Once

You can set the font style, weight, variant, size, line height, and family all at once Ⓐ. This is the way to go whenever possible so you can keep your style sheets lean.

To set all font values at once:

1. Type **font:**.

2. Optionally type **normal**, **italic**, or **oblique** to set the font style (see "Creating Italics").

3. Optionally type **normal**, **bold**, **bolder**, **lighter**, or a multiple of **100** (up to **900**) to set the font weight (see "Applying Bold Formatting").

4. Optionally type **normal** or **small-caps** to remove or set small caps (see "Using Small Caps").

5. Type the desired font size (see "Setting the Font Size").

6. If desired, type **/line-height**, where **line-height** is the amount of space there should be between lines (see "Setting the Line Height").

7. Type a space followed by the desired font family or families in order of preference, separated by commas, as described in "Choosing a Font Family."

Ⓐ This style sheet is equivalent to the one shown in Ⓐ in "Setting the Line Height," as is the resulting display Ⓑ. I've simply consolidated the **font** properties for the **body**, **h1**, and **h2** rules. Note that I didn't have to specify that the **font-weight** be **normal** for **h1** and **h2**, since **normal** is the default for the **font** property. Also, I couldn't consolidate the **p** element's declarations because **font** shorthand requires the family and size properties at a minimum. See examples in the first tip that include the **font-style**, **font-variant**, **font-weight**, and **line-height** in the **font** shorthand.

```
body {
    font: 100% "Palatino Linotype", Palatino,
    ⇢ serif;
}

h1,
h2 {
    font: 1.375em "Arial Black", Arial,
    ⇢ sans-serif;
}

h2 {
    font-size: .9375em;
}

p {
    /* Can't combine these into
       font shorthand unless declaring
       ⇢ the font family with them at the
       ⇢ same time. */
    font-size: .875em;
    line-height: 1.6;
}

em,
a:link,
a:hover {
    font-weight: bold;
}

/* Table of Contents navigation */
.toc a {
    font-size: .75em;
}
```

B This page is identical to the one shown in **B** in "Setting the Line Height."

TIP An example of combining the font-size, line-height, and font-family declarations into font shorthand is `font: .875em/1.6 "Palatino Linotype", Palatino, serif;`. The line height follows the size and forward slash. You can also include the `font-style`, `font-variant`, and `font-weight`. The following is an example with all possible properties in a font declaration: `font: italic small-caps bold .875em/1.6 "Palatino Linotype", Palatino, serif;`. The order of properties is important. You can use any combination of the properties as long as both the size and family are declared.

TIP You can also set each property separately, but you should combine the properties with the `font` shorthand whenever possible.

TIP The first three properties may be specified in any order or omitted. If you omit them, they are set to `normal`—which may not be what you expected **A**.

TIP The size and family properties must always be explicitly specified: first the size, then the family.

TIP The line height, which is optional, must come directly after the size and the forward slash.

TIP The `font` property is inherited.

Setting the Color

You can also change the color of the elements on your Web page **Ⓐ**.

To set the color:

1. Type **color:**.

2. Type **colorname**, where **colorname** is one of the predefined colors (see "CSS colors" in Chapter 7).

   Or type **#rrggbb**, where **rrggbb** is the color's hexadecimal representation. This is the most common way to specify colors.

   Or type **rgb(r, g, b)**, where **r**, **g**, and **b** are integers from 0–255 that specify the amount of red, green, and blue, respectively, in the desired color.

   Or type **rgb(r%, g%, b%)**, where **r**, **g**, and **b** give the percentage of red, green, and blue in the desired color.

   Or type **hsl(h, s, l)**, where **h** is an integer from 0–360 that specifies the hue, and **s** and **l** are percentages from 0 to 100 that specify the amount of saturation and lightness, respectively, in the desired color. (Generally, it's better to instead use hex or RGB for non-transparent colors.)

Ⓐ You can use color names, hexadecimals, or RGB, HSL, RGBA, or HSLA values to define your colors. Note that the **a:visited** and **a:hover** colors (**#909** and **#c3f**, respectively) use the abbreviation discussed in the second tip.

```css
body {
    color: #909;
    font: 100% "Palatino Linotype", Palatino,
      ⤷ serif;
}

h1,
h2 {
    color: navy;
    font: 1.375em "Arial Black", Arial,
      ⤷ sans-serif;
}

h2 {
    font-size: .9375em;
}

p {
    font-size: .875em;
    line-height: 1.6;
}

em {
    font-weight: bold;
}

/* Links */
a:link {
    color: #74269d;
    font-weight: bold;
}

a:visited {
    color: #909;
}

a:hover {
    color: #c3f;
    font-weight: bold;
}

/* Table of Contents navigation */
.toc a {
    font-size: .75em;
}
```

B The headings are navy blue, and the text is light purple. The links are dark purple but turn lighter after being visited, and they turn a pinkish purple when hovered over so as to stand out.

Or type **rgba(*r*, *g*, *b*, *a*)**, where *r*, *g*, and *b* are integers from 0–255 that specify the amount of red, green, and blue, and *a* is a decimal from 0 to 1 that specifies the amount of alpha transparency in the desired color.

Or type **hsla(*h*, *s*, *l*, *a*)**, where *h* is an integer from 0–360 that specifies the hue, *s* and *l* are percentages from 0 to 100 that specify the amount of saturation and lightness, and *a* is a decimal from 0 to 1 that specifies the amount of alpha transparency in the desired color.

TIP If you type a value higher than **255** for **r, g,** or **b, 255** will be used. Similarly a percentage higher than **100** will be substituted with **100**.

TIP You can also use **#rgb** to set the color where the hex values are repeated digits. In fact, I recommend it. So you could (and should) write **#FF0099** as **#F09** or **#f09**.

TIP The hex number should not be enclosed in double quotes.

TIP Keep in mind that Internet Explorer didn't support HSL, RGBA, and HSLA until IE9, so if you use any of those in your color declarations you'll have to define fallback colors for older versions of IE. See "CSS colors" in Chapter 7 for details.

TIP The **color** property is inherited.

Changing the Text's Background

You can set the background of individual elements, the whole page, or any combination of the two Ⓐ. In so doing, you can change the background of just a few paragraphs or words, links in their different states, sections of content, and more.

To change the text's background:

1. Type **background:**.

2. Type **transparent** or *color*, where *color* is a color name, or hex, rgb, hsl, rgba, or hsla color value (see "Setting the Color"). Hex colors are the most common.

3. If desired, type **url(**_image.gif_**)** to use an image for the background, where _image.gif_ is the path and file name of the image relative to the location of the style sheet.

   If desired, type **repeat** to tile the image both horizontally and vertically, or **repeat-x** to tile the image only horizontally, or **repeat-y** to tile the image only vertically, or **no-repeat** to not tile the image.

   If desired, type **fixed** or **scroll** to determine whether the background should scroll along with the canvas. (Leaving it out, as is usually the case, defaults to **scroll**.)

   If desired, type *x y* to set the position of the background image, where *x* and *y* can be expressed as an absolute distance or as a percentage from the upper-left corner. Or use the values **left**, **center**, or **right** for x and **top**, **center**, or **bottom** for y.

Ⓐ Setting the background color of the **body** element colors the background of the whole page. The background set on the element with the **toc** class distinguishes the table of contents from other parts of the page Ⓑ.

```
body {
    background: #eef;
    color: #909;
    font: 100% "Palatino Linotype", Palatino,
    → serif;
}


... [other CSS is here] ...


/* Table of Contents navigation */
.toc {
    background: #ebc6f9;
}

.toc a {
    font-size: .75em;
}
```

B The background of the **body** element is light blue. The background of the table of contents is light purple.

Multiple Backgrounds and More with CSS3

CSS3 introduces a handful of new background-related capabilities, including the long-awaited multiple backgrounds, background resizing, and more. You can learn about some of these in Chapter 14. See www.w3.org/TR/css3-background/ if you want to dig into all these features in the related CSS3 module.

TIP You can specify both a color and an image's URL for the background. The color will be used until the image is loaded—or if it can't be loaded for any reason—and will be seen through any transparent portions of the image. If you define a background image for an element, it's generally a good practice to define a background color that provides sufficient contrast between your text color and the background. This will ensure your text remains legible if your visitor has disabled images in his or her browser or if the image doesn't load for some reason. If you don't define an explicit background color, it'll be whatever color the element inherits from its parent, such as the default white of the body element. That would spell trouble if you were hoping to show light text on a dark background image. See the "More on Backgrounds" sidebar for more details.

TIP Create enough contrast between the background and the foreground so that your visitors can actually read the text. Not only does this help the average user, but it's important for accessibility. Contrast is especially important for color-blind visitors.

TIP The `background` property is not inherited.

More on Backgrounds

The **background** property is powerful, and you'll find lots of occasions to use it. Understandably, you might have been a little uncertain about how to leverage step 3 of "To change the text's background." Here is an example:

```
body {
    background: #foc url(bg-page.png) repeat-x scroll 0 0;
}
```

That's actually shorthand notation, just like you use the **font** property to combine **font-family**, **font-size**, **line-height**, and other properties in one declaration.

Moving left to right, that **background** shorthand notation could be rewritten as this:

```
body {
    background-color: #foc;
    background-image: url(bg-page.png);
    background-repeat: repeat-x;
    background-attachment: scroll;
    background-position: 0 0;
}
```

That's a lot of code, so you can see why shorthand is the way to go unless you have reason to split it up. In fact, you can even make our example a little shorter by removing the **scroll** and **0 0** default values:

```
body {
    background: #foc url(bg-page.png) repeat-x;
}
```

In practice, your URL will be something like **../img/bg-page.png**, because you won't want to keep your images in the same folder as your style sheets.

So, what does this do? Imagine that the background image, **bg-page.png**, is a repeating pattern that is 15 pixels wide and 600 pixels high. The example shorthand rule above says, "Repeat the image infinitely horizontally and show the color **#foc** infinitely wherever the image isn't." So, you'd see the image all the way across for the first 600 pixels of height. Wherever the content is taller than 600 pixels, you'll see **#foc** (hot pink, perfect for your Hello Kitty tribute site).

More on Backgrounds *(continued)*

Presumably, the image was designed to blend nicely into the color so visitors don't see an obvious line where the image ends and the color begins. And because the **background** was defined for **body**, all the page content sits on top of the image and background color. If you dig around the CSS of nearly any site, you're likely to find some variation of **background** set on **body**.

Here are a few more examples to give you a taste of the possibilities:

Black background color combined with image that repeats infinitely vertically.

```
body {
    background: #000 url(../../image/bg-page.png) repeat-y;
}
```

Background image that repeats infinitely in all directions. Yellow shows if image doesn't load or until image loads.

```
body {
    background: yellow url(../img/bg-smiley-faces.png);
}
```

Dark green background color with background image that doesn't repeat and that is positioned 200 pixels from the left edge of the page and 125 pixels from the top. Negative values are allowed too. Use **center** to center it in the page.

```
body {
    background: #3f8916 url(../../img/bg-gumby.png) no-repeat 200px 125px;
}
```

I've focused on **body** backgrounds because of their impact on designing your page, but you can apply **background** properties to any element. So if you really wanted to, you could set a photo of Telly Savalas as the background of all your paragraphs. In fact, I *encourage* it.

Controlling Spacing

You can add or reduce space between words (which is called tracking) or between letters (which is called kerning) 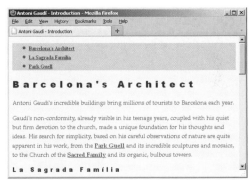.

To specify tracking:

Type **word-spacing: *length***, where ***length*** is a number with units, as in **0.4em** or **5px**.

To specify kerning:

Type **letter-spacing: *length***, where ***length*** is a number with units, as in **0.4em** or **5px**.

TIP You may use negative values for word and letter spacing.

TIP Word and letter spacing values may also be affected by your choice of alignment and font family.

TIP Use a value of `normal` or 0 to set the letter and word spacing back to their defaults (that is, to add no extra space).

TIP If you use an em value, only the resulting size (or "computed value") is inherited. So, a parent at 16 pixels with .1em of extra word-spacing will have 1.6 pixels of extra space between each word. And all child elements will also have 1.6 pixels of extra space between words, regardless of their font size. Set the extra spacing explicitly for the child elements if you need to override such a value.

TIP The word-spacing and letter-spacing properties are inherited.

A Here I've added .4em of extra space between the heading letters, which at a font size of 22 pixels will mean almost 9 pixels between each letter **B**.

```
body {
    background: #eef;
    color: #909;
    font: 100% "Palatino Linotype", Palatino,
    ⇥ serif;
}

h1,
h2 {
    color: navy;
    font: 1.375em "Arial Black", Arial,
    ⇥ sans-serif;
    letter-spacing: .4em;
}

h2 {
    font-size: .9375em;
}

... [rest of CSS] ...
```

B The heading letters now have more space between them.

Structuring Your Pages

The whole point of using CSS is to separate the formatting and styling rules from the content of your page. This makes your pages easier to maintain and gives them the flexibility to work well in different browsers, platforms, and devices, or even in print. Just as it does with styling text, CSS provides great variety in how you present the overall layout of your pages. You apply CSS to the content containers that represent a page's primary structural elements, which you learned about in Chapter 3 Ⓐ (on the next page). With CSS, your masthead, main content area, sidebar (or two), page-level footer, and so on come to life visually.

To structure your page:

1. Divide logical sections of your document into **article**, **aside**, **nav**, **section**, **header**, **footer**, and **div** elements, as appropriate. Apply ARIA landmark roles as desired. See Chapter 3 for more details on both. In Ⓐ, you have:

   ▸ *container* and *page* **div**s that are used to apply some design and wrap the page

   ▸ A **header** for the masthead, which contains the logo, slogan, search form, and main navigation

   ▸ A *main* **div** divided into multiple *entry* **section** elements to contain the main content

   ▸ A *sidebar* **div** to house a monthly opinion column and archive links in the right column

   ▸ A page-level **footer** element for an "about" blurb

(continues on page 282)

A This is the document I use throughout this chapter. There are four main sections (masthead, main, sidebar, and footer) enclosed in two outer wrapper containers (container and page). You can find the complete file on my Web site (www.bruceontheloose.com/htmlcss/examples/chapter-11/finished-page.html). By default, the page is plain but still functional **B**.

```
...
<body>
<div id="container">
    <div id="page">
        <!-- ==== START MASTHEAD ==== -->
        <header id="masthead" role="banner">
            <p class="logo "><a href="/">photobarcelona&hellip; <span>capturing barcelona's cultural
              treasures on film</span></a></p>

            <div>
                <nav role="navigation">
                    ... [list of links] ...
                </nav>

                <form method="get" role="search">
                    ...
                </form>
            </div>
        </header>
        <!-- end #masthead -->

        <!-- ==== START MAIN CONTENT ==== -->
        <div id="main" role="main">
            <h1>Recent Entries</h1>
            <!-- Start Entry #1 -->
            <section class="entry">
                <header>
                    <h2 lang="es">Hospital Sant Pau</h2>
                    <p class="date"><time datetime="2011-06-26" pubdate="pubdate">June 26, 2011</time></p>
                </header>

                ... [image] ...

                <div class="intro">
                    <p>The Saint Paul Hospital at the top ...</p>

                    <p class="continued"><a href="#">continued</a></p>
                </div>
            </section>
            <!-- end .entry #1 -->

            <!-- Start Entry #2 -->
            <section class="entry">
                ...
            </section>
            <!-- end .entry #2 -->
```

code continues on next page

Ⓐ *continued*

```
                <!-- Start Entry #3 -->
                <section class="entry">
                   ...
                </section>
                <!-- end .entry #3 -->
            </div>
            <!-- end #main content -->

            <!-- ==== START SIDEBAR ==== -->
            <div id="related" class="sidebar" role="complementary">
                <aside class="excerpt">
                    <h2>From my Window</h2>

                    ...
                </aside>

                <aside class="archive">
                    <nav role="navigation">
                    <h2>Archive</h2>
                        ... [list of links] ...


                        ...
                    </nav>
                </aside>
            </div>
            <!-- end #sidebar -->

            <!-- ==== START FOOTER ==== -->
            <footer id="footer" role="contentinfo">
                <h1>about this photoblog</h1>

                ...

                ... [list of images] ...
            </footer>
            <!-- end #footer -->
        </div>
        <!-- end #page -->
    </div>
    <!-- #container -->
    </body>
</html>
```

2. Put your content in an order that would be the most useful if the CSS were not used . For example, the masthead, followed by the main content, followed by one or more sidebars, followed by the page-level footer. This can make it easier for you to provide the most important content on top for visitors on smaller screens like smartphones and tablets (and for users on older mobile devices that don't support CSS). You want to get the main content to them without making them scroll too far. In addition, search engines "see" your page as if CSS weren't applied, so if you prioritize your main content, they'll be better able to properly index your site. Lastly, screen readers access content the same way—by the order of your HTML (users often hop between headings rather than listen to the entire page, but either way they'd reach your main content sooner).

3. Use heading elements (**h1–h2**) consistently to identify and prioritize information on your page within the sections.

4. Use comments as desired to identify different areas of your page and their contents. As **A** shows, my preference is to use a different format for comments that mark the start, rather than the end, of a section.

B Here's what our example looks like with no styles except the browser's default. Thanks to its solid semantics, it is perfectly usable and intelligible, if a bit spartan.

TIP You don't have to mark up your entire page before you apply CSS. In practice, it's not uncommon to do the HTML for a section and then some or all of its CSS, then the same for the next section, and so on. It's really a matter of personal preference and what process works best for you. For the example in this chapter, I've marked up all the content with HTML before styling it.

TIP You may have noticed I used `section` elements in the example Ⓐ to contain each partial blog entry. Had they been complete entries, I would have marked them up with `article` instead, just as I would for pages dedicated to individual, complete blog entries. My thinking in that case would be that I could potentially syndicate a complete blog posting, not just the introductory portion included in the example partial entries. Using `article` for these instead of `section` wouldn't be wrong, just an indication that the snippets would be appropriate for syndication. See Chapter 3 for a variety of examples that use `article` and `section` both together and individually.

Styling Elements with ARIA Landmark Roles in CSS Selectors Instead of `ids`

The example page Ⓐ includes ARIA landmark roles on appropriate elements. In Chapter 9, I suggested avoiding or minimizing your use of **id**s for styling purposes (see the sidebar in that chapter's "Selecting Elements by Class or ID" section).

It is possible to use the landmark roles in your CSS selectors in some cases where you might otherwise be inclined to reference **id**s.

Let's use the page footer from Ⓐ as an example. Here's the HTML:

```
<footer id="footer" role="contentinfo">
    ... page footer content ...
</footer>
```

And some abbreviated corresponding CSS that uses **id** selectors:

```
#footer {
    border-top: 2px dotted #b74e07;
    clear: both;
}

#footer h1 {
    margin-bottom: .25em;
}
```

Now, let's simplify the HTML by removing **id="footer"**, since it was only there to style the footer (rather than as an anchor link pointing to the footer).

```
<footer role="contentinfo">
    ... page footer content ...
</footer>
```

Styling Elements with ARIA Landmark Roles *(continued)*

Landmark roles are attributes, so you can use them in attribute selectors.

```
footer[role="contentinfo"] {
    border-top: 2px dotted #b74e07;
    clear: both;
}

footer[role="contentinfo"] h1 {
    margin-bottom: .25em;
}
```

The first rule says, "Find the **footer** element with a **role** attribute that equals **contentinfo**." The second rule says, "Find the **h1** element *within* the **footer** element with a **role** attribute that equals **contentinfo**."

The results are exactly the same as the previous CSS that used **id** selectors.

You can do the same thing with other elements that contain landmark roles, and I've provided a version of this chapter's example page that does just that: www.bruceontheloose.com/htmlcss/ examples/chapter-11/finished-page-selectors-with-landmark-roles.html. See a related discussion by Jeremy Keith at http://adactio.com/journal/4267/.

Please note that IE6 does not support attribute selectors, so this approach may not be for you, depending on your audience.

One important reminder: It's critical that you use the landmark roles only where appropriate within your pages. Do not add one simply to have a hook for applying styles to an element. Use a class in that instance instead. See "Improving Accessibility with ARIA" in Chapter 3 for a refresher on landmark roles.

Styling HTML5 Elements in Older Browsers

As you know, HTML5 introduces several new semantic elements, most of which you learned about in Chapters 3 and 4. In many cases, modern browsers support those elements natively. From a styling point of view, that means these browsers apply default styles to the new elements just as they do for HTML elements that have existed since the earliest days of the language. For example, elements such as **article**, **aside**, **nav**, and **section** (as well as some others) display on their own line, just like **div**, **blockquote**, **p**, and others that were defined as block-level elements in versions of HTML before HTML5.

You might be wondering, "What about older browsers? How can I use the new HTML5 elements if they didn't exist when those browsers were created?"

Well, the good news is that most browsers allow you to style elements that they don't yet support natively. Internet Explorer is the exception, but there's an easy workaround that I describe in step 2. So follow the three easy steps in the next section to begin styling pages that have HTML5 elements.

To style new HTML5 elements in all browsers:

1. Add the following code to your site's main style sheet file (the one that all pages use):

```
article, aside, figcaption,
→figure, footer, header,
→hgroup, menu, nav, section {
    display: block;
}
```

About the HTML5 Shiv

Unlike other mainstream browsers, Internet Explorer 8 and older *ignore* CSS on elements they don't support natively.

Fortunately, there's a way to make these versions of IE recognize the elements—you use JavaScript's `document.createElement("elementname")` for each element, a discovery made by Sjoerd Visscher. For instance, `document.createElement("aside")` makes IE understand the **aside** element, and then the style rule in step 1 of "To style new HTML5 elements in all browsers" (and any other styles you create) takes effect.

John Resig documented this approach, dubbing it the HTML5 shiv (it's also referred to as the HTML5 shim). But thankfully, you don't have to write that JavaScript for each new HTML5 element yourself, because Remy Sharp bundled John's approach into a JavaScript file and made it available to the community at html5shiv.googlecode.com/svn/trunk/html5.js. Subsequent contributors have enhanced it.

Using the HTML5 shiv couldn't be easier. Simply link to the file, as shown in the highlighted code in step 2 of "To style new HTML5 elements in all browsers." (The part of the code that reads **[if lt IE 9]** means that only versions *less than* IE9 load the file. This is known as a conditional comment.)

The HTML5 shiv has also been bundled into some JavaScript libraries, like Modernizr (www.modernizr.com/). So if you add Modernizr to your pages, you won't need to load the HTML5 shiv separately. Incidentally, Modernizr is a very handy library that allows you to detect whether a browser supports various HTML5 and CSS3 features. Check it out!

Why: Most browsers treat elements they don't recognize as inline elements by default. So this bit of CSS forces the new HTML5 "block-level-like" semantics to render on their own line (IE needs more help, described in the next step). `display: block;` is the same declaration applied to **div**, **blockquote**, **p**, and others by each browser's built-in default style sheet.

2. To get the styling of new HTML5 elements to work in Internet Explorer prior to version 9, add the following highlighted code to the **head** element (*not* the **header** element) of each of your pages, preferably after you link to your CSS files:

```
<!DOCTYPE html>
<html lang="en">
<head>
<meta charset="utf-8" />
<title>photobarcelona</title>
<link rel="stylesheet" href=
 ➝"assets/css/base.css" />
<!--[if lt IE 9]>
    <script src="http://html5shiv.
     ➝ googlecode.com/svn/trunk/
     ➝ html5.js"></script>
<![endif]-->
</head>
<body>
...
```

See the sidebar "About the HTML5 Shiv" to understand why this is necessary and what it does.

3. Now, style away with CSS as you please!

You may run into the occasional glitch while styling elements, but you'll be in good shape for the most part.

There is one drawback to this approach and these alternative options. Because styling HTML5 elements in IE6 through IE8 requires JavaScript, users whose browsers don't support JavaScript or have it disabled will see unstyled and possibly messy HTML5 elements. You might be OK with this risk if it's one of your own sites; many designers and developers are. However, if you're doing work for a client, you may want to get their clearance before you use the HTML5 elements that are intended to display as blocks. They may also have user analytics concerning browser usage to inform the decision.

Alternative approaches:

- If you aren't comfortable using **article**, **section**, **nav**, and the others listed in step 1 above, you can use **div** for all your containers instead. This is how people built sites before HTML5 was introduced. It's true that you'll reduce the semantic richness of your site, but it is an acceptable approach. Some even choose to use classes that mimic the new HTML5 element names to get accustomed to the new elements. For instance:

  ```
  <div class="header">...</div>

  <div class="article">...</div>

  <div class="section">...</div>
  ```

  and so on.

 The page in IE6 when JavaScript is disabled, preventing the HTML5 shiv JavaScript file from executing. The masthead area looks a little broken, but the page on the whole is intact.

- If you do use the new elements, you can write CSS selectors that target other elements as much as possible to reduce the impact when JavaScript is off. I've done that often with the page layout in this chapter. It doesn't look the same in IE6 when JavaScript is disabled, but it's not unusable either .

TIP You may download `html5.js` (the HTML5 shiv file) and add it to the files in your site instead of pointing to http://html5shiv. googlecode.com/svn/trunk/html5.js. But it is updated periodically, so it's not a bad idea to load it from Google Code instead by using the code in step 2 of "To style new HTML5 elements in all browsers."

Resetting or Normalizing Default Styles

As mentioned, each browser has a built-in style sheet that dictates the presentation of your HTML unless you write your own CSS to override it. The default browser styles are fairly similar on the whole, but they have enough differences that it's common for developers to level the playing field before they apply their own CSS.

There are two main ways to level the playing field:

- Begin the main style sheet with a CSS *reset*, like the Meyer reset created by Eric Meyer (http://meyerweb.com/eric/tools/css/reset/). There are also other reset style sheets available.

- Begin the main style sheet with **normalize.css**, created by Nicolas Gallagher and Jonathan Neal. Find it at http://necolas.github.com/normalize.css/ (follow the "Get the normalize.css file" link).

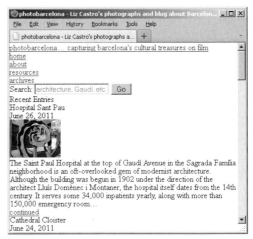

A Here's our example page with a reset applied to it. The most obvious differences are that all font sizes are the same and all margins and padding are set to zero.

continued

A CSS reset effectively sets all the default element styles to "zero" . The second method, **normalize.css**, takes a different approach. Instead of resetting everything, it tweaks the default styles so they look very similar across browsers .

You aren't required to use either of these approaches. It's perfectly fine if you just let the browser defaults remain and write your CSS accordingly.

For this chapter, I have used the Meyer reset and have styled the text to get the page started. So before applying the remaining styling described in this chapter, the page looks like . Because I've used the reset, you'll be able to see more explicitly how the CSS shown in this chapter affects the layout. And by following along in the chapter, you'll learn how to lay out a page when using a reset, a valuable skill given the popularity of this approach.

Here's the example page using **normalize.css** instead of the reset. It's similar to the unstyled, default rendering, but there are differences. More to the point, this version would look very similar if you were to view it in today's common browsers.

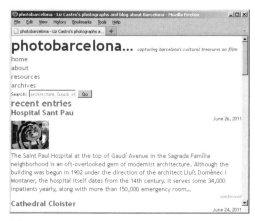

Here's the example page with the reset and text formatting applied. You'll begin styling the rest of the page from here, evolving it as you step through the chapter.

The Box Model

CSS treats your Web page as if every element it contains were enclosed in an invisible box. The box is made up of a content area, the space surrounding that area (padding), the outside edge of the padding (border), and the invisible space around the border that separates one element from the next (margin). It's sort of like a framed picture on a wall, where the picture is the content, the matting is the padding, the frame is the border, and the distance between that frame and the next one is the margin 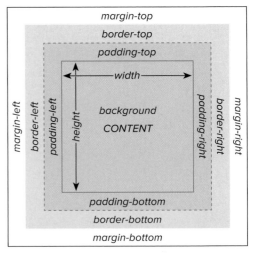.

You can use CSS to determine both the appearance and the position of each element's box, and in so doing, you have considerable control over the layout of your Web page **B**.

As discussed in Chapter 1, by default an element's box may be block-level (thereby starting on a new line like a new paragraph) or inline (not generating a new line). This trait governs the initial layout of the Web page: By default, elements are displayed in the same order as they appear in the HTML code from top to bottom—this is known as the *document flow*—with line breaks at the beginning and end of each element that is styled as block-level **A**.

A Each element's box has four important properties that determine its size: content area, padding, border, and margin. You can control each property individually.

The space between the content area and the border is the padding. (Here there is padding of 10 pixels on all sides.) The background color fills both areas.

The sidebar content area. No explicit width or height is specified in the CSS in this case.

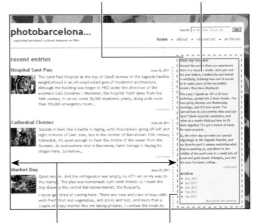

The margin is the invisible space beyond the border. (Here there's a left margin of 72 percent of the container around the entire page.)

The outside edge is the border. (This box has no border.)

B The box model in the context of the sidebar in our page.

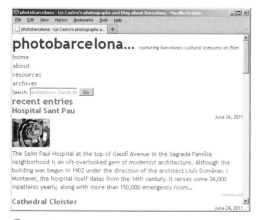

There are four principal ways to position an element box: You can leave the box in the flow (the default, also called *static*; this is what you'll do most of the time), you can remove the box from the flow and specify its exact coordinates with respect to either its parent element (*absolute*; to be used carefully) or the browser window (*fixed*; even less common in practice), or you can move the box with respect to its default position in the flow (*relative*; somewhere in between). In addition, if boxes overlap one another, you can specify the order in which they should do so (*z-index*).

You can also control its appearance, including its **background**, **padding**, **border**, **margin**, **width**, **height**, **alignment**, **color**, and more. We'll discuss all of these in this chapter.

Note that some layout properties, particularly em and percentage values, are relative to an element's parent. Remember that a parent is the element that contains the current element (see "Parents and Children" in Chapter 1).

Ⓒ Remember the example page from the beginning of the chapter before I applied any styles? This is the document flow of the page. And the order hasn't changed as a result of styling the text **Ⓓ**.

TIP The illustration in **Ⓐ** was inspired by Rich Hauck's box model diagram (which is itself inspired by the one in the CSS spec): www.mandalatv.net/itp/drivebys/css/.

Ⓓ Here's the styled page to this point. The normal flow is still intact because I've only styled the text so far.

Changing the Background

As you learned in Chapter 10 ("Changing the Text's Background" and "More on Backgrounds"), you can style the background of the entire page and individual elements Ⓐ. This includes nearly every element, even forms and images (yes, an image can have a background image!).

To use a background image:

1. Type **background-image:**.

2. Then type **url(*image.png*)**, where *image.png* is the path and name of the image that should be used for the background Ⓐ. Or type **none** to use no image at all, as in **background-image: none;** (you'd only use this when overriding another style rule that's applying a background image to the element).

To repeat a background image:

Type **background-repeat: *direction***, where *direction* is either **repeat** (to tile the image both horizontally and vertically), **repeat-x** (to tile the image horizontally), **repeat-y** (to tile the image vertically) Ⓐ, or **no-repeat** (to not tile the image at all).

Ⓐ First, you apply a background image to the outermost container, the **div** with **id="container"**. Then you repeat it vertically (the y-axis). This is the long way to define background styles—specifying each property in its own declaration. In order to keep my code as compact as possible, my style sheet actually uses the shorthand notation shown in Ⓑ instead. Either way, the results are not particularly attractive in the example page Ⓒ.

```
#container {
background-image:
→ url(../img/bg-bluebench.jpg);
    background-repeat: repeat-y;
}
```

Ⓑ You can use the shortcut **background** property described in Chapter 10 and on the next page to apply more than one background-related property at once. I recommend you use shorthand notation whenever possible, though there are situations where it makes sense to specify individual properties. Unrelated, the path to my background image is **../img/bg-bluebench.jpg** because my style sheet is in a folder that sits alongside the **/img/** folder. The paths to your own images could vary.

```
[code block figure]
#container {
background: url(../img/bg-bluebench.jpg)
→ repeat-y;
}
```

C This page is a bit of a disaster at the moment; the background image makes the text all but unreadable. We'll eventually cover the background image up so that the text is once again legible. Later on, we'll peel back the cover to let some of the background peek through.

To control whether the background image is attached:

1. Type `background-attachment:`.

2. Then type `fixed` to stick the background image to the browser window (meaning it will continue to show even if the visitor scrolls the page) or `scroll` to let it move when the visitor scrolls. `scroll` is the default value, so you don't have to specify it if that's the effect you want, which is typical.

To specify the position of an element's background image:

Type `background-position:` *x y*, where *x* and *y* can be expressed as a percentage or as an absolute distance, such as **20px 147px** (negative values are also allowed). Or use the values **left**, **center**, or **right** for *x* and **top**, **center**, or **bottom** for *y*. (See the "More on Backgrounds" sidebar in Chapter 10 for some examples.)

To change the background color:

1. Type **background-color:**.

2. Type **transparent** (to let the parent element's background show through) or *color*, where *color* is a color name, hex color, RGB color, RGBA color, HSL color, or HSLA color (see "CSS colors" in Chapter 7) (**D** through **F**).

To change all the background properties at once:

1. Type **background:**.

2. Specify any of the accepted background property values (as described beginning with "To use a background image" and continuing through "To change the background color") in any order (**B** and **D**).

TIP The default for **background-color** is **transparent**. The default for **background-image** is **none**. The default for **background-repeat** is **repeat**. The default for **background-attachment** is **scroll**. The default for **background-position** is **top left** (this is the same as **0 0**).

TIP When using the **background** shorthand property, you needn't specify all the properties. But be aware that if any non-specified properties are set to their defaults, they may override earlier style rules.

D The **background-color** property would work for each of these but is longer than necessary, so I went with the **background** shorthand again. The background for the **page div** will make the text legible. (I change this color to white a little later in the chapter.) Next, you add a background to links that are hovered over, in order to make it clear that they really are links. You override that effect for the linked site logo, giving it a transparent background so the page background shows through during a hover. Finally, you add a background color to the feature column in the **sidebar div**. I'm using a **class** so the style can be repurposed if another sidebar or item with similar styling is added later.

```
#container {
background: url(../img/bg-bluebench.jpg)
repeat-y;
}

#page {
background: #fef6f8;
}

a:focus,
a:hover,
a:active {
background: #f3cfb6;
}

.logo a:hover {
    background: transparent;
}

.sidebar {
background: #f5f8fa;
}
```

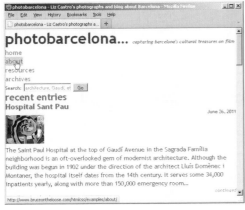

E The **page div**'s background completely covers our background image from **C**. We'll remedy that shortly (with **padding**). Notice how the links that are not being hovered over share the same background as **page**, while the hovered About link has a higher-contrast background to draw attention to it.

like me taking pictures. I confuse the locals by talk

from my window

Around the corner from our apartment there is a mosaics studio, and looked in wistfully, thinking how cool it would be to make sor displayed.

This year, I signed up. It's a 22 hour workshop, spread into 2 hour Wednesday mornings, and it's been great. I've learned how to cut for sandstone, and refers to a matte tile) and how to fit them tog projects.

So, the other day we make our annual pilgrimage to the Sagrada F watching what they're working on, and there in the middle of the gold mosaic triangles, just like the ones I've been cutting...

archive

May 2011
Apr 2011
Mar 2011
Feb 2011
Jan 2011

about this photoblog

F The background color for the **sidebar** is the lightest shade of blue I could manage—just enough to set it off.

TIP The **background** properties are not inherited. You only need to explicitly set default values like **transparent** or **scroll** when you want to override another style rule.

TIP If you use the **background-position** property with a **repeat**, the position specifies where the first image in the **repeat** starts. For example, from the **top right**, **0 20px**, and so on.

TIP You can use negative values with the **background-position** property. For example, **background-position: -45px 80px** positions the image to the left—not *from* the left—45 pixels (so you won't see the first 45 horizontal pixels of the image) and 80 pixels down from the top of the element.

TIP To create a background for the entire page, set the **background** property for the body element.

TIP If you specify both a color and a URL for the background, the color will be used until the image at the URL is loaded, will be seen through any transparent portions of the background image, and displays in any area of the element that the image doesn't cover.

TIP Choose your text and background colors (and images) carefully to allow sufficient contrast between the two. This is particularly important for vision-impaired users.

Setting the Height or Width for an Element

You can set a height and width on elements such as sectioning content, paragraphs, list items, **div**s, images, **video**, form elements, and more (**Ⓐ** and **Ⓑ**). Also, you can set phrasing content elements (which display as inline by default) to **display: block;** or **display: inline-block;** and then apply a width or height to them too. (See "Displaying and Hiding Elements" for more information about the **display** property.)

To set the height or width for an element:

1. Type **width:** *w*, where *w* is the width of the element's content area and can be expressed either as a length (with units like **px** and **em**) or as a percentage of the parent element. Or use **auto** to let the browser calculate the width (this is the default).

2. Type **height:** *h*, where *h* is the height of the element and can be expressed only as a length (with units like **px** and **em**). Or use **auto** to let the browser calculate the height (this is the default).

Ⓐ Limiting the **container div** width to 90% of the browser window gives it some air and helps it not look so cramped (it's the white space on the side in Ⓑ). By reducing the **page div** to 97.9167% of the **container div**, you see part of the background image on the side (see the comments in the example code on the book site to learn how I arrived at that percentage; also, feel free to use more conventional percentages). And by setting the **main div** to 71% of the **page div**, you leave room for the sidebar, which you'll move to the side later. The **input** style sets the width of the search form field. Lastly, the **.photo** dimensions control the size of the paragraphs around the images in the blog entries (it matches the width and height of the images themselves).

```
#container {
    background: url(../img/bg-bluebench.jpg)
    → repeat-y;
    width: 90%;
}

#page {
    background: #fef6f8;
    width: 97.9167%;
}

#main {
width: 71%;
}

input[type="text"] {
    width: 150px;
}

.photo {
height: 75px;
width: 100px;
}
```

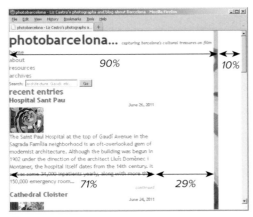

B The **container div**, which encloses the shaded **page div**, now occupies only 90% of the browser window. Part of its background image shows on the side because the **page div** width was reduced as well. The **main div** width is 71% of the **page div**, not the **container div** or browser window.

C The **max-width** property is ideal for setting the outside limit of our fluid layout. In our case, you don't want it to get too wide, even if visitors have huge displays. If you want to prevent an element from getting too narrow, you could apply the **min-width** property, though given the popularity of Web browsing on mobile phones and other smaller devices, choose wisely if you're inclined to set a **min-width**.

```
#container {
background: url(../img/bg-bluebench.jpg)
repeat-y;
max-width: 950px;
width: 90%;
}
```

TIP If you don't explicitly set the **width** or **height**, **auto** is used (see "Width, margins, and auto").

TIP Remember that a percentage value is relative to the width of the parent element— not to the original width of the element itself.

TIP The padding, borders, and margin are not included in the value of **width** (see "Width, margins, and auto").

TIP You can't set a **height** or **width** on elements that display as inline elements (like phrasing content) unless you set them to **display: inline-block** or **display: block**. See "Displaying and Hiding Elements" for more information about the **display** property.

TIP Widths and **heights** are not inherited.

TIP There are also **min-width**, **min-height**, **max-width**, and **max-height** properties **C**. (In the event that you want to support Internet Explorer 6 for your site, be aware that it doesn't support these properties.)

Width, margins, and auto

For most elements that display as block-level by default, the **auto** value for **width** is calculated from the width of the containing block minus the element's padding, borders, and margins. The *containing block* is the width that the element gets from its parent.

Elements like images have an **auto** width equal to their intrinsic value; that is, the actual dimensions of the external file (like the example page's images, which are 100 x 75). Floated elements have an **auto** width of 0. Non-floated inline elements ignore the **width** property altogether (meaning you can't set a width on elements like **em** and **cite** unless you set them to **display: inline-block** or **display: block**). See "Making Elements Float" to learn more about floats, and "Displaying and Hiding Elements" for more information about **display**.

D In this example, I've set the **width** of the parent **div** to 300 pixels. This will be our containing block. Then, both paragraphs have 10-pixel margins, 5-pixel padding, and 5-pixel borders on all sides. The first paragraph has the **width** set automatically, since **auto** is the default **width** value unless you specify otherwise. The second paragraph (which has **class="example"** in the HTML) is set at **200px**.

```
div {
background: yellow;
width: 300px;
}

p,
.example {
background: white;
border: 6px solid blue;
margin: 10px;
padding: 5px;
}

.example { /* the second paragraph */
background: white;
border-color: purple;
width: 200px;
}
```

Why min-height Is Often Preferable to height

Unless you're certain an element's content won't get taller, it's almost always best to avoid giving it a height in your style sheet. In most cases, you'll let the content and browser dictate the height automatically. This lets content flow as needed on the range of browsers and devices.

If you do set a height and the content grows, it could break out of the element's box, which might not be what you'd expect. Standards-compliant browsers do *not* expand the height automatically in this circumstance; they take your word for it when you specify a height, and they stick to it. (IE6 doesn't follow the standard, so it does expand the height.)

However, if you always want the element to be *at least* a certain height, set a **min-height**. If the content later grows, the element's height will grow automatically as desired. That is the difference between **height** and **min-height**, as well as **width** and **min-width**.

And in case you're wondering, there are a variety of reasons content might grow. Your content might come from a database or a feed or be user-generated. Also, your visitor may increase the font size in his or her browser, overriding the style you specified.

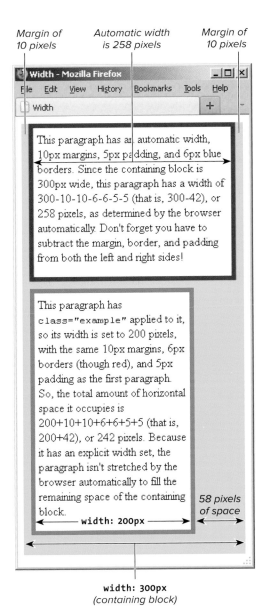

Margin of 10 pixels

Automatic width is 258 pixels

Margin of 10 pixels

This paragraph has an automatic width, 10px margins, 5px padding, and 6px blue borders. Since the containing block is 300px wide, this paragraph has a width of 300-10-10-6-6-5-5 (that is, 300-42), or 258 pixels, as determined by the browser automatically. Don't forget you have to subtract the margin, border, and padding from both the left and right sides!

This paragraph has class="example" applied to it, so its width is set to 200 pixels, with the same 10px margins, 6px borders (though red), and 5px padding as the first paragraph. So, the total amount of horizontal space it occupies is 200+10+10+6+6+5+5 (that is, 200+42), or 242 pixels. Because it has an explicit width set, the paragraph isn't stretched by the browser automatically to fill the remaining space of the containing block.

58 pixels of space

◄——— width: 200px ———►◄——►

width: 300px
(containing block)

E If the **width** is **auto**, as in the top paragraph, its value is derived from the width of the containing block (yellow) minus its own margins, padding, and border. If the **width** is set manually (as in the bottom paragraph), the right margin is usually adjusted to pick up the slack.

If you manually set the **width**, **margin-left**, and **margin-right** values, but together with the border and padding they don't equal the size of the containing block, something's got to give. And indeed, the browser will override you and set **margin-right** to **auto** (**D** and **E**).

If you manually set the **width** but set one of the margins to **auto**, then that margin will stretch or shrink to make up the difference.

However, if you manually set the **width** but leave *both* margins set to **auto**, *both* margins will be set to the same maximum value (resulting in your element being centered; for example, **#container { margin: 20px auto; }** centers the page). That's precisely what I've done for the example page, as shown in the next section, "Setting the Margins around an Element."

Setting the Margins around an Element

The margin is the amount of transparent space between one element and the next (A and B). See "The Box Model" for how it relates to an element's border and padding.

To set an element's margins:

Type **margin:** *x*, where *x* is the amount of desired space to be added, expressed as a length, a percentage of the width of the parent element, or **auto**.

> **TIP** If you use one value for **margin**, that value is applied to all four sides equally. If you use two values, the first value applies to the top and bottom and the second value applies to the right and left A. If you use three values, the first applies to the top, the second to the right and left, and the third to the bottom. If you use four values, they are applied to the top, right, bottom, and left, in clockwise order C.

> **TIP** You can also add one of the following suffixes to the **margin** property to apply a margin to a single side: **-top**, **-bottom**, **-left**, or **-right** C. There shouldn't be any space after **margin** (for example, **margin-top: 10px**).

A One of the principal margin adjustments is to the **container div**. When you set two values, the first is applied to the top and bottom margins, the second is applied to the left and right margins. You'll set the top and bottom margins to **20px** to give our design a little space. With an explicit width already defined on **container**, the left and right margins of **auto** cause the page to center horizontally in the browser B.

```
#container {
    background: url(../img/bg-bluebench.jpg)
        repeat-y;
    margin: 20px auto;
    max-width: 950px;
    width: 90%;
}
```

B The **auto** margin setting centers the layout in the window by dividing up the leftover 10% of the browser window width that is not used by the **container div** between the right and left margins. (Don't worry about the bullets sticking out the left side of the page; we'll take care of those later in the chapter.)

C The sidebar `div` (with `id="related"`) will have a left margin of 72% so it's farther from the left than the main content `div`, which has a width of 71%. The sidebar will continue to appear below the `main` content `div` until you float the latter a little later in the chapter **D**. I've added margins to several other elements too, like below the masthead, above the footer, and to the right and bottom of the partial blog entries to give them some breathing room **E**.

```
h1 {
    font-size: 1.5em; /* 24px/16px */
    margin-bottom: .75em;
    text-transform: lowercase;
}

aside h2 {
    font-size: .9375em; /* 15px/16px */
    margin-bottom: 3px;
    text-transform: lowercase;
}

#masthead {
    margin-bottom: 30px;
}

#footer {
    margin-top: 10px;
}

.entry { /* blog snippet */
    margin: 0 .5em 2em 0;
}

.continued {
    font-style: italic;
    margin-top: -5px;
}

#related { /* the sidebar */
    margin-left: 72%;
}
```

TIP The `margin` property's `auto` value depends on the value of the `width` property (see "Setting the Height or Width for an Element).

TIP If one element is placed above another, only the greater of the two touching margins—that is, the touching bottom and top margins of the elements—is used. The other one is said to collapse. Left and right margins don't collapse.

TIP Margins are not inherited.

TIP I set margins to a few more elements than shown in either **A** or **C**. You can see the complete code at www.bruceontheloose .com/htmlcss/examples/chapter-11/finished-page.html.

D The sidebar is now 72% from the left edge.

E Now there's more space between several of the elements.

Adding Padding around an Element

Padding is just what it sounds like: extra space around the contents of an element but inside the border. You might recall my analogy from before—padding is like the matting between a photo (the content) and a picture frame (the border). You can change the padding's thickness (Ⓐ, Ⓒ, and Ⓔ) but not its color or texture, but an element's background color and image do show in the padding area (Ⓑ, Ⓓ, Ⓕ, and Ⓖ).

To add padding around an element:

Type **padding:** *x*, where *x* is the amount of desired space to be added, expressed in units (typically in ems or pixels) or as a percentage of the width of the parent element (**20%**).

Ⓐ Similar to setting margins, when you set four values for **padding**, they are assigned to the top, right, bottom, and left, in that clockwise order. So here, there will be padding only on the top and right Ⓑ.

```
#container {
    background: url(../img/bg-bluebench.jpg)
    ⤷ repeat-y;
    margin: 20px auto;
    max-width: 950px;
    width: 90%;
    padding: 30px 10px 0 0;
}
```

Ⓑ When you add padding to the `container div`, space is created between its margin (because its border is 0 by default) and its contents (in this case, the **page div**). As a result, more of **container**'s background image is revealed.

Ⓒ Now you'll add padding to the contents of the **page div**—to the top, right, and bottom but not to the left.

```
#page {
    background: #fef6f8;
    max-width: 940px;
    padding: 10px 10px 10px 0;
    width: 97.9167%; /* 940px/960px */
}
```

Ⓓ With the padding added to the **page div**, notice the extra 10 pixels between "photobarcelona" and the top edge.

E I've replaced the page's temporary background color with white (#fff) **F**. I also added a little padding to all four sides of the sidebar so the content doesn't run to the edges, as well as padding to the left of the ordered list so the bullets indented **G**. (See Chapter 15 for more about lists.)

```css
#page {
    background: #fff;
    padding: 10px 10px 10px 0;
    max-width: 940px;
    width: 97.9167%; /* 940px/960px */
}

.sidebar {
    background: #f5f8fa;
    padding: 10px;
}

.archive ol {
    /* changes list items from numbers to
    → bullets */
    list-style: disc;
    /* indents bullets */
    padding-left: 18px;
}
```

TIP As with the `margin` property, if you use one value, the specified padding is applied to all four sides equally **E**. If you use two values, the first value applies to the top and bottom and the second value applies to the right and left. If you use three values, the first applies to the top, the second to the right and left, and the third to the bottom. If you use four values, they are applied to the top, right, bottom, and left, in clockwise order (**A** and **C**).

TIP You can also add one of the following suffixes to the `padding` property to apply padding to a single side: `-top`, `-bottom`, `-left`, or `-right`. There should be no space between the word `padding` and the suffix (for example, `padding-right: 1em`).

TIP Padding is not inherited.

F When the **page** background is set to white, it's clear why you didn't add padding to the left as well. I have made a number of other padding adjustments that you can study in the code files on the book's site.

from my window

Around the corner from our apartment there is a mosaic studio. Last year and the year before, I walked by and looked in wistfully, thinking how cool it would be to make some of the incredible mosaics they have displayed.

This year, I signed up. It's a 22 hour workshop, spread into 2 hour chunks. I've been going Monday and Wednesday mornings, and it's been great. I've learned how to cut ceramic tiles and also "gres" (their word for sandstone, and refers to a matte tile) and how to fit them together. I've got a bunch of ideas for more projects.

So, the other day we make our annual pilgrimage to the Sagrada Familia, and my favorite part is always watching what they're working on, and there in the middle of the work area is a small pile of green and gold mosaic triangles, just like the ones I've been cutting...
continued

archive
- May 2011
- Apr 2011
- Mar 2011
- Feb 2011
- Jan 2011

More from the archive

G The sidebar's background color shows through the **10px** of padding added to all four sides in **E**.

Making Elements Float

You can make elements float in a sea of text (or other elements). You can use this technique to make text wrap around images (A and B) or figures to create multi-column layouts and more.

To wrap text around elements:

1. Type `float:`.

2. Type `left` if you want the element on the left, and the rest of the content to flow to its right (A through G).

   Or type `right` if you want the element on the right, and the rest of the content to flow to its left.

A When you float an element to a side, the content that would normally display after it flows around it instead. Here, I've floated the image containers (a `p` with `class="photo"`) to the left in order to get the blog entry introductory text next to them. (You can also apply `float` directly to `img` elements.) As you can see in B, the text wraps around an image container when it's taller than it. This effect is desirable in many cases, but for this page I want the text to continue straight down, regardless of its length. I achieve this by adding a left margin to the container around the text C.

```
.photo {
    float: left;
    height: 75px;
    width: 100px;
}
```

B Since the `.photo` containers are floated left, the text scoots up alongside it and wraps around it when it's taller.

C By giving the container around the text a left margin of **110px**, its content always displays that far from the left edge, even when it's taller than the image container. As a result, it no longer wraps around it D. Unrelated to this task, I included the **-5px** top margin so the text would align with the top of the image to its left.

```
/* This class is on the div that contains
→ both the introductory text and the
→ "continue" link that follows it. */
.intro {
    margin: -5px 0 0 110px;
}
```

D The intro text doesn't wrap anymore. Next, you'll float the **main div** E so the sidebar appears alongside it F.

E Now, you'll use the same approach to float the main content to the left so the sidebar will appear next to it. (Earlier you pushed the sidebar off to the right of—but still below—the main content by applying a left margin to it.)

```
#main {
    float: left;
    width: 71%;
}

/* We applied this margin to the sidebar
  earlier. */
#related {
    margin-left: 72%;
}
```

F Here, the **main div** is floated left, so the sidebar simply flows along the right side of the floated left **main div**. In fact, the footer does as well **G**, because it follows the sidebar in the HTML immediately. (You'll get the footer back down where it belongs in the next section.) Note that it wasn't strictly necessary to give the sidebar (**#related**) a big left margin to get the float effect, just as it wasn't when you floated the blog text around the image containers (**A** and **B**). But in the same way that it prevented wrapping in **C** and **D**, the left margin prevents the sidebar text from wrapping underneath the **main div** if the sidebar ever gets taller than the **main div**. Also, the sidebar's background color would stretch across the entire **main div** if the sidebar lacked a left margin.

Or type **none** if you don't want the element to float at all. (**none** is the default value, so you'd only set it explicitly if you were overriding another rule that made an element float that you didn't want to in a particular circumstance.)

3. Use the **width** property (see "Setting the Height and Width for an Element") to explicitly set the width of the element.

TIP Remember, the direction you choose applies to the element you're floating, not to the elements that flow around it. When you **float: left**, the rest of the page flows to the right, and vice versa.

TIP Some elements (for example, phrasing content) without an explicit width may not float properly.

TIP The **float** property is not inherited.

G Since the **main div** is floated left, all of the other elements, including the footer, flow around it unless you say otherwise. And you *will* say otherwise in the next section.

Controlling Where Elements Float

You can control which elements an element can float next to and which it cannot. To keep an element from floating next to something you don't want it to, use the **clear** property **Ⓐ**.

To control where elements float:

1. Type **clear:** (**Ⓐ** and **Ⓑ**).

2. Type **left** to keep elements from floating to the left of the element you're styling **Ⓒ**.

   Or type **right** to keep elements from floating to the right of the element you're styling.

   Or type **both** to keep elements from floating to either side of the element you're styling.

   Or type **none** to let elements flow to either side of the element you're styling.

Ⓐ On the previous page, you saw that the footer flowed around the floated **main div**. Here, you apply **clear: both;** to prevent that **Ⓑ**. You could conceivably use **clear: left;** instead since the only floated element you have to worry about is floating on the left. But it doesn't hurt to clear both sides, and it may come in handy if the design grows more complex.

```
#footer {
    clear: both;
    margin-top: 10px;
}
```

Ⓑ The **clear** property indicates that the element in question (the footer in this case) must not flow around the floated element, but must instead be displayed after the floated element.

Ⓒ In styling the masthead, the logo (which includes the slogan) is floated left. The **div** surrounding the main navigation and search box is floated right. And within that **div**, each navigation list item is floated left so they appear next to each other instead of stacking vertically.

```
.logo {
    float: left;
    font-size: 2.5em; /* 40px/16px */
    margin: 0;
}

/* This div surrounds both the main
 → navigation and the search form. */
#masthead div {
    float: right;
}

/* :::: Site Nav :::: */
.nav li {
    float: left;
    font-size: .75em; /* 12px/16px */
    padding: 0 25px 0 3px;
}
```

D Most of the masthead's layout is fine, but the content below the masthead, especially the sidebar, has moved up because of the **float**s. That's because the height of the masthead's containing element (the **header**) has collapsed since it didn't account for the height of the floated elements within it.

E To clear the **float**s in the masthead so the main content and sidebar **div**s don't flow into it, you could add a **div** around both the main and sidebar **div**s and apply **clear: both;** to it. But you want to keep the HTML as lean as possible, so that's not ideal. Another way is to use a very popular solution known as **clearfix**. All it requires is to apply **class="clearfix"** to the masthead. Assuming the **.clearfix** CSS is already in the style sheet, the problem is solved **F**. See the sidebar on the next page for more details.

```
<div id="container">
    <div id="page">
        <header id="masthead" role="banner"
        → class="clearfix">
            ...
        </header>

        <div id="main" role="main">
            ...
        </div>
```

F The **clearfix** method magically clears the masthead's **float**s so the content that follows appears below it.

TIP You add the **clear** property to the element whose sides you want to be clear of floating objects (**D** through **F**). So if you want an element not to be displayed until the right side is clear of floating elements (and anything flowing to the side of it), add **clear: right;** to it (and *not* to the floating elements).

TIP A span surrounds the page's slogan. Though not shown, the style sheet contains a rule reading **.logo span { display: block; }**. This rule makes the **span** display on its own line, just like a paragraph or other elements that display as blocks by default. See "Displaying and Hiding Elements" for more information.

Other Methods for Clearing floats

There are a couple of other ways you could solve clearing the **float**s in the masthead so the main and sidebar content don't flow into it Ⓓ.

The overflow Method

The first and most simple way is to add this to your style sheet:

```
#masthead {

    overflow: hidden;

}
```

(The **overflow** property is covered later in the chapter.) Using **overflow: auto;** also works in some cases, but you might see a scroll bar, which is obviously undesirable. And in some cases, **overflow: hidden;** will cut off content, so keep an eye out for that. In my own work, I use **overflow** to solve float issues like the one in the masthead when it's able to do the job. When it isn't, I use **clearfix** Ⓔ. Generally, **clearfix** is the more consistent method, which is why I showed you how to do it in the example even though it's my last resort.

The clearfix Method

The CSS for **.clearfix** has gone through various permutations over the years as members of the Web community have refined it. The version shown below was taken from the excellent *HTML5 Boilerplate* (www.html5boilerplate.com), an effort started by Paul Irish and subsequently contributed to by a variety of community developers. I encourage you to check it out.

Nicolas Gallagher, who is now a core member of the project, contributed the following **clearfix** code. Simply copy and paste it into your style sheet and apply **class="clearfix"** to the element containing the **float**s Ⓔ.

```
.clearfix:before, .clearfix:after { content: ""; display: table; }

.clearfix:after { clear: both; }

.clearfix { zoom: 1; }
```

I won't explain what all that means since it's a little involved. You can read more about it at http://nicolasgallagher.com/micro-clearfix-hack/ (be warned that the discussion is pretty technical).

Summary

There's a subtle difference between using the **clear** property and using either the **overflow** or **clearfix** methods. With **clear**, you apply it to the element that you don't want flow around a floated element. The other two are methods that you apply to a container of the floated element or elements.

 You add a few more design touches by implementing these borders. In the case of the dotted border on the bottom of the masthead, it also helps visitors distinguish the masthead from the rest of the page at a glance.

```
#masthead {
    border-bottom: 2px dotted #1d3d76;
    margin-bottom: 30px;
    padding-bottom: 20px;
}

.entry {
    border-right: 2px dashed #b74e07;
    margin: 0 .5em 2em 0;
}

#footer {
    border-top: 2px dotted #b74e07;
    clear: both;
    margin-top: 10px;
}
```

B Notice that since a right border is applied to each **entry section** element and not the **main div**, it stops and starts for each entry. Unlike the masthead and footer borders, these are dashed.

C The footer has a top border that is the same style (dotted) as the one below the masthead but is a different color. And similar to that one, it helps to separate the footer visually from other content.

Setting the Border

You can create a border around or on individual sides of an element and then set its thickness, style, and color **A**. If you've specified any padding (see "Adding Padding around an Element"), the border encloses both the padding and the contents of the element.

To define the border style:

Type **border-style:** *type*, where *type* is **none**, **dotted**, **dashed**, **solid**, **double**, **groove**, **ridge**, **inset**, or **outset**.

To set the width of the border:

Type **border-width:** *n*, where *n* is the desired width, including abbreviated units (for example, **4px**).

To set the color of the border:

Type **border-color:** *color*, where *color* is a color name, hex value, or RGB, HSL, RGBA, or HSLA color (see "CSS colors" in Chapter 7).

To set one or more border properties at once with a shortcut:

1. Type **border**.

2. If desired, type **-top**, **-right**, **-bottom**, or **-left** to limit the effect to a single side.

3. If desired, type **-property**, where **property** is **style**, **width**, or **color**, to limit the effect to a single property.

4. Type **:** (a colon).

5. Type the appropriate values (as described in the three techniques on the previous page). If you skipped step 3, you can specify any or all of the three types of border properties (for example, **border:1px solid** or **border-right: 2px dashed green;**). If you specified a property type in step 3, use an accepted value for just that property (for example, **border-right-style: dotted;**).

TIP **Borders are not inherited.**

TIP **The individual border properties (border-width, border-style, and border-color) can have from one to four values. If you use one value, it is applied to all four sides. If you use two, the first is used for the top and bottom, and the second for the right and left. If you use three, the first is used for the top, the second for the right and left, and the third for the bottom. And if you use four, they are applied to the top, right, bottom, and left, in clockwise order.**

D In this example, I set the padding and default border for each paragraph. Then for the first paragraph, I set the border width for all four sides, and then the style for each side. For the four remaining paragraphs, it was easier to repeat the **10px** than to separate the style and color into two separate properties.

```
p {
    border: 10px solid red;
    padding: 15px;
}

p.ddd {
    border-width: 4px;
    border-style: dotted dashed double
    ⸴ solid;
}

p.inset {
    border: 10px inset blue;
}

p.outset {
    border: 10px outset green;
}

p.groove {
    border: 10px groove purple;
}

p.ridge {
    border: 10px ridge orange;
}
```

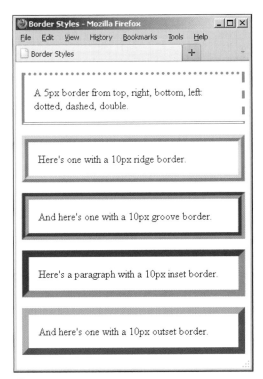

A 5px border from top, right, bottom, left: dotted, dashed, double.

Here's one with a 10px ridge border.

And here's one with a 10px groove border.

Here's a paragraph with a 10px inset border.

And here's one with a 10px outset border.

Ⓔ Each browser's treatment of the border styles isn't exactly the same, but this view of Firefox gives you a sense of the differences between the style types.

TIP You must define at least the style for a border to display. If there's no style, there will be no border. The default is `none`.

TIP If you use a shortcut, like `border` or `border-left` (and so on), the properties you don't give values for are set to their defaults. So `border: 1px black;` means `border: 1px black none;`, which means you won't get a border (even if you specified a style earlier with `border-style`).

TIP The default color is the value of the element's `color` property (see "Setting the Color" in Chapter 10).

TIP IE (up to and including version 7) cannot display very dark two-tone border styles like `groove`, `ridge`, `outset`, and `inset`. They come out solid.

TIP The `border` property can be used for tables and their cells.

TIP CSS3 introduces the `border-image` property. Browser support is good outside of Internet Explorer (see http://caniuse.com/#search=border-image). You can learn about `border-image` at www.sitepoint.com/css3-border-image/.

Offsetting Elements in the Natural Flow

Each element has a natural location in a page's flow . Moving the element with respect to this original location is called relative positioning (Ⓑ and Ⓒ). The surrounding elements are not affected at all Ⓒ.

To offset elements within the natural flow:

1. Type **position: relative;** (don't forget the semicolon; the space is optional).

2. Type **top**, **right**, **bottom**, or **left**.

   Then type **:v**, where **v** is the desired distance that you want to offset the element from its natural location, expressed either as an absolute or relative value (**10px** or **2em**, for example) or as a percentage.

3. If desired, repeat step 2 for additional directions, separating each property/value pair with a semicolon as usual.

Hospital Sant Pau

June 26, 2011

The Saint Paul Hospital at the top of Gaudí Avenue in the Sagrada Família neighborhood is an oft-overlooked gem of modernist architecture. Although the building was begun in 1902 under the direction of the architect Lluís Domènec i Montaner, the hospital itself dates from the

Ⓐ Although the date is aligned to the right, it is on a separate line from the heading and thus appears below it and too close to the entry text.

Ⓑ Remember to both specify the relative positioning and also give the offset. It can be either a positive or negative value. Using ems will keep the offset in proportion with the size of the text. Because 1em is equal to the element's font size, in this example the declaration moves the date up by that much (because of **-1em**) Ⓒ.

```
.entry .date {
    line-height: 1;
    margin: 0 1em 0 0;
    padding: 0;
    position: relative;
    top: -1em;
}
```

Hospital Sant Pau   June 26, 2011

The Saint Paul Hospital at the top of Gaudí Avenue in the Sagrada Familia
neighborhood is an oft-overlooked gem of modernist architecture.
Although the building was begun in 1902 under the direction of the
architect Lluís Domènec i Montaner, the hospital itself dates from the
14th century. It serves some 34,000 inpatients yearly, along with more

C By applying a negative offset to the date, you push it up into the preceding block's space. In this case, that results in the date being aligned with the section title. The succeeding elements are not affected at all.

TIP The "relative" in relative positioning refers to the element's original position, not the surrounding elements. You can't move an element with respect to other elements. Instead, you move it with respect to where it used to be. Yes, this is important!

TIP The other elements are not affected by the offsets—they flow with respect to the original containing box of the element. Depending on your `top`, `right`, `bottom`, or `left` values, your relatively positioned content may overlap other content.

TIP Use the `z-index` property to specify the stacking order of elements that overlap each other when positioned with `relative`, `absolute`, or `fixed`. See "Positioning Elements in 3D" for details.

TIP Offsets don't work unless you're also using the `position` property.

TIP Set an element to `position: static` to override a `position: relative` setting. `static` is the default value for elements, which is why they appear in the normal document flow. See an example in "Positioning Elements in 3D."

TIP Positioning is not inherited.

Positioning Elements Absolutely

As noted, the elements in your Web page generally flow in the order in which they appear in the HTML source code . That is, if the **img** element comes before the **p**, the image appears before the paragraph. You can take elements out of the normal flow—and position them absolutely—by specifying their precise position with respect to the **body** B or to the nearest positioned ancestor element D.

To position elements absolutely:

1. Type **position: absolute;** (don't forget the semicolon; the space is optional).

2. If desired, type **top**, **right**, **bottom**, or **left**.

   Then type **: v**, where **v** is expressed as the desired distance that you want to offset the element from its ancestor (**10px** or **2em**, for example) or as a percentage of the ancestor. (See the second tip for a related note.)

3. If desired, repeat step 2 for additional directions, separating each property/value pair with a semicolon as usual.

4. If desired, add **position: relative** to the *ancestor* element to which you want your absolutely positioned element to be offset D. If you skip this step B, the element will be offset with respect to the **bod**y C.

A Our search form is still sitting below the main navigation because it's part of the normal document flow. You want to shift it to the upper-right corner of the masthead that contains it.

B By positioning the form absolutely, I've taken it completely out of the document flow. It doesn't know other content exists, and vice versa. This code alone doesn't achieve our desired results because, unless you specify otherwise, an element with **position: absolute** is positioned relative to the **body** element, as you can see in **C**.

```
#masthead form {
    position: absolute;
    top: 7px;
    right: 0;
}
```

C The search form displays 7 pixels from the top of the **body** and 0 from the right, relative to the **body**.

D I set the form's **div** container to **position: relative;** so the form will be positioned absolutely relative to the **div**, not to the **body** element. This gets the search box where you want it, but it introduces another problem **E**.

```
/* This div srrounds both the search form and
→ the main navigation. */
#masthead div {
    float: right;
    position: relative;
}

#masthead form {
    position: absolute;
    top: 7px;
    right: 0;
}
```

E The search form now displays 7 pixels from the top edge of its container **div** and 0 from the right of it. (The extra white space above and to the right of it is the **10px** padding you set on **#page**.) However, it's sitting on top of the navigation. Not good. As mentioned, when an element is positioned absolutely it's taken out of document flow, so the navigation displays in the same place it would if the search form didn't exist at all. Let's resolve that **F**.

F A simple margin on the top of the navigation pushes it down below the search form and lines it up with the slogan in the logo **G**.

```
/* This div srrounds both the search form and
→ the main navigation. */
#masthead div {
    float: right;
    position: relative;
}

#masthead form {
    position: absolute;
    top: 7px;
    right: 0;
}

.nav {
    margin-top: 45px;
}
```

G The search form and navigation now display as you'd like. Better yet, their layout relative to one another remains intact when the page is narrower **H**. This is good news for visitors on mobile phones and other devices with narrower screens.

TIP Because absolutely positioned elements are taken out of the flow of the document, they can overlap each other and other elements **F**. (This is not always bad.)

TIP If you don't specify an offset for an absolutely positioned item, the item appears in its natural position but does not affect the flow of subsequent items.

TIP There is also a fixed positioning type. When a visitor scrolls in the browser window, the contents of the page usually move up or down. When you set an element to position: fixed;, it is affixed to the browser window so that it doesn't move when the visitor scrolls up or down. The rest of the page does scroll as usual. **IE6** doesn't support fixed.

TIP Use the z-index property to specify the stacking order of elements that overlap each other when positioned with relative, absolute, or fixed. See "Positioning Elements in 3D" for details.

TIP Set an element to position: static to override a position: absolute; setting. static is the default value for elements, which is why they appear in the normal document flow. See an example in "Positioning Elements in 3D."

TIP Positioning is not inherited.

H The search form and navigation move together as a unit because they are both contained in the same **div**. When the browser is narrow, they slide underneath the floated logo. The experience remains usable because the layout accounts for those conditions.

Positioning Elements in 3D

Once you start using relative, absolute, or fixed positioning, it's quite possible that you'll find that your elements have over-lapped, just as they did with the search form and main navigation. You can choose which element should display on top (Ⓐ through Ⓒ).

To position elements in 3D:

Type **z-index: *n***, where *n* is a number that indicates the element's level in the stack of positioned objects.

TIP The z-index property only works on positioned elements (that is, absolute, relative, or fixed). The example Ⓐ shows absolute elements only, but you can mix and match and the z-index settings will apply col-lectively, not separately, within the absolute, relative, and fixed elements.

TIP The higher the value of the z-index property, the higher up the element will be in the stack (Ⓐ and Ⓑ).

Ⓐ Here is quick sample HTML code followed by its style sheet Ⓑ, which renders as Ⓒ.

```
...
<body>
<div class="box1">
    <p>This is box 1</p>
</div>

<div class="box2">
    <p>This is box 2</p>
</div>

<div class="box3">
    <p>This is box 3</p>
</div>

<div class="box4">
    <p>This is box 4</p>
</div>
</body>
</html>
```

B This style sheet demonstrates that the absolutely (or relatively or fixed) positioned element with the highest **z-index** number always shows on top **C**, regardless of where it appears in the order of the HTML **A**. This also shows how **position: static;** can be handy. The first rule sets all four **div**s to **position: absolute;**, but then I override it on **.box3**, setting it back to the default value of **static**. This returns **.box3** to the normal document flow, so even though it has the highest **z-index** number, that has no effect and **.box3** will always be on the bottom.

```
div {
    background: #ccc;
    border: 1px solid #666;
    height: 125px;
    position: absolute;
    width: 200px;
}

.box1 {
    background: pink;
    left: 110px;
    top: 50px;
    z-index: 120;
}

.box2 {
    background: yellow;
    left: 0;
    top: 130px;
    z-index: 530;
}


.box3 {
    height: auto;
    min-height: 125px;
    position: static;

    /* Has no effect on stacking order
    ⇢ because the element is not
    ⇢ positioned as absolute, relative,
    ⇢ or fixed. */
    z-index: 1000;
}

.box4 {
    background: orange;
    left: 285px;
    top: 65px;
    z-index: 3;
}
```

TIP If you have nested items within an element that has a certain **z-index**, all those nested items are first ordered according to their own individual **z-index**es and then, as a group, ordered in the larger context.

TIP IE7 and earlier don't implement **z-index** as expected. Each positioned element starts its own stacking context rather than respecting the stacking order of all positioned elements within the whole page as it should. This issue and a fix are demonstrated at http://brenelz.com/blog/squish-the-internet-explorer-z-index-bug/. (Ignore the fact that the solution is shown in inline styles. Place your CSS in an external style sheet as you normally would.)

TIP The **z-index** property is not inherited.

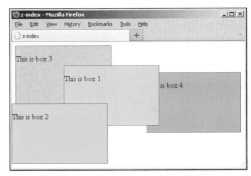

C The positioned boxes are stacked from highest **z-index** down to lowest. The third box is below all of them because it's in the normal document flow.

Determining How to Treat Overflow

Elements are not always contained in their boxes. Sometimes the box is simply not big enough. For example, an image that is wider than its container will spill out of it. Or perhaps you've positioned the content outside of the box, either with negative margins or absolute positioning. Regardless of the cause, you can control the area outside of the element's box with the `overflow` property.

To determine how the browser should treat overflow:

1. Type `overflow:`.

2. Type `visible` to expand the element box so that its contents fit. This is the default option.

   Or type `hidden` to hide any contents that don't fit in the element box.

   Or type `scroll` to always add scroll bars to the element so that the visitor can access the overflow if they so desire.

   Or type `auto` to have scroll bars appear only when necessary.

about this photoblog

This photoblog is the product of a love of computers, photography, and Barcelona. If you're interested in any of my photos, please contact me. The photographs on these pages are licensed under the Creative Commons Attribution-NonCommercial-NoDerivs License. To view a copy of this license, visit http://creativecommons.org/licenses/by-nc-nd/2.5/; or, (b) send a letter to Creative Commons, 543 Howard Street, 5th Floor, San Francisco, California, 94105, USA.

Ⓐ The images at the bottom of the footer wrap to multiple lines when the window is narrow. This is usually a good thing, because you want your content to adapt to different conditions. But just to show you how the **overflow** property works, you'll change this behavior temporarily (Ⓑ and Ⓒ).

Ⓑ In order to display a single line of images regardless of the browser width, you set the height of the **ul** element that contains the list of images to the height of the largest images and then set **overflow** to **hidden**.

```
.thumbnails {
    height: 33px;
    overflow: hidden;
}
```

about this photoblog

This photoblog is the product of a love of computers, photography, and Barcelona. If you're interested in any of my photos, please contact me. The photographs on these pages are licensed under the Creative Commons Attribution-NonCommercial-NoDerivs License. To view a copy of this license, visit http://creativecommons.org/ licenses/by-nc-nd/2.5/; or, (b) send a letter to Creative Commons, 543 Howard Street, 5th Floor, San Francisco, California, 94105, USA.

C Now the extra images are hidden. If you were to widen the browser, more images would show on the same line. Next, I'll show another approach **D**, though it's unsightly in this case **E**.

D If you want to restrict the viewable area of images to one line but allow visitors to access them all via a scroll bar **E** when they spill to multiple lines, use **overflow: auto;** in conjunction with the same height as before.

```
.thumbnails {
    height: 33px;
    overflow: auto;
}
```

about this photoblog

This photoblog is the product of a love of computers, photography, and Barcelona. If you're interested in any of my photos, please contact me. The photographs on these pages are licensed under the Creative Commons Attribution-NonCommercial-NoDerivs License. To view a copy of this license, visit http://creativecommons.org/ licenses/by-nc-nd/2.5/; or, (b) send a letter to Creative Commons, 543 Howard Street, 5th Floor, San Francisco, California, 94105, USA.

E I've scrolled down near the last line of images. Obviously, this isn't attractive in this context. But this technique can be handy in some circumstances, albeit with a taller height set on the container.

TIP In practice, I don't advocate hiding the images like in the examples, because it's preferable to allow users to view them regardless of the width of their browser (remember that mobile phones and tablets have narrower screens). Because the example was just for demonstration purposes, I've omitted the `height` and `overflow` declarations from the completed version of the page on the book site. Also, I wouldn't make a habit of including this many thumbnails in all my pages, because it's a lot of images to load. Again, I did so here in order to demonstrate the concepts.

TIP The `overflow` property is also handy for stopping `floats`. See "Other Methods for Clearing `floats`."

TIP Note that IE6 will incorrectly extend the parent to be as big as the child. The only exception is if you set the `overflow` property to any value except `visible` (the default), in which case the parent will shrink down to its normal size and let the `overflow` property do its job.

TIP The default value for `overflow` is `visible`. The `overflow` property is not inherited.

Aligning Elements Vertically

You can align elements in many different ways to make them look neater on the page than the default alignment (Ⓐ through Ⓒ).

To align elements vertically:

1. Type `vertical-align:`.

2. Type `baseline` to align the element's baseline with the parent's baseline.

   Or type `middle` to align the middle of the element with the middle of the parent.

   Or type `sub` to position the element as a subscript of the parent.

   Or type `super` to position the element as a superscript of the parent.

   Or type `text-top` to align the top of the element with the top of the parent.

   Or type `text-bottom` to align the bottom of the element with the bottom of the parent.

   Or type `top` to align the top of the element with the top of the tallest element on the line.

   Or type `bottom` to align the bottom of the element to the bottom of the lowest element on the line.

   Or type a percentage of the line height of the element, which may be positive or negative.

> **TIP** The `vertical-align` property works only on elements displayed inline, not on elements that display as a block. See Chris Coyier's explanation at http://css-tricks.com/2597-what-is-vertical-align/ for more details.

Ⓐ Images are aligned by default to the bottom of the line.

Ⓑ Notice that the alignment is set on the images themselves, not on the `li` items that contain them. (See more about lists in Chapter 15.)

```
.thumbnails img {
    vertical-align: middle;
}
```

Ⓒ Now the images are aligned to the middle of the line.

A When you point to the Home link, the cursor changes to a pointing hand and the link is highlighted, just as for any other link.

B I've assigned **class="current"** to the Home link when the visitor is on the homepage. By doing so, I can then change the default color and the cursor and background color for the hover states so the Home link doesn't look like a link. (Alternatively, you could remove the **a** element around the Home link from the navigation in this instance.)

```
a.current {
    color: #1d3d76;
}

a:hover.current {
    background: white;
    cursor: default;
}
```

C Although this continues to be a real, live link, it no longer looks like one. Since you are already on the page to which this link goes, that makes sense.

Changing the Cursor

Normally, the browser takes care of the cursor shape for you, using an arrow most of the time, a pointing finger to highlight links **A**, as well as some others. CSS lets you take the reins (**B** and **C**).

To change the cursor:

1. Type **cursor:**.

2. Type **pointer** for the cursor that usually appears over links (🖑), **default** for an arrow (⬉), or **crosshair** (+), **move** (✛), **wait** (⧖), **help** (⬉?), **text** (I), or **progress** (⬉⧖).

   Or type **auto** to get whatever cursor usually appears in that situation.

   Or type **x-resize** to get a double-sided arrow, where **x** is the cardinal direction one of the arrows should point—that is, **n** (north), **nw** (northwest), **e** (east), and so on. For example, the **e-resize** cursor might look like this: ↔.

TIP The cursors vary slightly from browser to browser and system to system.

Displaying and Hiding Elements

The sample page in Ⓐ helps demonstrate the difference between the **display** and **visibility** properties.

The **display** property is multifaceted. You can override an element's natural display type, such as changing it from **inline** to **block** (Ⓑ through Ⓓ) or vice versa. There is also a hybrid display type called **inline-block**, which allows an element to appear on the same line as other content while otherwise behaving like a block-level element. The **display** property is also useful for preventing an element and its content from occupying any visual space in the page (Ⓔ and Ⓕ). There are other values too (see the tips).

Meanwhile, the **visibility** property's primary purpose is to control whether an element is, well, visible. Unlike the **display** property, when you hide an element with **visibility**, a blank space shows where the element and its content would appear otherwise (Ⓖ and Ⓗ).

Ⓐ Here's the HTML: three simple **img** elements. The middle one has a **class** of **hide**, which I'll take advantage of in an example later. By default, **img** elements display inline Ⓑ.

```
...
<body>
    <img src="assets/img/top.jpg" width="300"
    ↳ height="125" alt="At the top" />
    <img src="assets/img/middle.jpg"
    ↳ width="300" height="100" alt="In the
    ↳ middle" class="hide" />
    <img src="assets/img/bottom.jpg"
    ↳ width="300" height="125" alt="At the
    ↳ bottom" />
</body>
</html>
```

Ⓑ No CSS is applied, so the images appear next to each other because **img** elements have a default style of **display: inline**, just like phrasing content elements. (If the browser were narrower, the images would wrap to fit.) It's simple to change their style so that each image occupies its own line instead Ⓒ.

Ⓒ By changing the images to **display: block;**, they now display on their own line just like paragraphs and other elements that display as blocks by default Ⓓ.

```
img {
    /* Make the elements display on their
    ↳ own line. */
    display: block;
}
```

D This looks like one image, but it's the same three **img** elements from the sample code **A**. The only difference is that they each display as a block instead of inline content thanks to the simple rule applied in **C**. I've left the browser at the same width so you can see the images appear on their own lines solely due to the change in their **display** property.

E You'll recall that the second **img** has the **hide** class applied to it **A**. When we set **hide** to have no display...

```
img {
    display: block;
}

.hide {
    /* Make all elements with this class not
    → display */
    display: none;
}
```

F ...no trace of the second image remains. (I've narrowed the browser, but that doesn't affect the result shown.)

To specify how elements should be displayed:

1. In your style sheet rule, type **display:**.

2. Type **block** to display the element as block-level (thus like starting a new paragraph) (**B** through **D**).

Or type **inline** to display the element as inline (not like starting a new paragraph).

Or type **inline-block** to display the element as inline but with block-level characteristics, meaning you can also assign the element properties, such as **width**, **height**, **margin**, and **padding**, on all four sides.

Or type **none** to hide the given element and completely remove it from the document flow (**E** and **F**).

See the tips for a link to other **display** values.

To control an element's visibility:

1. In your style sheet rule, type **visibility:**.

2. Type **hidden** to make the element invisible without removing it from the document flow (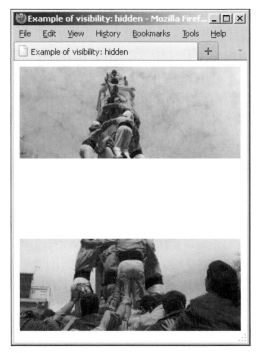 and).

   Or type **visible** to reveal the element.

TIP If you use display: none;, no visible trace remains of the element in the browser. There is no empty space . When you use visibility: hidden;, the space that the hidden element would have taken up still remains in the document flow . All content (including any descendants) within the elements is affected too. For instance, if you set display: none; to an article element that contains several p, figure, and img elements, none of them would display. If you set visibility: hidden; to the article instead, a blank space (probably large!) would show.

TIP See example in "Controlling Where Elements Float" for another example of setting display: block; to an element that has display: inline; as its default style. In that case, I applied it to the span element that is wrapped around the tagline within the site's logo.

TIP The display property has several other values as well, though IE6 and IE7 don't support some of them. See more information at http://reference.sitepoint.com/css/display (be sure to read the comments too).

TIP The visibility property doesn't have to be used in conjunction with the display property (or vice versa) as it is in .

TIP The visibility property has a third value (apart from inherit): collapse, which you use with certain parts of table elements. IE6 and IE7 don't support it. Learn more about collapse at http://reference.sitepoint.com/css/visibility.

When we remove the display: none; declaration from the **hide** class and change the **visibility** property to **hidden**...

```
img {
    display: block;
}

.hide {
    /* Hide all elements with this class */
    visibility: hidden;
}
```

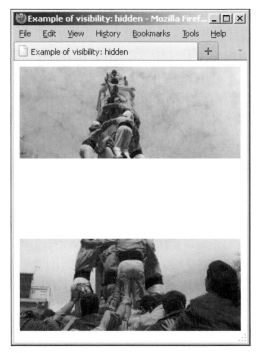

...an empty space remains where the hidden image used to be.

Style Sheets for Mobile to Desktop

A last-minute decision to go to the movies. A bet about the official language of Andorra. The phone number for a company where you're fifteen minutes late for a meeting. A map to the company, because the reason you're late is you can't find it.

We want information immediately, and with the proliferation of powerful mobile devices of all shapes and sizes, the Web can be in your pocket, purse, or backpack just as easily as it's at your desk or kitchen table. And today's mobile browsers are far superior to those of even just a few years ago, largely spurred on by the advent of Apple's Mobile Safari browser and the popularity of the iPhone.

So now it's up to you and me to build sites that make it possible for visitors to access information from any mobile phone, smartphone, tablet, laptop, desktop computer, game console, or future Web-enabled devices.

In this chapter, you'll learn how to build one site that works on the entire range of devices, adapting its layout according to the device's capabilities.

In This Chapter

Mobile Strategies and Considerations

Generally, there are two approaches for creating Web sites suitable for mobile devices:

- Build a dedicated site for mobile phones. That is, a site that is tailored for the mobile experience and that is separate from the site for desktop and tablet users. Sometimes tablets— especially the iPad—get their own version of a site, making a total of at least three sites.

- Build one site for all. Deliver all devices—from mobile phones to desktop computers—the same HTML, but style it differently so it's device-appropriate. With some additional trickiness, you can even deliver different image and video sizes so mobile-phone users aren't penalized by large downloads.

(Note that I'll often use "desktop" in this chapter to mean both desktop computers and laptops.)

There is no single correct approach that applies to every situation. However, recent advances in both technology and Web development techniques have brought the idea of a single-site approach to the forefront of discussion in the Web community; more on that in a bit.

A dedicated site for mobile phones

This approach revolves around the idea that the difference between a Web site for desktops and a site for mobile phones does not end with their display size. Most notably, the context is different. What a visitor might need when they're on the road with their phone will be quite different from what they're looking for from home or the office, this approach posits,

A Here is BART's site as seen on a desktop computer. Some other devices, such as the iPad, are delivered this version by default too. Though not shown, a link in the footer allows visitors to switch to the mobile version **B**.

B BART's main mobile site keeps its interface simple and omits the imagery found on the desktop site **A** so visitors can access information quickly. If you look closely at the footer, you'll notice a "Desktop" link, which points to the site shown in **A**, and another link to "Older Mobile Site," which points visitors to a simple mobile site at www.bart.gov/wireless/.

and simply miniaturizing the information from your desktop site won't be sufficient. Also, desktop computers tend to be more powerful and have faster Internet connections than their mobile-phone counterparts, so there's an opportunity to provide a richer experience.

This approach calls for deciding what information is particularly useful for mobile visitors and providing it to them on a mobile-specific site that requires the least scrolling, tapping, clicking, downloading, and waiting.

Although this approach is not exclusive to large companies or public services, you're more likely to find examples from them in the wild, in no small part because they can afford to develop and maintain multiple sites. Shopping sites like Amazon and Target greatly simplify their home pages and change their navigation strategies on their mobile sites. For instance, Target (www.target.com) gives their store locator much more prominence on their mobile site (sites.target.com/site/en/spot/mobile.jsp), figuring that a mobile-phone visitor is more likely to be out and about looking for a physical store. They also channel visitors through their vast array of products in a much different manner, reducing the number of top-level links for the small screen.

As an agency that provides a public transportation service, San Francisco Bay Area Rapid Transit (BART) serves a broad audience. They provide visitors three site options: a desktop site (www.bart.gov) **A**, a mobile site (m.bart.gov) **B**, and a further stripped-down mobile site for older devices (www.bart.gov/wireless/). Furthermore, they allow you to switch between the versions via a link in the footer **B**, putting control in their visitors' hands.

Nike provides no fewer than three distinct experiences, too—one for smartphones, one for the iPad, and one for the desktop—that are progressively more image rich. Similarly, Yahoo! has mobile, tablet, and desktop experiences.

One site for all

With new devices seemingly hitting the market each week and new *types* of devices no doubt being envisioned behind company walls, is it realistic—or even desirable—to build and maintain separate sites? We can't know what's around the corner, so this approach advocates building one site for all devices and then adapting its layout accordingly.

For most of us, a single site will likely serve our visitors well. Besides—part of the argument for a single site goes—today it's harder to predict someone's intentions when they visit our site, especially with smartphones and their browsers having become more robust. For instance, it's not always a safe bet that the mobile visitor is, in fact, mobile. I'm sure I'm not alone in browsing sites on my phone while lounging on my couch, even with my laptop just on the other side of the room. In most cases, I'm looking at full sites, not mobilized versions of the desktop experience.

However, there's no getting around the smaller screen sizes and reduced bandwidth of mobile phones, so it's still our job to deliver a site that is suitable for viewing in this context.

One site for all: making it happen

OK, if one site sounds great, how do you accommodate such a vast array of devices?

This is where progressive enhancement really shines. (Please review "Progressive

Ⓒ Believe it or not, the Food Sense home page shown here and in Ⓓ and Ⓔ are all from the same site, www.foodsense.is, not separate sites hosted at their own URLs. The site uses the responsive Web design approach so its layout changes based on the viewing conditions. The iPhone (shown here) and devices with similar screen sizes display the layout according to specific CSS rules. Different CSS rules target other, larger browser views (Ⓓ and Ⓔ), adjusting the layout accordingly.

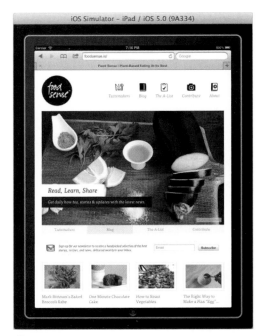

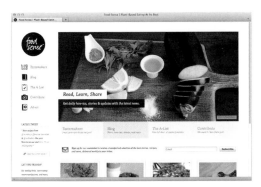

D Here is Food Sense as seen on the iPad and other devices with similar screen sizes. The CSS for this view changes the logo and navigation since the browser has more space to display content.

E This is the widest view of the site, shown on a desktop browser. The site has two other layouts not shown in any of the figures. You can view them by visiting www.foodsense.is on your computer and dragging the corner of the browser to make it narrower or wider.

Enhancement: A Best Practice" in the book's introduction for a refresher.) With your HTML separate from your CSS, you can provide styles that progressively evolve the layout for higher resolutions and more capable devices (**C** through **E**).

Ethan Marcotte has given us a blueprint for doing so, with an approach he dubbed *responsive Web design.* His article at www.alistapart.com/articles/responsive-web-design/ and his book *Responsive Web Design* (A Book Apart, 2011) are highly recommended. His approach is rooted in three things:

- A flexible, grid-based layout. This is the fluid layout approach you saw in Chapter 11, with some slight adjustments. A responsive site has all **width**, **margin**, and **padding** properties set in percentages so that all layout components are relative.

- Flexible images and media. Assets are also sized with percentages so that they scale up and down. (See Ethan's book excerpt at www.alistapart.com/articles/fluid-images/.) People have been developing techniques to deliver different-sized images based on a device's screen size so that visitors on mobile phones won't have to wait for large images to download.

- Media queries. A CSS3 component, these allow you to adjust the design based on media features such as the width of the browser's viewable page area (see the "Understanding the Viewport and Using the Viewport **meta** Element" sidebar in the next section). You'll learn about them in "Understanding and Implementing Media Queries" and then see them applied in "Building a Page that Adapts with Media Queries."

The Web community has rallied around the idea of building responsive sites, sharing techniques that build upon Ethan's foundation. And the approach isn't just for humble blogs. The *Boston Globe* (www.bostonglobe.com) became the talk of the town when it launched its new site, which was built on a foundation of responsive Web design.

We'll focus on this approach for the remainder of the chapter. You'll learn how to apply a mobile-first approach to the site from Chapter 11, progressively layering in CSS for larger screen resolutions with media queries(**C** through **E**).

Still, it is not a one-size-fits-all solution. As noted, there are cases where the context, desired content, navigation, appearance, and interactions are different enough to warrant a separate site.

TIP Luke Wroblewski began championing the notion of "mobile first" design in November of 2009 (www.lukew.com/ff/entry.asp?933). The premise is to design a site with the mobile experience in mind and then carry those principles to its desktop counterpart (if, in fact, those sites are different). By doing so, he suggests, you're more likely to identify which content is critical for users of all devices. You can watch his presentation on the topic at www.lukew.com/ff/entry.asp?1137. He's also written a book, aptly named *Mobile First* (A Book Apart, 2011).

TIP Jeremy Keith summed up the "one site for all" approach to excellent effect in his "One Web" presentation (www.vimeo.com/27484 362/). (For those of you who prefer to read, the transcript is available at www.adactio.com/articles/4938/.)

TIP Both videos are highly recommended. In fact, feel free to watch them now. I'll wait!

```
<!DOCTYPE html>
<html lang="en">
<head>
    <meta charset="utf-8" />
    <title>Media queries in link elements
    → </title>
    <meta name="viewport" content="width=
    → device-width, initial-scale=1.0" />
    <link rel="stylesheet" media="all"
    → href="base.css" />

    <!--
    The logic is only.
    The type is screen.
    The feature: value is min-width: 480px.
    -->
    <link rel="stylesheet" media="only
    → screen and (min-width: 480px)"
    → href="styles-480.css" />
</head>
<body>
...
```

Understanding and Implementing Media Queries

As you learned in the section "Using Media-Specific Style Sheets" in Chapter 8, you can target your CSS to specific media types in two ways. (There is a third way, the **@import** rule, that we didn't cover, because it affects performance.) To recap, the first way is via the **media** attribute of the **link** element; for example, **<link rel="stylesheet" href="global.css"** media="screen" **/>**, which goes in your page's **head**. The second way is with an **@media** rule in your style sheet:

```
/* Print style sheet */

@media print {

    header[role="banner"] nav,

    .ad {

        display: none;

    }

}
```

Media queries enhance the media type methods, allowing you to target your styles to specific device features Ⓐ. They're particularly handy for adjusting your site's presentation so that it adapts to different screen sizes. The following is a list of the media features you can include in media queries:

- **width**
- **height**
- **device-width**
- **device-height**
- **orientation**
- **aspect-ratio**
- **device-aspect-ratio**

- **color**
- **color-index**
- **monochrome**
- **resolution**
- **scan**
- **grid**

There are some non-standard media features too, such as

- **-webkit-device-pixel-ratio**
- **-moz-device-pixel-ratio**

For all but **orientation**, **scan**, and **grid**, you can include **min-** and **max-** prefixes. The **min-** prefix targets values that are "greater than or equal to," while **max-** targets values that are "smaller than or equal to." We'll focus on **min-width** and **max-width** in this chapter, because they are the two media features you'll use over and over for responsive pages. Descriptions for all media features are available in the CSS3 Media Queries spec (www.w3.org/TR/css3-mediaqueries/#media1).

Media queries enjoy great support among modern desktop and smartphone browsers. However, Internet Explorer 8 and below do not support them (see the first tip for a solution for **min-width** and **max-width**).

Media query syntax and examples

With a large nod to Peter Gasston's *The Book of CSS3* (No Starch Press, 2011), which summarizes this very well, here's the basic syntax for media queries.

- For a link to an external style sheet:

  <link rel="stylesheet" media=
  →"logic type and (feature:
  →value)" **href="your-stylesheet.**
  →**css" />**

- For a media query within a style sheet:

  @media logic type and (feature:
  →value) **{**

  /* your targeted CSS rules go
  →**here */**

  }

B This crude example contains default paragraph styling followed by changes to the paragraph text when the media query is **true**. I've saved this style sheet in **basic-media-query.css**, and I've loaded it into the page shown in **C**. You can see the results in **D** through **F**.

```
/* Your regular styles go here. Every device
→ gets them unless they are overridden by
→ rules in the media queries. */
body {
    font-size: 100%;
}

p {
    color: green;}

/*
The logic is only.
The type is screen.
The feature: value is min-width: 480px.
*/@media only screen and (min-width:
→ 480px) {
    /* Your styles for this condition go
→ here. */
    p {
        color: red;
        font-weight: bold;
    }
}
```

C This page links to the external style sheet in **B**, which contains a basic media query example.

```
<!DOCTYPE html>
<html lang="en">
<head>
    <meta charset="utf-8" />
    <title>Basic media query example</title>
    <meta name="viewport" content="width=
→ device-width, initial-scale=1.0" />
    <link rel="stylesheet" href="assets/
→ css/basic-media-query.css" />
</head>
<body>
    <p>Hi, I'm a paragraph. By default, I'm
→ green and normal. But get me in a
→ viewport that's at least 480px wide,
→ and I get red and bold!</p>
</body>
</html>
```

D Mobile Safari's viewport in portrait mode is 320 pixels wide, so the text remains green per the base styles in the style sheet. (It inherits the normal `font-weight` from the browser's default styles.) However, when the page is viewed on an iPad…

E …the text turns red and bold because the browser's viewport is 768 pixels wide in portrait view on the iPad, and the media query triggers when the width is 480 pixels or greater. It also takes effect on the iPhone in landscape mode, which has a viewport width of exactly 480 pixels.

I'll explain the syntax further shortly, but a couple of quick examples (**A** and **B**) will help put everything in context. The queries in the examples are identical, but the means by which they deliver the styles are different. The example in **A** translates to "Load and use the rules in `styles-480.css` only when the media type is `screen` and the minimum width of the viewport is 480 pixels." The example in **B** translates to "Use the following rules only when the media type is `screen` and the minimum width of the viewport is 480 pixels." (See the sidebar "Understanding the Viewport and Using the Viewport `meta` Element" to learn the meaning of *viewport*.) I've created a test page **C** that links to a style sheet that contains the code from **B**. You can see the results on an iPhone **D**, an iPad **E**, and a narrow desktop browser **F**.

Returning to the syntax, let's explore its components:

- The *logic* portion is optional and can have a value of either **only** or **not**. The **only** keyword ensures that older browsers don't try to read the rest of the media query, ignoring the linked style sheet altogether. The **not** keyword negates the result of the media query, making the opposite true. For example, `media="not screen"` will load the style sheet if the media type is anything other than `screen`.

- The *type* portion is the media type, such as `screen` or `print`.

- A *feature: value* pair is optional, but if present, it must be enclosed in parentheses and preceded by the word **and**. The *feature* is one of the pre-defined media features, like `min-width`, `max-width`, `orientation`, or the others. The *value* is optional for the `color`, `color-index`, and `monochrome` features.

You can chain together sets of features and values with **and**, as well as create a list of media queries by separating each media query with a comma. A whole media query list is true if any one of the media queries in the comma-separated list is true. 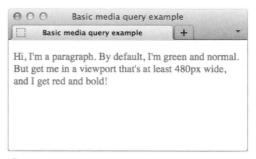 **G** and **H** show a variety of media queries.

To define a media query when linking to an external style sheet:

1. Type **<link rel="stylesheet"** in the **head** section of each HTML page in which you wish to use the style sheet.

2. Type **media="** to begin the media query.

3. Create your media query by following the steps in "To define a media query."

4. Type **"** to end the media query.

5. Type a space and then **href="*url.css*"**, where *url.css* is the path to and name of the style sheet that should be applied to the page when the media query is true.

6. Type a space and the final **/>**. (Or if you prefer, type no space and simply **>**. HTML5 allows both approaches, and the results are the same.)

To define a media query and associated rules within a style sheet:

1. Within your style sheet, type **@media** followed by a space.

2. Create your media query by following the steps in "To define a media query."

3. Type a space and **{**.

4. Optionally starting on a new line, create the style rules that should apply to the page when the media query is true.

5. Type **}** (optionally on a new line) to complete the media query block.

F Modern desktop browsers understand media queries too. Here is Firefox with the lower-right corner dragged in to make the viewport narrower than 480 pixels, so the text is green with a normal **font-weight**. If I were to stretch the window so it's at least 480 pixels, the text would turn bold and red immediately—no page refresh required.

G Examples of other media queries used to load external style sheets when **true**.

```
...
        <link rel="stylesheet" media="only
       screen and (min-width: 480px)
       and (max-width: 767px)" href=
       "styles.css" />

        <link rel="stylesheet" media="only
       screen and (orientation:
       landscape)" href="styles.css" />

        <link rel="stylesheet" media="only
       print and (color)" href="color-
       pages.css" />

        <link rel="stylesheet" media="only
       print and (monochrome)"
       href="monochrome-pages.css" />

        <link rel="stylesheet" media="only
       screen and (color), projection and
       (color)" href="styles.css" />
</head>
<body>
...
```

H These are the same media queries as in **G**, but they appear directly in a style sheet.

```
/* Base Styles
----------------------------- */

/* your base rules for all devices */


/* Begin Media Queries
----------------------------- */
@media only screen and (min-width: 480px)
→ and (max-width: 767px) {
    /* your rules */
}

@media only screen and (orientation:
→ landscape) {
    /* your rules */
}

@media only print and (color) {
    /* your rules */
}

@media only print and (monochrome) {
    /* your rules */
}

@media only screen and (color),
projection and (color) {
    /* your rules */
}
```

To define a media query:

1. Optionally, type **only** followed by a space. (Although this is optional, I recommend including it except when specifying **not**.) If you don't specify **only**, optionally type **not** followed by a space to indicate that you'd like the opposite of the media query result to be true.

2. Type *type*, where *type* is the media type (typically **screen** or **print**; see "Using Media-Specific Style Sheets" in Chapter 8).

3. Optionally, type a space, then **and**, then another space. Next type **(*feature*: *value*)**, where *feature* is one of the predefined media features: **width**, **height**, **device-width**, **device-height**, **orientation**, **aspect-ratio**, **device-aspect-ratio**, **color**, **color-index**, **monochrome**, **resolution**, **scan**, or **grid**, and where *value* is an appropriate *feature* value (oftentimes, but not exclusively, expressed in pixels or ems; see **B**, **G**, and **H** for examples). Where allowed and as desired, prefix the *feature* with **min-** to target a value that is "greater than or equal to" or with **max-** to target a value that is "smaller than or equal to." The *value* is optional for the **color**, **color-index**, and **monochrome** features.

4. If you'd like to create a list of media queries, type a comma and then repeat steps 2 and 3. Otherwise, your media query is complete.

continues on next page

TIP See "Rendering the media query styles in IE8 and below" to learn how to patch deficiencies in those versions of IE.

TIP Any base style rules you include outside the media queries are applied to all devices. You can override those as desired with media queries. To clarify, declarations within media query rules only write over *conflicting* declarations in the regular styles, such as `color: green;` in the case of Ⓑ. If the p rule before the media query had included `font-style: italic;`, paragraph text would still be italicized when the media query is true, because the p rule within the media query doesn't specify `font-style`.

TIP The iPhone increases a page's zoom level when you rotate the phone to landscape mode. As a result, some content typically is out of view, requiring visitors to manually zoom back down to get the width within the boundaries of the screen. There is a way to prevent this, but at the very unfortunate cost of also preventing visitors from being able to change the page's zoom level. However, if you must control the behavior, add the highlighted portions of this code: `<meta name="viewport" content="width=device-width, initial-scale=1.0,` `maximum-scale=1.0,` `user-scalable=no" />`. I advise against it, though. Instead, omit those two properties and let your visitors control zooming on your site.

TIP You can use Apple's free iOS Simulator to test the example pages on the iPhone and iPad. See the "Mobile Coding and Testing Tools" sidebar in the next section.

Understanding the Viewport and Using the Viewport meta Element

The *viewport* is the area within a browser that displays your page, both on desktop and mobile browsers. It doesn't include things like the browser's address bar or buttons, just the browsing area. The media query **width** feature maps to the viewport width. However, this is different than the **device-width** feature, which is the width of the screen.

These values are often different by default on mobile devices such as the iPhone. The viewport of Mobile Safari, which is the iPhone's browser, is 980 pixels wide by default, but the iPhone screen is only 320 pixels wide (it's 480 pixels high). So the iPhone takes what is akin to a desktop browser set to 980 pixels wide and scales it down to fit in the screen width of 320 pixels in portrait mode . As a result, when you navigate in Mobile Safari to most Web sites that have been built for desktop browsers, it displays a zoomed-out view of them. It does the same thing in landscape mode, but the width is 480 pixels. As you can see in ❶, pages are often hard to read without zooming in. (Be aware that the default viewport width varies among devices.)

Fortunately, there's a quick solution for fluid layouts (that is, layouts built with percentage widths in CSS). Simply add the viewport **meta** element to the **head** of your pages.

```
<!DOCTYPE html>
<html lang="en">
<head>
    <meta charset="utf-8" />
    <title>Fancy page title</title>
    <meta name="viewport" content="width=device-width, initial-scale=1.0" />
    ...
</head>
<body>
    ...
```

❶ My test page contains a green **div** that is 320 x 480. By default, Mobile Safari's viewport is 980 pixels wide, so the iPhone shrinks it to display it within the 320px-wide screen. That's why the green box occupies roughly a third of the screen's width (that is, 320/980).

The important part of this code is **width=device-width**. With that in place, the viewport width is set to be the same as the device width (for the iPhone, that's 320 pixels), so page content of that width fills the screen in portrait mode ❶. Without including this, you won't get the results you expect from your media queries that leverage **min-width** and **max-width**.

The **initial-scale=1.0** portion of the code has no bearing on the **width** and **device-width** values, but it's common to include it. It sets the initial page zoom level to 100%. You can also specify values less than or greater than **1.0**.

❶ This test page's code is exactly the same as in ❶ except it has the viewport **meta** element set to **width=device-width**. As you can see, the viewport width and the screen width are the same now.

Although not shown, three other properties exist. Set **minimum-scale** to a number greater than **0** and as high as **10.0** to effectively set the page's minimum zoom level. See the tips for information on the **maximum-scale** and **user-scalable** properties.

Building a Page that Adapts with Media Queries

The previous section explained how media queries work. Now you'll see how to apply them to a full page so that its layout adapts to a device's viewport size. This is the same technique used in Ethan Marcotte's responsive Web design approach. However, I do not adapt the image sizes, as responsive designs typically do (it isn't mandatory). I'll use our page from Chapter 11 as the example.

I'm not going to show you all the style rules I apply within each media query block, because those will be different from one site to another. The important thing is to know how to approach building a responsive site, and the types of media queries used to achieve that. You can view the completed page and its code at www.bruceontheloose.com/htmlcss/examples/.

Creating your content and HTML

Everything should begin with solid, carefully considered content. If you attempt to design and build your site with placeholder text (the vaunted *lorem ispum*), you may find that it doesn't hold together well when you drop in real content. So if possible, do the legwork up front so you can be confident you're designing and developing a site that will serve your visitors (and you) well.

The underlying HTML for the example page is the same as for the page in Chapter 11, with three exceptions:

- I added `<meta name="viewport" content="width=device-width, initial-scale=1.0" />` to the **head** element. See the sidebar "Understanding the Viewport and Using the Viewport

Ⓐ A sampling of the base styling I apply for all devices. The rules are just like others you've seen leading up to this chapter—they are not encased in media query blocks.

```
/* Base Styles
--------------------------------- */
body {
    color: #1d3d76;
    font: 100% "Trebuchet MS", Verdana,
    → sans-serif;
}

h1,
h2,
h3,
h4,
h5,
h6,
.logo {
    color: #b74e07;
    font-weight: bold;
}

h1 {
    font-size: 1.25em; /* 24px/16px */
    text-transform: lowercase;
}

.nav li {
    display: inline;
    font-size: .7em;
}

...
```

B The iPhone supports media queries, but I haven't added them to the style sheet yet. I've done the base styles only, so these screen shots are representative of what browsers that don't support media queries will render. The page layout is linear, with the portion in the image on the right appearing below the "recent entries." The page footer is below that, but not shown.

`meta` Element" for details about what this does. I recommend you include this `meta` element in your pages if you're implementing a flexible layout.

■ I removed the tiny thumbnail images at the very bottom of the page (there were more than 20 of them). Keeping bandwidth (and device capabilities) in mind, it was more images than I would recommend requiring all devices to load by default. If I wanted to get fancy, I could write some server-side code or JavaScript that loads the images dynamically for larger screens. That's beyond the scope of what we can cover here, however.

■ I added a call to `respond.js` near the bottom of the page to make the media queries work in IE8 and below. See "Rendering the media query styles in IE8 and below."

Choosing a design implementation approach

There are at least a couple of ways to approach building a responsive page. Both approaches use the same HTML, but some of the CSS is different. Here they are in summary:

Approach 1: Build a baseline for all devices, and then work your way up from small screen (mobile) to large (desktop)

1. First, provide baseline styles for all devices **A**. This usually includes basic font formatting, colors, and maybe tweaks to default margin and padding settings, but no floats or positioning of elements. Content will run top to bottom according to the normal document flow. The goal is for your site to be legible and presentable in a single column **B**. As a result, the site will

be accessible to all devices, new and old, that have a Web browser. It might look a little different from device to device, but that's to be expected and is perfectly fine.

2. Work your way up from there, using media queries to define styles for progressively larger screen sizes (or other media features, like **orientation**). The **min-width** and **max-width** media query features will be your main tools most of the time ( through ).

This approach is typically referred to as mobile-first responsive Web design.

Approach 2: Build for the desktop, and *then* address different device screen sizes

1. Style the desktop version of your site first (see Chapter 11).

2. Use media queries to override styles for other, smaller screen sizes.

The first approach has gained a lot of traction in Web circles because it embraces progressive enhancement. I'll use this approach in the example so you can see how it's done. You could test the second approach yourself by using the finished page from Chapter 11 as a starting point and adding media queries for smaller screen sizes based on what you learn here.

🅒 I add one rule for devices with a viewport that is at least 320 pixels wide. This makes the text wrap around the image in the blog entries 🅓. I didn't include this rule in the base styles because some mobile phones (even smartphones) have narrower screens that would make narrow text next to the image hard to read.

```
/* Base Styles
-------------------------------- */
...

/* 320px and up
-------------------------------- */
@media only screen and (min-width: 320px) {

    .photo {
        float: left;
    }
}

}
```

🅓 Text wraps around the images in the blog-entry intros, thanks to the media query defined in 🅒. The style takes effect in the iPhone because the viewport is 320 pixels wide in portrait mode.

E Now the style sheet has a media query that targets devices with a viewport of at least 480 pixels. This represents larger phones, like several Android models, as well as the iPhone in landscape mode **F**.

```
/* Base Styles
---------------------------------- */
...

/* 320px and up
---------------------------------- */
@media only screen and (min-width: 320px) {
    ...
}

/* 480px and up
---------------------------------- */
@media only screen and (min-width: 480px) {

    .intro {
        margin: -.9% 0 0 110px;
    }

    .entry .date {
        margin: 0;
        text-align: right;
        position: relative;
        top: -1em;
    }

    #main .continued {
        margin-top: -1%;
        text-align: right;
    }

}
```

F Here's the middle part of the page viewed at 480 pixels wide. Because there's more screen real estate, I stopped text from wrapping around the images and aligned the date and the "continued" link to the right.

Evolving your layout

OK, so you've got your content together, it's marked up with semantic HTML, and you've decided to go with Approach 1 to implement your design. **A** through **J** illustrate how I began with base styles for all devices and gradually worked my way up until I had a layout that is suitable for a range of viewport sizes and devices.

In responsive Web design lingo, you leverage media queries to define styles for each *breakpoint* in your page—that is, each width at which your content would benefit from adjustment. In the case of the example, I created style rules for the breakpoints in the list that follows. Keep in mind that for each minimum width case with no maximum width counterpart, the styles target devices at that **min-width** and *all the way up*, including the desktop.

- A minimum width of 320 pixels (**C** and **D**). This targets the iPhone, the iPod touch, and numerous Android and other mobile phones in portrait mode.

- A minimum width of 480 pixels (**E** and **F**). This targets larger mobile phones such as several HTC models, as well as many of the 320-pixel devices when in landscape mode (the iPhone, the iPod touch, and certain Android models among them).

- A minimum width of 600 pixels (**G** and **H**). I set these rules primarily for the benefit of narrow desktop browsers, but, as always, they apply to any device that displays at this minimum width.

- Within the range of a minimum width of 600 pixels and a maximum width of 767 pixels (**G** and **H**). The layout of the masthead was falling apart in this range—it was primarily viewable

continues on page 346

 These media queries start the transition of the masthead from the linear layout to the horizontal approach. It makes the page more presentable on desktop browsers when at a moderate width .

```
/* Base Styles
--------------------------------- */
...

/* 320px and up
--------------------------------- */
@media only screen and (min-width: 320px) {
    ...
}

/* 480px and up
--------------------------------- */
@media only screen and (min-width: 480px) {
    ...
}

/* 600px and up
--------------------------------- */
@media only screen and (min-width: 600px) {

    #container {
        background: url(../img/bg-bluebench.
        → jpg) repeat-y;
        margin: 20px auto;
        padding: 30px 10px 0 0;
        width: 90%;
    }

    .logo {
        float: left;
        font-size: 2em; /* 32px/16px */
    }

    ...
}

/* From 600px-767px, not beyond
--------------------------------- */
@media only screen and (min-width: 600px)
→ and (max-width: 767px) {

    .logo {
        background: #eee;
        font-size: 1.825em;
    }
}
```

code continues in next column

```
#masthead form {
    width: 235px;
}

input[type="text"] {
    width: 130px;
}

.nav li {
    font-size: .625em;
    font-weight: bold;
    padding-left: 1%;
}

...
}
```

 With the styles from , the page is inching ever closer to its complete form. The content layout is still a single column, but now the search field and main navigation are alongside the logo. Also, the background image around the page makes its first appearance.

I This is the final media query, targeting viewports that are at least 768 pixels wide. This is true for most desktop browsers (unless the user has made it narrower, as in H), but it also maps to the width of the iPad and some other tablets in portrait mode J.

```
/* Base Styles
----------------------------------- */
...

/* 320px and up
----------------------------------- */
@media only screen and (min-width: 320px) {
    ...
}

/* 480px and up
----------------------------------- */
@media only screen and (min-width: 480px) {
    ...
}

/* 600px and up
----------------------------------- */
@media only screen and (min-width: 600px) {
    ...
}

/* From 600px-767px, not beyond
----------------------------------- */
@media only screen and (min-width: 600px) and
→ (max-width: 767px) {
    ...
}

/* 768px
----------------------------------- */
@media only screen and (min-width: 768px) {

    #container {
        max-width: 950px;
    }

    #page {
        padding-left: 0;
        width: 97.9167%;
    }

    .nav li {
        display: list-item;
        float: left;
        font-size: .75em; /* 12px/16px */
    }
```

code continues in next column

```
    #main {
        float: left;
        width: 71%;
    }

    #related {
        margin-left: 72%;
    }

    #footer {
        clear: both;
    }

    ...
}
```

J With the styles from I, the page is complete. The iPad's rendering is shown here, but it looks similar on desktop browsers (though wider if the visitor has expanded the browser). The main content column and sidebar automatically stretch, because their widths are based on percentages.

when resizing a desktop browser—so I created these styles to clean that up and bridge the gap until the final breakpoint.

- A minimum width of 768 pixels (**I** and **J**). This suits desktops both old and new, as well as the iPad and other tablets.

Your breakpoints may be different from the ones I used. It depends on what is right for your content, design, and audience.

For instance, some people define a media query for **(min-width: 992px)**, and sometimes yet another beyond that for higher resolutions. Instead, I added **max-width: 950px;** to the **#container** selector of the example page **I**. With that defined, the layout is flexible up until 950 pixels but won't stretch beyond it, so I don't specify media queries greater than that width. Note that this **max-width** is of the layout *property* variety and is not a media query feature like **(max-width: 950px)**.

You also can stray from the breakpoints that align with the exact device viewport widths. If a media query based on **(min-width: 700px)** is best for presenting your content, use it. For that matter, you don't have to use pixels as the unit. You could create a media query that uses ems, like **(min-width: 20em)**.

Mobile Coding and Testing Tools

Testing your pages on mobile phones and tablets presents a special challenge because it can be difficult to get your hands on devices. Although there is nothing like testing on the real thing, there are some techniques and tools you can use while coding and conducting initial testing:

- Resize your desktop browser to approximate the viewport size of various mobile phones and tablets while you write your styles. This is a crude method to be sure, but it can help you get your styles in the ballpark so you'll have less refining to do after you've done proper testing on devices. However, *do* resize your browser in and out to test how your layout adjusts when viewed on the desktop.

- Use ProtoFluid (www.protofluid.com) during initial development. It's a free, browser-based tool that provides views that map to a few popular device sizes. Again, it's not for formal testing, because it doesn't behave like phones or the iPad, but it is helpful during initial coding. (A little warning that it's not the most intuitive tool to use. You might have to fiddle with it a bit to get the hang of it.) Your pages will need to be on a server for you to view them in ProtoFluid. It can be the server your Web hosting company provides (see Chapter 21) or one you run on your computer for development purposes (search online for "set up localhost server").

- Use Apple's free iOS Simulator for testing your pages for the iPhone and iPad. Now we're getting somewhere. This is the next best thing to testing on the actual devices. You'll notice I used it in some of the screen shots. However, it only works on OS X, and there is no Windows equivalent. The iOS Simulator is part of the free Xcode download, available at http://developer.apple.com/xcode/.

- Use Electric Mobile Simulator for Windows (www.electricplum.com/dlsim.html), which is perhaps the best tool of its kind for Windows. Just so there's no mistake, this is not equivalent to Apple's iOS Simulator.

- Use emulators and simulators for other devices and mobile browsers. Mobile Boilerplate maintains a list of links to mobile emulators and simulators for iOS, Android, Nokia Symbian, and more at https://github.com/h5bp/mobile-boilerplate/wiki/Mobile-Emulators-&-Simulators.

With any luck, you have some friends with a few different devices that you can test on, too. Ask around!

Rendering the media query styles in IE8 and below

There's one caveat to writing baseline styles and then adapting the design with media queries: Internet Explorer 8 and below don't support media queries. That means they only render the styles you define outside of media queries; namely, the baseline styles. Collectively, IE6, 7, and 8 still represent a healthy portion of traffic on most sites, so chances are you'll want those visitors to see your design as intended.

Scott Jehl set out to fix this problem, and he created a lightweight script, **respond.js**, that makes **min-width** and **max-width** media queries work in the older versions of IE. It's available at https://github.com/scott jehl/Respond. Activate the respond.min.js link to see the code, then copy it, paste it in your text editor, and save it as **respond.js**.

Although the script also makes **min-width** and **max-width** media queries work in other old browsers, there aren't any old browsers of significance. So you may want to use a conditional comment to instruct only IE8 and below to load the script, as shown in **K**.

Alternatively, if you plan to use Modernizr (www.modernizr.com) in your project, you can include **respond.js** with Modernizr's configuration build tool instead of downloading and calling it separately from your HTML page. See "Using Polyfills for Progressive Enhancement" in Chapter 14 for a little bit more about Modernizr, and see Chapter 19 for more on scripts.

K By putting the script element in this conditional comment, only Internet Explorer 8 and below will load **respond.js**. Replace the **assets/js/** part of the **src** value with the path (if different) to **respond.js** on your site. When all is set, IE8 and below will understand the media queries and render the styles accordingly.

```
...

        <footer id="footer"
role="contentinfo">
...
        </footer>
    </div>
</div>

<!--[if lte IE 8]>
    <script src="assets/js/respond.js">
    ↪</script>
<![endif]-->
</body>
</html>
```

To build a page that adapts with media queries:

1. Create your content and HTML.

2. In the **head** element of your HTML page, type `<meta name="viewport" content="width=device-width, initial-scale=1.0" />`. (See the sidebar "Understanding the Viewport and Using the Viewport **meta** Element" in the "Understanding and Implementing Media Queries" section.)

3. Choose a design implementation approach. I recommend you first create a baseline of styles for all devices and then work your way up with media queries as demonstrated in the example. However, you could implement the desktop layout first (see Chapter 11) and then apply media queries for smaller devices afterward if you prefer.

4. Adapt your layout for different viewport widths, as appropriate for your content. Identify breakpoints and create associated media queries according to the steps described in "Understanding and Implementing Media Queries" and as demonstrated in 🅒, 🅔, 🅖, and 🅘. Along the way, make your page's layout fluid by using percentages for **width**, **margin**, and **padding** whenever possible.

5. If you'd like IE8 and below to render style rules within **min-width** and **max-width** media queries, obtain **respond.js** (as explained in "Rendering the media query styles in IE8 and below").

continues on next page

6. If you performed step 5, link to **respond.js** from your page by typing the following code above the **</body>** end tag Ⓚ.

```
<!--[if lte IE 8]>
    <script src="path/respond.js">
    ↪ </script>
<![endif]-->
```

The **path** equates to the location of the JavaScript file on your site, and **respond.js** equals the name of the JavaScript file you saved. The conditional comments around the **script** element are optional.

7. Test away! (See the "Mobile Coding and Testing Tools" sidebar.)

8. Refine your CSS and media queries in step 4 as necessary, and test until the page renders as desired across a range of devices.

TIP As shown in Ⓒ, Ⓔ, Ⓖ, and Ⓘ, all of the example page styles are in one style sheet. Alternatively, you could use the instructions found in "Understanding and Implementing Media Queries" to link to separate style sheets. Generally, a single file is better for performance as long as it isn't abnormally large, because the fewer the files the browser has to download, the sooner it will render the page.

TIP Eivind Uggedal's http://mediaqueri.es site is an ever-expanding gallery of responsive sites in the wild. It's worth a look for inspiration.

TIP Mobile Boilerplate (www.html5boilerplate.com/mobile) is a Web page starter template that incorporates many mobile best practices. The team behind it has also provided a handy matrix of specifications for modern mobile devices (both smartphones and tablets) at https://github.com/h5bp/mobile-boilerplate/wiki/Mobile-Matrices. As the page notes, the information can be helpful when crafting media queries.

TIP If you want to target styles for high-pixel-ratio devices such as the iPhone 4 and phones using the Opera Mobile 11 browser, use the following media query:

```
@media only screen and (-webkit-min-
→ device-pixel-ratio: 1.5), only
→ screen and (-o-min-device-pixel-
→ ratio: 3/2), only screen and
→ (min-device-pixel-ratio: 1.5) {
    /* your rules */
}
```

This recommendation comes courtesy of Mobile Boilerplate.

TIP 320 and Up (http://stuffandnonsense.co.uk/projects/320andup/), created by Andy Clarke and Keith Clark, is another starter template. It mirrors the methodology shown here, starting with a set of default styles and scaling up the layout from there with media queries.

TIP Luke Wroblewski nicely sums up the current state of affairs regarding building responsive sites at http://www.lukew.com/ff/entry.asp?1436. His article also contains several links for further reading.

TIP Maximiliano Firtman maintains a matrix of HTML5 and CSS3 support among modern mobile devices at http://mobilehtml5.org. (A lot of the information pertains to the advanced HTML5 features not covered in this book.)

TIP If `respond.js` isn't working, take a look at the "Support & Caveats" section at https://github.com/scottjehl/Respond. If you're still having trouble, try putting the highlighted code from Ⓚ just above your page's `</head>` end tag instead of before the `</body>` end tag.

TIP Learn more about conditional comments at www.quirksmode.org/css/condcom.html.

13

Working with
Web Fonts

Over the past few years, we have observed a renaissance in using fonts on the Web. Whereas we used to have a very limited choice of typefaces, now, thanks to Web fonts, we have myriad options for choosing typefaces for Web projects. Watching this change unfold is both fascinating and extremely exciting.

Choosing a font used to be relatively simple. By default, you were limited as to what fonts you could expect users to have installed on their computers. This is the reason most Web sites have their **body** copy set in Georgia, Arial, Verdana, or Trebuchet. These typefaces all look reasonably nice at small text sizes, and they come installed on any Mac or Windows computer.

It's not silly or an exaggeration to say that now we're in a whole new world.

In This Chapter

What Is a Web Font?

Web fonts are made possible thanks to the `@font-face` CSS rule, which allows CSS to link to a font on a server for use in a Web page.

Many people think Web fonts are new. In fact, Web fonts have been around since 1998. Netscape Navigator 4 and Internet Explorer 4 both adopted this technology, but neither of their implementations supported standard font file formats, so they didn't see much use. It wasn't until nearly a decade later that browsers started adopting this standard with more common font file types and that the use of Web fonts started to become commonplace.

Web font file formats

Web fonts come in an array of file types.

- Embedded OpenType (.eot). Internet Explorer 8 and earlier support only Embedded OpenType for use with `@font-face`. A Microsoft proprietary format, Embedded OpenType uses digital rights management technology to prevent unlicensed use of the font.

- TrueDoc. Originally used by Netscape Navigator 4.0, but no longer used or supported.

- TrueType (.ttf) and OpenType (.otf). The standard font file types used for desktop computers, TrueType and OpenType are widely supported by Mozilla Firefox (3.5 and later), Opera (10 and later), Safari (3.1 and later), Mobile Safari (iOS 4.2 and later), Google Chrome (4.0 and later), and Internet Explorer (9 and later). These formats do not use digital rights management.

- Scalable Vector Graphics (.svg). This format is used in special situations where other formats aren't supported, such as on earlier versions of mobile Safari.

- Web Open Font Format (.woff). This newer standard is designed specifically for use as a Web font. A Web Open Font Format font is a TrueType or OpenType font that has been compressed. The WOFF format also allows additional metadata to be attached to the file; this can be used by font designers or vendors to include licensing or other information beyond what is present in the original font. Such metadata does not affect the rendering of the font in any way, but it may be displayed to the user on request. The Web Open Font Format is supported by Mozilla Firefox (3.6 and later), Opera (11.1 and later), Safari (5.1 and later), Google Chrome (6.0 and later), and Internet Explorer (9 and later). Considering the wide support for Web Open Font Format, it seems to be the standard that the industry is settling on.

Web font browser support

The support for Web fonts across modern browsers is robust. Because earlier browsers support only specific font formats, working with these earlier browsers requires a bit of extra leg work on the part of the Web developer, but the reward for your efforts is rich typography in all modern desktop browsers, even most mobile smartphone browsers.

Legal issues

Fonts are, at a technical level, little pieces of software. I know people who make their living designing and building fonts, and it's a painstaking and detailed creative process that is not for the faint of heart. For this reason, it's understandable that it might ruffle some feathers that the `@font-face` feature even exists in the first place. After all, if a browser can link to and download a font, then that means anybody can download and install that font onto their computers, whether they've purchased it or not. This is why we, as Web designers and developers, must make

sure that any fonts we use in our Web sites are properly licensed for use on the Web. Most foundries and font services offer this licensing as a part of the purchase of a font or as an à la carte option. Alternatively, you can restrict the fonts you use to the free ones, such as those available at Font Squirrel (www.fontsquirrel.com) or The League of Moveable Type (www. theleagueofmoveabletype.com). Either way, make sure you're solidly in the right when it comes to using Web fonts in a project. You can do this by taking a look at the license for any fonts you purchase. As this is a pretty hot topic these days, this information is often mentioned on the Web site of the foundry you are purchasing from. When in doubt, contact the foundry to see what is allowed.

If you have purchased a font, and you know for sure that you can use it as a Web font, one tool that might come in handy is Font Squirrel's free `@font-face` generator (www.fontsquirrel.com/fontface/generator). This tool converts your font to all the Web font file types you will need for using it on the Web.

Where to Find Web Fonts

You have two options for using Web fonts in a Web site: self-hosting and Web font services. Both are perfectly valid options; however, they are quite different, with their own pros and cons to consider. As you weigh these pros and cons, you will also find that not all Web fonts are available everywhere. You may find that even though you want to go with self-hosting, the font you need is only available from a Web font service. This may require finding a close substitute or rethinking your approach. It pays to be flexible and to weigh all your options before you commit to a direction.

Self-hosting

Self-hosting a Web font is the more traditional approach and the one that we will cover in the step-by-step portion of this chapter. The fonts are served up from your own server, much like any other asset (such as an image or a CSS file). If there's a cost associated with the font, it's usually a one-time purchase, and it's up to you to upload the font files and include the code on your site.

It's relatively easy to find Web fonts for self-hosting, because there are plenty of them out there. And they come in a wide range of qualities and prices (some are even free). Some of the more popular ones are

- Font Squirrel (www.fontsquirrel.com)
- MyFonts (http://myfonts.com)
- The League of Moveable Type (www.theleagueofmoveabletype.com)
- FontShop (www.fontshop.com)

Web font services

Web font services typically offer a subscription approach to Web fonts. Instead of buying the fonts outright, you pay monthly or annually for the rights to use the fonts. These services host the fonts and give you a small piece of code to put into your Web pages. Depending on the service, this code is JavaScript or CSS. It includes all the necessary code for the font files to be served up from a remote server and displayed on your site. Many favor this approach because it's usually cheaper than purchasing fonts individually and it lets you try many different fonts.

A few of the more popular Web font services are

- Typekit (https://typekit.com)
- Fontdeck (http://fontdeck.com)
- Fonts.com (www.fonts.com)
- WebINK (www.webink.com)
- Google Web Fonts (www.google.com/webfonts)

By nature, Web font services are able to offer more features than self-hosting. Everything is hosted on the server, including the font files. If better font files or improved code for serving them become available, the services can easily provide it.

Additionally, many of these services use JavaScript to embed the code for serving up Web fonts. This comes with some benefits—and a few drawbacks too. JavaScript can do a lot in this process, like detecting which browser is loading the page and giving added control over the loading of the fonts themselves. This kind of control can lead to a genuinely better experience, because it lets Web font services customize the font formats and the code to serve them up. For instance, Typekit recently

A This screenshot composite shows the same code rendered by Internet Explorer 6 (top) and Chrome 15 (bottom). Notice that in Internet Explorer, the letters are lighter and not as smooth.

announced that they are serving up some of their display fonts using PostScript-based outlines (just to Windows browsers) to make the rendering smoother (http://blog.typekit.com/2011/09/15/improved-windows-rendering-for-more-typekit-fonts/). This kind of thing just isn't available without JavaScript.

The cost of this luxury, of course, is that you're relying 100 percent on JavaScript. If a user doesn't have JavaScript enabled on their browser, they will not be able to view your Web fonts. Additionally, JavaScript can affect the performance of a page. The user will have to wait for the JavaScript to load before any of the Web fonts load on the page. These are things to keep in mind as you decide how to bring Web fonts to your site.

Web font quality and rendering

Unfortunately, not all Web fonts are created equal. There can be noticeable differences in how Web fonts look across Web browsers. This is most apparent in some fonts that just don't look good in earlier versions of Internet Explorer.

As you select your fonts, do your best to vet potential Web font choices by examining how they will look in a variety of browsers **A**. This has gotten easier because many Web font companies are now providing live examples of the Web fonts, and some companies provide screenshots of the fonts on a variety of browsers and platforms.

TIP If you are stuck doing these tests on your own, try out the resource available from Web Font Specimen (http://webfontspecimen.com). It's a tool that lets you see how your Web fonts will look in a variety of contexts and sizes.

Downloading Your First Web Font

Downloading a free Web font is quick and easy. We will be using Font Squirrel; they even provide a `demo.html` file for you to see how these fonts look in action.

In the next section, we will explore the `@font-face` syntax and how to integrate a few Web fonts in a page.

To download a Web font from Font Squirrel:

1. Go to the `@font-face` Kits section of Font Squirrel (www.fontsquirrel.com/fontface), and select a font you want to use. I've selected League Gothic.

2. Click the Get Kit link **A**, and your download should immediately begin. The download is a ZIP archive.

3. Once the download is finished, open the archive, and you should have a folder containing Web fonts, a CSS file, and a `demo.html` file **B**.

A If you want to browse a bit further before downloading, feel free to click View Font to see a bit more about any of the fonts, along with download options. If you click View @ff Demo, you can see a full sampling of the font rendered as a Web font; this is a quick way to test how the font renders in a few different browsers.

B The expanded ZIP archive of League Gothic. As you can see, we have a `demo.html` file, four Web fonts, a license, and a style sheet.

Font-face Demo for the League Gothic Font

League Gothic Regular - Lorem ipsum dolor sit amet, consectetur adipisicing elit, sed do eiusmod tempor incididunt ut labore et dolore magna aliqua. Ut enim ad minim veniam, quis nostrud exercitation ullamco laboris nisi ut aliquip ex ea commodo consequat. Duis aute irure dolor in reprehenderit in voluptate velit esse cillum dolore eu fugiat nulla pariatur. Excepteur sint occaecat cupidatat non proident, sunt in culpa qui officia deserunt mollit anim id est laborum.

C Behold, the Web fonts rendering in all their glory!

To view the selected fonts in the demo.html file:

Open the **demo.html** file from the down-loaded font in your browser **C**. (See "Viewing Your Page in a Browser" in Chapter 2.)

This demo file shows that the Web font does indeed work. This is very exciting! Before you declare victory and call it a day, we'll explore more about how this works in the next section.

TIP Need some inspiration on which fonts to choose for your next project? The team at Typekit writes a wonderful blog with lots of great information on Web fonts and on typography in general. Try the "Sites we like" series for starters (http://blog.typekit.com/category/sites-we-like/).

TIP Do you need to use any of these fonts to mock something up in Photoshop? Install the TrueType (.ttf) font that comes with the Web font kit onto your computer. Once you install it, you can use it just like any other font on your computer.

Working with @font-face

You have downloaded the Web font kit and have tested the **demo.html** file in a browser. Now it's time to look under the hood and see how this works. Let's look at the code for **stylesheet.css** Ⓐ.

As you can see, the style sheet is fairly simple, with just one rule. Admittedly, that one rule is a big one!

The **@font-face** syntax is a bit different from traditional CSS. For one, it doesn't appear to follow the traditional method of a selector followed by property/value pairs that you read about in the beginning of Chapter 8. This rule starts with that odd-looking **@font-face** declaration.

One way to wrap your head around how **@font-face** works is to understand that a **@font-face** rule is just setting up a *tool* that can be used by the rest of your CSS. This rule doesn't affect the style of any specific element, but it does provide for the use of Web fonts for your CSS.

The first line in this rule is for the font family: **font-family: 'LeagueGothicRegular';**.

This establishes the name for this particular Web font. In this case, we are using **LeagueGothicRegular**, but it can be whatever you choose. You could choose **Banana** or **The Best Font Ever**. It's up to you.

The next few lines in the rule are for telling the browser where the font files live. These include the font file formats that give support to all the different browsers that support Web fonts. This syntax can look a little scary, but for our purposes it's not necessary to understand it completely. If you do want to dig a little deeper and find out why this looks the way it does, I recommend one of Ethan Dunham's

Ⓐ This is the **@font-face** rule that Font Squirrel provides in the kit. You may notice that it uses single quotes instead of the double quotes shown in CSS examples throughout the book. Single quotes and double quotes work the same way in CSS, so use whichever method you prefer.

```
@font-face {
font-family: 'LeagueGothicRegular';
src: url('League_Gothic-webfont.eot');
src: url('League_Gothic-webfont.eot?#iefix')
format('embedded-opentype'),
        url('League_Gothic-webfont.woff')
        ▸ format('woff'),
        url('League_Gothic-webfont.ttf')
        ▸ format('truetype'),
        url('League_Gothic-webfont.
        ▸ svg#LeagueGothicRegular')
        ▸ format('svg');
font-weight: normal;
font-style: normal;
}
```

B This is the CSS from the top of the `demo.html` file. Font Squirrel puts it here for demonstration purposes, but in practice, it's best to keep all your CSS in an external style sheet.

```
h1.fontface {
    font: 60px/68px 'LeagueGothicRegular',
    ↪Arial, sans-serif;
letter-spacing: 0;
}

p.style1 {
    font: 18px/27px 'LeagueGothicRegular',
    ↪Arial, sans-serif;
}
```

posts on Fontspring (www.fontspring.com/blog/further-hardening-of-the-bulletproof-syntax), where he explains the latest thinking on `@font-face` syntax.

Incorporating Web fonts into a Web page

We've covered the `@font-face` syntax, but we haven't actually put the Web fonts onto a page yet. Look at the code for `demo.html`, and let's examine the CSS code toward the top of the page B.

The included rules style the HTML with the League Gothic Web fonts. In the first rule, **60px/68px** specifies the font size and line height. Our example uses pixels for sizing, but you are welcome to specify in other units. The sizing is followed by specifying **'LeagueGothicRegular', Arial, sans-serif**. As you learned in "Specifying Alternate Fonts" in Chapter 10, when we specify multiple font families separated by commas like this, it is what's called a font stack. If a browser doesn't support the first font in a stack, it tries the next one down the line. Since we are using Web fonts here, it's a pretty good chance that the browser will just render the Web font; however, it's still a good practice to use a font stack. After all, not every browser supports Web fonts.

In this CSS, the **font** property refers to **LeageGothicRegular**, based on the **font-family** name that was set in the **@font-face** rule. What's more, it refers to it just as it would any other font. In the eyes of the browser, League Gothic may as well be installed on the computer that is visiting the Web site.

Now that you have tasted success, perhaps you want to try this with a few more Web fonts?

For our next task, we will use League Gothic for our main headline, and Crimson for the rest of the text on the page.

To work with multiple Web fonts:

Head back to Font Squirrel, and download the Crimson Web font kit, which includes six different fonts **C**.

To use multiple Web fonts in the same project:

1. There are a lot of fonts in the folder. For our purposes, we only need a few. Select the four Web font files for Crimson-Roman-webfont, and copy them over to the League Gothic folder in which we were working before. The results should look like **D**.

2. In **stylesheet.css**, type the following rule:

```
@font-face {
    font-family: "CrimsonRoman";
    src: url("Crimson-Roman-
    → webfont.eot");
    src: url("Crimson-Roman-
    → webfont.eot?#iefix")
    → format("embedded-opentype"),
        url("Crimson-Roman-webfont.
        → woff") format("woff"),
        url("Crimson-Roman-webfont.
        → ttf") format("truetype"),
        url("Crimson-Roman-webfont.
        → svg#CrimsonRoman")
        → format("svg");
}
```

This looks strikingly familiar, I'm sure. Now our style sheet has rules for League Gothic and Crimson Roman. The next step is to add the selectors to bring Crimson to the page.

C Just as you did before, click Get Kit to download the ZIP archive of the Web font kit. Once it has downloaded, expand the archive.

D Now we have two Web fonts in the same folder. Well done! (See the last tip regarding organizing files.)

3. After the **@font-face** rule you just typed, type the following on a new line:

```
body {
    font-family: "CrimsonRoman",
    → Georgia, serif;
}
```

4. On a new line, type the following rule to style an **h1**:

```
h1 {
    font-family: "LeagueGothic
    → Regular", Arial, sans-serif;
    font-size: 4em;
    font-weight: normal;
}
```

Next, we will create a new HTML document.

5. Inside the same folder, create a new HTML file called **demo2.html**.

6. Type the following code into your **demo2.html** page (notice how we are linking to the **stylesheet.css** that we were just editing):

```
<!DOCTYPE html>
<html lang="en">
<head>
    <meta charset="UTF-8" />
    <title>Our Awesome Web Font
    → Examples</title>
    <link rel="stylesheet"
    → href="stylesheet.css" />
</head>
<body>
<article>
    <h1>Headlines Are Very
    → Important</h1>
```

continues on next page

```
<p>There is more to Philadel
  phia than cheesesteaks,
  Rocky and the Liberty Bell.
  Did you know that Phila
  delphia used to be the
  capital of the United States?
  You will also find that
  Philadelphia has our nation's
  first Post Office, Hospital,
  and free library. That Ben
  jamin Franklin was one busy
  fellow!</p>

</article>

</body>

</html>
```

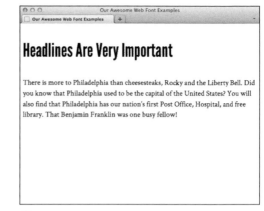

Ⓔ The headline uses League Gothic, and the rest of the page is rendered with Crimson.

7. Open **demo2.html** in a Web browser Ⓔ (see "Viewing Your Page in a Browser" in Chapter 2). Your fonts should be looking pretty good now.

TIP We used the font family names that came with the kit from Font Squirrel, such as LeagueGothicRegular. That is a nice, descriptive name, but another school of thought is to use a more *semantic* naming scheme, such as font-family: "Headline";. One benefit to choosing this scheme is that if you change your mind and decide to use a different Web font (instead of League Gothic), you only need to replace this @font-face rule with your new one and give it the font family name Headline.

TIP Although the steps and examples assume the font files, style sheet, and HTML page are in the same directory, it's good practice to organize them in folders (see "Organizing Files" in Chapter 2). Just make sure to change the paths to your style sheet in the HTML and to the Web fonts in the CSS, as necessary (see "URLs" in Chapter 1).

Styling Web Fonts and Managing File Size

Web fonts are a bit more complicated than working with regular fonts, so there are a few things you might want to watch out for when working with them.

One potential risk with Web fonts, especially when using more than one or two of them, is that they can start to weigh down the page. I'm not talking about bacon and doughnuts here—I'm talking about kilobytes and megabytes.

All of those fonts need to be downloaded to the user's computer before they can be rendered on the page. If you have half a dozen fonts on a page, this can slow down the Web site, especially for mobile users. My recommendation to you is to be prudent with your Web font choices. If you find yourself using seven Web fonts, then look for ways to consolidate your font choices.

One way to save some page weight is through *subsetting*. Subsetting is a way to trim down the size of the actual font by only including the characters you know you will use. For instance, if you are using League Gothic for headlines, but the design of the site requires that the headlines are always in all caps, then there is no need for lowercase letters. Using subsetting, you can remove those letters from the font, and the font's file size will be measurably smaller.

Additionally, you can select language-specific subsets for many fonts. If you are browsing the fonts at Font Squirrel, just click View Font instead of Get Kit for a particular font. From that font's page, choose **@font-face** Kit to see the language-specific options before downloading the kit. Explaining the nuts and bolts of subsetting is beyond the scope of this book, but Font Squirrel does have a tool that helps you do expert-level subsetting (www.fontsquirrel.com/fontface/generator).

Another situation in which Web fonts can act a little strangely is when you want to do what seems like the most basic styling of them. The thing to keep in mind is that Web fonts come in only one weight and one style per font. If you want to use bold or italic, you need to create separate rules for them, each with its own Web font file.

To add italic and bold:

1. Update the first paragraph of the **demo2.html** file with the following highlighted code:

```
<p>There is more to Philadelphia
 than cheesesteaks, Rocky and
 the Liberty Bell. <em>Did you
 know</em> that Philadelphia
 used to be the capital of the
 United States? You will also
 find that Philadelphia has
 our nation's first Post Office,
 Hospital, and free library.
 That Benjamin Franklin was one
 <b>busy</b> fellow!</p>
```

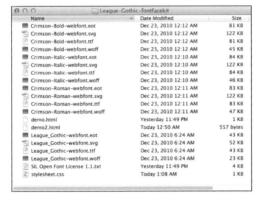

This is fake italic. It is not real.

This is not fake italic. It is real.

(A) Which one is the fake? Take note of the lowercase "k", "a," and "f."

⬤ ⬤ ⬤	League-Gothic-fontfacekit	
Name ▲	**Date Modified**	**Size**
▣ Crimson-Bold–webfont.eot	Dec 23, 2010 12:12 AM	81 KB
▣ Crimson-Bold–webfont.svg	Dec 23, 2010 12:12 AM	122 KB
▤ Crimson-Bold–webfont.ttf	Dec 23, 2010 12:12 AM	81 KB
▣ Crimson-Bold–webfont.woff	Dec 23, 2010 12:12 AM	45 KB
▣ Crimson-Italic–webfont.eot	Dec 23, 2010 12:10 AM	84 KB
▣ Crimson-Italic–webfont.svg	Dec 23, 2010 12:10 AM	122 KB
▤ Crimson-Italic–webfont.ttf	Dec 23, 2010 12:10 AM	84 KB
▣ Crimson-Italic–webfont.woff	Dec 23, 2010 12:10 AM	46 KB
▣ Crimson-Roman–webfont.eot	Dec 23, 2010 12:11 AM	83 KB
▣ Crimson-Roman–webfont.svg	Dec 23, 2010 12:11 AM	122 KB
▤ Crimson-Roman–webfont.ttf	Dec 23, 2010 12:11 AM	83 KB
▣ Crimson-Roman–webfont.woff	Dec 23, 2010 12:11 AM	47 KB
▢ demo.html	Yesterday 11:49 PM	1 KB
▢ demo2.html	Today 12:50 AM	557 bytes
▣ League_Gothic–webfont.eot	Dec 23, 2010 6:24 AM	43 KB
▣ League_Gothic–webfont.svg	Dec 23, 2010 6:24 AM	52 KB
▤ League_Gothic–webfont.ttf	Dec 23, 2010 6:24 AM	43 KB
▣ League_Gothic–webfont.woff	Dec 23, 2010 6:24 AM	23 KB
▢ SIL Open Font License 1.1.txt	Yesterday 11:49 PM	4 KB
▤ stylesheet.css	Today 1:08 AM	1 KB

(B) My, it's getting a bit crowded in here! The new bold and italic files for Crimson should be right at home next to the roman files. (See the last tip.)

2. Refresh your Web browser.

It appears that there are bold and italic right there in the paragraph. However, not everything is quite as it seems. In fact, the Web font for Crimson Roman doesn't have bold and italic built in, and the browser is faking the bold and italic by making the regular text a little fatter for the bold and a bit more slanted for the italic.

The fake effect is noticeable, even for the average viewer (A). What we want it to do is to use the proper bold and italic that were designed for the font. Great news—this is actually pretty easy!

To use the proper bold and italic for Crimson, we must get those Web font files and copy them over to this folder, just as we did in the section "To use multiple Web fonts in the same project."

3. Locate the Crimson-Bold and Crimson-Italic Web font files and copy all the formats of each (eight files total) over to the demo project folder (B).

Next, just as before, we need to add some new **@font-face** rules to bring in the bold and italic files.

continues on next page

4. Type the following into **stylesheet.css**:

```
@font-face {
    font-family: "CrimsonBold";
    src: url("Crimson-Bold-webfont.
    ⇢ eot");
    src: url("Crimson-Bold-webfont
    ⇢ .eot?#iefix") format(
    ⇢ "embedded-opentype"),
        url("Crimson-Bold-webfont.
        ⇢ woff") format("woff"),
        url("Crimson-Bold-webfont.
        ⇢ ttf") format("truetype"),
        url("Crimson-Bold-
        ⇢ webfont.svg#CrimsonBold")
        ⇢ format("svg");
}


@font-face {
    font-family: "CrimsonItalic";
    src: url("Crimson-Italic-
    ⇢ webfont.eot");
    src: url("Crimson-Italic-
    ⇢ webfont.eot?#iefix")
    ⇢ format("embedded-opentype"),
        url("Crimson-Italic-webfont.
        ⇢ woff") format("woff"),
        url("Crimson-Italic-webfont.
        ⇢ ttf") format("truetype"),
        url("Crimson-Italic-webfont.
        ⇢ svg#CrimsonItalic")
        ⇢ format("svg");
}
```

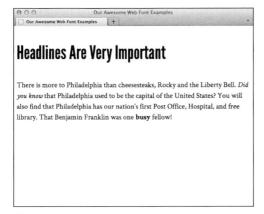

Headlines Are Very Important

There is more to Philadelphia than cheesesteaks, Rocky and the Liberty Bell. *Did you know* that Philadelphia used to be the capital of the United States? You will also find that Philadelphia has our nation's first Post Office, Hospital, and free library. That Benjamin Franklin was one **busy** fellow!

Ⓒ Multiple Web fonts, all styled properly.

5. Add the following rules to `stylesheet.css`:

```
b {
    font-family:"CrimsonBold",
      Georgia, serif;
    font-weight: normal;
}


em {
    font-family:"CrimsonItalic",
      Georgia, serif;
    font-style: normal;
}
```

The first rule styles the **b** element, giving it the font family of Crimson Bold, and setting the font weight to normal. If you forget to set **font-style** to **normal**, and you leave the font weight as is, then the browser will try to make the bold bolder, which just makes things worse! You handle the **em** element in the same way—changing the font family and also setting **font-style** to **normal**.

That should do it.

6. Take a look at **demo2.html** in your Web browser to see the proper italic and bold Ⓒ.

TIP You can apply bold and italic formatting with a Web font to any element containing text, not just those shown in the examples and steps. As always, choose the HTML element that best describes your content, and style it as desired.

TIP Remember that each style and weight that requires a new font file adds to the file size that the browser needs to download. This can affect performance. For this reason, many designers choose to use Web fonts only for headlines.

continues on next page

TIP There is a somewhat cleaner approach to writing the `@font-face` code that lets you have the extra variations in weight without having to write extra rules for `b`, `em`, or whichever elements you wish to style as bold or italic. However, it comes with some extra risks and isn't as compatible with Internet Explorer. To learn how to do it, check out this blog post by Roger Johansson: www.456bereastreet.com/archive/201012/font-face_tip_define_font-weight_and_font-style_to_keep_your_css_simple/.

TIP If you use Typekit or other Web font services that use JavaScript, check how they apply font styles, because they may have their own way to write the selectors for styling.

TIP Although the steps and examples assume the font files, style sheet, and HTML page are in the same directory **B**, it's good practice to organize them in folders (see "Organizing Files" in Chapter 2). Just make sure to change the paths to your style sheet in the HTML and to the Web fonts in the CSS, as necessary (see "URLs" in Chapter 1).

Enhancements with CSS3

One of the challenges faced by Web site authors over the years has been the limited number of options for producing rich layouts using CSS. In most cases, it meant using additional HTML and CSS and a lot of images. Combined, this resulted in pages that were more complicated, were less accessible, took longer to download and display in the browser, and were simply more fragile and difficult to maintain.

Browsers' rapid adoption of many new CSS3 properties in recent years has changed things for the better. Today, it's possible to create rounded corners, gradients, and drop shadows; adjust transparency; and more by using only CSS, resulting in Web pages that use less markup and fewer images. Perhaps most importantly, these pages download and display faster on less powerful devices such as smartphones as well as on desktop and laptop computers.

As CSS continues to evolve, the challenge that remains is that not all new CSS properties receive exactly the same level of support across browsers.

In this chapter, I'll look at several popular and useful CSS3 properties for rounding corners, creating shadows and gradients, using multiple backgrounds on a single element, and adjusting transparency. I'll also show you how browser makers and enterprising Web professionals are using the philosophy of progressive enhancement to bridge the gaps between browsers through vendor prefixes and JavaScript-based polyfills.

The code examples shown in this chapter are available on the book's site at www.bruceontheloose.com/htmlcss/examples/. The site also includes an extra example that combines the CSS3 effects discussed in this chapter.

A An example of the `border-radius` property, which requires using vendor prefixes (as in the first two declarations shown) to support older versions of Firefox and of Webkit-based browsers such as Chrome and Safari. The latest versions of those browsers no longer use the prefixed property and instead use the non-prefixed property (that is, simply `border-radius: 10px;`). As always, the last competing declaration in a rule takes precedence, which is why the non-prefixed version should be last.

```
div {
    -moz-border-radius: 10px;
    -webkit-border-radius: 10px;
    border-radius: 10px;
}
```

Understanding Vendor Prefixes

Although much of what falls under the umbrella of CSS3 has not yet reached the W3C's Candidate Recommendation stage (which would mean that the specifications are complete), many parts have already been implemented in recent versions of Firefox, Internet Explorer, Chrome, Safari, and Opera.

In order to future-proof unfinished (and occasionally competing) CSS implementations that are subject to change, those that require it have been implemented in browsers using what are called vendor prefixes. These allow each browser to introduce its own support for a property without conflicting with the final specification or with other browsers. Additionally, vendor prefixes provide a way to ensure that, once a specification has matured or been finalized, existing Web sites using the experimental implementations do not break.

Each of the major browsers has its own prefix: `-webkit-` (Webkit/Safari/Chrome), `-moz-` (Firefox), `-ms-` (Internet Explorer), `-o-` (Opera), and `-khtml-` (Konqueror). They are used, as you might guess, by placing the prefix before the CSS property name, but you should keep in mind that you don't need all the prefixes all the time. In most cases, you'll only need the `-moz-` and `-webkit-` prefixes, as you'll see throughout the examples in this chapter. To future-proof your work, it's recommended that you include a non-prefixed version as the last declaration **A**.

In practice, and as you'll see throughout this chapter, this means less HTML but more CSS to achieve a desired effect.

While vendor prefixes often add a considerable amount of repetition in your CSS, it's a small price to pay for progress—and one that Web professionals have largely accepted, if only because they've found ways to automate the tedious work of adding prefixed properties to their code (see the last tip) .

TIP Not all CSS3 properties, such as `text-shadow` and `opacity`, require the use of prefixes for any browser (see "Adding Drop Shadows to Text" and "Setting the Opacity of Elements," respectively). In addition, not all browsers require the use of a specific prefix for a property.

TIP If a property's syntax changes before being finalized, you can include multiple versions in your CSS. You can find examples of this in this chapter's demonstrations of the `border-radius` and `gradient` properties (see "Rounding the Corners of Elements" and "Using Gradient Backgrounds," respectively). Each browser will interpret only the specific syntax it understands, ignoring the rest.

TIP Although there is no defined order in which you should include prefixed properties, always include a non-prefixed version of the property last in order to future-proof your work **A**. This will ensure that nothing breaks once browsers begin to support the non-prefixed properties.

TIP Services such as the CSS3 Generator (www.css3generator.com) can make short work of creating these properties, saving you time and a lot of typing. See www.bruceon theloose.com/tools/ for a list of other tools that generate code for you.

B The CSS3 Generator (www.css3generator.com) can be a beneficial learning tool while also removing the repetitious work of writing prefixed and non-prefixed CSS properties for browsers that support them.

border-radius	1.0	9.0	1.0	3.0	10.3
box-shadow	3.5	9.0	1.0	3.0	10.5
text-shadow	3.0	10.0	1.0	1.1	10.0
multiple backgrounds	3.6	9.0	1.0	1.3	10.0
gradients	3.6	10.0	2.0	4.0	11.1
opacity	1.0	9.0	1.0	2.0	10.0

Ⓐ This table illustrates when browser support was first introduced for each of the CSS properties discussed in this chapter. For a more detailed breakdown, look up each property at www. caniuse.com or www.findmebyip.com/litmus/.

A Quick Look at Browser Compatibility

Because the pace at which browsers are evolving has increased significantly in recent years, it's important to understand when you can expect reliable support for these new CSS properties. Here's a snapshot of when browsers began providing basic support for each of the properties covered in this chapter Ⓐ.

Using Polyfills for Progressive Enhancement

A commonly accepted approach to creating Web sites today is based on what is known as *progressive enhancement*, which emphasizes creating content and functionality that is accessible to all users at a basic level regardless of Web browser while providing more capable browsers an enhanced experience. In simpler terms, progressive enhancement means that it's perfectly acceptable for Web sites to look and behave differently in different Web browsers as long as the content is accessible.

An example of this in practice is the Dribbble site (http://dribbble.com) , which uses CSS3 to provide a richer experience for more modern browsers through progressive enhancement. Older browsers, such as Internet Explorer 8 **B**, are presented a slightly different visual experience with no loss of functionality.

There may be times when you want to bridge the limits of a less-capable browser with the capabilities of another by using *polyfills* (or *shims*, as they're often called).

Typically implemented using JavaScript, polyfills enable a degree of support for HTML5 and CSS3 APIs and properties in less-capable browsers while silently falling back to official support when the capabilities exist natively in a browser. It's important to note that these generally incur a performance penalty, because JavaScript is measurably slower in less-capable Web browsers (particularly in older versions of Internet Explorer).

A The Dribbble site uses several CSS3 properties, such as **border-radius** and CSS3 gradient backgrounds, to provide a richer experience for users with more-modern browsers, but it is built with less-capable browsers in mind.

B When viewed in older browsers (such as Internet Explorer 8) that do not support **border-radius**, the experience changes. Rounded corners, such as those in the pill-shaped navigation buttons, are simply squared off with no loss of functionality. Everything still works. This is one aspect of progressive enhancement in action.

You can find out more about progressive enhancement, the many types of polyfills, and responsibly bridging the gap between older browsers and new Web technologies on the site for Modernizr (www.modernizr.com), a JavaScript library C. Faruk Ateş created Modernizr in 2009, and now Paul Irish, Alex Sexton, and Ryan Seddon are part of the team. See the tips for more about Modernizr.

C Modernizr is a JavaScript library that allows you to detect whether a browser supports specific HTML5, CSS3, and other features to create Web site experiences that are optimized based on available capabilities.

D You can find a growing list of JavaScript polyfills to bridge HTML5 and CSS3 features in older browsers that do not support them natively.

TIP Today, Web browsers include functionality that either encourages users to download updated versions periodically (as Firefox, Safari, and Internet Explorer do) or downloads updates silently in the background (as Chrome does).

TIP JavaScript-based tools such as Modernizr assist by providing clues when (among other things) new or experimental CSS is available in a browser, allowing you to use CSS and JavaScript to progressively enhance pages and create a richer experience for more-capable browsers without leaving others behind.

TIP You can find a community-managed list of useful JavaScript polyfills at GitHub (https://github.com/Modernizr/Modernizr/wiki/HTML5-Cross-Browser-Polyfills) D, as part of the Modernizr project. The ones listed in the "CSS3 Styles" section will be of particular interest, especially Jason Johnston's PIE (www.css3pie.com), which provides support to Internet Explorer 6–9 for many of the CSS3 effects discussed in this chapter (of them, IE9 requires PIE to display linear gradients only; it has native support for the others). Be aware that using PIE may affect your site's performance in these older browsers.

Rounding the Corners of Elements

Using CSS3, you can round the corners of most elements, including form elements, images, and even paragraphs of text, without needing additional markup or images (Ⓐ and Ⓑ). Like the **margin** and **padding** properties, the **border-radius** property has both long- and short-form syntaxes. Refer to Ⓔ for some basic examples showing different ways you can use the **border-radius** property.

To round all corners of an element equally:

1. Type **-moz-border-radius: *r***, where ***r*** is the radius value of the corners, expressed as a length (with units) Ⓒ.

2. Type **-webkit-border-radius: *r***, where ***r*** is the radius value of the corners, using the same value from step 1.

3. Type **border-radius: *r***, where ***r*** is the radius value of the corners, using the same value from step 1. This is the standard short-form property syntax.

Ⓐ This document contains example **div**s with **class** attributes. Each is used to illustrate a different use of **border-radius** and the different syntaxes for setting all corners equally, for setting a single corner individually using the long-form syntax, for creating an elliptical corner, and for shapes such as circles.

```
...
<body>
<div class="all-corners"></div>
<div class="one-corner"></div>
<div class="elliptical-corners"></div>
<div class="circle"></div>
</body>
</html>
```

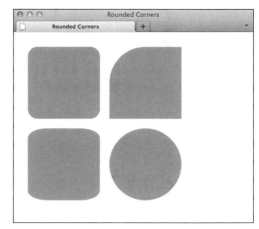

Ⓑ Browsers that support the **border-radius** property with or without vendor prefixes should render the examples similarly to these. Note that there are subtle visual differences between implementations, particularly in older versions of Safari and Firefox.

The CSS for the four **border-radius** examples, including the vendor-prefixed properties necessary to support older versions of Firefox and Safari. Note that Opera 10.5 and Internet Explorer 9 do not require a prefixed property. Refer to ⒟ for more information.

```
div {
    background: #999;
    float: left;
    height: 150px;
    margin: 10px;
    width: 150px;
}

.all-corners {
    border-radius: 20px;
}

.one-corner {
    -moz-border-radius-topleft: 75px;
    -webkit-border-top-left-radius: 75px;
    border-top-left-radius: 75px;
}

.elliptical-corners {
    -moz-border-radius: 40px / 20px;
    -webkit-border-radius: 40px / 20px;
    border-radius: 40px / 20px;
}

.circle {
    -moz-border-radius: 75px;
    -webkit-border-radius: 75px;
    border-radius: 75px;
}
```

To round one corner of an element:

1. Type **-moz-border-radius-topleft: *r***, where ***r*** is the radius value of the top-left corner, expressed as a length (with units). This is the older, non-standard syntax used by versions of Firefox prior to 4.0 (see the second-to-last tip). You may skip this step if you don't mind that these older versions will display square corners ⒞.

2. Type **-webkit-border-top-left-radius: *r***, where ***r*** is the same value as in step 1.

3. Type **border-top-left-radius: *r***, where ***r*** is the radius value of the top-left corner, expressed as a length (with units). This is the standard long-form property syntax.

Note that these steps describe how to style the top-left corner only, but you can style the other corners individually too. Here's how:

- To round the top-right corner: Replace **top-left** in steps 2 and 3 with **top-right**. Optionally, replace **topleft** in step 1 with **topright**.

- To round the bottom-right corner: Replace **top-left** in steps 2 and 3 with **bottom-right**. Optionally, replace **topleft** in step 1 with **bottomright**.

- To round the bottom-left corner: Replace **top-left** in steps 2 and 3 with **bottom-left**. Optionally, replace **topleft** in step 1 with **bottomleft**.

To create elliptical corners:

1. Type `-moz-border-radius: x / y`, where *x* is the horizontal radius value of the corners and *y* is the vertical radius value of the corners, expressed as a length (with units) **C**. The values should be separated by a forward slash.

To create a circle using border-radius:

1. Type `-moz-border-radius: r`, where *r* is the radius value of the element (with length units). To create a circle, you can use the short-form syntax, and the value of *r* should be half the height or width of the element **C**.

2. Type `-webkit-border-radius: r`, where *r* is the radius value of the element (with length units). This adds support for older versions of Webkit-based browsers such as Chrome and Safari.

3. Type `border-radius: r`, where *r* is the radius value of the element (with length units). This is the standard non-prefixed syntax.

TIP Older browsers that don't support `border-radius` will simply render the element with square corners.

TIP Like the CSS `border`, `margin`, and `padding` properties, `border-radius` can be specified using either a long- or short-form style, depending on whether you need to specify different values for each corner.

Firefox Firefox 3.6	-moz-border-radius-topleft -moz-border-radius-topright -moz-border-radius-bottomleft -moz-border-radius-bottomright
Webkit Safari 3 and 4 Chrome 3	-webkit-border-top-left-radius -webkit-border-top-right-radius -webkit-border-bottom-left-radius -webkit-border-bottom-right-radius
Standard CSS3 Syntax Firefox 4 Chrome 4 Safari 5 Internet Explorer 10 Opera 10.5	border-top-left-radius border-top-right-radius border-bottom-left-radius border-bottom-right-radius

D The different long-form `border-radius` syntaxes required to support Firefox 3.6 and Webkit (Safari/Chrome), along with the official unprefixed syntax used by the most recently released browser versions.

ⓔ These examples show just a few ways you can specify the **border-radius** values—either using a pair of values or by specifying all four corners individually. Using the short-form syntax also removes the need to worry about the more complex long-form syntax, particularly if you need to support versions of Firefox prior to 4.0.

```
div {
    /* Makes the radius of the top-left and
    → bottom-right corners 5px and the top-
    → right and bottom-left corners 10px */
    border-radius: 5px 10px;
}

div {
    /* Makes the radius of the top-left
    → corner 5px, the top-right corner 10px,
    → the bottom-right corner 0, and the
    → bottom-left corner 20px */
    border-radius: 5px 10px 0 20px;
}

div {
    /* Makes the radius of the top-left
    → corner 20px, the top-right corner 0,
    → the bottom-right corner 0, and the
    → bottom-left corner 0 */
    border-radius: 20px 0 0 0;
}

div {
    /* Makes the radius of the top-left
    → corner 30px */
    -moz-border-radius-topleft: 30px;
    -webkit-border-top-left-radius: 30px;
    border-top-left-radius: 30px;
}
```

TIP If you want to round all four corners of an element by the same radius value, you can use the simpler **border-radius** shorthand syntax, just as you would for setting basic border style properties ⓔ. For example, **border-radius: 12px;** gives all four corners of an element a radius of 12 pixels.

TIP The **border-radius** property is not inherited.

TIP Although it's possible to specify the radius of a rounded corner using percentages, this is generally not recommended, because some browsers may treat this inconsistently based on the calculated dimensions of an element.

TIP When **border-radius** support was added to Firefox and Safari, Firefox initially used a non-standard, long-form syntax (**-moz-border-radius-topleft, -moz-border-radius-topright, -moz-border-radius-bottomleft, -moz-border-radius-bottomright**) for specifying the property for individual corners of an element ⓓ, but as of Firefox 4.0 it has followed the recommended syntax (**border-top-left-radius, border-top-right-radius, border-bottom-left-radius, border-bottom-right-radius**). The most recent versions of all browsers now support the non-prefixed **border-radius** property.

TIP If writing CSS for **border-radius** seems confusing or tedious, don't worry. Web-based services such as the CSS3 Generator (www.css3generator.com) by Randy Jensen can help make short work of creating rounded corners and save you a lot of typing. You enter radius values, and it displays the results on a sample element so you can see if it's the effect you want. Better yet, it writes all the CSS for you, which you can copy and paste into your style sheet. It does the same for other CSS3 properties. Much easier!

Adding Drop Shadows to Text

Iriginally included as part of the CSS2 specification, removed in CSS2.1, and later resurrected in CSS3, the **text-shadow** property allows you to add dynamic drop-shadow effects to text in elements such as paragraphs, headings (Ⓐ through Ⓒ), and more without first needing to render the text using an image.

To add a drop shadow to an element's text:

1. In the CSS, type **text-shadow:**.

2. Type the four values for **x-offset**, **y-offset**, **color**, and **blur radius** (with length units) without commas separating them; for example, **2px 2px 5px #999**. (See the tips for more about what values are allowed.)

3. Type **;** (a semicolon).

To add multiple drop shadow styles to an element's text:

1. In the CSS, type **text-shadow:**.

2. Type the four values for **x-offset**, **y-offset**, **color**, and **blur radius** (with length units) without commas separating them. (See the tips for more about what values are allowed.)

3. Type **,** (a comma).

4. Repeat step 2 using different values for each of the four properties.

5. Type **;** (a semicolon).

Ⓐ Two example implementations that demonstrate the use of **text-shadow**.

```
...
<body>
<h1>Text Shadow</h1>
<h1 class="multiple">Multiple Text Shadows
↪ </h1>
</body>
</html>
```

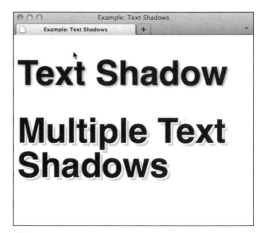

Ⓑ What the two examples should look like when displayed in a browser that supports the **text-shadow** property.

It's possible to add more than one drop shadow to a single element by separating the sets of property values with a comma, as shown applied to the `.multiple` class selector. This allows you to combine drop shadows to create unique and interesting effects.

```
h1 {
    font-family: Helvetica, Arial,
sans-serif;
    font-size: 72px;
    line-height: 1em;
    text-shadow: 2px 2px 5px #999;
}

.multiple {
    text-shadow: 2px 2px 0 rgba(255,255,
     255,1), 6px 6px 0 rgba(50,50,50,.25);
}
```

To reset text-shadow back to its default value:

1. In the CSS, type `text-shadow:`.

2. Type `none`.

3. Type `;` (a semicolon).

TIP Vendor prefixes are not needed for the `text-shadow` property.

TIP Although the syntax may appear similar, it's not possible to individually specify the four property values for `text-shadow` as you can for borders and backgrounds.

TIP The initial property value is `none` if not set.

TIP The `text-shadow` property is inherited.

TIP The property accepts four values: `x-offset` with length units, `y-offset` with length units, an optional `blur radius` with length units, and finally a `color` value. If you do not specify the blur radius, it is assumed to be zero.

TIP The `x-offset` and `y-offset` values can be positive or negative integers; that is, both `1px` and `-1px` are valid. The `blur radius` value must be a positive integer. All three values can also be zero.

TIP Color can be specified using hex, RGB, RGBA, or HSLA values (see "CSS colors" in Chapter 7) and can be placed first or last in the order of property values.

TIP It's possible to achieve advanced effects by applying multiple shadows to a single element. To do so, separate the individual shadow properties with a comma; for example, `text-shadow: 2px 2px 0 #999, 6px 6px 0 rgba(50,50,50,.25);` ⑤. The shadows are stacked in reverse order, with the first being the topmost and any subsequent shadows stacking one after another below.

Adding Drop Shadows to Other Elements

The **text-shadow** property allows you to apply shadows to an element's text, but the **box-shadow** property allows you to add shadows to the elements themselves (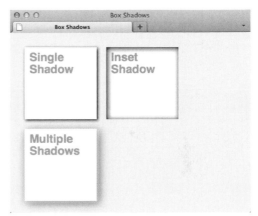 **A** and **B**). Although based on the same basic set of attributes, **box-shadow** allows two more optional attributes—the **inset** keyword attribute, and the **spread** attribute to expand or shrink the shadow.

The **box-shadow** property also differs from its **text-shadow** counterpart in that it is less widely supported and requires vendor prefixes for some browser versions.

Although you'll most often use only four, the **box-shadow** property accepts six values: **x-offset** and **y-offset** with length units, an optional **inset** keyword, an optional **blur-radius** with length units, an optional **spread** value with length units, and a **color** value. If you do not specify the **blur-radius** or **spread** values, they are assumed to be zero.

A This document contains three **div**s that demonstrate using **box-shadow** to add one or more shadows.

```
...
<body>
<div class="shadow">
<h1>Single Shadow</h1>
</div>

<div class="inset-shadow">
<h1>Inset Shadow</h1>
</div>

<div class="multiple">
<h1>Multiple Shadows</h1>
</div>
</body>
</html>
```

B What the three examples should look like when displayed in browsers that support the **box-shadow** property.

C The CSS used to create the three examples. Note the two additional vendor-prefixed properties required to ensure that it displays correctly in older Firefox and Webkit browsers. Browsers that don't understand **box-shadow** will simply ignore those CSS rules, and pages will render without the shadows.

```
div {
    background: fff;
    float: left;
    height: 150px;
    margin: 10px;
    width: 150px;
}

.shadow {
    background: #ccc;
    -moz-box-shadow: 2px 2px 5px #000;
    -webkit-box-shadow: 2px 2px 5px #000;
    box-shadow: 2px 2px 5px #000;
}

.inset-shadow {
    -moz-box-shadow: inset 2px 2px 10px
    → #000;
    -webkit-box-shadow: inset 2px 2px
    → 10px #000;
    box-shadow: inset 2px 2px 10px #000;
}

.multiple {
    -moz-box-shadow: 2px 2px 10px
    → rgba(0,255,0,.75), 5px 5px 20px
    → rgba(125,0,0,.5);
    -webkit-box-shadow: 2px 2px 10px
    → rgba(0,255,0,.75), 5px 5px 20px
    → rgba(125,0,0,.5);
    box-shadow: 2px 2px 10px
    → rgba(0,255,0,.75), 5px 5px 20px
    → rgba(125,0,0,.5);
}
```

To add a drop shadow to an element:

1. In the CSS, type `-moz-box-shadow:`.

2. Type the values for **x-offset**, **y-offset**, **blur-radius** (all with length units), and **color** **C**.

3. Type `-webkit-box-shadow:` and repeat step 2.

4. Type **box-shadow:** and repeat step 2 again.

To create an inset shadow:

1. In the CSS, type `-moz-box-shadow:`.

2. Type **inset** after the colon, followed by a space.

3. Type the values for **x-offset**, **y-offset**, **blur-radius** (all with length units), and **color**; for example, **2px 2px 5px #000**.

4. Type `-webkit-box-shadow:` and repeat steps 2 and 3.

5. Type **box-shadow:** and repeat steps 2 and 3 again.

To apply multiple shadows
to an element:

1. In the CSS, type **-moz-box-shadow:**.

2. Type the values for **x-offset**, **y-offset**, **blur-radius** (all with length units), and **color**; for example, **2px 2px 5px #000**.

3. Type **,** (a comma).

4. Repeat step 2 using different values for each of the properties Ⓒ.

5. Type **-webkit-box-shadow:** and repeat steps 2 through 4.

6. Type **box-shadow:** and repeat steps 2 through 4 again.

To reset box-shadow back
to its default value:

1. In the CSS, type **-moz-box-shadow: none**.

2. Type **-webkit-box-shadow: none**.

3. Type **box-shadow: none**.

TIP Firefox 3.5 and 3.6 require the -moz-vendor prefix for the box-shadow property, and some older versions of the Webkit-based browsers such as Safari and Chrome require the –webkit- prefix. Opera 10.5 and Internet Explorer 9 support the box-shadow property, so they do not require a vendor prefix. You can find detailed information on when vendor prefixes are needed for box-shadow at http://css3please.com.

TIP The initial property value is none if not set.

TIP The box-shadow property is not inherited.

TIP Color can be specified using hex, RGB, RGBA, or HSLA values (see "CSS colors" in Chapter 7) and can be placed first or last in the order of property values.

TIP The x- and y-offset values can be positive or negative integers; that is, both 1px and -1px are valid. The blur radius value must be a positive integer. The values for each of these three attributes can also be zero.

TIP It's possible to achieve advanced effects by applying multiple shadows to a single element. To do so, separate the individual shadow properties with a comma; for example, box-shadow: 2px 2px 0 #999, 6px 6px 0 rgba(50,50,50,.25); ⒞. The shadows are stacked in reverse order, with the first being the topmost and any subsequent shadows stacking one after another below.

TIP It's possible to create drop shadows in older versions of Internet Explorer by using the proprietary filter and -ms-filter properties, but this also requires additional HTML markup and CSS rules to resolve the issues created by using the filter.

Applying Multiple Backgrounds

One of the most sought-after features in CSS has been the ability to specify multiple backgrounds on a single HTML element (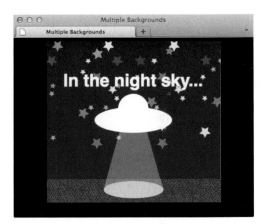 and ⒸⒸ). This simplifies your HTML code by reducing the need for elements whose sole purpose is to attach additional images using CSS, making it easier to understand and maintain. Multiple backgrounds can be applied to just about any element.

To apply multiple background images to a single element:

1. Type **background-color: *b***, where *b* is the color you want applied as the fallback background for the element Ⓓ.

2. Type **background-image: *u***, where *u* is a comma-separated list of absolute or relative path image references.

3. Type **background-position: *p***, where *p* is a comma-separated set of positive or negative **x-** and **y-offset** pairs with length units. There should be one set of coordinates for each background image.

4. Type **background-repeat: *r***, where *r* is a comma-separated list of **repeat-x**, **repeat-y**, or **no-repeat** values (see "Changing the Text's Background" in Chapter 10), one for each image.

Ⓐ Applying multiple backgrounds.

```
...
<body>
<div class="night-sky">
    <h1>In the night sky...</h1>
</div>
</body>
</html>
```

Ⓑ Browsers that support multiple backgrounds will render our example by layering the images on top of each other, with the first one in the comma-separated list at the top of the stacking order. Adding multiple background images to a single element is straightforward, but to ensure that the content is still accessible, you need to provide a simple fallback in the CSS rules by using **background-color**.

In the night sky...

C This is what you will see in browsers that do not support the multiple background image syntax. If you adhere to the philosophy of progressive enhancement, you should include either a **background-color** or single **background-image** property before the **background-image** rule as a safety net for less-capable browsers.

D To use multiple backgrounds, you need to use the four individual long-form background properties: **background-color**, **background-image**, **background-position**, and **background-repeat**. Using each, you can adjust how images are positioned and repeated.

```
.night-sky {
    background-color: #333;
    background-image: url(ufo.png),
    → url(stars.png), url(stars.png),
    → url(sky.png);
    background-position: 50% 102%, 100%
    → -150px, 0 -150px, 50% 100%;
    background-repeat: no-repeat,
    → no-repeat, no-repeat, repeat-x;
    height: 300px;
    margin: 0 auto;
    padding-top: 36px;
    width: 75%;
}
```

TIP Vendor prefixes are not required when specifying multiple backgrounds.

TIP You can use the standard short-form syntax with multiple background images by separating each set of background parameters with a comma. For example, you can use background: url(image.jpg) 0 0 no-repeat, url(image2.jpg) 100% 10% no-repeat; to accomplish the same thing as the more repetitive long-form syntax.

TIP Background images are layered on top of each other, with the first image at the top and the last image at the bottom of the stacking order.

TIP If a background-color value is specified, it will be applied as the final background layer behind any images and will be used by browsers that do not support multiple background images.

TIP Browsers that do not support multiple background images will ignore the background-image property and attempt to fall back to the value for background-color.

Using Gradient Backgrounds

Gradient backgrounds, also new in CSS3, allow you to create transitions from one color to another without using images (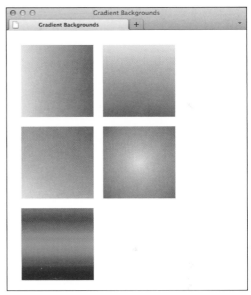(A)

and (B)). The specification is still in flux, but browser support is increasing as the specification is inching closer to being finalized.

Although the background gradient syntax requires vendor prefixes to support the widest array of browsers, I'll ease you into using gradients by demonstrating them using the non-prefixed properties. Additional information can be found in the tips for this section, and you can find complete examples, including the required vendor-prefixed properties, in the code download for this chapter.

In keeping with the philosophy of progressive enhancement, it's a good idea to include a fallback option for browsers that don't support the background gradient property. This can be a simple background color or image and can be specified as a separate rule prior to the background gradient rule in your CSS.

There are two primary styles of gradients (linear and radial) that can be created using CSS, each with a different set of required and optional parameters ((C) and (D)).

(A) Five ways to implement gradients using only CSS.

```
<body>
<div class="horizontal"></div>
<div class="vertical"></div>
<div class="diagonal"></div>
<div class="radial"></div>
<div class="multi-stop"></div>
</body>
```

(B) Browsers that support gradient backgrounds should render the five examples similarly to what is shown, provided the appropriate vendor prefixes are appended to the example code. Current browsers all require vendor prefixes for background gradients. Browsers that do not understand the gradient syntax will use the fallback **background** property, if specified.

C A simple two-color horizontal gradient using the standard linear gradient syntax and also containing a simple fallback color for browsers that don't support CSS gradients.

```
div {
    float: left;
    height: 150px;
    margin: 10px;
    width: 150px;
}

.horizontal {
    background: #cedce7;
    background: linear-gradient(left,
    → #cedce7,#596a72);
}
```

D Creating a vertical gradient is just a matter of changing the first property to have a value of **top** or **bottom**.

```
.vertical {
    background: #cedce7;
    background: linear-gradient(top,
    → #cedce7,#596a72);
}
```

E It's possible to create angled gradients by simply changing the value of the first property, which sets the origin of the gradient to an angle value. Angles are specified as the angle between a horizontal line and the gradient line in a counterclockwise direction; for example, **0deg** creates a left-to-right horizontal gradient, whereas **90deg** creates a bottom-to-top vertical gradient.

```
.diagonal {
    background: #cedce7;
    background: linear-gradient(45deg,
    → #cedce7, #596a72);
}
```

To create a fallback background color:

Type **background-color:** *color*, where *color* is any of the supported color names or hex, RGB, RGBA, or HSL values.

To define the type of gradient:

Type **background:** *type***(**, where *type* is **linear-gradient** or **radial-gradient**.

To define where the gradient starts:

Type **left** followed by **,** to start the gradient from the left side of the element.

Or type **right** followed by **,** to start the gradient from the right side of the element.

Or type **top** followed by **,** to start the gradient from the top side of the element.

Or type **bottom** followed by **,** to start the gradient from the bottom side of the element.

Or type an **angle** value (like **0deg**, **45deg**, or **120deg**) followed by **,** to change the angle of the gradient. Angles are specified as the angle between a horizontal line and the gradient line in a counterclockwise direction **E**.

Or type **center** (for radial gradients only) followed by **,** to start the gradient from the center of the element **F**.

F Radial gradients include additional optional parameters, but the simplest example uses the same parameters as a linear gradient. In this case, the origin for the gradient is the center of the element, denoted by the **center** keyword.

```
.radial {
    background: #cedce7;
    background: radial-gradient(center,
    → #cedce7,#596a72);
}
```

To specify the starting and ending colors:

Type **c1, c2**), where **c1** and **c2** are the starting and ending colors in the gradient. Colors can be specified using color names or hex, RGB, RGBA, or HSL values.

To create a gradient with multiple colors:

1. Repeat the first two techniques for creating either a linear or radial gradient by specifying the type of gradient and the starting point (**B** through **D**).

2. Then type **c1 p1, c2 p2, c3 p3**), where **c#** is a color (specified using color names or hex, RGB, RGBA, or HSL values) and **p#** is the position of the color (specified as a percentage from 0 to 100) **G**.

TIP Earlier versions of Webkit-based browsers (for example, Safari 4) used a non-standard syntax to specify gradient backgrounds. Safari 5 and new versions of Chrome both support the same syntax as Firefox but at the moment still require the `-webkit-` and `-moz-` vendor prefixes.

TIP You can find the most current and detailed information on using the gradient properties from the teams at Mozilla (https://developer.mozilla.org/en/CSS/-moz-radial-gradient) and Webkit (http://webkit.org/blog/1424/css3-gradients/).

TIP You can create multicolor gradients by specifying more than two colors and then using one of the additional optional parameters (`color-stop`) in the gradient syntax **G**.

G Multi-step gradients (those that use more than two colors) follow the same pattern but require the **color-stop** position, which is specified using a percentage value from 0 to 100.

```
.multi-stop {
    background: url(multi-stop-gradient.jpg)
    → 0 0 repeat-x;
    background: linear-gradient(top, #ff0000
    → 0%, #00ff00 50%, #0000ff 100%);
}
```

TIP Color can be specified using color names or hex, RGB, RGBA, or HSLA values.

TIP Although support is improving in the latest versions of Web browsers, the gradient syntax is still in flux and requires vendor prefixes, including ones for Internet Explorer and Opera.

TIP You can use visual tools like ColorZilla's gradient generator (http://colorzilla.com/gradient-editor/) or Microsoft's CSS gradient background maker (http://ie.microsoft.com/testdrive/graphics/cssgradientbackground maker/) to take the tedious work out of creating CSS gradient code. These tools will also automatically generate all the vendor prefix properties for you to ensure the maximum level of compatibility with older browser versions.

TIP Internet Explorer 10 includes support for CSS gradients natively. Versions prior to 10 can use the proprietary `filter: progid:DXImageTransform.Microsoft. gradient` filter to create gradients, or they can be created by using additional HTML markup and SVG (as is the case for Internet Explorer 9). Tools such as the ColorZilla gradient editor mentioned in the previous tip can produce all the code you need for this, so don't worry about having to write it yourself.

TIP You should accommodate unsupported browsers by specifying either a `background-color` or a `background-image`, but you should keep in mind that images in the CSS will be downloaded by browsers whether they are used or not.

TIP Firefox and Webkit additionally support prefixed `repeating-linear-gradient` and `repeating-radial-gradient` capabilities.

Setting the Opacity of Elements

Using the **opacity** property, you can change the transparency of elements, including images (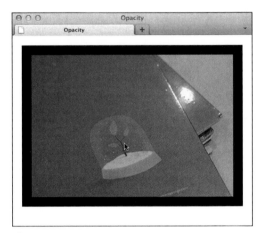 A and B).

To change the opacity of an element:

Type **opacity:** *o*, where *o* is the level of opaqueness of the element to two decimal places (without units).

TIP The default value of opacity is 1. Values can be set in two-decimal-place increments from 0.00 (completely transparent) to 1.00 (completely opaque) (C and D).

TIP You can produce some interesting and practical effects by using the opacity property along with the :hover pseudo-property. For example, you can change the opacity of an element when a user mouses over it, or give an element such as an optional form field the appearance of being disabled.

A This document contains a **div** element with an image enclosed.

```
...
<body>
<div class="box">
     <img src="sleeves.jpg" width="420"
height="296" alt="Record Sleeves" />
</div>
</body>
</html>
```

B Here's what our example looks like with the **div** element's **opacity** set to the default value of 1.

C By making the **opacity** value less than 1, you can make an element and its children transparent. In this case, I changed the opacity to 50 percent, or .5. Including a zero before the decimal point is not required.

```
img {
     vertical-align: top;
}

.box {
     background: #000;
     opacity: .5;
     padding: 20px;
}
```

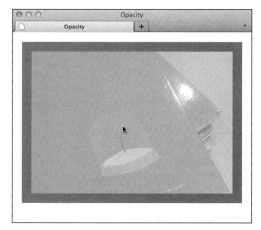

D Here's what our example looks like with the **div** element's **opacity** value set to .5 (50 percent opaque). Notice that the solid black background of the **div** element is now gray and that the image is semi-transparent.

E This simple example demonstrates how you can apply Internet Explorer's proprietary filters for versions prior to 9, which don't natively support opacity. The **-ms-filter:** declaration covers IE8, while the simpler **filter:** declaration supports IE versions 5 through 7.

```
div {
    /* Sets the element's opacity to 50% and
    → includes the optional proprietary
    → filter declarations for Internet
    → Explorer prior to version 9 and also
    → ensures the element hasLayout for
    → those older versions of Internet
    → Explorer by using the zoom: 1
    → declaration */
    -ms-filter: progid:DXImageTransform.
    → Microsoft.Alpha(opacity=50);
    filter: alpha(opacity=50);
    opacity: .5;
    zoom: 1;
}
```

TIP As with the opacity values for **RGBA** and **HSLA** color units, you do not need to include a leading zero before the decimal point when setting a value for opacity.

TIP Despite how it may appear, opacity is not an inherited property. Children of an element with an opacity of less than 1 will also be affected, but the opacity value for those child elements will still be 1.

TIP The opacity property does not natively work in Internet Explorer versions prior to 9, but it is possible to achieve by using the proprietary -ms-filter: progid:DXImageTransform.Microsoft. Alpha(opacity=50); and filter: alpha(opacity=50); properties in addition to zoom: 1; on the element that triggers hasLayout in the browser **E**. You can find out more about these filters at CSS Tricks (http://css-tricks.com/64-css-transparency-settings-for-all-broswers/), and you can find out more about where hasLayout came from and how it may affect you at http://haslayout.net/haslayout.

15

Lists

HTML contains elements specifically for creating lists of items. You can create plain, numbered, or bulleted lists, as well as lists of descriptions. You can also nest one list (or more) inside another one.

All lists are formed by a principal element to specify what sort of list you want to create (**ul** for *unordered list*, **ol** for *ordered list*, and **dl** for *description list*, known as a definition list before HTML5) and secondary elements to specify what sort of list items you want to create (**li** for a list item in an **ol** or **ul**, and **dt** for the term with **dd** for the description in a **dl**).

Of these, the unordered list is the most common across the Web, as it's the de facto standard for marking up most kinds of navigation (there are several examples of this throughout the book). But all three list types have their place, which you'll learn about in this chapter.

In This Chapter

Creating Ordered and Unordered Lists

The ordered list is perfect for providing step-by-step instructions on how to complete a particular task (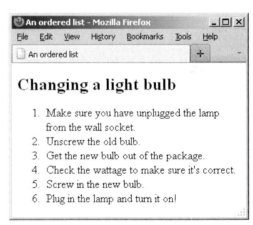**A** and **B**) or for creating an outline (complete with links to corresponding sections, if desired) of a larger document. It is also the proper choice for marking up breadcrumb navigation (see the tips). In short, any list of items for which the order is meaningful.

Unordered lists may be the most widely used lists on the Web, because they're used to mark up navigation (**C** and **D**).

To create lists:

1. Type **<ol>** for an ordered list or **<ul>** for an unordered list. For an ordered list, you can include any of the optional attributes **start**, **type**, and **reversed**. (See "Choosing Where to Start List Numbering" regarding **start**, "Choosing Your Markers" regarding **type**, and the last tip to learn about **reversed**, which is not yet supported and so has no visible effect.)

2. Type **<li>** (that's the first two letters of the word "list") to begin the first list item. For an ordered list, you can include the optional **value** attribute (see "Choosing Where to Start List Numbering" for details).

3. Add the content (such as text, links, or **img** elements) to be included in the list item.

4. Type **</li>** to complete each list item.

5. Repeat steps 2 through 4 for each new list item.

6. Type **</ol>** or **</ul>**, to match the start tag (from step 1) and complete the list.

A There is no official way to format a list's title. Most of the time, a regular heading (see Chapter 3) or a paragraph (see Chapter 4) is the appropriate lead-in to a list like the one in this example. It's conventional, but not required, to indent the list items to indicate that they are nested in an **ol** (the same is true when using a **ul**). That doesn't make them indent when displayed, though; that's purely a function of the CSS applied to the list.

```
...
<body>
<h1>Changing a light bulb</h1>
<ol>
    <li>Make sure you have unplugged the
    ↪ lamp from the wall socket.</li>
    <li>Unscrew the old bulb.</li>
    <li>Get the new bulb out of the
    ↪ package.</li>
    <li>Check the wattage to make sure
    ↪ it's correct.</li>
    <li>Screw in the new bulb.</li>
    <li>Plug in the lamp and turn it
    ↪ on!</li>
</ol>
</body>
</html>
```

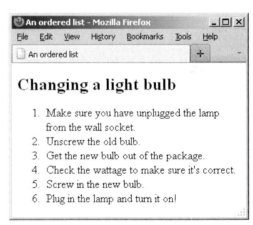

B This list uses the default option of Arabic numerals to create a numbered ordered list. You can change this with CSS. Both ordered and unordered lists display indented by default, whether or not they are indented in the HTML itself **A**.

C The list item element of unordered lists is identical to those of ordered lists. Only the `ul` element is different.

```
...
<body>
<h1>PageWhacker, version 12.0: Features</h1>
<ul>
    <li>New or improved features marked
    ⇥ with a solid bullet.</li>
    <li>One-click page layout</li>
    <li>Spell checker for 327 major
    ⇥ languages</li>
    <li>Image retouching plug-in</li>
    <li>Special HTML filters</li>
    <li>Unlimited Undo's and Redo's</li>
    <li>Automatic book writing</li>
</ul>
</body>
</html>
```

D Unordered lists have solid round bullets by default. You can change these with CSS.

TIP Don't make the decision about which list type to use based on which marker style you want next to your content. After all, you may always change that with CSS (yes, you can even show bullets on an ordered list). Instead, think about your list's meaning—would it change if the order of the list items changed? If the answer is yes, mark up the list as an ordered list. Otherwise, use an unordered list.

TIP Regarding using lists to mark up groups of links, use unordered lists to mark up most groups of links, such as your main navigation, a list of links to videos or related stories, or the links in your footer. Use ordered lists to mark up breadcrumb navigation, since the links represent a distinct sequence of links (in other words, the order is meaningful). Breadcrumb navigation is often displayed horizontally above the main content area to indicate where the current page exists in the site's navigation path. For instance, on a page providing the details of a particular mobile phone, it could be: Home > Products > Phones > The Fone 3.0. Each item in the list except the last would be a link, since the visitor is on the page for The Fone 3.0. I've included this example in Figure **E** of "Styling Nested Lists" (the breadcrumb navigation is between the main navigation on top and the large product name heading).

TIP The completed sample Web page in Chapter 11 demonstrates lists used and presented in a variety of ways. It includes an unordered list for the navigation (styled horizontally and with bullets), an unordered list for a list of images (styled horizontally with no markers), and an ordered list for a list of chronological monthly archive links (styled with bullets). Chapter 3 also has examples that include a `ul` as navigation.

TIP Unless you specify otherwise with CSS, items in ordered lists will be numbered with Arabic numerals (1, 2, 3, and so on) **A**.

TIP Items in unordered lists have solid round bullets by default **B**. You can choose different bullets (see "Choosing Your Markers") or even create your own (see "Using Custom Markers").

continues on next page

TIP Be sure to place list content only within `li` elements. For instance, you aren't allowed to put content between the start `ol` or `ul` tag and the first `li` element.

TIP You can nest various types of HTML elements in `li` elements, such as any of the phrasing content elements (like `em`, `a`, `cite`, and so on). Nesting paragraphs and `div`s in list items is valid too, though there are fewer cases in which you'd have occasion to do so.

TIP You may create one list inside another—known as *nesting* lists—even mixing and matching ordered and unordered lists. Be sure to nest each list properly, using all the required start and end tags. See examples of nested ordered and unordered lists in "Styling Nested Lists."

TIP Lists are indented from the left margin by default, though you can remove the indentation (or add more) with CSS. Depending on how much you reduce the left margin, your bullets might stick outside your content or disappear beyond the left edge of the window. (You can see an example of them sticking out in Chapter 11.)

TIP If you specify your content direction as right-to-left, as you would if the page's base language were Hebrew, for instance, the lists are indented from the right margin instead of the left. To achieve this, set the `dir` attribute on your page's `html` element: `<html dir="rtl" lang="he">`. In this case, `lang` is set to he for Hebrew. You also can set `dir` and `lang` on elements within the `body` to override the settings on the `html` element. The `dir` attribute defaults to `ltr`.

TIP At the time of this writing, browser support for the Boolean `reversed` attribute is non-existent, but its purpose is to indicate a descending ordered list (you can specify it with either `<ol reversed>` or `<ol reversed="reversed">`).

Ⓐ Here is our simple ordered list, to which we will apply capital Roman numerals (**upper-roman**).

```
...
<body>
<h1>The Great American Novel</h1>
<ol>
    <li>Introduction</li>
    <li>Development</li>
    <li>Climax</li>
    <li>Denouement</li>
    <li>Epilogue</li>
</ol>
</body>
</html>
```

Ⓑ You can apply the **list-style-type** property to any list item. If you had two lists on this page, one of which was unordered, you could apply capital Roman numerals to just the ordered one by changing the selector in this example to **ol li**.

```
li {
    list-style-type: upper-roman;
}
```

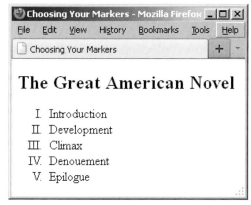

Ⓒ Now the ordered list has capital Roman numerals. Note that most browsers align numeric markers to the right (but to the left of the list item content, as shown).

Choosing Your Markers

When you create a list, be it ordered **Ⓐ** or unordered, you can also choose what sort of markers (that is, bullets, numbers, or images) should appear to the left of each list item.

To choose your markers:

In the style sheet rule, type **list-style-type:** *marker*, where *marker* is one of the following values:

- **disc** (●)
- **circle** (○)
- **square** (■)
- **decimal** (1, 2, 3, ...)
- **upper-alpha** (A, B, C, ...)
- **lower-alpha** (a, b, c, ...)
- **upper-roman** (I, II, III, IV, ...) (**Ⓑ** and **Ⓒ**)
- **lower-roman** (i, ii, iii, iv, ...)

To display lists without markers:

In the style sheet rule, type
`list-style-type: none`.

TIP By default, unordered lists use discs for the first level, circles for the first nested level, and squares for the third and subsequent level lists. See "Styling Nested Lists" for more on this topic.

TIP The disc, circle, and square bullets vary slightly in size and appearance from one browser to another.

TIP You may apply any of the marker styles to both `ol` and `ul` with `list-style-type`. In other words, an `ol` could have square markers and a `ul` decimal markers.

TIP You can also specify an ordered list's marker type with the `type` attribute, although I recommend defining the list style type in CSS instead whenever possible. The acceptable values for `type` are A, a, I, i, and 1, which indicate the kind of numeration to be used (1 is the default). For example, `<ol type="I">` specifies uppercase Roman numerals.

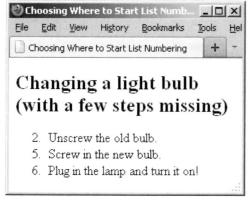

Ⓐ In this example, I've omitted some steps but want to maintain the original numbering of the remaining steps. So I start the whole list at **2** (with `start="2"`) and then set the value of the second item to **5** (with `value="5"`). Both attributes are optional and don't have to be used together as they are here.

```
...
<body>
<h1>Changing a light bulb (with a few steps
↪ missing)</h1>
<ol start="2">
    <li>Unscrew the old bulb.</li>
    <li value="5">Screw in the new bulb.
    ↪ </li>
    <li>Plug in the lamp and turn it on!
    ↪ </li>
</ol>
</body>
</html>
```

Ⓑ Notice that not only are the first and second items numbered as we've specified, but the third item ("Plug in the lamp and turn it on!") is also affected.

Choosing Where to Start List Numbering

You might want to start a numbered list with something other than a default **1** Ⓐ.

To determine the initial value of an entire list's numbering scheme:

Within the `ol` start tag, type `start="n"`, where **n** represents the list's initial value.

To change the numbering of a given list item in an ordered list:

In the desired `li` item, type `value="n"`, where **n** represents the value for this list item. The `value` is always specified numerically and is converted by the browser automatically to the type of marker specified with CSS or with the `type` attribute (see "Choosing Your Markers").

TIP If you use `start`, always give it a numeric value even if you decide to have the list display with letters or Roman numerals (see "Choosing Your Markers"). Browsers will display the markers as intended.

TIP The `value` attribute overrides the `start` value.

TIP When you change a given list item's number with the `value` attribute, the subsequent list items are also renumbered accordingly.

TIP Using `value` also is handy to indicate that two or more items hold the same spot in an ordered list. Take, for example, a list with the top five finishers in a road race. Normally, they would display as 1, 2, 3, 4, 5. But if there were a tie for second, by specifying the *third* list item as `<li value="2">`, the list would display as 1, 2, 2, 3, 4.

TIP Your list can include more than one `li` with a `value` attribute.

Using Custom Markers

If you get tired of circles, squares, and discs, or even Roman numerals, you can create your own custom marker with an image. You don't have to change your HTML to do so Ⓐ, just the CSS Ⓑ.

To use custom markers:

1. In the rule for the desired list or list item, type **list-style: none;** to turn off normal markers.

2. In the rule for the desired list, set the **margin-left** and/or **padding-left** properties to dictate how much the list items will be indented. (Both properties are usually necessary to achieve similar results across browsers.) Settings of **margin-left: 0;** and **padding-left: 0;** remove all indentation. Note that if you've set **dir="rtl"** for your content, you should adjust the **margin-right** and **padding-right** properties instead. See the tips in "Creating Ordered and Unordered Lists" for more details about **dir**, **lang**, and right-to-left languages in these list types.

3. In the rule for the **li** elements within the desired list, type **background: url(_image.ext_) _repeat-type horizontal vertical_;**, where **_image.ext_** is the path and file name of the image you'd like to use as the custom marker; **_repeat-type_** is a value of **no-repeat** (typical), **repeat-x**, or **repeat-y**; and **_horizontal_** and **_vertical_** are values for the position of the background within the list items Ⓑ.

   Type **padding-left: _value_;**, where **_value_** is at least the width of the background image in order to prevent the list item content from overlapping the custom marker.

Ⓐ This is just like any ordinary unordered list, but with a little CSS Ⓑ we can make it look different Ⓒ.

```
...
<body>

<h1>PageWhacker, version 12.0: Features</h1>
<ul>
      <li>One click page layout</li>
      <li>Spell checker for 327 major
       · languages</li>
      <li>Image retouching plug-in</li>
      <li>Unlimited Undo's and Redo's</li>
      <li>Automatic book writing</li>
</ul>
</body>
</html>
```

Ⓑ First you turn off the default markers (so you don't see both bullets and the arrows) and adjust how far the list items will be indented. Then you assign the arrow background image to each list item, positioning it a couple of pixels from the top of the **li** and being sure to add left padding so the text doesn't overlap the arrows. Be sure to include the proper path to your image in the **url** part of the **background**. The **url** should be where the image is located relative to the style sheet, not to the HTML page (see "Changing the Text's Background" in Chapter 10 for related information).

```
ul {
      /* turn off the default markers */
      list-style: none;

      /* set indentation of list items. */
      margin-left: 0;
      padding-left: 15px;
}

li {
      /* show image 2 pixels from top of item */
      background: url(arrow-right.png)
       · no-repeat 0 2px;

      /* bump the text over to make room for
       · the arrow */
      padding-left: 25px;
}
```

C The default bullets are replaced by the arrow image.

TIP There should be no space between `url` and the opening parenthesis **B**. Quotes around the URL are optional.

TIP Note that relative URLs are relative to the location of the style sheet, not the Web page.

TIP Apply a class to one or more `li` elements and define a style rule for it if you want to apply a custom marker to certain list items within a list. Depending on the look you want, you may need to adjust the left margin of the `li` items with the class rather than the margin and padding of the parent `ol` or `ul` element.

TIP Another way to display custom markers is with the `list-style-image` property. Here's an example: `li { list-style-image: url(image.png); }`. However, it never quite lived up to its promise, because browsers don't render them consistently. Plus, you have more control over the placement of image markers with the method shown in **B**, which is why people tend to favor that approach. The `list-style-image` property overrides `list-style-type`. But if for some reason the image cannot be loaded, the marker specified with `list-style-type` is used.

Controlling Where Markers Hang

By default, lists are indented from the left margin (of their parent). Your markers can either begin halfway to the right of that starting point 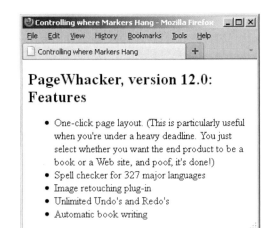, which is the default, or flush with the rest of the text (called inside) (**B** and **C**).

To control where markers hang:

1. In the style sheet rule for the desired list or list item, type `list-style-position:`.

2. Type `inside` to display the markers flush with the list item text **B**, or `outside` to display the markers to the left of the list item text (the default).

> **TIP** By default, markers are hung outside the list paragraph.

> **TIP** The `list-style-position` property is inherited.

A This demonstrates how browsers render wrapped text in a list item relative to the marker by default. The markers are outside the content. You can change this with CSS. I've added a bit more text to the first feature so that the effect of hanging markers inside is obvious (**B** and **C**).

B Setting `list-style-position` to `inside` changes the display.

```
li {
    list-style-position: inside;
}
```

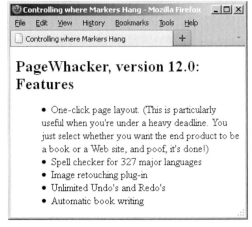

C The markers for the lines that wrap begin at the left margin of the list item, instead of outside it to the left.

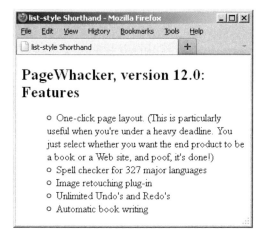

Ⓐ This style rule is equivalent to setting the `list-style-position` to `inside` and the `list-style-type` to `circle`. It's just shorter. You may also specify the `list-style-image` in the shorthand (see the first tip).

```
li {
    list-style: inside circle;
}
```

Ⓑ The result is the same as in Ⓒ in the "Controlling Where Markers Hang" section, except I've switched the markers to circles.

Setting All List-Style Properties at Once

Just as it has shorthand properties for **background**, **border**, **font**, **outline**, and more, CSS has one for the **list-style** features Ⓐ.

To set all the list-style properties at once:

1. Type **list-style:**.
2. If desired, specify the kind of markers that should appear next to the list items, if any (as described in "Choosing Your Markers").
3. If desired, specify the custom marker that should be used for list items (as described in the last tip of "Using Custom Markers").
4. If desired, specify whether markers should be hung outside the list paragraphs or flush with the text (as described in "Controlling Where Markers Hang").

TIP If you want to specify a **list-style-image** in the shorthand property, the example in Ⓐ would instead be typed as **li { list-style: url(arrow-right.png) inside square; }**.

TIP You may specify any or all of the three **list-style** properties. Ⓐ shows two.

TIP You might think that by omitting one of the three properties, you won't be affecting it, but that's not always the case. Any properties not explicitly set are returned to their defaults (**disc** for **list-style-type**, **none** for **list-style-image**, and **outside** for **list-style-position**).

TIP The properties may be specified in any order.

TIP The **list-style** property is inherited.

Styling Nested Lists

You may insert one type of list in another; the inner list is known as a *nested* list. You can do this with ordered and unordered lists (together or independently). There's also another kind of nested list; see "Creating Description Lists" for an example.

Nesting lists is particularly useful with an outline structured as ordered lists—where you may want several levels of items (Ⓐ through Ⓒ)—or for navigation with sub-menus structured as unordered lists (Ⓓ and Ⓔ; see the sidebar for more details). You can style nested lists a variety of ways, as the examples demonstrate.

To style nested lists:

1. For styling the outermost list, type *toplevel* li {*style_rules*}, where *toplevel* is the list type of the outermost list (for example, **ol**, **ul**, or **dt**) and *style_rules* are the styles that should be applied.

2. For the second-level list, type *toplevel 2ndlevel* li {*style_rules*}, where *toplevel* matches the *toplevel* in step 1 and *2ndlevel* is the list type of the second-level list.

3. For the third-level list, type *toplevel 2ndlevel 3rdlevel* li {*style_rules*}, where *toplevel* and *2ndlevel* match the values used in steps 1 and 2 and *3rdlevel* is the kind of list used for the third nested list.

4. Continue in this fashion for each nested list that you wish to style.

Ⓐ There are four nested lists here, one in the Introduction list item, one in the Development item, one in the Climax item and one, highlighted and in bold, inside the "Boy gives Girl ultimatum" item (which is inside the Climax item).

```
...
<body>

<h1>The Great American Novel</h1>
<ol>
    <li>Introduction
        <ol>
            <li>Boy's childhood</li>
            <li>Girl's childhood</li>
        </ol>
    </li>
    <li>Development
        <ol>
            <li>Boy meets Girl</li>
            <li>Boy and Girl fall in love
            ⇥</li>
            <li>Boy and Girl have fight
            ⇥</li>
        </ol>
    </li>
    <li>Climax
        <ol>
            <li>Boy gives Girl ultimatum
                <ol>
                    <li>Girl can't believe
                    ⇥her ears</li>
                    <li>Boy is indignant at
                    ⇥Girl's indignance</li>
                </ol>
            </li>
            <li>Girl tells Boy to get
            ⇥lost</li>
        </ol>
    </li>
    <li>Denouement</li>
    <li>Epilogue</li>
</ol>

</body>
</html>
```

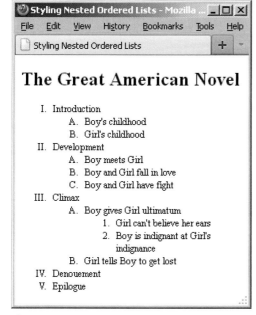

B You can format each level of a nested list separately. If you use ems or percentages for the font size of the list text, be sure to add the `li li {` `font-size: 1em; }` (or **100%** instead of **1em**) so that it doesn't shrink to the point of being illegible in the nested lists (see the last tip).

```
ol li {
    font-size: .75em;
    list-style-type: upper-roman;
}

ol ol li {
    list-style-type: upper-alpha;
}

ol ol ol li {
    list-style-type: decimal;
}

li li {
    font-size: 1em;
}
```

C The first-level lists (**ol li**) have capital Roman numerals. The second-level lists (**ol ol li**) have capital letters. The third-level lists (**ol ol ol li**) have Arabic numerals.

TIP Your selectors should reflect the types of nested lists in your document; that is, you might need something like `ul ul ol li`.

TIP Alternatively, you could add a class to each nested list and style it accordingly. But the method shown here allows you to control the styling without changing the HTML.

TIP Ordered lists always use Arabic numerals (1, 2, 3) by default, regardless of their nesting position. Use `list-style-type` to specify other numbering schemes (see "Choosing Your Markers"). According to *The Chicago Manual of Style,* the correct nesting order for lists is I, A, 1, a (and the 1 and a levels are repeated from then on).

TIP By default, the first level of an unordered list will have solid round bullets, the next will have empty round bullets, and the third and subsequent levels will have square bullets. Again, use `list-style-type` to specify the type of bullets you want (see "Choosing Your Markers").

TIP Since list items (`li` elements) can be nested within other list items, you have to be a bit careful with font sizes specified in relative values. If you use something like `li {font-size: .75em; }`, the font size of the outermost list item will be 75% of its parent element; so if the parent is a default 16 pixels high, the outermost list item will be 12 pixels, and not a problem. However, the font size of the first *nested* list item will be 75% of *its* parent (the first list item, which is 12 pixels) and thus will be only 9 pixels high. Each level gets worse quickly. One solution is to add `li li {font-size: 1em; }` **B** (or 100% instead of 1em). Now nested list items will always be the same size as top-level ones **C**. (Thanks to Eric Meyer, www.meyerweb.com.)

continues on next page

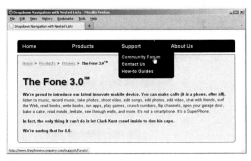

D Here's another example of nested lists. In this case, a navigation menu is structured as an unordered list with two nested unordered lists for sub-navigation. Note that each nested **ul** is contained within its parent start tag **<li>** and end tag **</li>**. With a little CSS, you can lay out the navigation horizontally, hide the sub-menus by default, and show them based on the visitor's interaction **E**.

```
...
<body>
<nav role="navigation">
    <ul class="nav">
        <li><a href="/">Home</a></li>
        <li><a href="/products/">Products</a>
            <ul>
                <li><a href="/products/phones.html">Phones</a></li>
                <li><a href="/products/accessories.html">Accessories</a></li>
            </ul>
        </li>
        <li><a href="/support/">Support</a>
            <ul>
                <li><a href="http://www.thephoneycompany.com/support/forum/">Community Forum
                → </a></li>
                <li><a href="/support/contact-us.html">Contact Us</a></li>
                <li><a href="/support/how-to-guides.html">How-to Guides</a></li>
            </ul>
        </li>
        <li><a href="/about-us/">About Us</a></li>
    </ul>
</nav>
...
</body>
</html>
```

E Both the Products and Support list items contain sub-menus in nested **ul**s, but neither shows by default because of the CSS I've applied. In this case, the Support sub-menu displays because I've hovered over the **li** that contains both the Support link and the related sub-menu nested list **D**. The complete CSS is available on the book site.

Using Nested Lists for Drop-Down Navigation

One use for nested lists is to structure drop-down (or fly-out) navigation menus **D**. You can style the navigation with CSS so that each sub-menu shows only when the visitor hovers over the parent list item **E** and hides again when the visitor moves the pointer away.

You can implement this effect a few ways, but it always involves leveraging the **:hover** pseudo-class as part of the selector that reveals the sub-menu. Here's one such approach to hide the nested lists by default and then reveal them when the visitor hovers:

```
/* Default state of sub-menus */

.nav li ul {
    left: -9999em; /* moves sub-menus off-screen */
    position: absolute;
    z-index: 1000;
}


/* State of sub-menus when parent li hovered upon */

.nav li:hover ul {
    display: block; /* for older versions of IE */
    left: auto; /* puts sub-menus back in natural spot */
}
```

The corresponding HTML is shown in **D**. You'll need more CSS than this to implement the horizontal layout, remove the bullets from the list items, and otherwise adjust the presentation to meet your needs. The complete HTML and CSS for the page shown in **E** is available on the book site at www.bruceontheloose.com/htmlcss/examples/chapter-15/dropdown-nav.html. I've also included several comments in the code.

You can use a similar approach for a vertical navigation with fly-out sub-menus that appear to the side.

Creating Description Lists

HTML provides a type of list specifically for describing an association between names (or terms) and values in groups. Dubbed *description lists* in HTML5, they were known as definition lists in previous versions of HTML.

According to the HTML5 specification, "Name-value groups may be terms and definitions, metadata topics and values, questions and answers, or any other groups of name-value data." Each list is contained in a **dl**, and each name-value group within it has one or more **dt** elements (the names or terms) followed by one or more **dd** elements (their values). **A** shows a basic description list example. Aside from some boldfacing applied with a simple style rule **B**, it renders by default as **C**.

B You may want to add formatting to the terms in the **dt** elements to help them stand out **C**.

```
dt {
    font-weight: bold;
}
```

C By default, the name (the **dt**) is aligned to the left, and the value (the **dd**) is indented. The names are in bold thanks to the simple rule in **B**. Otherwise they'd appear as normal text.

A This is the most basic type of definition list, with one **dt** matched with one **dd** in each name-value group. Each group is separated by a blank line merely for legibility when reading the code. The space between groups isn't required, doesn't change the meaning of the content, and doesn't affect its rendering.

```
...
<body>

<h1>List of Horror Movie Legends</h1>

<dl>
    <dt>Boris Karloff</dt>
    <dd>Best known for his role in <cite>Frankenstein</cite> and related horror films, this
      ↪ scaremaster's real name was William Henry Pratt.</dd>

    <dt>Christopher Lee</dt>
    <dd>Lee took a bite out of audiences as Dracula in multiple Hammer horror classics.</
    dd>

    ...
</dl>

</body>
</html>
```

D This example includes multiple **dt**s paired with a single **dd** in each name-value group because the defined terms have more than one spelling but share the same definition.

```
...
<body>

<h1>Defining words with multiple spellings</h1>

<dl>
    <dt><dfn>bogeyman</dfn>, n.</dt>
    <dt><dfn>boogeyman</dfn>, n.</dt>
    <dd>A mythical creature that lurks under
    → the beds of small children.</dd>

    <dt><dfn lang="en-gb">aluminium
    → </dfn>, n.</dt>
    <dt><dfn>aluminum</dfn>, n.</dt>
    <dd>...</dd>
</dl>

</body>
</html>
```

E This will add more space between the name-value groups than they have by default.

```
dd + dt {
    margin-top: 1em;
}
```

F Now you can tell where one group of descriptions stops and the next starts. The rule in **E** works because "aluminium, n." is contained in a **dt** right after the **dd** from the previous name-value group.

All of the following arrangements are valid for a group of **dt** and **dd** elements within a **dl**:

- A single **dt** grouped with a single **dd** **A**. (Also see **G** under Director and in the nested description list under Cast.) This is the most common occurrence.

- A single **dt** grouped with multiple **dd** elements. See Writers in **G**.

- Multiple **dt** elements grouped with a single dd **D**. (With sample styling adjustments shown in **E** and **F**.)

- Multiple **dt** elements grouped with multiple **dd** elements. An example of this would be if bogeyman/boogeyman in **D** had more than one definition.

Use the **dfn** element around the names in the **dt**s to indicate that the list is defining terms, such as in a glossary **D**. (See "Defining a Term" in Chapter 4 for more about **dfn**.)

continues on next page

You may also nest description lists G and style them with CSS as you please H. When a **dl** is nested in another one, it automatically indents another level by default I (you can also change that with CSS, of course).

To create description lists:

1. Type **<dl>**.

2. Type **<dt>**.

3. Type the word or short phrase that will be described or defined, including any additional semantic elements (such as **dfn**).

4. Type **</dt>** to complete the name in the name-value group.

5. Repeat steps 2 through 4 as necessary if the group has more than one name or term D.

6. Type **<dd>**.

7. Type the description of the term that was entered in step 3.

8. Type **</dd>** to complete the description (the value) in the name-value group.

9. Repeat steps 6 through 8 as necessary if the group has more than one value to define (see the Writers group in G).

10. Repeat steps 2 through 9 for each group of terms and descriptions.

11. Type **</dl>** to complete the list of definitions.

G Here's an example of a description list that describes a film's director, writers, and cast, with the cast member names and their characters in a nested description list. You can style the nested list differently, as desired H.

```
...
<body>
<h1>Credits for <cite>Am&eacute;lie</cite></h1>

<dl>
    <dt>Director</dt>
    <dd>Jean-Pierre Jeunet</dd>

    <dt>Writers</dt> <dd>Guillaume Laurant
    → (story, screenplay)</dd>
    <dd>Jean-Pierre Jeunet (story)</dd>

    <dt>Cast</dt>
    <dd>
        <!-- Start nested list -->
        <dl>
            <dt>Audrey Tautou</dt> <!-- Actor/
            → Actress -->
            <dd>Am&eacute;lie Poulain</dd>
            → <!-- Character -->

            <dt>Mathieu Kassovitz</dt>
            <dd>Nino Quincampoix</dd>
            ...
        </dl>
        <!-- end nested list -->
    </dd>
    ...
</dl>
</body>
</html>
```

H I want to distinguish the terms in the main list from those nested within it, so I style **dt** elements with uppercase text and then return any **dt** elements in a nested **dl** back to normal (the **text-transform: none;** declaration). However, note that all terms display as bold **I** because the declaration in the first rule applies to all **dt** elements and I didn't turn that off in the nested list.

```
dt {
    font-weight: bold;
    text-transform: uppercase;
}

/* style the dt of any dl within another
→ dl */
dl dl dt {
    text-transform: none;
}

dd + dt {
    margin-top: 1em;
}
```

TIP Browsers generally indent descriptions (values) on a new line below their terms (names) **C**.

TIP You'll notice from the examples (**A**, **D**, and **G**) that you don't have to—or more to the point, *shouldn't*—mark up single paragraphs of text as p elements within the dd elements. However, if a *single* description is more than one paragraph, *do* mark it up with p elements inside one dd instead of splitting up each paragraph (without p elements) into its own dd.

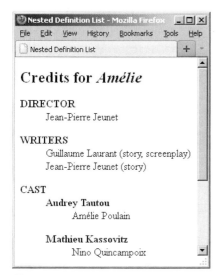

I When a **dl** is nested in another one, it automatically indents another level by default. With the styles from **H** applied, the first-level **dt** elements are in uppercase letters, while the ones in the nested list are normal. All are bold.

16

Forms

Until now, all the HTML you have learned has helped you communicate *your* ideas to your visitors. In this chapter, you'll learn how to create forms that enable your visitors to communicate with you.

There are two basic parts of a form: the collection of fields, labels, and buttons that the visitor sees on a page and hopefully fills out; and the processing script that takes that information and converts it into a format that you can read or tally.

Constructing a form's fields and buttons is straightforward and similar to creating any other part of the Web page. Some of these form field types include text boxes, special password boxes, radio buttons, checkboxes, drop-down menus, larger text areas, and even clickable images. Each element has a name that will serve as a label to identify the data once it is processed. You can use CSS to style the placement and formatting so the form is clear and easy to use.

In This Chapter

Using forms often requires using a server-side language to receive the submitted information. It requires code on the Web server that listens for form responses and processes the information in the response by storing information in a database, sending it in an email, or redirecting the user to new information. I recommend using PHP to start. It is easy and straightforward and perfectly suited to making Web pages interactive.

There are plenty of other server-side languages for processing forms. Server-side languages are beyond the scope of this book, and even explaining how to use existing scripts stretches the limits a bit, so I have provided some ready-made scripts to help you get started.

```
<form method="post" action="showform.
php">
    <fieldset>
        <h2 class="account">Account</h2>
        <ul>
            <li>
                <label for="first_name">First
                → Name:</label>
                <input type="text" id="first_
                → name" name="first_name"
                → class="large" />
            </li>
            <li>
                <label for="last_name">Last
                → Name:</label>
                <input type="text" id="last_
                → name" name="last_name"
                → class="large"/>
            </li>
...
        <input type="submit"
        → class="create_profile"
        → value="Create Account">
    </fieldset>
</form>
```

Creating Forms

A form has three important parts: the `form` element, which includes the URL of the script that will process the form and its method (post or get); the form elements, like fields and select boxes (checkboxes, drop-down menus, and radio buttons); and the submit button, which triggers sending the data to the script listening on the server **A**.

There are many details about choosing whether your form should be `method="post"` or `method="get"`. In general, I recommend using `method="post"`, because you can send more data to the server, and the information in your form is not shown in the URL. So if you're saving, adding, and deleting data in a database, **post** is the correct choice. If your form is `method="get"`, your form data will show in your browser's address bar, so the user can bookmark the results. Most search engines use `method="get"` in their search forms so you can save a search query or send it to a friend.

To create a form:

1. Type `<form method="post"`.

2. Type `action="script.url">`, where `script.url` is the location on the server of the script that will run when the form is submitted.

3. Create the form's contents (including a submit button), as described in the sections starting with "Creating Text Boxes."

4. Type `</form>` to complete the form.

continues on next page

TIP You can download the `showform.php` script from the book's Web site (www.bruceon theloose.com/htmlcss/examples/) and use it in step 2 to test your forms as you go through this chapter. It is also shown in Ⓐ in "Processing Forms."

TIP In order for your visitor to send you the data in the form, you'll need to include a button.

TIP You can use CSS to lay out your form elements Ⓑ. The form example that I demonstrate with illustrations throughout this chapter is shown in Ⓒ.

TIP You can also use the `get` method to process information gathered with a form. However, since the `get` method limits the amount of data that you can collect at one time and this form has a file upload, I recommend using `post`.

Ⓑ Here is a portion of the style sheet used to format the form. You can find the full style sheet on the book's Web site (www.bruceontheloose.com/ htmlcss/examples/).

```
fieldset {
    background-color: #f1f1f1;
    border: none;
    border-radius: 2px;
    margin-bottom: 12px;
    overflow: hidden;
    padding: 0 10px;
}

ul {
    background-color: #fff;
    border: 1px solid #eaeaea;
    list-style: none;
    margin: 12px;
    padding: 12px;
}

ul li {
    margin: 0.5em 0;
}

label {
    display: inline-block;
    padding: 3px 6px;
    text-align: right;
    width: 150px;
    vertical-align: top;
}

input, select, button {
    font-size: 100%;
}

.small {
    width: 75px;
}
.medium {
    width: 150px;
}
.large {
    width: 250px;
}
```

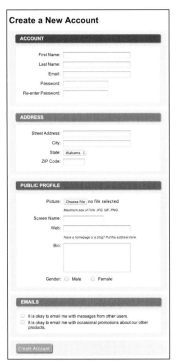

Ⓒ Here is the complete New Account form discussed in this chapter.

Server Side vs. Client Side

PHP is a *server-side* language, which means it runs on the computer that serves your Web pages (aptly called a *server*), not on your visitor's computer where the page is viewed. Your script must be uploaded to a server to work. In addition, that server must have PHP installed for the script to be interpreted. Server-side languages are needed for many functions of a professional Web site, such as storing data and sending emails.

Client-side languages, like JavaScript, work inside the browser. They can do many tasks without interacting with the server at all. They are great for manipulating the browser window, checking that all the data has been entered before submitting a form, and other tasks that happen without the server (or before the server gets involved).

Processing Forms

A form gathers the information from your visitor, and the script processes that information. The script can log the information to a database on the server, send the information via email, or perform any number of other functions.

In this chapter, since the focus is on creating Web forms, we'll use a very simple PHP script to echo the data back to the visitor when they fill out and submit a form **Ⓐ**. I'll also give you a script that you can use to submit a form's contents to your email address **Ⓑ**.

About PHP

PHP (which is a recursive abbreviation that stands for PHP: Hypertext Preprocessor) is an open-source scripting language that was written specifically for making Web pages interactive. It is remarkably simple

Ⓐ Here is the script used to process the forms in this chapter. Notice that the PHP script lives right in an HTML page. (You can find a commented version of this script at www.bruceontheloose.com/htmlcss/examples/.)

```
<!DOCTYPE html>
<html lang="en">
    <head>
    <meta charset="utf-8" />
        <title>Processing Form Data</title>
    <style type="text/css">
    body {
        font-size: 100%;
        font-family: Arial, sans-serif;
    }

    </style>
</head>
<body>
<p>This is a very simple PHP script that outputs the name of each bit of information (that
→ corresponds to the <code>name</code> attribute for that field) along with the value that was sent
→ with it right in the browser window.</p>
<p>In a more useful script, you might store this information in a MySQL database, or send it to your
→ email address.</p>
```

code continues on next page

and straightforward. (I highly recommend Larry Ullman's excellent *PHP for the Web: Visual QuickStart Guide, Fourth Edition* [Peachpit Press, 2011] for more information on using PHP.) While it's true that my scripts are not very complicated, that's sort of the point. I was able to get them to do what I needed without having to jump through a lot of hoops.

PHP is suited for basic server-side Web tasks as well as for such complex Web applications as WordPress and Drupal, which are popular blogging and content-management systems. PHP is both an

A *continued*

```
<table>
<tr><th>Field Name</th><th>Value(s)</th></tr>

<?php
if (empty($_POST)) {
    print "<p>No data was submitted.</p>";
} else {

foreach ($_POST as $key => $value) {
    if (get_magic_quotes_gpc()) $value=stripslashes($value);
    if ($key=='extras') {

    if (is_array($_POST['extras']) ){
        print "<tr><td><code>$key</code></td><td>";
        foreach ($_POST['extras'] as $value) {
            print "<i>$value</i><br />";
            }
            print "</td></tr>";
        } else {
        print "<tr><td><code>$key</code></td><td><i>$value</i></td></tr>\n";
        }
    } else {

    print "<tr><td><code>$key</code></td><td><i>$value</i></td></tr>\n";
    }
}
}
?>
</table>
</body>
</html>
```

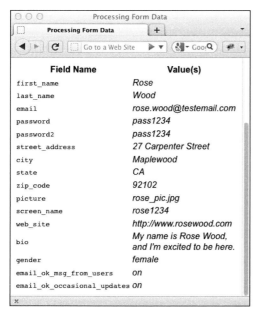

Field Name	Value(s)
first_name	*Rose*
last_name	*Wood*
email	*rose.wood@testemail.com*
password	*pass1234*
password2	*pass1234*
street_address	*27 Carpenter Street*
city	*Maplewood*
state	*CA*
zip_code	*92102*
picture	*rose_pic.jpg*
screen_name	*rose1234*
web_site	*http://www.rosewood.com*
bio	*My name is Rose Wood, and I'm excited to be here.*
gender	*female*
email_ok_msg_from_users	*on*
email_ok_occasional_updates	*on*

B The script shown in **A** outputs the name and values for each field in a table in the browser window.

entry-level programming language and a professional programming language. As your skills grow, PHP can keep up!

In addition to being easy to learn, PHP has a number of characteristics that make it ideal for processing HTML forms. First of all, PHP is an *interpreted*, or *scripting*, language, which means that it does not need to be compiled first. You write it, and off you go. PHP scripts can be independent text files, but they are often written right inside the HTML page itself, making PHP extremely convenient for Web designers.

Finally, because PHP was designed for the Web, it's good at the tasks that Web pages require and coordinates well with HTML. There are hundreds of built-in functions that you can take advantage of. In this chapter, we'll touch briefly on PHP's form-processing tools. You can find PHP's official site at www.php.net.

Security

When you're sending information to the server, you need to be very careful with security. Never assume anything about your data. Just because you built safeguards into your form doesn't mean the bad guys won't create their own form that calls your script in order to send out millions of spam messages with it. Check your data explicitly and make sure that it is what it should be, with no extra bits lurking about.

Alternatives to PHP

There are many alternatives to PHP for processing forms, such as Microsoft's ASP.NET, Adobe's ColdFusion, JSP (JavaServer Pages), and Ruby on Rails.

Sending Form Data via Email

If you don't feel like messing with server-side scripts and can deal with not having your data perfectly formatted (or preprocessed by a script), you can have a visitor's data sent to you via email **Ⓐ**.

Ⓐ Here is a script used to send form data via email. You can find a commented version of this script on the book's Web site.

```
...
<body>

<?php
//This is a very simple PHP script that ...
if (empty($_POST)) {
    print "<p>No data was submitted.</p>";
    print "</body></html>";
    exit();
}

function clear_user_input($value) {
    if (get_magic_quotes_gpc())
    → $value=stripslashes($value);
    $value= str_replace( "\n", '',
    → trim($value));
    $value= str_replace( "\r", '',
    → $value);
    return $value;
    }

$body ="Here is the data that was
→ submitted:\n";

foreach ($_POST as $key => $value) {
    $key = clear_user_input($key);
    $value = clear_user_input($value);
    if ($key=='extras') {
```

code continues in next column

Ⓐ *continued*

```
        if (is_array($_POST['extras']) ){
            $body .= "$key: ";
            $counter =1;
            foreach ($_POST['extras'] as
            → $value) {
                //Add comma and space until
                → last element
                if (sizeof($_POST['extras'])
                → == $counter) {
                    $body .= "$value\n";
                    break;}
                else {
                    $body .= "$value, ";
                    $counter += 1;
                    }
                }
            } else {
            $body .= "$key: $value\n";
            }
        } else {

        $body .= "$key: $value\n";
        }
}

extract($_POST);
$email = clear_user_input($email);
$first_name = clear_user_input
→ ($first_name);

$from='From: '. $email . "(" . $first_
→ name . ")" . "\r\n" . 'Bcc: yourmail@
→ yourdomain.com' . "\r\n";


$subject = 'New Profile from Web Site';


mail ('yourmail@yourdomain.com', $subject,
→ $body, $from);
?>

<p>Thanks for your signing up!</p>
</table>
</body>
</html>
```

B Except for an updated action field, this form is identical to **C** in "Creating Forms."

C It's always a good idea to give your visitor feedback about what just happened.

D Here is the email that was received after the form was submitted.

To send form data via email:

1. Type `<form method="post"`.

2. Type `action="emailform.php"`, where *emailform.php* is the script that will send the form data to your email.

3. Type `>`.

4. Create the form's contents, as described in the sections starting with "Creating Text Boxes."

5. Type `</form>`.

TIP You might want to ask for the email address to be entered twice. Then, have the script compare the two fields and return an error if they're not identical. This validation will prevent typos that keep you from receiving the form data.

TIP You can find the code for this script on the book's Web site (www.bruceontheloose. com/htmlcss/examples/). You are welcome to use it on your own site.

TIP If this script doesn't work on your server, it may be that your server doesn't have PHP installed. Contact your Web host and ask them (or check their support pages).

Organizing the Form Elements

If you have a lot of information to fill out on a form, you can use a **fieldset** element to group related elements and make the form easier to follow Ⓐ. The easier it is for your visitors to understand the form, the more likely they are to fill it out correctly. You can also use the **legend** element to give each **fieldset** a caption that describes the purpose of each grouping Ⓑ.

To organize the form elements:

1. Below the **form** start tag but above any form elements that you wish to have contained in the first group, type **<fieldset>**.

2. If desired, type **<legend**.

3. If desired, type **align="*direction*"**, where ***direction*** is **left** or **right**.

4. Type **>**.

5. Type the text for the legend.

6. Type **</legend>** to complete the legend.

7. Create the form elements that belong in the first group. For more information, see the sections beginning with "Creating Text Boxes."

8. Type **</fieldset>** to complete the first group of form elements.

9. Repeat steps 1 through 8 for each group of form elements.

Ⓐ I have added styles to the **fieldset** element and a **class** attribute to each **h2** element to facilitate applying styles to each group of form elements.

```
<form method="post" action="showform.php">
<fieldset>
     <legend>Account</legend> </fieldset>
<fieldset>
     <legend class="address">Address
     ⸱ </legend>
</fieldset>
<fieldset>
     <legend class="public-profile">Public
     ⸱ Profile</legend>
</fieldset>
```

Ⓑ I gave all the **fieldset** elements a margin, a background color, and padding, along with special background colors for each heading.

```
fieldset {
     background-color: #f1f1f1;
     border: none;
     border-radius: 2px;
     margin-bottom: 12px;
     overflow: hidden;
     padding: 0 10px;
}

legend {
     background-color: #dedede;
     border-bottom: 1px solid #d4d4d4;
     border-top: 1px solid #d4d4d4;
     border-radius: 5px;
     box-shadow: 3px 3px 3px #ccc;
     color: #fff;
     font-size: 1.1em;
     margin: 12px;
     padding: 0.3em 1em;
     text-shadow: #9FBEB9 1px 1px 1px;
     text-transform: uppercase;
}

legend.account { background-color: #0B5586; }
legend.address { background-color: #4494C9; }
legend.public-profile { background-color:
     ⸱ #377D87; }
legend.emails { background-color: #717F88; }
```

TIP The `legend` element limits the power of CSS to position it; this is the reason its styling is limited in most browsers **C**. I recommend re-creating the legend effect with an aptly styled p or h1–h6 element (**D** through **F**).

TIP Organizing your form into `fieldset` elements is optional.

E Here I style the **legend h2** with a background, a border, and other CSS3 features that you'll learn about later.

```
h2 {
    background-color: #dedede;
    border-bottom: 1px solid #d4d4d4;
    border-top: 1px solid #d4d4d4;
    border-radius: 5px;
    box-shadow: 3px 3px 3px #ccc;
    color: #fff;
    font-size: 1.1em;
    margin: 12px;
    padding: 0.3em 1em;
    text-shadow: #9FBEB9 1px 1px 1px;
    text-transform: uppercase;
}
```

C Browsers limit our ability to style the **legend** element. If you'd like greater control of its formatting, instead use a heading or a **p** element with a class name.

D Because of most browsers' lack of visual control over the **legend** element, I recommend using a regular heading element.

```
<form method="post" action="showform.php">
    <fieldset>
        <h2 class="account">Account</h2>
```

F Now the legends have more styling options.

Creating Text Boxes

Text boxes can contain one line of freeform text—that is, anything that the visitor wants to type—and are typically used for names, addresses, and the like.

There are many ways to separate your form elements from each other. In these examples, we are using unordered lists **A**, but you can also use the **div**, **p**, or **br** elements to organize your form elements.

B Text boxes can be different sizes to accommodate different types of fields. In our example, we're using CSS styles to set the width with classes. You can also set the width with the **size="n"** attribute on the HTML element.

A While it's essential to set the **name** attribute for each text box, you only have to set the **value** attribute when you want to add default values for a text box.

```
<form method="post" action="showform.php">
<fieldset>
    <h2 class="account">Account</h2>
    <ul>
        <li>
            <label for="first_name">First
            → Name:</label>
            <input type="text" id="first_
            → name" name="first_name"
            → class="large" required=
            → "required" placeholder="Enter
            → your first name" />
        </li>
        <li>
            <label for="last_name">Last Name:
            → </label>
            <input type="text" id="last_
            → name" name="last_name"
            → class="large"/>
        </li>
```

New HTML5 Form Input Attributes

Forms is one area of HTML that most developers find painstaking, because it often requires extra effort with CSS and JavaScript to make them function well. HTML5 has ventured to make this easier by adding plenty of enhancements, many of which you can use today.

These attributes include **autofocus**, **required**, **placeholder**, **maxlength**, and **pattern**. In the coming examples, you will learn about each of these features.

Older browsers that don't support these newer features simply ignore the attribute. Many developers use JavaScript to bridge the gap in functionality for these browsers.

For more information about the state of HTML5 forms, along with browsers that support each feature, please visit http://wufoo.com/html5.

C Text boxes can be designated as required for a form to submit. You can set a field as required by adding the **required** or **required="required"** attribute. This is a new feature in HTML5, so older browsers will ignore it. You should still validate your form on the server side, and you can add JavaScript to check the field in the browser.

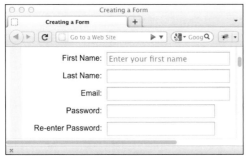

D Placeholders are a great way to give users a hint or extra instructions for filling out the form. The **placeholder** attribute will put text in a light gray color inside your text box. When the user begins to input text in the field, the light gray text will disappear, and it will come back if the user leaves the field without entering any information. This is another new feature in HTML5, and older browsers will simply ignore it.

To create a text box:

1. If desired, type the label that will identify the text box to your visitor (for example, **Name:**).

2. Type **<input type="text"**.

3. Type **name="*label*"**, where ***label*** is the text that will identify the input data to the server (and your script).

4. Type **id="*label*"**, where ***label*** is the text that will identify the element to its matching label element, which I will explain soon. It's also used for JavaScript to add functionality to your form. Although it's not required, many programmers make the **id** and the **name** identical.

5. If desired, type **value="*default*"**, where ***default*** is the data that will initially be shown in the field and that will be sent to the server if the visitor doesn't type something else.

6. If desired, type **required="required"** to not allow the form to submit unless the field has a value **C**.

7. If desired, type **placeholder="*hinttext*"**, where ***hinttext*** is the data that will initially be shown in the field to give instructions to the user **D**. When the input element has focus, the text will disappear to allow the user to type.

continues on next page

8. If desired, type **autofocus="autofocus"** Ⓔ. If it's the first input element to have this attribute, the input element will by default have focus when the page loads.

9. If desired, define the size of the box on your form by typing **size="*n*"**, where *n* is the desired width of the box, measured in characters. You can also use CSS to set the width on an input box.

10. If desired, type **maxlength="*n*"**, where *n* is the maximum number of characters that can be entered in the box.

11. Finish the text box by typing a final **/>**.

TIP Even if your visitor skips the field (and you haven't set the default text with the **value** attribute), the **name** attribute is still sent to the server (with an undefined, empty **value**).

TIP The default for **size** is 20. However, visitors can type up to the limit imposed by the **maxlength** attribute. Still, for larger, multi-line entries, it's better to use text areas.

TIP Don't confuse the **placeholder** attribute with the **value** attribute. They both have text appear in the text box by default, but the **placeholder** text will disappear on its own and will not be sent to the server; the **value** will not disappear when the input has focus, and that content will be sent to the server.

Ⓔ When your page loads, it's helpful to have the focus on a field automatically so the user can begin typing right away. Use the **autofocus= "autofocus"** attribute to have the browser put the cursor in the first form element.

```
<input type="text" id="first_name" name=
→ "first_name" class="large" required=
↳ "required" placeholder="Enter your first
↳ name" autofocus="autofocus" />
```

(A) The **password** attribute identifies the password when you compile the data. The **id** attribute is used for styling and for reference to the label. The **type** attribute must be **password**, but the **id** and name can have any values as long as they don't have spaces.

```
<li>
    <label for="password">Password:</label>
    <input type="password" id="password"
    ⇢ name="password" />
</li>
<li>
    <label for="password">Re-enter Password:
    ⇢ </label>
    <input type="password" id="password2"
    ⇢ name="password2" />
</li>/>
```

(B) When the visitor enters a password in a form, the password is hidden with bullets or asterisks.

Creating Password Boxes

The only difference between a password box and a text box is that whatever is typed in the former is hidden by bullets or asterisks **(A)**. The information is not encrypted when sent to the server.

To create a password box:

1. Type a label to identify the password box to your visitor (for example, **<label for="*label*"> Password</label>**), where ***label*** matches the label in step 4. You will learn about labels in the "Labeling Form Parts" section.

2. Type **<input type="password"**.

3. Type **name="*label*"**, where ***label*** is the text that will identify the input data to the server (and your script).

4. Type **id="*label*"**, where ***label*** is the text that will identify the input field to its label and JavaScript.

5. If desired, type **required="required"** to ensure that the form will not submit unless this field has a value.

6. Define the a form box's size by typing **size="*n*"**, where ***n*** is the width of the box, measured in characters.

7. Type **maxlength="*n*"**, where ***n*** is the maximum character count.

8. Finish the text box by typing a final **/>**.

> **TIP** Even if nothing is entered in the password box, the **name** is still sent to the server (with an undefined **value**).

> **TIP** A password box only keeps onlookers from seeing a user's password as it's typed. To really protect passwords, use a secure server (https://).

Creating Email, Telephone, and URL Boxes

The email, telephone, and URL input types are new to HTML5. They look exactly like text boxes but have small but very helpful features added for validation and inputting content ( through). Support for these new fields is growing, and older browsers will treat these fields as text boxes .

To create email, URL, and telephone boxes:

1. If desired, type the label that will identify the box to your visitor (for example, **<label for="*idlabel*">Email</label>**), where *idlabel* matches the **idlabel** in step 4. You will learn about labels in the next section.

2. Type **<input type="email" />** for an email box, **<input type="url" />** for a URL box, or **<input type="tel" />** for a telephone box.

Ⓐ When the visitor enters text into the Email field, the browser will check to make sure the format is valid for emails. An empty field will pass validation unless you add the **required** attribute.

Ⓑ When the visitor enters text into the Web field, the browser will check to make sure the format is valid for a URL. Notice that www.cnn.com is not a valid URL, because a URL must begin with http:// or https://. This is a good place to use a **placeholder** to help the visitor.

C When the visitor enters text into the Phone field, the browser will check to make sure the format matches the regular expression in the **pattern** field, with the format XXX-XXX-XXXX. Also, this field is handy in Safari on iOS, because it will bring up the number keyboard instead of the normal qwerty format.

D The **type** attribute identifies the email, URL, and telephone boxes. The **pattern** attribute is for custom validation. It uses regular expressions to restrict the content that a user puts into the box. Don't worry about the unusual syntax of regular expressions; you can find common ones at http://html5pattern.com.

```
<li>
    <label for="email">Email:</label>
    <input type="email" id="email"
    → name="email" class="large" />
</li>
<li>
    <label for="web_site">Web:</label>
    <input type="url" id="web_site"
    → name="web_site" class="large" />
    <p class="instructions">Have a homepage
    or a blog? Put the address here.</p>
</li>
<li>
    <label for="phone">Phone:</label>
    <input type="tel" id="phone"
    → name="phone" placeholder=
    → "xxx-xxx-xxxx" class="large"
    → pattern="\d{3}-\d{3}-\d{4}" />
</li>
```

3. Type **name="label"**, where *label* is the text that will identify the input data to the server (and your script).

4. Type **id="idlabel"**, where *idlabel* is the text that will identify the input field to its label and JavaScript.

5. If desired, type **required="required"** to ensure the form will not submit unless this field has a value.

6. If desired, type **pattern="regex"**, where *regex* is the regular expression that limits the text entered into the input box to a specific format.

7. If desired, define the size of the box on your form by typing **size="*n*"**, where *n* is the desired width of the box, measured in characters.

8. If desired, type **maxlength="*n*"**, where *n* is the maximum number of characters that can be entered in the box.

9. Finish the input box by typing a final **/>**.

TIP Regular expressions are outside the scope of this book, but there are many resources on the Web for finding patterns. Be sure to clearly state to the user what pattern you want them to follow. If you're not careful, visitors might give up and never submit the form. Don't let this happen!

Labeling Form Parts

HTML provides a method for marking up labels so that you can formally link them to the associated element and use them for scripting or other purposes. In the examples so far, you've seen that the explanatory information for each form element is inside a **label** element with a **for** attribute.

For example, you might have "First Name:" before the text field where the visitor should type his or her first name **Ⓐ**.

Placeholders are sometimes incorrectly used as a replacement for the **label**. Be sure to use the **placeholder** as a hint only.

To formally label form parts:

1. Type **<label**.

2. If desired, type **for="*idname*">**, where ***idname*** is the value of the **id** attribute in the corresponding form element.

3. Type the contents of the label.

4. Type **</label>**.

Ⓐ Marking field labels in a formal way gives you an easy way to identify them in a CSS style sheet. If you use the **for** attribute in the **label**, the value must match the **id** attribute of the form element.

```
<fieldset>
    <h2 class="account">Account</h2>
    <ul>
        <li>
            <label for="first_name">First
            → Name:</label>
            <input type="text" id="first_
            → name" name="first_name"
            → class="large" />
        </li>
        <li>
            <label for="last_name">Last Name:
            → </label>
            <input type="text" id="last_
            → name" name="last_name"
            → class="large"/>
        </li>
    </ul>
</fieldset>
```

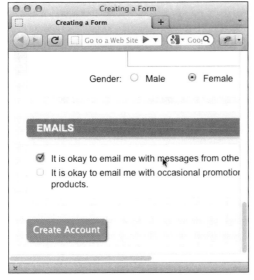

B Styling field labels is a great way to make your form more beautiful and user friendly.

```
label {
    display: inline-block;
    padding: 3px 6px;
    text-align: right;
    width: 150px;
    vertical-align: top;
}
```

C Labels for radio buttons and checkboxes allow the user to click the label as well as the form element to modify the state.

TIP If you use the `for` attribute, you must also add the `id` attribute to the associated form element's start tag in order to mark it with a `label`. (Otherwise, the document will not validate.)

TIP If you omit the `for` attribute, no `id` attribute is required in the element being labeled. The label and the element, in that case, are then associated by proximity or perhaps by being placed in a common `li` element.

TIP Another labeling technique is to use the `title` attribute. For more information, consult "Adding the Title Attribute to Elements" in Chapter 3. The `placeholder` attribute, however, is not a sufficient replacement for a label.

TIP You can use CSS to format your labels **B**.

Creating Radio Buttons

Remember those old-time car radios with big black plastic buttons—push one to listen to WFCR; push another for WRNX? You can never push two buttons at once. Radio buttons on forms work the same way (except you can't listen to the radio).

To create radio buttons:

1. If desired, type the introductory text for your radio buttons. You might use something like **Select one of the following**.

2. Type **<input type="radio"**.

3. Type **name="*radioset*"**, where **radioset** identifies the data sent to the script and also links the radio buttons together, ensuring that only one per set can be selected.

4. Type **id="*id*"**, where **id** identifies the unique radio button that you link to the label. Unlike the **name** value, which must be the same for all radio buttons in a set, the **id** for each element on the page must be unique.

(A) The **name** attribute serves a dual purpose for radio buttons: It links the radio buttons in a given set, and it identifies the **value** when it is sent to the script. The **value** attribute is crucial, since the visitor has no way of typing a value for a radio button.

```
<fieldset class="radios">
<ul>
    <li>
        <input type="radio" id="gender_male"
        → name="gender" value="male" />
        <label for="gender_male">Male</label>
    </li>
    <li>
        <input type="radio" id="gender_
        → female" name="gender" value=
        → "female" />
        <label for="gender_female">Female
        → </label>
    </li>
</ul>
</fieldset>
```

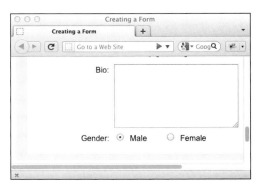

B This CSS sets the unordered list to display its list items horizontally. The labels have a right margin of 25 pixels to separate the radio button/label pair.

```
.radios {
     background: none;
     display: inline;
     margin: 0;
     padding: 0;
}

.radios ul {
     border: none;
     display: inline-block;
     list-style: none;
     margin: 0;
     padding: 0;
}

.radios li {
     margin: 0;
     display: inline-block;
}

.radios label {
     margin-right: 25px;
     width: auto;
}

.radios input {
     margin-top: 3px;
}
```

5. Type **value="*data*"**, where *data* is the text that will be sent to the server if the radio button is selected, either by you **C** or by the visitor.

6. If desired, type **checked="checked"** to make the radio button active by default when the page is opened. You can do this to only one radio button in the set. (The **="checked"** is optional in HTML.)

7. Type the final **/>**.

8. Type **<label for="*id*">*radio label* </label>** where *id* matches the **id** value in your radio button, and *radio label* identifies the radio button to the visitor. This is often the same as **value**, but it doesn't have to be.

9. Repeat steps 2 through 8 for each radio button in the set.

TIP If you don't set the **value** attribute, the word "on" is sent to the script. It's not particularly useful, since you can't tell which button in the set was pressed.

C The radio buttons themselves are created with the HTML input elements. The labels (Male and Female) are label elements; clicking the label will select the corresponding radio button.

Creating Select Boxes

Select boxes are perfect for offering your visitors a choice from a given set of options. They are most often rendered as drop-down lists. If you give the user the option to select multiple answers, the select box will render as a box of items with a scroll bar 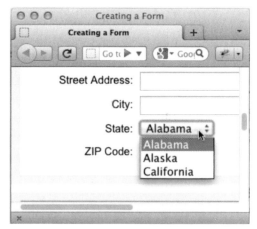.

To create select boxes:

1. If desired, type the text that will describe your menu.

2. Type **<select**.

3. Type **name="*label*"**, where ***label*** will identify the data collected from the menu when it is sent to the server.

4. Type **id="*idlabel*"**, where ***idlabel*** is the text that will identify the input field to its label and JavaScript.

5. If desired, type **size="*n*"**, where *n* represents the height (in lines) of the select box.

6. If desired, type **multiple="multiple"** to allow your visitor to select more than one menu option (with the Control key or the Command key).

7. Type **>**.

8. Type **<option**.

9. If desired, type **selected="selected"** to specify that the option be selected by default.

10. Type **value="*label*"**, where ***label*** identifies the data that will be sent to the server if the option is selected.

11. If desired, type **label="*menu option*"**, where ***menu option*** is the word that should appear in the menu.

12. Type **>**.

Ⓐ Select boxes are made up of two HTML elements: **select** and **option**. You set the common **name** attribute in the **select** element, and you set the **value** attribute in each of the **option** elements.

```
<label for="state">State:</label>
<select id="state" name="state">
     <option value="AL">Alabama</option>
     <option value="AK">Alaska</option>
     ...
</select>
```

Ⓑ We'll use CSS again to adjust the font size. You can adjust the **width**, **color**, and other attributes using CSS, but each browser displays drop-down lists slightly differently.

```
select {
     font-size: 100%;
}
```

Ⓒ A visitor will not be able to *not* make a selection in a menu unless you set the **size** attribute. The default selection is either the first option in the menu or the one you've set as **selected** in the HTML.

D Each sub-menu has a title, specified in the **label** attribute of the **optgroup** start tag, and a series of options (defined with **option** elements and regular text).

```
<label for="referral">Where did you find out
→ about us?</label>
<select id="referral" name="referral">
<optgroup label="On-line">
    <option value="social_network">Social
    → Network</option>
    <option value="search_engine">Search
    → Engine</option>
</optgroup>
<optgroup label="Off-line">
    <option value="postcard">Postcard
    → </option>
    <option value="word_of_mouth">Word of
    → Mouth</option>
</optgroup>
</select>
```

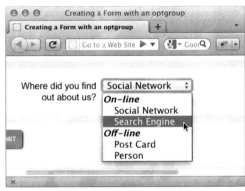

E Browsers generally don't create true sub-menus, but rather group the items in a single menu with sub-groups.

13. Type the option name as you wish it to appear in the menu.

14. Type **</option>**.

15. Repeat steps 8 through 14 for each option.

16. Type **</select>**.

If you have a particularly large menu with many options, you may want to group the options into categories.

To group select box options:

1. Create a select box as described in "To create select boxes."

2. Before the first **option** element in the first group that you wish to place together in a sub-menu, type **<optgroup**.

3. Type **label="*submenutitle*">**, where ***submenutitle*** is the header for the sub-menu.

4. After the last **option** element in the group, type **</optgroup>**.

5. Repeat steps 2 through 4 for each sub-menu.

TIP If you add the **size** attribute, the select box appears more like a list, and there is no automatically selected option (unless you use **selected**).

TIP If **size** is bigger than the number of options, visitors can deselect all values by clicking in the empty space.

Creating Checkboxes

Whereas radio buttons can accept only one answer per set, a visitor can select as many checkboxes in a set as they like. Like radio buttons, checkboxes are linked by the value of the **name** attribute.

To create checkboxes:

1. If desired, type the introductory text (something like **Select one or more of the following**) for your checkboxes.

2. Type **<input type="checkbox"**.

3. Type **name="*boxset*"**, where *boxset* identifies the data sent to the script and also links the checkboxes together.

4. Type **value="*data*"**, where *data* is the text that will be sent to the server if the checkbox is marked (either by the visitor, or by you as described in).

5. Type **checked="checked"** to make the checkbox selected by default when the page opens. You (or the visitor) may select as many checkboxes as desired. (The **="checked"** is optional in HTML.)

6. Type **/>** to complete the checkbox.

7. Type **<label for="*id*">*checkbox label*</label>**, where *id* matches the **id** value in your checkbox element, and *checkbox label* identifies the checkbox to the visitor. This is often the same as **value**, but it doesn't have to be.

8. Repeat steps 2 through 7 for each checkbox in the set.

TIP If you use PHP, you can automatically create an array (called **$_POST['boxset']**) out of the checkbox values by using name= **"*boxset*[ ]"** in Ⓐ, where *boxset* identifies the data sent to the script.

Ⓐ Notice that the label text (not highlighted) does not need to match the **value** attribute. That's because the label text identifies the checkboxes to the visitor in the browser, whereas the **value** identifies the data to the script. The empty brackets are for PHP (see the tip).

```
<ul class="checkboxes">
<li>
        <input type="checkbox" id="email_
        → ok_msg_from_users" name="email_
        → signup[]" value="user_emails" />
        <label for="email_ok_msg_from_users">
        → It is okay to email me with
        → messages from other users.</label>
</li>
<li>
        <input type="checkbox"
        → id="email_ok_occasional_
        → updates" name="email_signup[]"
        → value="occasional_updates" />
        <label for="email_ok_occasional_
        → updates">It is okay to email me
        → with occasional promotions about
        → our other products.</label>
</li>
</ul>
```

Ⓑ For checkboxes, it is often the case that you need to style the label differently, since it comes after the input form element.

```
.checkboxes label {
    text-align: left;
    width: 475px;
}
```

Ⓒ The visitor can select as many boxes as necessary. Each corresponding value will be sent to the script, along with the name of the checkbox set.

Ⓐ The **value** attribute is not used with the **textarea** element. Default values are set by adding text between the start and end tags.

```
<label for="bio">Bio:</label>
<textarea id="bio" name="bio" rows="8"
  cols="50" class="large"></textarea>
```

Ⓑ The font properties do not always inherit by default, so you must explicitly set them for **textarea**.

```
textarea { font: inherit; width: 250px; }
```

Ⓒ The visitor can type many lines of text right into the box.

Creating Text Areas

If you want to give visitors room to write questions or comments, use text areas. They will expand as needed Ⓒ.

To create text areas:

1. If desired, type the explanatory text that will identify the text area.

2. Type **<textarea**.

3. Type **name="*label*"**, where *label* is the text that will identify the input data to the server (and your script).

4. If desired, type **maxlength="*n*"**, where *n* is the maximum number of characters that can be entered in the box. This attribute is new to **textarea**s in HTML5, so its behavior varies across browsers (http://wufoo.com/html5/attributes/03-maxlength.html).

5. Type **rows="*n*"**, where *n* is the height of the text area in rows.

6. Type **cols="*n*"**, where *n* is the width of the text area in characters.

7. Type **>**.

8. Type the default text, if any, for the text area.

9. Type **</textarea>** to complete the text area.

TIP There is no use for the **value** attribute with text areas. The value instead is the text that appears between the start and end **textarea** tags.

TIP Visitors can enter up to 32,700 characters in a text area. Scroll bars will appear when necessary.

TIP A better way to set the height and width for a **textarea** is to use CSS.

Allowing Visitors to Upload Files

Sometimes you might want your users to upload a file, such as a photograph or a résumé, to your server.

To allow visitors to upload files:

1. Type **<form method="post" enctype= "multipart/form-data"**. The **enctype** attribute ensures that the file is uploaded in the proper format.

2. Next, type **action="*upload.url*">**, where ***upload.url*** is the URL of the script that processes incoming files. You'll need a special script for this.

3. Type the label for the file upload area so your visitors know what to upload. Something like **<label for="picture"> Picture:</label>** is common.

4. Type **<input type="file"** to create a file upload box and a Browse button .

5. Type **name="*title*"**, where ***title*** identifies the files being uploaded.

6. Type **id="*label*"**, where ***label*** identifies the form element to its label and is unique to the page.

7. If desired, type **size="*n*"**, where ***n*** is the width of the field in which the visitor will enter the path and file name. You can also use CSS to set the width.

8. Type the final **/>**.

9. Complete the form as usual, including the submit button and **</form>** end tag.

TIP You can't use the **get** method for forms that allow uploading.

TIP Servers need to be properly configured to store files before they can accept them.

A To allow visitors to upload files, you must set the proper **enctype** attribute and create the **input type="file"** element.

```
<form method="post" action="showform.php"
  ↪ enctype="multipart/form-data">
...
<label for="picture">Picture:</label>
<input type="file" id="picture" name=
  ↪ "picture" />
<p class="instructions">Maximum size of 700k.
  ↪ JPG, GIF, PNG.</p>
...
</form>
```

B The file upload area provides a way for the user to select a file on their system.

Ⓐ When you create a hidden field, you use the variables from your script to set the value of the field to what the visitor originally entered.

```
<form method="post" action="whatever.php">
<input type="hidden" name="name" value=
▸ "<?= $name ?>" />
<input type="submit" value="submit data" />
```

When to Use a Hidden Field?

Imagine you have a form and want to be able to give your visitors a chance to review what they've entered before they submit it. Your processing script can show them the submitted data and at the same time create a form with hidden fields containing the same data. If the visitor wants to edit the data, they simply go back. But if they want to submit the data, the hidden fields will already be filled out, saving them the task of entering the data again.

Creating Hidden Fields

Hidden fields are used to store data in the form without showing it to the visitor. You can think of them as invisible text boxes. They are often used by processing scripts to store information gathered from an earlier form so that it can be combined with the present form's data **Ⓐ**.

To create hidden fields:

1. Type `<input type="hidden"`.

2. Type `name="label"`, where *label* is a short description of the information to be stored.

3. Type `value="data"`, where *data* is the information itself that is to be stored. It is often a variable from the form processing script **Ⓐ**.

4. Type `/>`.

TIP It doesn't matter where the hidden fields are located in your form markup, because they won't be visible in the browser. As long as they are within the start and end `form` tags, you're OK.

TIP To create an element that will be submitted with the rest of the data when the visitor clicks the submit button but that is also visible to the visitor, create a regular form element and use the `readonly` attribute.

Creating a Submit Button

None of the information that your visitors enter will be any good to you unless they send it to the server. You should always create a submit button for your forms so that the visitor can deliver the information to you . (You can also use images to submit form data—see "To create a submit button that has an image.")

To create a submit button:

1. Type **<input type="submit"**.

2. If desired, type **value="*submit message*"**, where ***submit message*** is the text that will appear in the button.

3. Type the final **/>**.

To create a submit button that has an image:

1. Type **<button type="submit">**.

2. Type the text, if any, that should appear on the left side of the image in the button.

3. Type **<img src="*image.url*"**, where ***image.url*** is the name of the image that will appear on the button.

4. Type **alt="*alternate text*"**, where ***alternate text*** is what appears if the image doesn't.

5. If desired, add any other image attributes.

6. Type **/>** to complete the image.

7. Type the text, if any, that should appear on the right side of the image in the button.

8. Type **</button>**.

Ⓐ If you leave out the **name** attribute, the name/value pair for the submit button will not be passed to the script. Since you usually don't need this information, that's a good thing.

```
<input type="submit" class="create_profile"
→ value="Create Account">
```

Ⓑ I apply a background, font formatting, and some CSS3 features to the submit button by using a class.

```
.create_profile {
    background-color: #DA820A;
    border: none;
    border-radius: 4px;
    box-shadow: 2px 2px 2px #333;
    cursor: pointer;
    color: #fff;
    margin: 12px;
    padding: 8px;
    text-shadow: 1px 1px 0px #CCC;
}
```

Ⓒ The submit button activates the script that collects the data from the form. You can personalize the button's contents with the **value** attribute. (The phrase Create Account would be clearer to your visitors than the default text, Submit Query.)

D You can create a submit button that has an image next to the text by using the **button** element.

```
<button type="submit" class="create_profile">
  Create Account</button>
```

E The code for a submit button that has an image is slightly more complicated, but it gives you more control over composing and styling the element.

TIP If you leave out the `value` attribute, the submit button will be labeled Submit Query by default.

TIP The name/value pair for the submit button is only sent to the script if you set the name attribute. Therefore, if you omit the `name` attribute, you won't have to deal with the extra, usually superfluous, submit data.

TIP If you have multiple submit buttons, you can give a `name` attribute and a `value` attribute to each one so that your script can tell which one was pressed.

TIP You can also use the `button` element to create a submit button without an image.

TIP HTML5's `button` element lets you create prettier submit buttons, because you can compose the button with other HTML elements instead of just using a simple text value. Please know that there are some inconsistencies among browsers in how they render these elements, so you will have to work through them with lots of testing and CSS workarounds if you want things perfectly consistent.

Using an Image to Submit a Form

You may use an image alone as an input element to submit a form. Sometimes the designer creates a button that is beyond the capabilities of CSS3, even with its fancy gradients, shadows, and rounded corners .

To use an image to submit a form:

1. Create a PNG, GIF, or JPEG image.

2. Type `<input type="image"`.

3. Type `src="image.url"`, where *image.url* is the location of the image on the server.

4. Type `alt="description"`, where *description* is what will appear if the image does not.

5. Type the final `/>` to finish the active image definition for the form.

Ⓐ If you use an image, you don't need a submit button.

```
<input type="image" alt="Create Account"
    src="blue-submit-button.png" />
```

Ⓑ Use an image to submit a form when CSS isn't enough.

Ⓐ Here, I use JavaScript and the `disabled` attribute to make the Other text area inaccessible until the Other radio button is selected.

```
<li>
    <input type="radio" name="how" value=
    → "facebook" id="facebook" onclick=
    → "document.getElementById('other_
    → description').disabled = true;" />
    <label for="facebook">Facebook</label>
</li>
<li>
    <input type="radio" name="how" value=
    → "other" id="other" onclick="document.
    → getElementById('other_description').
    → disabled = false;" />
    <label for="other">Other</label>
</li>
<li>
    <textarea id="other_description"
    → disabled="disabled"></textarea>
</li>
```

Ⓑ When the Other radio button is not selected, the text area is grayed out and disabled, so the user cannot select the box and enter text.

Disabling Form Elements

In some cases, you may not want visitors to use certain parts of your form. For example, you might want to disable a submit button until all the required fields have been filled out Ⓐ.

To disable a form element:

In the form element's tag, type `disabled="disabled"` (or simply `disabled` since either is fine).

TIP You can change the contents of a disabled form element with a script. You'll also need some JavaScript expertise. The very simplistic way I've handled it here is to add `onclick="document.getElement ById('other_description').disabled = false;"` to each radio button. This enables or disables the text area, depending on which radio button is selected. This is just a demo; it is bad practice to mix your JavaScript with your HTML as in Ⓐ. See Christian Heilmann's www.onlinetools.org/articles/unobtrusive javascript/ for the proper approach.

Ⓒ When the visitor chooses the Other radio button, the text area turns white and the user can enter text to be submitted to the server—thanks to the JavaScript.

New HTML5 Features and Browser Support

HTML5 has many new features that make creating and using forms easier, and we've seen some of these features already. The new specification introduces a lot of new functionality, with new form elements, attributes, input types, validation handling, and styling capabilities.

There are more features that are still not widely supported or whose implementation is incomplete. In some cases, even the specification from the W3C is not finished.

Since the older browsers don't support these new capabilities, you have to know what to do as a fallback option so you can use these features today.

For instance, you can use a new form element called **output** that is now widely supported. It's used to show calculations from other form elements. For instance, if you have a shopping cart and change the number of items you want to buy, the **output** element could show the revised total for your order. This element is often used with JavaScript.

For a complete list of these new features and their levels of support in various browsers, please visit Wufoo's site *The Current State of HTML5 Forms* at http://wufoo.com/html5/.

Video, Audio, and Other Multimedia

One of the things that has made the Web so popular is that you can add graphics, sound, animations, and movies to your Web pages. Although in the past the prohibitive size of such files limited their effectiveness, newer technologies like streaming audio and video, along with broadband Internet connections, have opened the door for multimedia Web pages.

Some of those multimedia Web pages may serve as a base for an audio or video podcast; others may be advertisements or interactive displays. Still other Web pages may take advantage of occasional multimedia files to provide a richer experience to their visitors. I'll show you how to add multimedia to your Web pages for all these purposes and more.

Prior to HTML5, the only method of adding multimedia to your Web pages was through third-party plugins such as Adobe Flash Player or Apple's QuickTime. HTML5 changes all that with the introduction of native multimedia—where the browser takes care of it all.

In This Chapter

Because the Web population is so diverse, it can sometimes be tricky ensuring that all your visitors can view and hear the files that you provide (or the largest number of them possible). You need to think about the file format necessary for viewing or listening. The fact that the developers of multimedia technologies can't seem to agree on standards makes it a bit more complicated.

Please note that this chapter is meant to be an introduction to multimedia Web files, with a strong emphasis on the HTML5 code you need. It does not teach you how to create the multimedia content, only how to make it available to your visitors.

Third-Party Plugins and Going Native

As mentioned, prior to the introduction of HTML5, the only way to add media such as audio and video to your Web page was through a third-party plugin.

These third-party plugins can be a bit of a black box, and you're relying on the user to actually have them installed. With something like Flash Player, it was quite likely the user would have it installed, because it has a wide market share and is installed on a lot of user systems.

But there were problems. The code for embedding a Flash video in one browser didn't necessarily work in another, and there weren't any elegant ways around it. Plus, there was always a speed issue, because the browser hands off the playing of the media content to the plugin.

With such things in mind, native multimedia was added to the HTML5 specification. This brings a number of benefits: speed (anything native to the browser is bound to be quicker than a plugin), the native controls are built into the browser, and the reliance on plugins is drastically reduced (but not entirely gone—as you'll see later).

As with any set of standards, there are issues with HTML5's native multimedia

and the file formats it supports. Initially, the HTML5 specification named two media formats—one for audio and one for video—that an HTML5-compatible browser must support. This would have been very useful, but not all vendors wanted to be told what to do. Both Nokia and Apple disagreed with the choice of mandatory media format, and so the requirement was dropped from the specification. This means that you need to provide your media in more than one format for it to be playable by HTML5-capable browsers. We'll look at this in detail later.

The usefulness of HTML5 and native media was enhanced when Apple announced that they were not going to support Flash on their mobile devices, including iPhone and iPad. With these devices becoming more widespread every day, this showed that the past reliance on Flash for playing media files was fast disappearing and that the need to provide a different solution was at hand. This is where HTML5 native multimedia steps in and shows its strength, because the browser on Apple's mobile devices does indeed support HTML5.

Without further ado, let's see how you can go about adding native video to your Web pages.

Video File Formats

There are a number of different video file formats, or codecs, that are supported by HTML5.

HTML5 supports three main video codecs. Here are those three and the browsers that support them:

- Ogg Theora uses either the .ogg or .ogv file extension and is supported by Firefox 3.5+, Chrome 5+, and Opera 10.5+.

- MP4 (H.264) uses the .mp4 or .m4v file extension and is supported by Safari 3+, Chrome 5-?, Internet Explorer 9+, iOS, and Android 2+.

- WebM uses the .webm file extension and is supported by Firefox 4+, Chrome 6+, Opera 11+, Internet Explorer 9+, and Android 2.3+.

TIP You need to provide your video in at least two different formats—MP4 and WebM—in order to ensure that all HTML5-compatible browsers are supported. Which is not too bad!

TIP Google will drop support for MP4 in an upcoming release of Chrome, but they have yet to confirm when that will be.

What's a Codec?

A *codec* is a computer program that uses a compression algorithm to encode and decode a digital stream of data, making it more suitable for playback.

The objective of the codec is usually to try to maintain the highest audio and video quality it can while aiming for a smaller file size.

Of course, some codecs are better than others at performing this.

Converting between File Formats

Showing you how to create your own video resources is outside the scope of this chapter, but should you already have a video resource and wish to convert it to any or all of the file formats listed, there are a number of free tools that can help you with this. Here are two:

Miro Video Converter, at www.mirovideoconverter.com

HandBrake, at http://handbrake.fr

```
<body>
    <video src="paddle-steamer.webm"></video>
</body>
```

Adding a Single Video to Your Web Page

In order to add a video to your Web page in HTML5, you need to use the new **video** element. Doing so couldn't be simpler Ⓐ.

To add a single video to your Web page:

1. Obtain your video resource.

2. Type **<video src="*myVideo.ext*">** **</video>**, where *myVideo.ext* is the location, name, and extension of the video file.

   And that's it!

TIP Both Apple and Microsoft have taken and twisted the idea of native multimedia. In order for native multimedia to work on Safari (and Chrome, since it's also based on WebKit), QuickTime must be installed on the user's device; Internet Explorer 9 requires Windows Media Player to be installed. Such is life.

Exploring Video Attributes

What other attributes can you use with the **video** element? Let's take a look at Table 17.1.

As you can see, there are quite a number of attributes, which gives you a lot of flexibility with your video.

TABLE 17.1 Video Attributes

Attribute	Description
`src`	Specifies the URL to the video file.
`autoplay`	Automatically starts playing the video as soon as it can.
`controls`	Adds the browser's default control set to the video.
`muted`	Mutes the video's audio (not currently supported by any browser).
`loop`	Plays the video in a loop.
`poster`	Specifies an image file to display (instead of the first frame of the video) when it loads. Takes a URL to the required image file.
`width`	The width of the video in pixels.
`height`	The height of the video in pixels.
`preload`	Hints to the browser how much of the video it is to load. It can take three different values: **none** doesn't load anything. **metadata** loads only the video's metadata (e.g., length and dimensions). **auto** lets the browser decide what to do (this is the default setting).

Ⓐ Adding a single WebM video file, this time with controls

```
<body>
    <video src="paddle-steamer.webm"
    → controls="controls"></video>
</body>
```

Boolean Attributes

Boolean attributes, such as **controls**, don't need to have a value specified for them, because their existence within the media element is sufficient.

The examples in this book specify values for these Boolean attributes, but the controls in Ⓐ could also be written as

```
<video src="paddle-steamer.webm"
→ controls></video>.
```

Adding Controls and Autoplay to Your Video

So far, I've shown you the simplest possible method for adding video to your Web page, and the video in that example will not even start playing, because we haven't told it to. Also, if the browser you view this code sample in doesn't support the video file format you're using, then the browser will display either an empty rectangle (at 300 x 150 if dimensions haven't been specified) or the poster image, if one is indicated (via the **poster** attribute).

The short code sample in "Adding a Single Video to Your Web Page" won't add any controls to the video, but you can do so easily enough Ⓐ.

The **controls** attribute informs the browser to add a set of default controls to the video.

continues on next page

Each browser has its own set of default controls, which look very different from each other (B through F).

The following example illustrates how you can use some of the video attributes from Table 17.1 G.

To add controls to a video:

Type `<video src="myVideo.ext" controls="controls"></video>`.

To add autoplay to a video:

1. Obtain your video source.

2. Type `<video src="`*`myVideo.ext`*`" autoplay="autoplay" controls= "controls"></video>`, where *`myVideo.ext`* is the location, name, and extension of the video file.

B The video controls in Firefox

C The video controls in Safari

D The video controls in Chrome

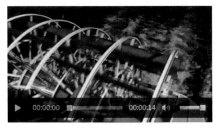

F The video controls in Internet Explorer 9

G A single WebM video set to play automatically on load

```
<body>
    <video src="paddle-steamer.webm"
    → autoplay="autoplay" controls=
    → "controls"></video>
</body>
```

E The video controls in Opera

Ⓐ A single WebM video set to play automatically and then loop

```
<body>
    <video src="paddle-steamer.webm"
    → autoplay="autoplay" loop="loop">
    → </video>
</body>
```

Ⓑ A single WebM video with controls and a specified poster image that will display when the page loads and displays the video

```
<body>
    <video src="paddle-steamer.webm"
    → poster="paddle-steamer-poster.jpg"
    → controls="controls"></video>
</body>
```

Ⓒ A video displaying a poster image. In this case, the image is a screenshot taken from within the video itself.

Looping a Video and Specifying a Poster Image

As well as setting your video to play automatically, you can also set it to play continuously until stopped Ⓐ. (This isn't recommended, though—think of your poor users!)

You simply use the **autoplay** and **loop** attributes.

Note, however, that the **loop** attribute is not supported by Firefox.

Normally, the browser will display the first frame of the video on loading. You may want to change this and specify your own image, which you can do via a poster image.

To add autoplay and loop a video:

1. Obtain your video source.
2. Type **<video src="*myVideo.ext*" autoplay="autoplay" loop="loop"> </video>**, where *myVideo.ext* is the location, name, and extension of the video file.

To specify a poster image for a video:

1. Obtain your video source.
2. Type **<video src="*myVideo. ext*" controls="controls" poster="*myPoster.jpg*"></video>**, where *myVideo.ext* is the location, name, and extension of the video file and *myPoster.jpg* is the image that you want to use as the poster image.

Preventing a Video from Preloading

If you think it unlikely that a user will view your video (e.g., it's not the main content on your page), you can ask the browser to not bother preloading it, which will save on bandwidth **Ⓐ**.

To instruct the browser to not preload a video:

1. Obtain your video source.

2. Type **<video src="*myVideo.ext*"**
   preload="none" controls="controls">
   </video>, where *myVideo.ext* is the location, name, and extension of the video file.

Ⓐ A single WebM video that won't load when the page fully loads. It won't load until the user attempts to play it.

```
<body>
    <video src="paddle-steamer.webm"
      preload="none"  controls="controls">
     </video>
</body>
```

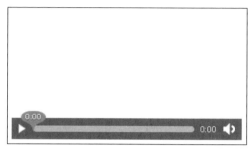

Ⓑ A video with **preload** set to **none**. As you can see, nothing is being displayed, because the browser has no information about the video (not even the dimensions) and no poster image was specified.

Ⓐ Two sources are defined here for the video: an MP4 file and a WebM file. Older browsers will only display the message contained within the **p** element.

```
<body>
    <video controls="controls">
        <source src="paddle-steamer.mp4"
        ↪ type="video/mp4">
        <source src="paddle-steamer.webm"
        ↪ type="video/webm">
        <p>Sorry, your browser doesn't
        ↪ support the video element</p>
    </video>
</body>
```

Using Video with Multiple Sources

This is all great, but you'll have noticed that all the preceding examples use only one video file, and therefore one format.

You've already seen that in order to support all HTML5-capable browsers, you need to supply video in at least two different formats: MP4 and WebM.

So how do you do that? This is where the HTML5 **source** element comes in.

Basically, the **source** element allows you to define more than one source for a media element, in this case **video**.

Any number of **source** elements can be contained within a **video** element, so defining two different formats for our video example is quite easy Ⓐ.

To specify two different video sources:

1. Obtain your video sources (two this time).

2. Type **<video controls="controls">** to open the **video** element with the default control set.

3. Type **<source src="*myVideo.mp4*" type="video/mp4">**, where *myVideo.mp4* is the name of the MP4 video source file.

4. Type **<source src="*myVideo.webm*" type="video/webm">**, where *myVideo.webm* is the name of the WebM video source file.

5. Type **<p>Sorry, your browser doesn't support the video element</p>** to display a message for browsers that don't support HTML5 video.

6. Type **</video>** to close the **video** element.

Multiple Media Sources and the Source Element

We'll go into the various attributes available for the **source** element in a moment, but let's first quickly look at why specifying multiple sources for the same media actually works.

When the browser comes across the **video** element, it first looks to see if there's a **src** defined in the **video** element itself. Since there isn't, it then checks for **source** elements. It goes through each one in turn looking for one that contains something it can play. Once it finds one, it plays it and ignores the rest.

In our previous example, Safari will play the MP4 file and won't even see the WebM file, whereas Firefox will note that it can't play the MP4 source and move on to the WebM one, which it can play .

Any browser that recognizes neither the **video** element nor the **source** element (that is, a browser that is not HTML5 capable) will ignore those tags entirely when parsing the document; it will simply display the text entered just before closing the **video** element.

Let's take a quick look at the **source** element attributes (**Table 17.2**).

> **TIP** If you specify a value in the **src** attribute of the **video** element itself, it will automatically override anything specified in any **source** elements.

A The video will load on all HTML5-capable browsers because we have specified both a WebM and MP4 source for it.

TABLE 17.2 Source Attributes

Name	Description
src	The URL to the video source.
type	Specifies the type of the video, which aids the browser in deciding whether it can play the video or not. As the example in the "Using Video with Multiple Sources" section shows, the value of this attribute reflects the format or codec of the video (e.g., video/mp4, video/webm, or video/ogg).
media	Allows you to specify a CSS3 media query for the video source, thus allowing you to specify different (e.g., smaller) videos for devices with different screen capabilities.

Ⓐ MP4 and WebM sources are specified for the video, with older browsers displaying a download link to the MP4 file.

```
<body>
    <video controls="controls">
        <source src="paddle-steamer.mp4"
        ↪ type="video/mp4">
        <source src="paddle-steamer.webm"
        ↪ type="video/webm">
        <a href="paddle-steamer.mp4">
        ↪ Download the video</a>
    </video>
</body>
```

Download the video

Ⓑ Internet Explorer 8 ignores the **video** and **source** elements and simply displays the download link.

Adding Video with Hyperlink Fallbacks

Not all browsers will be able to play HTML5 video (such as Internet Explorer 8 and below). A fallback solution is needed for these browsers.

It may have already occurred to you that the way the **video** and **source** elements work together in the example in the previous section is ideal.

And you'd be right.

You can take advantage of the fact that browsers that don't understand the **video** and **source** elements will simply ignore them.

In that example, you added a text message that would be displayed to visitors using a browser that is not HTML5 capable. You can replace that piece of text with a standard hyperlink to the video, allowing the user to download the file and view it at their leisure.

In this example Ⓐ, I have chosen to include a download link to the MP4 version of our video, but I could just as easily have linked to the WebM file or even to both.

To add a hyperlink fallback to a video:

1. Obtain your video sources.

2. Type **`<video controls="controls">`** to open the **`video`** element with the default control set.

3. Type **`<source src="`***`myVideo.mp4`***`"`** **`type="video/mp4">`**, where ***`myVideo. mp4`*** is the name of the MP4 video source file.

4. Type **`<source src="`***`myVideo.webm`***`"`** **`type="video/webm`**, where ***`myVideo. webm`*** is the name of the WebM video source file.

5. Type **`<a href="`***`myVideo.mp4`***`">Download`** **`the video</a>`** (where ***`myVideo.mp4`*** is the name of the video source file) to specify a fallback video file hyperlink from which the user can download the video.

6. Type **`</video>`** to close the **`video`** element.

Ⓐ Browsers that don't support HTML5 video will revert to the Flash fallback player and play the specified MP4 video file instead.

```
<body>
    <video controls="controls">
        <source src="paddle-steamer.mp4"
        → type="video/mp4">
        <source src="paddle-steamer.webm"
        → type="video/webm">
        <object type="application/
        → x-shockwave-flash" data=
        → "player.swf?videoUrl=paddle-
        → steamer.mp4&controls=true">
            <param name="movie" value=
            → "player.swf?videoUrl=paddle-
            → steamer.mp4&controls=true" />
        </object>
    </video>
</body>
```

Flash Fallback Player

The Flash fallback player (**player.swf**) that's mentioned in the code snippets is available with the downloadable code accompanying this chapter. The player itself is the excellent JW Player, from LongTail Video (www.longtailvideo.com/players/jw-flv-player).

Adding Video with Flash Fallbacks

As well as providing a download link, you could (and probably should) embed a Flash fallback player that can play the MP4 video file.

Yes, I'm afraid that despite all this great work with HTML5 and native multimedia, you still may want to resort to embedding Flash content, just for those older browsers that can't cope. That said, you do want to reach as many users as possible, so at least there's an option!

In the past, you could embed your Flash fallback player and video into your Web page using either the **object** element or the **embed** element, but neither was strictly valid HTML, because neither was in the specification.

The HTML5 specification does contain the **embed** and **object** elements, so at least now they're valid HTML.

We will use the **object** element here because it offers a more complete solution, as any content in the **object** element will be rendered even if the browser doesn't support the plugin that the **object** element specifies. This allows you to specify another fallback, should it be required. A fallback within a fallback!

I also recommend downloading an open source Flash video player (such as JW Player or Flowplayer), which makes it a lot easier to embed your video in this way Ⓐ. It's ideal if the player can play MP4 files, so you can re-use one of your existing video source files; if not, you may have to convert it to a SWF or FLV file.

To add a Flash fallback to a video:

1. Obtain your video files.

2. Type **<video controls="controls">** to open the **video** element with the default control set.

3. Type **<source src="*myVideo.mp4*" type="type/mp4">**, where *myVideo.mp4* is the name of the MP4 video source file.

4. Type **<source src="*myVideo.webm*" type="video/webm">**, where *myVideo.webm* is the name of the WebM video source file.

5. Type **<object type="application/ x-shockwave-flash" data= "*player.swf*?videoUrl=*myVideo.mp4* &controls=true">** (where *myVideo.mp4* is the name of the MP4 video source file) to specify that it's a Flash fallback player and to specify the player and video file to use. Note that the parameters specified here are specific to the *player.swf* used throughout this chapter.

6. Type **<param name="movie" value="*player.swf*?videoUrl= *myVideo.mp4*&controls=true" />** (where *myVideo.mp4* is the name of the video source file) to specify the player and video for browsers that don't understand the information in the opening **object** element definition. Note that the parameters specified here are specific to the *player.swf* used throughout this chapter.

7. Type **</object>** to close the **object** element.

8. Type **</video>** to close the **video** element.

Ⓑ Flash fallback player in Internet Explorer 8

```
<body>
    <video controls="controls">
        <source src="paddle-steamer.mp4"
         → type="video/mp4">
        <source src="paddle-steamer.webm"
         → type="video/webm">
        <object type="application/
         → x-shockwave-flash" data=
         → "player.swf?videoUrl=paddle-
         → steamer.mp4&controls=true">
            <param name="movie" value=
             → "player.swf?videoUrl=paddle-
             → steamer.mp4&controls=true" />
        </object>
        <a href="paddle-steamer.mp4">
         → Download the video</a>
    </video>
</body>
```

 Browsers that don't support HTML5 video will revert to the Flash fallback player, which will play the specified MP4 video file instead. The download link will also be displayed, and browsers that don't have Flash installed will still offer this option.

You could also add a video file download link (as in an earlier example) after the Flash object, just before closing the **video** element. This would be an even further fallback, allowing users to download the video file **C**. However, the Flash fallback player will be displayed alongside the download link on browsers that don't support HTML5 video.

To add Flash and a hyperlink fallback to a video:

1. Obtain your video files.

2. Type **<video controls="controls">** to open the **video** element with the default control set.

3. Type **<source src="*myVideo.mp4*" type="type/mp4">**, where *myVideo.mp4* is the name of the MP4 video source file.

4. Type **<source src="*myVideo.webm*" type="video/webm">**, where *myVideo.webm* is the name of the WebM video source file.

5. Type **<object type="application/ x-shockwave-flash" data= "*player.swf*?videoUrl=*myVideo.mp4* &controls=true">** (where *myVideo.mp4* is the name of the video source file) to specify the player and video file to use. Note that the parameters specified here are specific to the ***player.swf*** used throughout this chapter.

6. Type **<param name="movie" value= "*player.swf*?videoUrl=*myVideo.mp4* &controls=true" />** (where *myVideo .mp4* is the name of the video source file) to specify the player and video for browsers that don't understand the information in the opening **object** element definition.

continues on next page

7. Type **</object>** to close the **object** element.

8. Type **<a href="***myVideo.mp4***">Download the video</a>** (where *myVideo.mp4* is the name of the video source file) to specify a fallback video file download hyperlink.

9. Type **</video>** to close the **video** element.

TIP If a browser supports HTML5 video but is unable to find a file it can play, it will *not* revert to the Flash fallback player .

TIP An excellent resource on how to make video available to everybody is "Video for Everybody" by Kroc Camen (http://camendesign.com/code/video_for_everybody). It's definitely worth checking out, as is Jonathan Neal's *Video for Everybody Generator* (http://sandbox.thewikies.com/vfe-generator/).

D Firefox display (with default control set) when it can't find a video file it is able to play—it doesn't revert to the Flash fallback player or display the download link.

Providing Accessibility

Another advantage of having native multimedia is that the content can be made more keyboard accessible by taking advantage of the natural accessibility of modern browsers.

Or so you'd think.

Opera is currently the only modern browser whose default control set for HTML5 media is keyboard accessible.

For the other browsers, the only way to have an accessible media player is by creating your own control set, for which you need the JavaScript Media API (also part of HTML5), but that is outside the scope of this chapter.

HTML5 also specifies a new file format that allows you to include text subtitles, captions, descriptions, chapters, and so on in video content.

The WebVTT (Web Video Text Tracks) file format is intended for marking up external text track resources, such as subtitles.

No browser supports this format just yet, but there are a number of JavaScript libraries (such as Playr and Captionator) that you can use to harness WebVTT and its functionality.

Further discussion of WebVTT and captioning is outside the scope of this chapter, but you can find out more at www.iandevlin.com/blog/2011/05/html5/webvtt-and-video-subtitles.

TIP Ian Devlin's *HTML5 Multimedia: Develop and Design* (Peachpit Press, 2011) has chapters dedicated to showing you how to create your own accessible control set and how to use WebVTT.

Adding Audio
File Formats

Now that you can add video to your Web page using HTML5 native media, let's take a look at how to add audio. As with HTML5 video, there are a number of different file formats (codecs) that are supported.

There are five main audio codecs that you can use. Here they are, along with the browsers that support them:

- Ogg Vorbis uses the .ogg file extension and is supported by Firefox 3.5+, Chrome 5+, and Opera 10.5+.

- MP3 uses the .mp3 file extension and is supported by Safari 5+, Chrome 6+, Internet Explorer 9+, and iOS.

- WAV uses the .wav file extension and is supported by Firefox 3.6+, Safari 5+, Chrome 8+, and Opera 10.5+.

- AAC uses the .aac file extension and is supported by Safari 3+, Internet Explorer 9+, iOS 3+, and Android 2+.

- MP4 uses the .mp4 extension and is supported by Safari 3+, Chrome 5+, Internet Explorer 9+, iOS 3+, and Android 2+.

You will remember that MP4 was also listed as a video codec, but it can also be used to encode audio data only.

TIP As with video, your content needs to be in two different formats to ensure support across all HTML5-capable browsers. The two best formats in which to provide your content are Ogg Vorbis and MP3.

TIP The Miro Video Converter application mentioned in the "Converting between File Formats" sidebar can also be used for converting audio.

Ⓐ A simple Ogg-encoded audio file with no controls

```
<body>
    <audio src="piano.ogg"></audio>
</body>
```

Adding a Single Audio File to Your Web Page

Let's move on to actually placing an audio file in your Web page. The process is very similar to adding a video, but this time you'll use the **audio** element Ⓐ.

To add a single audio file to your Web page:

- Obtain your audio file.

- Type **<audio src="*myAudio.ext*">** **</audio>**, where *myAudio.ext* is the location, name, and extension of the audio file.

Adding a Single Audio File with Controls to Your Web Page

As the preceding example showed, it's quite easy to add a single audio file to your Web page. But this doesn't actually display anything, since an audio file is not visual, so you need to add some controls by using the **controls** attribute .

To add a single audio file with controls to your Web page:

1. Obtain your audio file.

2. Type **<audio src="myAudio.ext" controls="controls"></audio>**.

Of course, as with the video controls, each browser has its own idea of how these controls should look (B through F).

A A simple Ogg-encoded audio file with the default control set specified

```
<body>
    <audio src="piano.ogg" controls=
    ⤷"controls"></audio>
</body>
```

B The audio controls in Firefox

C The audio controls in Safari

D The audio controls in Chrome

E The audio controls in Opera

F The audio controls in Internet Explorer 9

TABLE 17.3 Audio Attributes

Name	Description
`src`	Specifies the URL to the audio file.
`autoplay`	Automatically starts playing the audio as soon as it can.
`controls`	Adds the browser's default control set to the audio.
`muted`	Mutes the audio (not currently supported by any browser).
`loop`	Plays the audio in a loop.
`preload`	Hints to the browser how much of the audio it is to load. It can take three different values:
	none doesn't load anything.
	metadata loads only the audio's metadata (e.g., length).
	auto lets the browser decide what to do (this is the default setting).

Exploring Audio Attributes

As with the **video** element, there are a number of attributes that you can use with the **audio** element. They are listed in **Table 17.3**.

Adding Controls and Autoplay to Audio in a Loop

Using the **controls** and **autoplay** attributes, adding controls and specifying that the audio file is to start playing on load is quite simple (Ⓐ and Ⓑ).

You can also indicate that you want the audio to play in a loop by using the **loop** attribute Ⓒ.

To add controls to an audio file and to start the audio playing automatically:

1. Obtain your audio file.

2. Type **<audio src="***myAudio.ext***" autoplay="autoplay" controls= "controls"></audio>**, where ***myAudio.ext*** is the location, name, and extension of the audio file.

To play an audio file in a loop:

1. Obtain your audio file.

2. Type **<audio src="***myAudio.ext***" loop="loop" controls="controls"> </audio>**, where ***myAudio.ext*** is the location, name, and extension of the audio file.

> **TIP** Firefox doesn't support the **loop** attribute.

> **TIP** Just because you can play audio automatically and in a loop doesn't mean that you should.

Ⓐ An Ogg audio file (with the default control set) that will automatically start playing when the page loads

```
<body>
    <audio src="piano.ogg" autoplay=
     "autoplay" controls="controls">
     </audio>
</body>
```

Ⓑ An audio file (with controls) that began to play automatically on load

Ⓒ An Ogg audio file (with the default control set) that will loop

```
<body>
    <audio src="piano.ogg" loop="loop"
     controls="controls"></audio>
</body>
```

A This Ogg audio file should have only its metadata (e.g., length) loaded when the page loads.

```
<body>
    <audio src="piano.ogg" preload=
    ▸"metadata" controls="controls">
    ▸</audio>
</body>
```

B This Ogg audio file allows the browser to decide for itself how much of the file to load.

```
<body>
    <audio src="piano.ogg" preload="auto"
    ▸controls="controls"></audio>
</body>
```

Preloading an Audio File

You can request that the browser preload the audio file in different ways by using the different **audio** element attributes (**A** and **B**) in Table 17.3.

To ask the browser to preload only the audio's metadata:

1. Obtain your audio file.

2. Type **<audio src="***myAudio.**
   ext***" preload="metadata"**
   controls="controls"></audio>, where
   myAudio.ext is the location, name, and
   extension of the audio file.

To ask the browser to decide how to preload the audio file:

1. Obtain your audio file.

2. Type **<audio src="***myAudio.**
   ext***" preload="auto"**
   controls="controls"></audio>, where
   myAudio.ext is the location, name, and
   extension of the audio file.

TIP Specifying a value for the `preload` attribute does not guarantee the browser's behavior; it's merely a request.

TIP Specifying that the audio file play automatically via the `autoplay` attribute overrides any `preload` attribute setting, because the audio file must load in order to play.

Providing Multiple Audio Sources

As mentioned, in order to support all HTML5-capable browsers, you need to provide your audio in more than one format. This is achieved in exactly the same way as it is with the **video** element: using the **source** element **Ⓐ**.

The whole process works in the same way as specifying multiple video source files. The browser ignores what it can't play and plays what it can.

To specify two different audio sources:

1. Obtain your audio files.

2. Type **<audio controls="controls">** to open the **audio** element with the default control set.

3. Type **<source src="*myAudio.ogg*" type="audio/ogg">**, where *myAudio.ogg* is the location, name, and extension of the Ogg Vorbis audio file.

4. Type **<source src="*myAudio.mp3*" type="audio/mp3">**, where *myAudio.mp3* is the location, name, and extension of the MP3 audio file.

5. Type **</audio>** to close the **audio** element.

> **TIP** The **type** attribute helps the browser decide whether it can play the source file. For audio formats, the value is always **audio/** followed by the format itself: **audio/ogg, audio/mp3, audio/aac, audio/wav,** and **audio/mp4.**

Ⓐ Two audio sources are defined for this **audio** element (which also has a default control set defined): one encoded as Ogg and the other as MP3.

```
<body>
    <audio controls="controls">
        <source src="piano.ogg" type=
        → "audio/ogg">
        <source src="piano.mp3" type=
        → "audio/mp3">
    </audio>
</body>
```

Ⓐ Two audio sources are defined for this **audio** element, and browsers that are not HTML5 capable will simply display the hyperlink to the downloadable MP3 version of the audio file.

```
<body>
    <audio controls="controls">
        <source src="piano.ogg" type=
        ➥ "audio/ogg">
        <source src="piano.mp3" type=
        ➥ "audio/mp3">
    <a href="piano.mp3">Download the
    ➥ audio</a>
    </audio>
</body>
```

Adding Audio with Hyperlink Fallbacks

At the risk of repeating myself, the fallback method for audio works exactly the same way as it does for video.

You define your multiple sources using the **audio** and **source** elements, and then you add the fallback for browsers that are not HTML5 capable before you close the **audio** element Ⓐ.

To add a hyperlink fallback to your audio:

1. Obtain your audio files.

2. Type **<audio controls="controls">** to open the **audio** element with the default control set.

3. Type **<source src="***myAudio.ogg***"** **type="audio/ogg">**, where *myAudio. ogg* is the location, name, and extension of the Ogg Vorbis audio file.

4. Type **<source src="***myAudio.mp3***"** **type="audio/mp3">**, where *myAudio. mp3* is the location, name, and extension of the MP3 audio file.

5. Type **<a href="***myAudio.mp3***">Download** **the audio</a>** (where *myAudio.mp3* is the location, name, and extension of the MP3 audio file) to provide a hyperlink audio download for browsers that are not HTML5 capable.

6. Type **</audio>** to close the **audio** element.

Adding Audio with Flash Fallbacks

Just as with video, Flash is often the plugin of choice for embedding audio content. And again, just as with video, you can provide a Flash fallback player for browsers that are not HTML5 capable, such as Internet Explorer 8.

To provide a Flash fallback for your audio:

1. Obtain your audio files.

2. Type **<audio controls="controls">** to open the **audio** element with the default control set.

3. Type **<source src="*myAudio.ogg*" type="audio/ogg**, where *myAudio.ogg* is the location, name, and extension of the Ogg Vorbis audio file.

4. Type **<source src="*myAudio.mp3*" type="audio/mp3">**, where *myAudio.mp3* is the location, name, and extension of the MP3 audio file.

5. Type **<object type="application/x-shockwave-flash" data="*player.swf*?audioUrl=*myAudio.mp3*&controls=true">** (where *myAudio.mp3* is the location, name, and extension of the audio file) to specify that it's a Flash fallback player and to specify the player and audio file to use. In this instance, **player.swf** is the same Flash fallback player that was used in the sections on video. Note that the parameters specified here are specific to the *player.swf* used throughout this chapter.

Ⓐ Two audio sources are defined for this **audio** element, and browsers such as Internet Explorer 8 will revert to using the specified Flash fallback player, which uses the MP3 file as its audio source.

```
<body>
    <audio controls="controls">
        <source src="piano.ogg" type=
        "audio/ogg">
        <source src="piano.mp3" type=
        "audio/mp3">
        <object type="application/
        x-shockwave-flash"
            data="player.swf?audioUrl=
            piano.mp3&controls=true">
            <param name="movie" value=
            "player.swf?audioUrl=
            piano.mp3&controls=true" />
        </object>
    </audio>
</body>
```

B Audio Flash fallback player in Internet Explorer 8

6. Type **<param name="movie" value="*player.swf*?audioUrl= *myAudio.mp3*&controls=true" />** (where *myAudio.mp3* is the location, name, and extension of the audio file) to specify the player and audio for browsers that don't understand the information in the opening **object** element definition.

7. Type **</object>** to close the **object** element.

8. Type **</audio>** to close the **audio** element B.

TIP **A browser such as Internet Explorer 8 will simply ignore the audio and source elements and will go straight to the Flash fallback player. As long as the user has Flash installed, the audio content will play.**

Adding Audio with Flash and a Hyperlink Fallback

You can provide a download link after the Flash fallback player to provide an extra fallback **Ⓐ**.

To add Flash and a hyperlink fallback to your audio:

1. Obtain your audio files.

2. Type **`<audio controls="controls">`** to open the **audio** element with the default control set.

3. Type **`<source src="myAudio.ogg" type="audio/ogg">`**, where *myAudio.ogg* is the location, name, and extension of the Ogg Vorbis audio file.

4. Type **`<source src="myAudio.mp3" type="audio/mp3">`**, where *myAudio.mp3* is the location, name, and extension of the MP3 audio file.

5. Type **`<a href="myAudio.mp3">Download the audio</a>`** (where *myAudio.mp3* is the location, name, and extension of the audio file) to provide a hyperlink audio download for browsers that are not HTML5 capable.

Ⓐ Two audio sources are defined for HTML5 browsers, and a Flash fallback player is defined for browsers, such as Internet Explorer 8, that do not support Flash. A further fallback is provided via a simple hyperlink to the MP3 version of the audio file.

```
<body>
    <audio controls="controls">
        <source src="piano.ogg" type=
         "audio/ogg">
        <source src="piano.mp3" type=
         "audio/mp3">
        <object type="application/
         x-shockwave-flash" data=
         "player.swf?audioUrl=piano.mp3
         &controls=true" width="280">
            <param name="movie" value=
             "player.swf?audioUrl=piano.mp3
             &controls=true" />
        </object>
        <a href="piano.mp3">Download the
         audio</a>
    </audio>
</body>
```

B Audio Flash and hyperlink fallback in Internet Explorer 8

6. Type **<object type="application/x-shockwave-flash" data="*player.swf*?audioUrl=*myAudio.mp3*&controls=true">** (where *myAudio.mp3* is the location, name, and extension of the audio file) to specify that it's a Flash fallback player and to specify the player and audio file to use. Note that the parameters specified here are specific to the *player.swf* used throughout this chapter.

7. Type **<param name="movie" value="*player.swf*?audioUrl=*myAudio.mp3*&controls=true" />** (where *myAudio.mp3* is the location, name, and extension of the audio file) to specify the player and audio for browsers that don't understand the information in the opening **object** element definition.

8. Type **</object>** to close the **object** element.

9. Type **<a href="myAudio.mp3">Download the audio</a>**.

10. Type **</audio>** to close the **audio** element.

Getting Multimedia Files

The most common multimedia files embedded on Web pages are sounds and videos. You can create sounds with a microphone and digitizing software (like Sound Recorder for Windows or Amadeus for Mac). And there are many programs that create MP3s from CDs.

With the advent of smartphones and their cameras (which just keep improving), getting video on the Web has become easier. Even if the video isn't in the format you require, tools such as Miro Video Converter and HandBrake allow you to easily convert the files to the required format.

You can also find sounds and movies on the Web, although you should read the corresponding license agreements carefully.

But don't limit yourself to audio and video. Even though the HTML5 **canvas** element, with the aid of its JavaScript API, allows you to create animations and so forth, you can still embed Flash animations in the same way as before—using the **object** element. Despite the enhancements that HTML5 media brings, Flash still has its place.

Considering Digital Rights Management (DRM)

One thing you'll no doubt have noticed with all this embedding of audio and video files is the fact that the URLs to the source files are available for anyone to download and "steal" your content—just as embedded images and HTML, JavaScript, and CSS source files are.

There's nothing you can do about this.

HTML5 doesn't provide any method to protect your media content in any way, although it may in the future.

So if you are concerned about protecting your media files, for now don't use either HTML5 native multimedia or the fallback Flash methods shown in this chapter, because DRM needs the media file embedding and the DRM tools to be already baked into the source material.

Embedding Flash Animation

Adobe Flash software allows you to create animations, movies, and other media that are widely used on the Web. The accompanying plugin was often used to embed video and audio in a Web page. But Flash was and is used for more than that. Since animations are often created using Adobe Flash, and although they won't display on devices such as iPads and iPhones, there are still occasions when you will decide to use them.

You saw earlier how Adobe Flash is used to embed audio and video as a fallback for older browsers using a downloaded Flash fallback player. Here you'll see how to embed an actual Adobe Flash animation SWF file (A and B).

A To embed Flash animation, set the MIME type to **application/x-shockwave-flash**.

```
<head>
<title>Embed Flash Movie</title>
</head>
<body>
<object type="application/x-shockwave-
  flash" data="http://www.sarahsnotecards
  .com/catalunyalive/minipalau.swf"
  width="300" height="240">
<param name="movie" value="http://
  www.sarahsnotecards.com/catalunyalive/
  minipaulau.swf" />
</object>
</body>
```

B The Flash animation is embedded on the page by using the **object** element.

To embed Flash animation:

1. Type **<object** to begin the **object** element.

2. Type **type="application/x-shock wave-flash"** to indicate the MIME type for Flash animations.

3. Type **data="*filename.swf*"**, where *filename.swf* is the name and location of the Flash animation on your server.

4. Specify the dimensions of your animation with **width="*w*" height="*h*"**, where *w* and *h* are values in pixels.

5. Type **>** to finish opening **object** tag.

6. Type **<param name="movie" value="*filename.swf*" />**, where *filename.swf* matches what you used in step 3.

7. Type **</object>** to complete the object.

TIP This technique is based on the article "Flash Satay" by Drew McLellan on *A List Apart* (www.alistapart.com/articles/flashsatay).

TIP Drew figured out a way to use small reference movies to help Flash animations stream properly with this technique. See his article for details.

TIP Many people use a combination of the **object** tag and the **embed** tag to insert Flash animation on a Web page, both of which are now valid in HTML5. For more details, search for "embed Flash" on Adobe's Web site (www.adobe.com).

Embedding YouTube Video

YouTube (and other services) now offer a server where you can upload your video files (which tend to be of considerable size) and make them available to your visitors.

To embed YouTube video:

1. Go to YouTube and view the video you want to use (www.youtube.com).

2. Copy the movie code from the address bar. It comes right after the **v=** and continues until the first ampersand (**&**).

3. Follow the instructions for embedding Flash in the section "To embed Flash animation." In the two places where you must insert the URL for the Flash animation, type **http://www.youtube.com/v/ moviecode**, where *moviecode* is what you copied from the address bar in step 2.

TIP When you grab the movie code for a YouTube movie, it comes after v=. But when you construct your URL for referencing the movie, you use v/.

Using Video with Canvas

Another great thing about having native multimedia with HTML5 is that it can work with a lot of the other new features and functionality that either come with or are related to HTML5.

One of the new features is the **canvas** element.

The **canvas** element and its corresponding JavaScript API allow you to draw and animate objects on your Web pages.

You can also use the API in conjunction with HTML5 video, because the **video** element can be treated just like any other HTML element and is therefore accessible to **canvas**.

With the JavaScript API, you can capture images from a playing video and redraw them in the **canvas** element as an image, thus allowing you to, for example, take screenshots from the video.

You can manipulate individual image pixels via the API, and since you can create images in **canvas** from your video, this allows you to also manipulate the video pixels. For example, you could convert them all to grayscale.

This gives you only a small idea of what **canvas** can do with the **video** element, and a thorough discussion of it is outside the scope of this book. For further information on **canvas** and its JavaScript API, see the section "Further Resources" at the end of this chapter.

Coupling Video with SVG

Another technology that people have begun to take more notice of with the dawn of HTML5 is SVG (Scalable Vector Graphics).

SVG has been around for ages (since 1999), but HTML5 brings with it the **svg** element, which allows SVG definitions to be embedded within the Web page itself.

SVG allows shapes and graphics to be defined in XML, which the browser interprets and uses to draw the actual shapes. All that the SVG definition contains is a bunch of instructions on how and what to draw.

The graphics produced by SVG are also vector-based rather than raster-based. This means that they scale well, because the browser simply uses the drawing instructions to draw the shape to the required size. Raster graphics contain pixel data, and if you want to redraw the image at a greater size than the original, there is not enough pixel data for the new size, leading to a loss in picture quality.

A complete discussion of SVG is well outside the scope of this chapter, but it's mentioned here so you know that video can be used in conjunction with SVG definitions. Shapes created by SVG can be used to mask videos—that is, to show only the underlying video through the shape (a circle, for example).

There are also a number of SVG filters that you can apply to HTML5 video, such as black and white conversion, Gaussian blurs, and color saturation. For further information on SVG, see the next section, "Further Resources."

Further Resources

This chapter covered only the basics of HTML5 multimedia. There's a lot more to learn, so here are a number of resources that you can check out at your leisure.

Online Resources

- "Video on the Web" (http://diveinto .html5doctor.com/video.html)

- *HTML5 Video* (http://html5video.org)

- "WebVTT and Video Subtitles" (www .iandevlin.com/blog/2011/05/html5/ webvtt-and-video-subtitles)

- "HTML5 Canvas: The Basics" (http://dev.opera.com/articles/view/ html-5-canvas-the-basics)

- "Learning SVG" (http://my.opera.com/ tagawa/blog/learning-svg)

Books

- Ian Devlin. *HTML5 Multimedia: Develop and Design*. Peachpit Press, 2011. (http://html5multimedia.com)

- Shelley Powers. *HTML5 Media*. O'Reilly Media, 2011.

- Silvia Pfeiffer. *The Definitive Guide to HTML5 Video*. Apress, 2010.

18

Tables

We're all familiar with tabular data in our daily lives. It takes many forms, such as financial or survey data, event calendars, bus schedules, or TV schedules. In most cases, this information is presented in columns, or row headers, along with the data itself.

The **table** element—along with its child elements—is described in this chapter. I'll focus on basic **table** structuring and styling. HTML tables can get quite complex, though you'll likely have few occasions to implement them unless you have a data-rich site. The links below show code examples for complex table structures, and emphasize how to make tables accessible:

- "Bring On the Tables" by Roger Johansson (www.456bereastreet.com/archive/200410/bring_on_the_tables/)

- "Accessible Data Tables" by Roger Hudson (www.usability.com.au/resources/tables.cfm)

- "Techniques for Accessible HTML Tables" by Stephen Ferg (www.ferg.org/section508/accessible_tables.html)

In This Chapter

Structuring Tables

The kind of information you put in a spread-sheet is usually suitable for presentation in an HTML table.

At the most fundamental level, a **table** element is made up of rows of cells. Each row (**tr**) contains header (**th**) or data (**td**) cells, or both. You may also provide a table **caption** if you think it'll help your visitors better understand the **table**. Furthermore, the **scope** attribute—also optional, but recommended—informs screen readers and other assistive devices that a **th** is the header for a table col-umn (when **scope="col"**), for a table row (when **scope="row"**), and more (see the last tip) **A**.

By default, browsers display tables only as wide as their information demands within the available space on the page **B**. As you would expect, you can change table format-ting with CSS, as I'll demonstrate shortly.

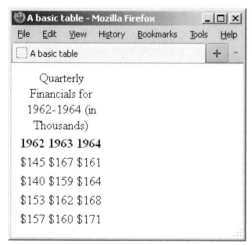

B By default, **th** text is bold, **th** and **caption** text is centered, and the table is only as wide as its content.

A Each row is marked by a **tr** element. This very simple table has one row that contains the headers (the **th** elements) and three more rows with cells of data (the **td** elements). If you include a **caption**, it must be the first element inside the **table** (**caption** may also include **p** and other text elements).

```
...
<body>
<table>
    <caption>Quarterly Financials for
     1962-1964 (in Thousands)</caption>
    <tr>
        <th scope="col">1962</th>
        <th scope="col">1963</th>
        <th scope="col">1964</th>
    </tr>
    <tr>
        <td>$145</td>
        <td>$167</td>
        <td>$161</td>
    </tr>
    <tr>
        <td>$140</td>
        <td>$159</td>
        <td>$164</td>
    </tr>
    <tr>
        <td>$153</td>
        <td>$162</td>
        <td>$168</td>
    </tr>
    <tr>
        <td>$157</td>
        <td>$160</td>
        <td>$171</td>
    </tr>
</table>
</body>
</html>
```

C I defined the table's sections explicitly with **thead**, **tbody**, and **tfoot**. Next, I added a **th** at the beginning of each row; the ones in the **tbody** and **tfoot** have **scope="row"** to indicate they are row headers.

```
...
<body>
<table>
    <caption>Quarterly Financials for
    ➝ 1962-1964 (in Thousands)</caption>
    <thead> <!-- table head -->
        <tr>
            <th scope="col">Quarter</th>
            <th scope="col">1962</th>
            <th scope="col">1963</th>
            <th scope="col">1964</th>
        </tr>
    </thead>
    <tbody> <!-- table body -->
        <tr>
            <th scope="row">Q1</th>
            <td>$145</td>
            <td>$167</td>
            <td>$161</td>
        </tr>
        <tr>
            <th scope="row">Q2</th>

            <td>$140</td>
            <td>$159</td>
            <td>$164</td>
        </tr>
        ... Q3 and Q4 rows ...
    </tbody>
    <tfoot> <!-- table foot -->
        <tr>
            <th scope="row">TOTAL</th>
            <td>$595</td>
            <td>$648</td>
            <td>$664</td>
        </tr>
    </tfoot>
</table>
</body>
</html>
```

The table from **A** is missing something, though. How do you know what each row of data represents? It would be easier to tell if the table had headers *alongside* each row too. Adding those is simply a matter of adding a **th** as the first element in each row. And whereas the column headers have **scope="col"**, each row **th** that precedes a **td** is given **scope="row"** **C**.

I also used **C** as an opportunity to introduce a few other elements that are specific to defining tables: **thead**, **tbody**, and **tfoot**. The **thead** element explicitly marks a row or rows of headers as the table head section. The **tbody** element surrounds all the data rows. The **tfoot** element explicitly marks a row or rows as the table foot section. You could use **tfoot** for column calculations, like in **C**, or to repeat the **thead** headings for a long table, such as in a train schedule (some browsers may also print the **tfoot** and **thead** elements on each page if a table is multiple pages long). The **thead**, **tfoot**, and **tbody** elements don't affect the layout and are not required (though I recommend using them), except that **tbody** is required whenever you include a **thead** or **tfoot**. You can also target styles with all three of them.

As you saw **B**, tables can appear a little squished by default. With some basic CSS applied **D**, you can add space in the cells to spread things out (via **padding**), add borders to indicate cell boundaries (via **border**), and format text, all to improve comprehension of your table **E**.

To structure a table:

1. Type **<table>**.

2. If desired, type **<caption>***caption content***</caption>**, where *caption content* describes your table.

3. If desired, before the first **tr** element of the section you want to create, type **<thead>**, **<tbody>**, or **<tfoot>**, as appropriate.

4. Type **<tr>** to define the beginning of a row.

5. Type **<th scope="***scopetype***">** to begin a header cell (where *scopetype* is **col**, **row**, **colgroup**, or **rowgroup**), or type **<td>** to define the beginning of a data cell.

6. Type the contents of the cell.

7. Type **</th>** to complete a header cell or **</td>** to compete a data cell.

8. Repeat steps 5 through 7 for each cell in the row.

9. Type **</tr>** to complete the row.

D This simple style sheet adds a **border** to each data cell, and **padding** within both the header and data cells. It also formats the table **caption** and content. Without **border-collapse: collapse;** defined on the **table**, a space would appear between the border of each **td** and the border of its adjacent **td** (the default setting is **border-collapse: separate;**). You can apply borders to **th** elements too, as shown in "Spanning Columns and Rows."

```css
body {
    font: 100% arial, helvetica, serif;
}

table {
    border-collapse: collapse;
}

caption {
    font-size: .8125em;
    font-weight: bold;
    margin-bottom: .5em;
}

th,
td {
    font-size: .875em;
    padding: .5em .75em;
}

td {
    border: 1px solid #000;
}

tfoot {
    font-style: italic;
    font-weight: bold;
}
```

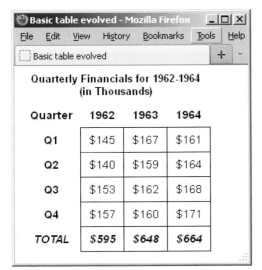

E Now the table has headers for columns and rows, and it has a row with column totals, enclosed in a **tfoot** element. The styling for our border, cell padding, **caption** content, and **tfoot** content is displayed too.

10. Repeat steps 4 through 9 for each row in the section.

11. If you started a section in step 3, close the section with **</thead>**, **</tbody>**, or **</tfoot>**, as appropriate.

12. Repeat steps 3 through 11 for each section. Note that a table may have only one **thead** and **tfoot** but may have multiple **tbody** elements.

13. To finish the table, type **</table>**.

TIP If a **table** is the only element other than a **figcaption** nested in a **figure** element, omit the **caption** and describe the **table** with the **figcaption** instead (see "Creating a Figure" in Chapter 4). To clarify, don't nest the **figcaption** in the **table**, but in the **figure**, as usual.

TIP Although not shown in the CSS example **D**, you can define a **background**, a **width**, and more in your style sheet for the **table**, **td**, or **th** elements. In short, most of the text and other formatting you use to style other **HTML** elements applies to tables too (see "Spanning Columns and Rows" for another example). You may notice slight display differences among browsers, especially Internet Explorer.

TIP You can assign the **scope** attribute to a **th** that is the header for an entire group of columns (**scope="colgroup"**) or an entire group of rows (**scope="rowgroup"**). See an example of the latter in the next section.

Spanning Columns and Rows

You may span a **th** or **td** across more than one column or row with the **colspan** and **rowspan** attributes, respectively. The number you assign to the attributes specifies the number of cells they span (**A** and **B**).

To span a cell across two or more columns:

1. When you get to the point at which you need to define the cell that spans more than one column, type **<td** followed by a space.

2. Type **colspan="*n*">**, where *n* equals the number of columns the cell should span.

3. Type the cell's contents.

4. Type **</td>**.

5. Complete the rest of the table as described in "Structuring Tables." If you create a cell that spans two columns, you will need to define one cell fewer in that row; if you create a cell that spans three columns, you will need to define two cells fewer in that row; and so on.

A I've indicated that *Celebrity Hoedown* runs on both Tuesday and Wednesday at 8 p.m. by applying **colspan="2"** to the **td** that contains the show. Similarly, I added **rowspan="2"** to the **td** containing *Movie of the Week*, because it runs for two hours. Note, too, that the Time **th** has **scope="rowgroup"**, because it is the header for every header in the group of row headers directly beneath it.

```
...
<body>
<table>
    <caption>TV Schedule</caption>
    <thead> <!-- table head -->
        <tr>
            <th scope="rowgroup">Time</th>
            <th scope="col">Mon</th>
            <th scope="col">Tue</th>
            <th scope="col">Wed</th>
        </tr>
    </thead>
    <tbody> <!-- table body -->
        <tr>
            <th scope="row">8 pm</th>
            <td>Staring Contest</td>
            <td colspan="2">Celebrity Hoedown
            → </td>
        </tr>
        <tr>
            <th scope="row">9 pm</th>
            <td>Hardy, Har, Har</td>
            <td>What's for Lunch?</td>
            <td rowspan="2">Movie of the Week
            → </td>
        </tr>
        <tr>
            <th scope="row">10 pm</th>
            <td>Healers, Wheelers &amp;
            ▸ Dealers</td>
            <td>It's a Crime</td>
        </tr>
    </tbody>
</table>
</body>
</html>
```

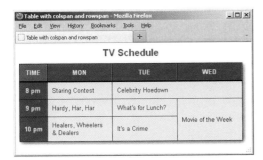

TV Schedule

TIME	MON	TUE	WED
8 pm	Staring Contest	Celebrity Hoedown	
9 pm	Hardy, Har, Har	What's for Lunch?	Movie of the Week
10 pm	Healers, Wheelers & Dealers	It's a Crime	

B It may have been a little hard to tell by glancing at the code, but when viewed in the browser it's clear how **colspan** and **rowspan** affect the table's display. I also styled the table with CSS. The style sheet is available on the book's site at www.bruceontheloose.com/htmlcss/examples/.

To span a cell across two or more rows:

1. When you get to the point at which you need to define the cell that spans more than one row, type **<td** followed by a space.

2. Type **rowspan="*n*">**, where *n* equals the number of rows the cell should span.

3. Type the cell's contents.

4. Type **</td>**.

5. Complete the rest of the table as described in "Structuring Tables." If you define a cell with a **rowspan** of 2, you will not need to define the corresponding cell in the next row; if you define a cell with a **rowspan** of 3, you will not need to define the corresponding cells in the next two rows; and so on.

TIP Each row in a table must have the same number of cells defined. Cells that span across columns count for as many cells as the value of their **colspan** attribute.

TIP Each column in a table must have the same number of cells defined. Cells that span across rows count for as many cells as the value of their **rowspan** attribute.

Working with Scripts

While HTML defines your Web page's content and CSS defines its presentation, JavaScript defines special behavior.

You can write simple JavaScript programs to show and hide content, and you can write more complicated ones that load data and dynamically update your page. You can drive custom HTML5 **audio** and **video** element controls, and create browser-based games that use HTML5's **canvas** element. And you can write full-blown Web applications that leverage some of the most powerful features in HTML5 and related technologies (they're advanced topics, so they aren't covered in this book).

In This Chapter

As you can see, JavaScript has quite a range of possibilities, and its use has exploded. JavaScript libraries like jQuery (jquery.com), MooTools (mootools.net), YUI (yuilibrary.com), and others have made it easier to add both simple interactivity and sophisticated behavior to pages, while helping them behave consistently across browsers. Of these, jQuery enjoys the most widespread use, largely because beginners find it easier to learn, it has good online documentation, and it has a large community behind it.

Browser vendors have spent considerable time making their browsers process JavaScript significantly faster than their versions of even just a few years ago. JavaScript also works in tablet and modern mobile browsers, though for performance reasons you'll want to be smart about how much you load in pages for these devices.

Alas, JavaScript is its own, large topic, so we won't cover it in this book. In this chapter, I'll stick to explaining how to insert scripts, once created, into your HTML documents. I'll also pass along some basic advice about how to do that in a way that minimizes the impact on your page's rendering time, and I'll give you a quick look at event handlers.

A The **src** attribute of the **script** element references the script's URL. Most of the time, it is best to load scripts at the very end of your page, just before the **</body>** end tag. You may also load scripts in your page's **head** element **B**, but it can affect how quickly your page displays. See the "Scripting and Performance Best Practices" sidebar for more information.

```
<!DOCTYPE html>
<html lang="en">
<head>
    <meta charset="utf-8" />
    <title>Loading an External Script</title>
<link rel="stylesheet" href="css/base.css" />
</head>
<body>
... All of your HTML content is here ...

<script src="behavior.js"></script>
</body>
</html>
```

B This example shows a script loaded in the **head** instead. It is after the **link** element, so it won't block the CSS file from beginning to load sooner. See the "Scripting and Performance Best Practices" sidebar to learn why you want to minimize how often you load scripts from the **head**.

```
<!DOCTYPE html>
<html lang="en">
<head>
    <meta charset="utf-8" />
    <title>Loading an External Script</title>
<!-- Load style sheets before any JS files -->
<link rel="stylesheet" href="base.css" />
<script src="behavior.js"></script>
</head>
<body>
... All of your HTML content is here ...
</body>
</html>
```

Loading an External Script

There are two primary kinds of scripts—those that you load from an external file (in text-only format) and those that are embedded in your page (covered in the next section). It's the same concept as external and embedded style sheets.

And just as with adding style sheets to your pages, it's generally better to load scripts from an external file **A** than to embed them in your HTML. You reap some of the same benefits, in that a single JavaScript file can be loaded by each page that needs it. You can edit one script rather than updating similar scripts in individual HTML pages.

Whether loading an external script or embedding a script, you use the **script** element.

To load an external script:

Type **<script src="*script.js*"></script>**, where ***script.js*** is the location on the server and the file name of the external script. Place each script element directly before the **</body>** end tag whenever possible **A**, instead of in the document's **head** element **B**.

continues on next page

TIP Your page may load multiple JavaScript files and contain multiple embedded scripts (see Ⓐ in "Adding an Embedded Script"). By default, browsers will load (when necessary) and execute scripts in the order in which they appear in your HTML. See the sidebar to learn why to avoid multiple scripts when possible.

TIP Browsers that don't understand JavaScript (these are admittedly rare) or that have it disabled by the user will ignore your JavaScript file. So be sure that your page doesn't rely on JavaScript to provide users access to its content and basic experience.

TIP To keep your files organized, it's common to place your JavaScript files in a sub-folder (`js` and `scripts` are popular names). Your `src` attribute values would need to reflect this, just like any URL that points to a resource. For instance, if the file in Ⓐ were in a folder named `assets/js/`, you could type `<script src="assets/js/behavior.js"></script>`. (That's just one example; there are other ways to represent the URL. See "URLs" in Chapter 1.)

TIP The JavaScript file in the examples (Ⓐ and Ⓑ) is called `behavior.js`, but you can specify other valid file names as long they have the `.js` extension.

TIP Technically, there is a third way to add JavaScript to a page: inline scripts. An *inline script* is a small bit of JavaScript assigned to certain element attributes directly in your HTML. I hesitate to mention them except to point out that you should avoid using them, just as you would avoid inline style sheets. Just as inline style sheets mix your HTML and CSS, inline scripts inextricably intertwine your HTML and JavaScript, rather than keeping them separate per best practices.

Scripting and Performance Best Practices

A full discussion of best practices pertaining to scripts and page performance is beyond the scope of this book, but I'll touch on a few points that are high impact.

First, it helps to understand how a browser handles scripts. As a page loads, by default the browser downloads (for external scripts), parses, and executes each script in the order in which it appears in your HTML. As it's processing, the browser neither downloads nor renders any content that appears after the **script** element—not even text. This is known as *blocking behavior*.

This is true for both embedded and external scripts, and as you can imagine, it can really affect the rendering speed of your page, depending on the size of your script and what actions it performs.

Most browsers do this because your JavaScript may include code on which another script relies, code that generates content immediately, or code that otherwise alters your page. Browsers need to take all of that into account before they finish rendering.

So how do you avoid this? The easiest technique to make your JavaScript non-blocking is to put all **script** elements at the end of your HTML, right before the **</body>** end tag. If you've spent even just a little time viewing source on others' sites, no doubt you've also seen scripts loaded in the **head** element. Outside of the occasional instance where that may be necessary, it's considered a dated practice that you should avoid whenever possible. (One case in which it is necessary is loading the HTML5 shiv, as described in Chapter 11.) If you do load scripts from the **head**, place them after all **link** elements that load CSS files (again, for performance reasons).

Another quick way to speed up your script loading is to combine your JavaScript into a single file (or into as few as possible) and minify the code. Typically, minified code doesn't have line breaks, comments, or extra whitespace (among other possible differences from un-minified code). Imagine writing the code in one long line without ever pressing Return or Enter.

You may use tools such as the following to minify your scripts:

- Google Closure Compiler:
  http://code.google.com/closure/compiler/ (download and documentation)
  http://closure-compiler.appspot.com (online version of tool)

- YUI Compressor:
  http://developer.yahoo.com/yui/compressor/ (download and documentation)
  http://refresh-sf.com/yui/ (unofficial online version of tool)

Each will reduce your file size, but results will vary from script to script. Generally, it's faster for a browser to load one file than two (or more), even if the single file is larger than the combined size of the individual files (unless the one file is *much* larger).

Those are two common and powerful methods, but they only scratch the surface of what's possible. For in-depth discussions of script-loading methods and optimization, I highly recommend *Even Faster Web Sites* (O'Reilly Media, 2009) by Steve Souders, as well as his site, www.stevesouders.com. Be forewarned—some of the discussions get a little technical.

Adding an Embedded Script

An embedded script exists in your HTML document, much in the way an embedded style sheet does. An embedded script is contained in a **script** element **Ⓐ**. Embedding a script is not the preferred method (see "Loading an External Script"), but sometimes it's necessary.

To add an embedded script:

1. In your HTML document, type **<script>**.

2. Type the content of the script.

3. Type **</script>**.

> **TIP** Each **script** element is processed in the order in which it appears in the **HTML**, whether it's an embedded script or an external one (see "Loading an External Script").

> **TIP** Even though the **script** element requires an end tag (**</script>**), you cannot embed code between it and the start tag when a **src** attribute is present (see "Loading an External Script"). In other words, **<script src="behavior.js">**Some function in here**</script>** is invalid. Any given **script** element may only either load an external script with **src**, or embed a script and not have a **src**.

Ⓐ An embedded script doesn't have a **src** attribute. Instead, the code is in the page. If you embed a script, do so directly before the **</body>** end tag whenever possible. It's also possible to embed a script in the **head** **Ⓑ**, but it's less desirable from a performance standpoint.

```
<!DOCTYPE html>
<html lang="en">
<head>
    <meta charset="utf-8" />
    <title>Adding an Embedded Script</title>
<link rel="stylesheet" href="css/base.css" />
</head>
<body>
... All of your HTML content is here ...

<script>
/*
Your JavaScript code goes here
*/
</script>
</body>
</html>
```

Ⓑ This example shows a script embedded in the **head**. It appears after the **link** element so that the CSS file will load faster. See the "Scripting and Performance Best Practices" sidebar to learn why you want to minimize how often you embed scripts in the **head**.

```
<!DOCTYPE html>
<html lang="en">
<head>
    <meta charset="utf-8" />
    <title>Loading an External Script</title>
<!-- Load style sheets before any JS files -->
<link rel="stylesheet" href="base.css" />
<script>
/*
Your JavaScript code goes here
*/
</script>
</head>
<body>
... All of your HTML content is here ...
</body>
</html>
```

JavaScript Events

In this chapter's introduction, I noted that diving into JavaScript was beyond the scope of the book. However, I do want to give you a tiny peek at JavaScript events so you'll have a basic sense of what Java-Script can do for you.

You can write JavaScript to respond to specific, predefined events that either your visitor or the browser triggers. The list that follows is just a small sample of the event handlers available to you when you write scripts. HTML5 introduces numerous other ones, many of which revolve around events related to the **audio** and **video** elements. Some touchscreen devices have gotten in on the action too, with special touch-based event handlers.

Please note that "mouse" in this list means any "pointing device." For example, **onmousedown** occurs if a visitor uses a digital pen, an actual mouse, or a similar device.

- **onblur**. The visitor leaves an element that was previously in focus (see **onfocus**).
- **onchange**. The visitor modifies the value or contents of the element. This is most commonly used on form fields (see Chapter 16 for more on forms).
- **onclick**. The visitor clicks the specified area or hits the Return or Enter key while focused on it (like on a link).
- **ondblclick**. The visitor double-clicks the specified area.
- **onfocus**. The visitor selects, clicks, or tabs to the specified element.
- **onkeydown**. The visitor presses down on a key while in the specified element.

continues on next page

- **onkeypress**. The visitor presses down and lets go of a key while in the specified element.

- **onkeyup**. The visitor lets go of a key after typing in the specified element.

- **onload**. The browser finishes loading the page, including all external files (images, style sheets, JavaScript, and so on).

- **onmousedown**. The visitor presses the mouse button down over the specified element.

- **onmousemove**. The visitor moves the mouse cursor.

- **onmouseout**. The visitor moves the mouse away from the specified element after having been over it.

- **onmouseover**. The visitor points the mouse at the element.

- **onmouseup**. The visitor lets the mouse button go after having clicked the element (the opposite of **onmousedown**).

- **onreset**. The visitor clicks the form's reset button or presses the Return or Enter key while focused on the button.

- **onselect**. The visitor selects one or more characters or words in the element.

- **onsubmit**. The visitor clicks the form's submit button or presses the Return or Enter key while focused on the button.

You can see a complete list of HTML5 event handlers at http://dev.w3.org/html5/spec-author-view/global-attributes.html. The touch-based event handlers that some touchscreen devices (like smartphones and tablets) contain include **touchstart**, **touchend**, **touchmove**, and more (https://dvcs.w3.org/hg/webevents/raw-file/tip/touchevents.html).

Testing & Debugging Web Pages

So, you've written a brand new page and fired it up in your browser only to find that it doesn't look anything like you expected. Or it doesn't display at all. Or maybe it looks great in your default browser, but when you or your clients check it in others, it looks, well, kind of funny.

Between HTML, CSS, and the multitude of browsers (especially older ones) and platforms, it's easy to have trouble here and there. This chapter will alert you to some common errors and will also help you weed out your own homegrown variety.

Some of these debugging techniques will seem pretty basic, but problems with Web pages are often pretty basic too. Before you go looking for a big problem, make sure you don't have any little ones. I'll show you how in the first section.

Once your code is correct, you should thoroughly test your site on a few browsers, in one or more platforms, to see if each page works the way you want it to (see the section "Testing Your Page" and the sidebar "Which Browsers Should You Test?").

In This Chapter

Trying Some Debugging Techniques

Here are some tried and true techniques for getting the kinks out of a Web page.

- Check the easy stuff first.

- Be observant and methodical.

- Work incrementally. Make small changes, and test after each change. That way, you'll be able to pinpoint the source of a problem if one occurs.

- When you're debugging, start with what you know works. Only then should you add the hard parts chunk by chunk—testing the page in a browser after each addition—until you find the source of the problem.

- Use the process of elimination to figure out which chunks of your code are giving you trouble. For example, you can comment out half of the code to see if the problem is in the other half ⓐ. Then comment out a smaller portion of the offending half, and so on, until you find the problem. (See "Adding Comments" in Chapter 3 and "Adding Comments to Style Rules" in Chapter 7.)

- Be careful about typos. Many perplexing problems can end up being simple typing mistakes—for instance, you spelled a class name one way in your HTML but a different way in your CSS.

- In CSS, if you're not sure whether the problem is with the property or with the selector, try adding a very simple declaration to your selector, like **color: red;** or **border: 1px solid red;** (or choose

ⓐ I've commented out the middle section of this code to see if it's the culprit. Note that many HTML and CSS editors include syntax highlighting, which is automatic color-coding of elements, selectors, and the like. This can aid your debugging. Mistype the name of a CSS property, for example, and the editor won't show it in the expected color: a hint that it isn't valid.

```
...

.entry {
    border-right: 2px dashed #b74e07;
    margin: 0 .5em 2em 0;
}

.entry h2 {
    font-size: 1.25em;
    line-height: 1;
}

/*
.continued,
.entry .date {
    text-align: right;
}

.entry .date {
    line-height: 1;
    margin: 0 1em 0 0;
    padding: 0;
    position: relative;
    top: -1em;
}

.intro {
    margin: -5px 0 0 110px;
}
*/

.photo {
    float: left;
    height: 75px;
    width: 100px;
}

.photo a {
    margin: 0;
    padding: 0;
}

...
```

an uncommon site color like **pink** if **red** is part of your design). If the element turns red, the problem is with your property; if it doesn't, the problem is with your selector (assuming you don't have another selector that's more specific or that comes after the current one).

- Take a break. Sometimes you can get much more done in the fifteen minutes after an hour-long walk than you would have if you'd worked during that hour. I've also solved problems in my head while taking brief naps.

- Test changes to your HTML or CSS directly in the browser by using one or more of the developer toolbars at your disposal. Or inspect the code with these tools to try to locate the problem. (See the "Browser Developer Tools" sidebar.)

Browser Developer Tools

Browsers either include debugging tools or have them available as extensions. Many tools' features are similar. The feature you will find yourself returning to time and again is the ability to change CSS or HTML and see it affect your page immediately. This allows you to quickly test changes before incorporating them in your code.

Following is a round-up of the tools used most often for each browser:

- Chrome: Developer Tools (http://code.google.com/chrome/devtools/docs/overview.html).
- Firefox: The extremely popular Firebug add-on (http://getfirebug.com). Also, Web Developer (http://chrispederick.com/work/web-developer/) is a slightly different type of tool, but it is very handy. It's also available for Chrome at the same link.
- Internet Explorer: IE8+ has Developer Tools (http://msdn.microsoft.com/en-us/ie/aa740478) built in. For IE6 and IE7, you can install the Internet Explorer Developer Toolbar (www.microsoft.com/download/en/details.aspx?id=18359).
- Opera: Dragonfly (www.opera.com/dragonfly/).
- Safari: Web Inspector (http://developer.apple.com/technologies/safari/developer-tools.html).

Documentation and videos showing how to use many of these tools are available online.

See examples of Firebug and Web Inspector in action in "Checking the Easy Stuff: HTML" and "Checking the Easy Stuff: CSS," respectively.

Checking the Easy Stuff: General

While the difference you see between browsers *might* be due to some obscure browser bug or some new technique you're using, often it's just something simple. Everyone from novices to experts makes the occasional simple mistake that trips them up. For instance, it's easy to think the source of a problem is in the code and spend a lot of time debugging it, only to find that you're changing one file but uploading and viewing a different one from your server!

Many of the following suggestions apply to testing your site from the site's URL on your server.

To check the general easy stuff:

- Validate your code as described in "Validating Your Code." This is a great place to start, because you can eliminate coding syntax and related errors as the cause of the problem you're noticing.

- Make sure you've uploaded the file you want to test.

- Make sure you've uploaded the file to the location where it belongs.

- Make sure you've typed the URL that corresponds to the file you want to test. Or if you've tried to browse to the page from another page, make sure the URL you coded in the link to the page matches its file name and location.

- Make sure you've saved the file—including the very latest changes—before you upload it.

- Make sure you've uploaded any auxiliary files—CSS, images, music, videos, and so on.

- Make sure the upper- and lowercase letters in your URL exactly match the upper- and lowercase letters in your file names. (By the way, this is one reason I recommend using only lowercase letters; it reduces the room for error when typing URLs—for both you and your visitors.) And make sure you haven't used spaces in file names (use hyphens instead).

- If you disabled any of the browser features, such as JavaScript support, during previous testing, make sure you haven't neglected to re-enable them.

- Make sure the problem is not the browser's fault. The easiest way to do that is to test the page in another browser.

In the next two sections, I'll tell you how to check the easy stuff in HTML and CSS.

Checking the Easy Stuff: HTML

Sometimes the problem is in your HTML.

To check the easy stuff in HTML:

- A simple typo or two can be easy to miss **A**. Make sure you've spelled everything correctly and that you've assigned valid values to attributes **B**. Use one of the HTML validators to expose these so you can correct them quickly (see "Validating Your Code").

- Be careful about element nesting. For instance, if you open **\<p>** and then use ****, make sure the end **** comes before the final **\</p>**.

- If accented characters or special symbols are not displaying properly, make sure **\<meta charset="utf-8" />** (or the right character encoding if different than UTF-8) appears right after the document **head** element starts, and be sure your text editor is configured to save your HTML files in the same encoding. If you're still having trouble, try using the appropriate character reference.

- Be sure attribute values are enclosed in straight, not curly, quotes. An attribute's value can contain single quotes if the value is enclosed in double quotes **C**, which is the norm. If the value itself contains double quotes, use character references for the inner quotes **D**.

A Can you see where the problems are? I've misspelled **src** and included a unit type in the **width** and **height** values. The HTML validators will flag these types of errors, saving you the time of trying to hunt them down elsewhere if you don't notice your typos.

```
<img scr="woody.jpg" width="200px"
  height="150px" alt="Woody the cat" />
```

B The corrected version shows the **src** attribute spelled correctly, and I've removed the **px** from the **width** and **height** values.

```
<img src="woody.jpg" width="200"
  height="150" alt="Woody the cat" />
```

C If an attribute's value contains a *single* quote, you can just enclose it in double quotes as usual.

```
<img src="jungle.jpg" width="325" height="275"
  alt="Llumi's jungle" />
```

D If an attribute's value contains *double* quotes, use character references around the quoted text within the value.

```
<img src="cookie-the-cat.jpg" width="250"
  height="200" alt="Cookie's saying,
  &quot;Enough!&quot;" />
```

E Don't include an end tag on void elements, like **img**. The HTML validators will flag this example as an error.

```
<img src="jungle.jpg" width="325" height="275"
→ alt="Llumi's jungle"></img>
```

F With Firebug installed in Firefox, you can right-click (or Control-click on a Mac) content and choose Inspect Element. That displays in Firebug the underlying structure of the content **G**.

G When you inspect the paragraph with Firebug, you can see that Firefox structured the HTML as `<p>We've <fm>really got a problem here</fm>.</p>` when it encountered the code error in **H**.

H This **em** element has a typo in the start tag. When a browser like Firefox parses the HTML, it tries to make sense of the mistake and changes the underlying structure of the document when displaying the page, as shown in **G**. The HTML validators will flag this error too.

```
<p>We've <fm>really</em> got a problem here.
→ </p>
```

- Make sure all appropriate elements have start and end tags. And don't use separate start and end tags for void (empty) elements **E**. (Technically, browsers may render elements correctly if you omit the end tag or include one on a void element, but play it safe.)

- Use the browser developer tools to inspect the document structure as it appears after the browser has parsed it **F**, and compare it with the nesting of elements that you were expecting **G**. This may help pinpoint the location of a malformed tag, an unclosed element, or an element you closed too soon. (See the "Browser Developer Tools" sidebar.)

Checking the Easy Stuff: CSS

While CSS syntax is pretty straightforward, it has some common pitfalls, especially if you're more accustomed to writing HTML. A CSS validator will flag syntax errors like the ones discussed in this section, so validate your style sheets before you go digging through your CSS looking for errors.

To check the easy stuff in CSS:

- Make sure you separate properties from their values with a colon (:), not an equals sign (as you do in HTML) (Ⓐ and Ⓑ).

- Be sure to complete each property/value pair (a *declaration*) with a semicolon (;). Make sure there are no extra semicolons (Ⓒ and Ⓓ).

- Don't add spaces between numbers and their units (Ⓔ and Ⓕ).

- Don't forget to close your curly braces.

- Make sure you're using an accepted value. Something like **font-style: none;** isn't going to work, since the "none" value for this property is called **normal**. You can find a list of CSS properties and values in Appendix B (see the book's site).

Ⓐ Oops. It can be hard to break the habit of separating properties and values with the equals sign.

```
p {
    font-size=1.3em;
}
```

Ⓑ Much better. Always use a colon between the property and the value. It doesn't matter if you add extra spaces before and after the colon, but it's common to include one after the colon.

```
p {
    font-size: 1.3em;
}
```

Ⓒ Another error. You must put one and only one semicolon between each property/value pair. Here, there's one missing and one extra.

```
p {
    font-size: 1.3em font-style: italic;;
  → font-weight: bold;
}
```

Ⓓ The error is easier to spot when each property/value pair occupies its own line, because the semicolons aren't lost in a sea of properties, values, and colons.

```
/* Still wrong, but easier to spot */
p {
    font-size: 1.3em;;
    font-style: italic
    font-weight: bold;
}

/* Here's the correct version */
p {
    font-size: 1.3em;
    font-style: italic;
    font-weight: bold;
}
```

E And yet another error. Never put spaces between the number and the unit.

```
p {
    font-size: .8275 em;
}
```

F This will work. Note that the space between the colon and the value is optional (but common).

```
p {
    font-size: .8275em;
}
```

G I've inspected the `<h1>Recent Entries</h1>` code with Safari's Web Inspector. The CSS applied to the element displays in the panel on the right. It shows a line through a *font-size* setting to indicate it has been overridden by another rule (the one listed above it). This result is what I wanted in this case, but you can use this technique to track down why a style might not have been applied as expected. You can also edit the rules in the right-hand panel to test different CSS.

- Don't forget the `</style>` end tag for embedded style sheets.

- Make sure you've linked the HTML document to the proper CSS file, and that the URL points to the desired file.

- Watch the spaces and punctuation between the selectors.

- Make sure the browser supports what you're trying to do, particularly with CSS3, because browser support is still evolving as CSS3 matures. See Appendix B (on the book's site) for URLs related to checking browser support for specific properties and values. A CSS validator won't tell you if a particular browser supports a CSS feature, but it *will* indicate if you've typed a selector, property, or value that doesn't exist in CSS.

- Use the browser developer tools to inspect the style rules as parsed by the browser—as well as the currently computed element styles—to quickly highlight which code isn't being parsed as expected or to see how specificity rules have been applied **G**. (See the sidebar "Browser Developer Tools.")

Validating Your Code

One great way to find errors on a page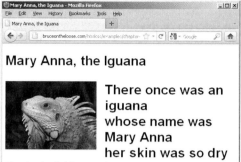
is to run it through a validator B. An HTML
validator compares your code against the
rules of the language, displaying errors or
warnings for any inconsistencies it finds. It
will alert you to syntax errors; invalid elements, attributes, and values; and improper
nesting of elements C. It can't tell if you've
marked up your content with the elements
that best describe it, so it's still up to you
to write semantic HTML (see "Semantic
HTML: Markup with Meaning" in Chapter 1).
CSS validators work similarly.

You aren't required to make your pages
pass the validators error-free before you
put them on the Web. Indeed, most sites
have some errors. Also, the W3C's CSS
validator will mark vendor prefixes used on
property names as errors but that doesn't
mean you should remove the vendor
prefixes from your style sheets (learn about
vendor prefixes in Chapter 14).

Browsers are built to handle many types
of errors (and ignore some others) and display your page the best they can. So even
if your page has a validation error, you
might not see the difference. Other times,
the error directly affects a page's rendering A or behavior. So, use the validators
to keep your code as free from errors as
possible.

See "Checking the Easy Stuff: HTML" and
"Checking the Easy Stuff: CSS" for examples of errors validators catch.

To validate your code:

1. First check your HTML with either
   http://html5.validator.nu (B and C) or
   the W3C's http://validator.w3.org. See
   the first two tips for more information.

A That text to the right of the image isn't
supposed to be so big. I've already looked
through my CSS to rule out that it's coming from
an unintentionally large **font-size** setting. What's
the problem?

B I've pasted the URL I want to check in the
Address field. I also selected the Show Source
option (it is deselected by default), so my HTML
source code will appear underneath any errors
the validator catches, with the errant parts of the
HTML highlighted.

2. Fix any HTML errors that are flagged, save the changes, and, if necessary, upload the file to your server again. Then repeat step 1.

3. You can check for CSS errors with http://jigsaw.w3.org/css-validator/. Be sure to select CSS level 3 from the Profile drop-down if your style sheet includes any CSS3 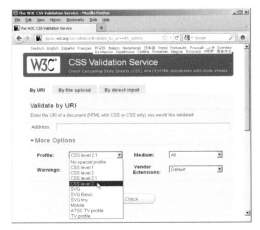. Otherwise, the validator will flag more errors than your style sheet really contains.

C The error found on Line 9 is the problem—instead of an **</h1>** end tag, I've used another **<h1>** start tag by mistake. The other errors are caused by the first error, so once I fix that, the page will be error-free.

D The validator defaults to the CSS level 2.1 profile. Select CSS level 3 if your style sheet contains any CSS3. Otherwise, the validator will display more errors, because the CSS3 features aren't part of CSS 2.1.

TIP The W3C's validator (http://validator.w3 .org/) uses the validation engine from http:// html5.validator.nu/, so use whichever you prefer. The W3C's error messages are easier to read, but they don't highlight the errant portions of the HTML source code.

TIP You can validate your HTML by entering the URL **A**, uploading the HTML file, or pasting the HTML into the validator. With the file upload or copy-paste methods, you can check files without uploading them to your server.

TIP One HTML error can cause several in a validator's results. For example, a missing end tag can trigger lots of error messages **C**. Fix the end tag, and all of those subsequent errors go away. Start at the top, fixing a few errors at a time, and then immediately revalidate the file to see if other problems are resolved.

TIP HTML5 is pretty lenient about how you format certain parts of your code. For instance, it doesn't care if you close void elements like img, so both <img src="iguana.jpg" alt="Mary Anna, the Iguana" /> and <img src="iguana.jpg" alt="Mary Anna, the Iguana"> are valid. The validators will not tell you if your code is consistent in these areas. If you like being sure your code *is* consistent, you can run each HTML page through HTML Lint (http://lint.brihten.com/html/). It has options for checking that empty elements are closed, start and end tags are lowercase, attributes are lowercase, and more.

Testing Your Page

Even if your code validates, your page still may not work the way you want it to  **A**. Or it may work properly in one browser, but not in the next. It's important to test your page in a variety of browsers and platforms (see the sidebar "Which Browsers Should You Test?").

To test your HTML pages:

1. Validate your HTML and CSS (see "Validating Your Code"), and make any necessary changes.

2. Open a browser, and choose File > Open File. Find the Web page that you want to test, and click Open. The page appears in the browser.

3. Go through the whole page, and make sure it looks exactly the way you want it. For example:

   ▸ Does the formatting look the way you want it to?

   ▸ Does each URL in your links point to the proper page or asset? (You can test the URLs by activating the links and seeing if the right thing happens.)

   ▸ Is your CSS file referenced properly (**A** through **C**)?

   ▸ Do all of your images appear? Are they placed and aligned properly?

4. Without closing the page in the browser, open the appropriate HTML or CSS document and make any necessary changes.

5. Save the changes.

6. Switch back to the browser and refresh or reload to see the changes.

7. Repeat steps 3 through 6 until you are satisfied with your Web page. Don't get discouraged if it takes several tries.

A This page validates, but it doesn't look anything like it's supposed to. What's the problem **B**?

B The problem is the link to the CSS file—the file is named **styles.css**, and here I'm linking to **style.css**. The browser can't find the CSS and thus displays the page wrong **A**. After fixing the file name in the code, the style sheet loads.

```
<!DOCTYPE html>
<html lang="en">
<head>
    <meta charset="utf-8" />
    <title>Mary Anna, the Iguana</title>
    <link rel="stylesheet" href=
  ➝ "css/style.css" />
</head>
<body>

...

</body>
</html>
```

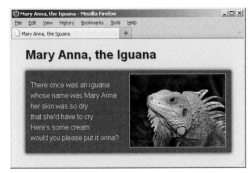

C Now that the link to the CSS is corrected, the page is displayed properly.

Revalidate the code to make sure you haven't introduced any new errors.

8. Beginning with step 2, perform the same testing procedure in other browsers until you are satisfied and think your page is ready to go live on your site.

9. Upload the files to the server.

10. Return to the browser, type your page's URL in the address bar, and press Return or Enter. The page will appear in the browser.

11. With your page on the server, go through your page again to make sure everything is all right. Don't forget to test it on mobile devices too, if visitors will be accessing your site on them.

TIP I recommend testing your site's local version thoroughly before you upload your files to your server. Once they are uploaded, test them thoroughly again, but from your server—regardless of how much testing you did of your local version during development—because that's the version your visitors will see.

TIP Again, if you can, test your HTML documents in several browsers on various platforms (see the sidebar "Which Browsers Should You Test?"). You never know what browser (or computer) your visitors will use.

TIP See "Building a Page that Adapts with Media Queries" in Chapter 12 for information on mobile device browser testing.

TIP If your HTML code instead of your page displays in the browser, be sure your file has either a .html or .htm extension (and not one like .txt).

TIP Sometimes it's not your fault—especially with styles. Make sure a browser supports the feature you're having trouble with before assuming the problem is with your code. See Appendixes A and B (on the book's site) for links to resources that contain information about browser support for HTML and CSS features, respectively.

Which Browsers Should You Test?

Generally, most people developing sites verify them in the following browsers:

- Chrome's latest version. Chrome updates itself automatically on your computer. A new release occurs about once every six weeks. Download Chrome at www.google.com/chrome.

- Firefox 3.6+. Firefox has a rapid release schedule, like Chrome, though updates are not automatic. Firefox is already several versions beyond version 3.6, so 3.6 won't be a priority for much longer. Download Firefox at www.firefox.com.

- Internet Explorer 7+. Download IE at http://windows.microsoft.com/en-US/internet-explorer/downloads/ie.

- Safari 5+. In most cases, limit your testing to the Mac version. Although Safari is available on Windows, it has a very small user base, so it isn't particularly worth testing on it. Download Safari at www.apple.com/safari/.

- Opera 11+. Opera has a small market share in many parts of the world, but it also has excellent HTML5 support and tools. Download Opera at www.opera.com/.

Browser capabilities have exploded in recent years due to HTML5, CSS3, improved JavaScript engines, and other technologies. Most of the browsers listed here will render your CSS similarly (exceptions mostly involve CSS3). Internet Explorer 7 and 8 are much older and, so, more prone to differences (and bugs). So it's OK if your site looks a little different on IE7 and IE8 as compared with modern browsers.

And what of Internet Explorer 6? It's been a thorn in the side of designers and developers for years because of its numerous quirks and bugs. Thankfully, its share of the market has shrunk significantly (see www.ie6countdown.com). Nowadays, it's less common for site owners to put special effort into getting their sites to behave in IE6, but it all depends on a site's audience. Some large corporations aren't yet willing to abandon it entirely, but people have generally moved away from it, and you'll have little to gain by expending much energy on IE6 with your sites. But know your audience. Some areas of the world, like parts of Asia (China especially), still have a large IE6 user base. Additionally, some large organizations use IE6 as their default browser.

It's a little challenging to get access to all these browsers and platforms. See Addy Osmani's article for ideas about how to test your pages on a variety of browsers, especially the range of Internet Explorer versions: http://coding.smashingmagazine.com/2011/09/02/reliable-cross-browser-testing-part-1-internet-explorer/. Also, friends and family members can help you test your pages if they have browsers you don't. If you're tight on time or resources and need to narrow your testing, check your pages on the latest versions of Chrome and Firefox and on IE7+ if at all possible.

The browser market moves fast: By the time you read this, people may be testing newer versions of these browsers. Still, if you follow the principle of progressive enhancement, your sites can offer a simple experience in older browsers and an enhanced one in modern browsers.

With this in mind, Yahoo! introduced the concept of Graded Browser Support (http://yuilibrary.com/yui/docs/tutorials/gbs/), which it applies to the testing of YUI, their JavaScript and CSS framework (www.yuilibrary.com). The idea is to categorize browsers into grade levels, which define what is expected of them during testing. You could adopt their approach and categorize browsers, as appropriate, for your project.

Google takes a different approach with Google Apps, supporting the two most recent versions of most browsers (http://googleenterprise.blogspot.com/2011/06/our-plans-to-support-modern-browsers.html). Similarly, your project's needs may vary.

A The file name for the image is `iguana.jpg`, but in the HTML, it is incorrectly referenced as `Iguana.jpg` (with a capital I). As result, it doesn't display when you check the page from your server **B**.

```
...
<body>
<h1>Mary Anna, the Iguana</h1>

<p><img src="Iguana.jpg" width="220" height=
   "165" alt="Mary Anna, the Iguana" /> There
   once was an iguana ...</p>
</body>
</html>
```

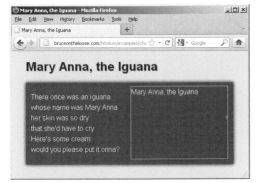

B The page may look fine on your computer if it isn't picky about upper- and lowercase letters. But when the page is published to the server, which is case sensitive, the image cannot be found and the `alt` text displays instead.

When Images Don't Appear

Little red x's, broken image icons, alternate text, or nothing at all—these are all signs that your images aren't loading properly (**A** and **B**). It's a drag if what you really wanted was a picture of an iguana!

To fix missing images:

- First, check that the file name of the image on the server *exactly* matches the name you've referenced in the `img` element, including upper- and lowercase letters and the extension **A**.

- Don't include spaces in file names. See "File Names" in Chapter 1.

- Make sure the image's URL is correct in the `img` element's `src` attribute. One easy test is to put an image in the same directory as the HTML page. Then you'll just need the proper file name and extension in the `img` element, but no path information. If the image shows up, the problem was probably in the path. However, it isn't good practice to keep images in the same directory as HTML files, because your site will quickly become disorganized. So after your test, remove the image from the HTML page directory, and fix the `src` path that points to it. See "URLs" in Chapter 1.

- If the image shows up when you view your page on your computer but not when you upload the page to the server, make sure you've uploaded the image to the server.

- Have you saved the image as a PNG, JPEG, or GIF? If so, all browsers will display it, which is not true for a BMP or TIFF. See Chapter 5 for more information.

Still Stuck?

Don't think I'm being patronizing when I suggest you go take a break. Sometimes the best thing you can do for a problem is leave it alone for a minute. When you come back, the answer may be staring you in the face. If it's not, let me offer you these additional suggestions.

1. Check again for typos. Revalidate your code (see "Validating Your Code").

2. Check the easy pieces first. Check the stuff you think you know really well before you investigate the less familiar things in search of the problem.

3. Simplify the problem. Go back to the most recent version of the page that worked properly. (Related to that, make copies of your page as you progress through building it so you will have versions to go back to if necessary.) Then test the page as you add each new element bit by bit.

4. For resources that your page links to, type the URL for that CSS, image, JavaScript, or media file directly in the browser's address bar to make sure it exists where you are expecting it.

5. Read through this chapter again—you may have missed something the first time, or it might trigger an idea.

6. There are numerous sites where you can search for solutions or ask for guidance. Stack Overflow (www.stackoverflow.com) and SitePoint (www.sitepoint.com/forums/forumdisplay.php?40-design-your-site) are just two examples. You can turn up others by searching online.

Publishing Your Pages on the Web

Once you've finished your masterpiece and are ready to present it to the public, you have to transfer your pages to your Web host server so that people can get to them.

You may also want to ask your Web host or Internet Service Provider (ISP) about the best way to upload your files. Typically, they have a set of instructions that let you know how to connect to their servers and where to upload files.

Be sure to test your pages thoroughly both before and after publishing them. For more details, see Chapter 20.

In This Chapter

Getting Your Own Domain Name

Before visitors can see your site, you need a domain name to associate with it . You can register your own domain name and then find a Web host to serve your site to anyone who visits the domain in a browser (see "Finding a Host for Your Site"). If you ever decide to change your Web host (or if they go out of business), you can move your domain to another Web host's server and all of your URLs will stay exactly the same.

To get your own domain name:

1. Point your browser at a domain registrar (see www.internic.net/alpha.html for a list) to see if the domain you want is available **B**. (Many Web hosts also allow you to search on their sites for available domains.)

2. Once you've found a domain name, either register it yourself (more common) or register it through the Web host you'll use. Charges vary from registrar to registrar, but about $10 a year for a .com domain is not uncommon (other extensions may have a different price). Some Web hosts offer domain registration as part of a discounted hosting fee.

TIP See the sidebar "Connecting Your Domain and Your Web Host" in the next section for an important configuration that's required to make your site display when someone visits your URL.

A Only certain companies are accredited registrars of domain names (this view and the one below are from www.namecheap.com, no endorsement implied). You can use one of their sites to see if a desired domain name is available, or you can check through a Web host's site.

Popular Extensions

☑	☆	catalancats.com	Available
☐	☆	catalancats.net	Available
☐	☆	catalancats.org	Available
☐	☆	catalancats.cm	Available
☐	☆	catalancats.mobi	Available
☐	☆	catalancats.us	Available
☐	☆	catalancats.biz	Available
☐	☆	catalancats.info	Available
☐	☆	catalancats.tv	Available

Additional Extensions

☐	☆	catalancats.co	Available
☐	☆	catalancats.me	Available
☐	☆	catalancats.co.uk	Available
☐	☆	catalancats.org.uk	Available
☐	☆	catalancats.me.uk	Available

Search All Extensions ...

Add to Cart

B If the name is available, you can either register it through the third-party registrar site where you checked it or register it through a Web host. (And now you know that the very useful www.catalancats.com domain can be yours!)

Your ISP as Web Host

If you have Internet access, you may already have a small amount of Web space through your ISP. It might not be enough for your entire Web site, but it's certainly enough to get used to putting pages on the Web. Ask your ISP for details. However, keep in mind that these types of hosting spaces typically don't allow you to put your site at a unique domain name. Instead, they are in a sub-domain or sub-directory of the ISP's domain, like www.someisp.com/your-site/ instead of www.yourdomain.com. In other words, if you have professional ambitions for your site, you wouldn't want it to be hosted on the free space your ISP may provide.

Finding a Host for Your Site

Unless you have your own server, you'll probably have to pay someone to host your site. Web hosts provide a piece of their server for your site's files and provide other services, like allowing you to create email addresses that are associated with your domain name (such as *yourname@yourdomain*.com).

There are hundreds of companies that provide Web site hosting. Most charge a monthly fee that depends on the services they offer. Some offer free Web hosting in exchange for advertising from your site. Although you can search on the Internet for a Web host, I recommend talking to friends to see if they use a host that they like—or maybe the author of a blog you trust has noted what company he or she uses as a host.

When considering a host, there are a number of things—besides price—to keep in mind.

- How much disk space will they let you have for your Web site? Don't pay for more than you need. Having said that, usually even the most basic accounts will have plenty of space for your site. Remember that HTML files take up very little space, whereas images, audio files, and videos take up successively larger quantities.

continues on next page

- How much data transfer (bandwidth) per month do their accounts allow? This represents the total size of data—the HTML, CSS, images, media files, and so on—they will serve to your visitors, rather than how much they'll allow you to store on their server. So if you expect visitors to access a lot of large files from your site, you'll need a larger monthly transfer allotment.

- Do they have plans that cater to sites with a lot of traffic, to ensure the site won't crash?

- How many mailboxes can you create for your domain? (Hosting companies often allow plenty.)

- Does the account allow you to host more than one domain, or is a separate account required for each site?

- What kind of technical support do they offer? Is it by phone, by email, or by online chat? How long will it take them to get back to you? Also, do they have a lot of support information available on their site? (You can probably check the quality of that content before becoming a customer.)

- How often do they back up data on their servers (in case there's a problem)?

- What kind of server-side languages and software packages come with the account? Do they use PHP, MySQL, WordPress, or other advanced features?

- Do they offer Web analytics reports that let you know how many people have visited your site, as well as other useful data?

Connecting Your Domain and Your Web Host

Once you've registered a domain and found a Web host, an important step is required to tie them together: You must point your domain to your Web host so that your site loads when visitors type in your site's URL.

To make this work, you configure what is known as the name server associated with your domain. Your Web host provides you the name server information to use in the configuration.

The actual configuration is done in one of two places, depending on where you registered your domain (see "Getting Your Own Domain Name"). If you registered it with a domain registrar, log in to your account with them and set the name server information for your domain (your domain registrar will provide instructions). If you registered your domain through your Web host, you would log in to your account there to update the settings.

Don't worry if all this sounds a little confusing. Your Web host and domain registrar (if different) will provide instructions on how to do this, and they will usually provide hands-on help if you need it.

One other point to keep in mind: When you change the name server settings, it usually takes 24 to 48 hours (72 at the very most) for the update to propagate across the Web. But this change doesn't take hold at the same time everywhere. So if you've updated your domain's name server (and uploaded your site's files as described in "Transferring Files to the Server"), your friends might be able to access your site fine from where they live, even though you don't see it right away (or vice versa). Your site should show for everyone before too long.

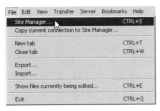

(A) To enter information about a new server, select File > Site Manager from the main FileZilla window. Site Manager is where you configure the FTP connection details for each site.

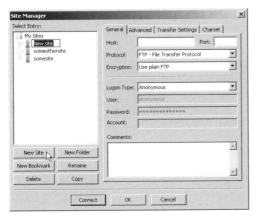

(B) When you click the New Site button in Site Manager, a temporary name appears under My Sites.

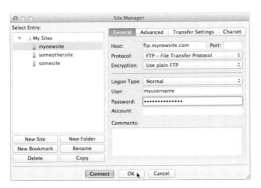

(C) Replace the temporary name with a name of your choice, and then configure the connection details in the General tab. The Connect button saves the information and establishes a connection with the server right away. The OK button saves the information only.

Transferring Files to the Server

In order for other people on the Internet to see your pages, you have to upload them to your Web host's server. One easy way to do that is with an FTP client such as FileZilla (http://filezilla-project.org), which is free for Windows, Mac OS X, and Linux (see the tips for other FTP clients). Many Web page editors also include FTP capabilities, so you can publish pages right from there instead of using a program like FileZilla.

Typically, your Web host emails FTP connection information to you after you sign up for a hosting account. (Contact them if you didn't receive it.) Once you have that information, you can configure your server connection and save it under a name (**A** through **C**) for easy access anytime you want to publish files (or download them from your site's server).

continues on next page

Then, connecting to your server  and transferring files (**E** and **F**) are straightforward.

Note that FileZilla looks different on Mac OS and Windows, but the interfaces are configured very similarly (the figures show a mix of the operating systems). Except where noted, the steps for using them are identical.

To define a new FTP site's properties:

1. Choose File > Site Manager from FileZilla's main menu **A**.

2. In the Site Manager window, click the New Site button **B**. A temporary name for your site appears under My Sites.

3. Type a name for the site (replacing the temporary name). It doesn't have to be the same as your domain name; it's just a label. Follow the information provided by your Web host to fill out the appropriate fields under the General tab. At a minimum, this usually involves entering the host URL, choosing Normal for the Logon Type option, and entering your user name and password (usually created when you set up the account) **C**.

4. Once you've finished indicating the connection details, either click the Connect button to save the information and connect to your server right away or click the OK button to save the information and connect later **C**.

D Now that your site's connection information is saved in the Site Manager, you can connect to your Web host's FTP server without retyping everything each time. On Mac or Windows, return to the Site Manager (via the server icon or the menu in **A**), select your site from the list, and select Connect **C**. Alternatively on Windows, as shown in the bottom figure here, you can activate the down arrow next to the server icon (on the far left) and then choose your site's name from the menu that displays. FileZilla will connect to the server.

E In the right part of the window, select the server's destination directory. In the left part of the window, navigate to the directory on your computer that contains the files you want to upload. Then right-click the file or folder you wish to upload to the server, and select Upload.

F The newly transferred folder appears in the frame on the right side of the window. Follow the same process for all the files and folders you want to transfer to your site. Or, to transfer several at once, select multiple files or folders and then right-click to select Upload.

G Choose Server > Disconnect once you're finished.

To transfer files to the server with FileZilla:

1. Open FileZilla.

2. Select the down arrow next to the server icon (on the far left, just below the main menu). Then choose your site's name from the menu that displays D. FileZilla will establish a connection with your server.

3. On the right side of the window, navigate to the server directory to which you want to upload files.

4. On the left side of the window, navigate to the directory on your computer that has the files you want to upload.

5. Right-click the desired file or folder in the left frame, and choose Upload from the menu that appears E. The files are transferred F (this will take longer for large files, like videos). You may also transfer files in the other direction (see the first tip).

6. Your site updates are live now. Browse your site at www.*yourdomain.tld* (where *yourdomain.tld* is the domain you registered; .tld is the top-level domain, which will be .com unless you registered a domain with a different extension) to make sure everything is working properly. Edit any of the files on your computer as necessary, and upload them to your server by following steps 3 through 5 (you may need to do step 2 again if a lot of time has passed). Repeat this step until the site is as you intend it.

7. Close FileZilla or choose Server > Disconnect from the main menu once you've finished transferring files G.

continues on next page

TIP You can also transfer files from your site's server to your computer. To do so, right-click files or folders in the right-hand frame and choose Download from the menu that appears.

TIP FileZilla is just one of many FTP clients available. Some other popular ones for Mac OS X are CyberDuck (free, http://cyberduck.ch), Transmit (www.panic.com/transmit), and Fetch (http://fetchsoftworks.com). Mac OS X also has built-in FTP capability (see http://osxdaily .com/2011/02/07/ftp-from-mac/). Search online for "FTP client" to find more for both Windows and Mac. They all work similarly, but some have more features than others.

TIP When you transfer files and folders, they are copied to the destination folder. The source location retains its version of the assets.

TIP Your FTP program might prompt you (FileZilla does) to be sure you want to over-write a file or folder if you transfer one that the destination already contains. Each FTP client is different, though, so it's possible it won't ask for your permission. Try it on a test file to learn how your FTP client handles such a situation.

TIP Relative URLs in your code are main-tained when you transfer a folder to the server.

TIP If your site doesn't load when you visit its URL, it could be a few things. First, double-check that you uploaded the files to the proper directory. Often, your pages belong in a directory called *public_html*, *www*, or some-thing similar. Your Web host's instructions should specify the proper location; ask them if you aren't sure. If you've got the files in the right place and the site still doesn't show, the problem might be your domain's name server settings (see the "Connecting Your Domain and Your Web Host" sidebar).

TIP If you've uploaded a new version of a file to your server but don't see the change when you visit your site, clear your browser's cache and check the page again. Search the browser's Help section if you aren't sure how to clear the cache.

TIP You can resize the window of most FTP clients to show more (or fewer) files at a time. Just click and drag the lower-right corner.

Index

/*, */, using for CSS comments, 182
: (colon) versus = (equals) sign, 205
; (semicolon), using with CSS properties, 205
`<!--`, `-->`, using for HTML comments, 97
3D, positioning elements in, 318–319
320 and Up, 351

A

a element. *See* anchors
AAC audio file format, 468
abbr element, 118–119
abbreviations, explaining, 118–119
absolute versus relative URLs, 21–23
accessibility. *See also* ARIA (Accessible Rich
     Internet Applications), and screen readers
   advocates, 91
   explained, 11
   HTML5 media, 467
active links, 230
:active pseudo-class, 231
address element
   defining contact information with, 102–103
   using with **article** element, 70
Adobe Fireworks, 153, 155
Adobe Photoshop, 153–155
   finding image sizes, 159
   mockups, 359
   scaling images, 161
::after pseudo-element, 229

aligning
   elements vertically, 322
   text, 268–269
alt attribute, 157
alternate text, 157
anchors. *See also* links
   creating, 172–173, 175–177
   linking to, 174
animated images, saving, 151
Apple's Link Maker, 177
ARIA (Accessible Rich Internet Applications),
     88–91. *See also* accessibility
   form role, 91
   landmark roles, 88–89
   role="banner" definition, 89
   role="complementary" definition, 90
   role="contentinfo" definition, 90
   role="main" definition, 89
   role="navigation" definition, 89
   screen reader test results, 90
   spec, 91
ARIA landmark roles. *See* landmark roles
   versus **id**s, 284–285
   overlap with HTML5 elements, 88
   recommendation, 90
   styling elements with, 284–285
article element, 68–71
   address element, 70
   children of, 15

content. *See also* text content
   separating from presentation, 276
   syndicated, 57
controls
   audio attribute, 471–472
   video attribute, 454–456
corners
   elliptical, 380
   rounding, 378–381
Coyier, Chris, 322
Creative Commons licenses, 152
CSS (Cascading Style Sheets)
   adjacent sibling combinator, 226
   colliding rules, 184–187
   comments for style rules, 182–183
   style rules, 181
CSS code, viewing, 212
CSS colors, 190. *See also* color
   HSL, 193–196
   HSLA, 193–196
   RGB, 191
   RGBA, 192–196
CSS errors, checking, 515
CSS properties
   bare numbers, 189
   hexadecimal colors, 191
   inherit value, 188
   lengths, 188–189
   percentages, 188–189
   predefined values, 188
   URLs, 190
   using ; (semicolon) with, 205
CSS reset, beginning main style sheet
   with, 290
CSS Tricks, 395
CSS troubleshooting
   browser support, 513
   curly braces, 512
   declarations, 512
   developer tools, 513
   linking HTML documents, 513
   property/value pairs, 512
   punctuation, 513
   separating properties from values, 512
   spaces, 512–513
   `</style>` end tag, 513
   values, 512

CSS1, introduction of, 8
CSS3
   backgrounds, 388–389
   browser compatibility, 375
   drop shadows, 382–387
   general sibling combinator, 226
   gradient backgrounds, 390–393
   opacity elements, 394–395
   polyfills for progressive enhancement,
      376–377
   rounding corners of elements, 378–381
   vendor prefixes, 373–374
CSS3 Generator, 374
CSS3 selectors, resource for, 239
cursor property
   auto value, 323
   crosshair value, 323
   default value, 323
   move value, 323
   pointer value, 323
   progress value, 323
   text value, 323
   wait value, 323
   x-resize value, 323
cursors, changing, 323
custom markers. *See also* markers
   displaying, 405
   URLs (Uniform Resource Locators), 405
   using, 404–405
CyberDuck FTP client, 528

D

datetime attribute, 106–108
debugging techniques
   checking HTML, 510–511
   syntax highlighting, 506–507
default page, specifying, 33–34. *See also*
   HTML pages; Web pages
default styles. *See also* styles
   normalizing, 290–291
   resetting, 290–291
default.htm page, 33
defining terms, 120
del element, 124–127
deleting, borders from images, 156
description list (**dl**). *See also* lists
   creating, 414–415

dt and dd elements, 413
name-value groups, 412
nesting, 415
Devlin, Ian, 467, 487
dfn (definition) element, 120
Digital Rights Management (DRM), 481
disabled attribute, 447
display property, 324
block value, 325
inline value, 325
inline-block value, 325
none value, 325
div element
applying styles to, 85
best practices, 86
examples, 87
as generic container, 84–87
versus span element, 85
structuring pages with, 279
surrounding content, 84
using with JavaScript, 85
dl (description list). See also lists
creating, 414–415
dt and dd elements, 413
name-value groups, 412
nesting, 415
DOCTYPE
case insensitivity, 45
rendering in browsers, 45
for XHTML Strict document, 45
<!DOCTYPE html> declaration, 4, 24
document outline, 50–55
algorithm, 57
assistive technologies, 54
explicit semantics, 53
h1-h6 hierarchy, 51
screen readers, 54
sectioning elements, 51–52, 55
document structure, inspecting, 511
document.createElement(), 287
documents. See also HTML documents; Web
pages
ending, 5
saving, 35
structuring, 278
domain name
connecting to Web host, 524
getting, 522

Dribbble site, 376
DRM (Digital Rights Management), 481
drop shadows
adding to elements, 384–387
adding to text, 382–383
drop-down navigation, using nested lists for,
411
Dunham, Ethan, 360–361

E
editing Web pages, 35
edits, noting, 124–127
Electric Mobile Simulator for Windows, 347
element box
controlling appearance of, 293
positioning, 293
elements, 13–14. See also pseudo-elements
adding padding around, 304–305
aligning vertically, 322
ancestors, 221
applying styles to groups of, 236–237
auto value for width, 300
contents of, 13
descendants, 221
displaying, 324–326
empty, 13
end and start tags, 511
end tag, 13
floating, 306–310
formatting, 93
hiding, 324–326
naming with classes or IDs, 92–94
nesting, 15
offsetting in natural flow, 314–315
overlap with landmark roles, 88
positioning absolutely, 316–317
positioning in 3D, 318–319
rounding corners of, 378–381
selecting based on adjacent sibling, 226
selecting based on ancestors, 222–223
selecting based on attributes, 232–235
selecting based on child, 224–226
selecting based on parents, 223–224
selecting based on type, 217
selecting by class or id, 218–220
selecting by context, 221–226
selecting by name, 216–217

Google Apps, 518
Google Closure Compiler, 501
Google WebFonts, 356
Graded Browser Support, 518
gradient backgrounds, 390–393. *See also*
    backgrounds
gradient generator, 393
grouping
    headings, 58–59
    selectors, 237
groups of elements, specifying, 236–237

H

H.264 video file formats, 452
h1 heading, using, 9
h1-h6 elements, 48
    sizes of, 49
    using consistently, 49, 55
HandBrake video converter, 452
hanging indent, creating, 265
hasLayout, 395
head element
    explained, 44
    indenting code nested in, 45
header element, 61–63, 279
headers
    creating, 61–63
    versus headings, 63
    nav element, 63
    restrictions, 63
    using, 63
headings, 282
    adding **id**s to, 49
    creating, 48–49
    grouping, 58–59
    versus headers, 63
    lang attribute in, 49
    in search engines, 49
    using, 9, 48
height: property
    versus **min-height**, 300
    setting, 298–299
height video attribute, 454
hexadecimal colors, 191
hgroup element, 58–59
hh:mm:ss format, 108

hidden fields
    creating, 443
    readonly attribute, 443
hiding files, 34
highlighting text, 116–117
homepage, specifying, 33–34
host, finding for sites, 523–524
hover links, 230
:hover pseudo-class, 231
href attribute
    beginning with **#**, 172
    values in, 15
HSL and HSLA color, 193–196
HSL Color Picker, 194–195
.htm and **.html** extensions, 19, 30–31
HTML
    checking, 514
    markup, 6
    semantic, 6, 24
    start and end tags, 511
    validating, 515
HTML code, viewing, 39
HTML comments. *See also* comments
    adding, 96–97
    restrictions, 97
    syntax, 97
HTML documents, beginning, 24. *See also*
    documents
HTML elements
    block-level, 7
    displaying, 6–8
    inline, 7
HTML forms. *See* forms
HTML Lint, 515
HTML markup, components, 24. *See also*
    markup
HTML pages. *See also* default page; Web
    pages
    above **<body>** start tag, 4
    basic page, 3
    carriage returns, 3
    DOCTYPE, 4, 24
    ending documents, 5
    foundation, 43
    h1 heading, 9
    headings, 9
    images, 9
    links, 10

Johnston, Jason, 377
JPEG format, 148, 150
jQuery JavaScript library, 498
JW Player, 463

K

kbd element, 129
Keith, Jeremy, 332
kerning, specifying, 264
-khtml- prefix, 373
Kiss, Jason, 91
Kissane, Erin, 27

L

label element
   example of, 14
   using with forms, 434
landmark roles
   versus **id**s, 284–285
   overlap with HTML5 elements, 88
   recommendation, 90
   styling elements with, 284–285
lang attribute, 43
   in headings, 49
   using with **q** element, 114
layout with styles. *See also* styles
   approaches, 277–278
   background color, 296
   background images, 294–295
   background properties, 296–297
   box model, 292–293
   browsers, 276–277
   content and presentation, 276
layouts
   elastic, 278
   fixed, 277
   fluid, 277–278
The League of Moveable Type, 355–356
"Learning SVG," 487
legend element, 426–427
letter spacing, setting, 264
li (list item) elements, 398–400
line break, creating, 133, 137
line height, setting, 255
line spacing, fixing, 123

linking thumbnail images, 177
links, 17. *See also* anchors
   active, 230
   block-level, 168–170
   changing appearance of, 230
   creating, 167–170
   defining, 10
   defining rules for, 231
   designating for navigation, 65
   destination, 166
   focus, 230
   hover, 230
   labels, 166, 170
   LVFHA mnemonic, 231
   marking up groups of links with, 399
   nesting in **nav** element, 64
   opening, 171
   selecting based on states, 230–231
   structuring in **ul** and **ol** elements, 65
   target attribute, 171
   visited, 230
   wrapping in **nav** element, 66–67
list content, placement of, 400
list item (**li**) elements, 398–400
list numbering, starting, 403
list type, choosing, 399
lists. *See also* **dl** (description lists); nested lists
   choosing markers, 401–402
   creating, 398–400
   custom markers, 404–405
   displaying without markers, 402
   hanging markers, 406
   indenting, 400
   nesting, 400
   ordered (**ol**), 398–400
   right-to-left content direction, 400
   start value, 403
   unordered (**ul**), 398–400
   value attribute, 403
list-style properties, setting, 407
list-style-type property, 401
loop
   audio attribute, 471
   video attribute, 454
lowercase value, using with **text-transform**,
   270

M

mailto scheme, 20
Marcotte, Ethan, 331
margins
    auto value, 302–303
    setting around elements, 302–303
    setting values for, 301
mark element, 116–117
markers. *See also* custom markers
    choosing for lists, 401
    controlling hanging, 406
    inside value, 406
    outside value, 406
markup, defined, 1, 6. *See also* HTML markup
math element, 129
mathML element, 129
max-width property, setting, 299
McLellan, Drew, 483
@media at-rule, using in style sheets, 208–209
media queries
    building pages adapting with, 349–350
    chaining features and values, 336
    content and HTML, 340–341
    declarations in rules, 338
    defining, 336–337
    design implementation, 341–342
    evolving layout, 343–346
    examples, 334–336, 344–345
    feature: value pair, 335
    features of, 333–334
    iPhone 4, 351
    logic portion, 335
    min-width and max-width, 348
    Opera Mobile 11 browser, 351
    rendering styles in Internet Explorer, 348
    syntax, 334–336
    type portion, 335
    width feature, 338
media sources, source element, 460
media-specific style sheets, 208–209
meta element, 339
meter element
    versus progress element, 143
    using, 142–143
Meyer, Eric, 290
min-height versus height, 300
Miro Video Converter, 452

Mobile Boilerplate, 347, 350
mobile coding tools, 346
mobile devices, HTML5 and CSS3 support for, 351
"mobile first" design, 332
mobile phones. *See also* responsive Web design
    base styling, 340
    building baseline for, 341–342
    building for desktop, 342
    building sites for, 328–332
    testing pages on, 347
Mobile Safari's viewport, 335
Modernizr JavaScript library, 287, 348, 377
monospaced font, rendering, 129
MooTools JavaScript library, 498
-moz- prefix, 373, 378–379
MP3 audio file format, 468
MP4
    audio file format, 468
    video file formats, 452
-ms- prefix, 373
multimedia files, getting, 480
multimedia resources, 487
muted
    audio attribute, 471
    video attribute, 454
MyFonts, 356

N

nav element, 64–67
    in headers, 63
    nesting links in, 64
    placing footer links in, 65
    restrictions, 65
    role attribute, 64
    using with screen readers, 65
    wrapping links in, 66–67
navigation
    with keyboard, 170
    marking, 64–67
Neal, Jonathan, 123, 290, 466
nested lists. *See also* lists
    drop-down navigation, 411
    :hover pseudo-class, 411
    selectors, 409
    styling, 408–411

none value, using with **text-transform**, 270
normalize.css, 123, 290–291
Notepad text editor, using, 28–30
NVDA screen reader, 91

O

Ogg Theora video file formats, 452
Ogg Vorbis audio file format, 468
ol (ordered list)
    Arabic numerals, 409
    creating, 398–400
    marker types, 402
    using with links, 65
onblur JavaScript event, 503
onchange JavaScript event, 503
onclick JavaScript event, 503
ondblclick JavaScript event, 503
"One Web" presentation, 332
onfocus JavaScript event, 503
onkeydown JavaScript event, 503
onkeypress JavaScript event, 504
onkeyup JavaScript event, 504
online resources
    320 and Up, 351
    Apple's Link Maker, 177
    ARIA spec, 91
    BOM, 32
    browser compatibility, 375
    browser developer tools, 507
    Coda text editor, 29
    collapse value for **visibility**, 326
    ColorZilla's gradient generator, 393
    conditional comments, 351
    Creative Commons licenses, 152
    CSS error checking, 515
    CSS Tricks, 395
    CSS3 Generator, 374
    CSS3 selectors, 239
    developer tools, 507
    Electric Mobile Simulator for Windows, 347
    event handlers, 504
    Firebug for Firefox, 212
    Font Squirrel, 355–356, 358, 366
    Fontdeck service, 356
    Fonts.com service, 356
    FontShop, 356
    Fontspring, 361

online resources *(continued)*
    forms, 428
    Google Apps, 518
    Google Closure Compiler, 501
    Google WebFonts, 356
    Graded Browser Support, 518
    gradient backgrounds, 392
    gradient generator, 393
    HandBrake, 452
    hasLayout, 395
    HTML forms, 428
    HTML Lint, 515
    "HTML5 Canvas: The Basics," 487
    HTML5 Video, 487
    HTML5's new features, 448
    iOS Simulator, 347
    JavaScript events, 504
    JavaScript libraries, 498
    jQuery JavaScript library, 498
    JW Player, 463
    The League of Moveable Type, 355–356
    "Learning SVG," 487
    Meyer reset, 290
    Miro Video Converter, 452
    Mobile Boilerplate, 347, 350
    mobile devices, 351
    "mobile first" design, 332
    Modernizr, 287, 348, 377
    MooTools JavaScript library, 498
    multimedia, 487
    MyFonts, 356
    normalize css, 123
    "One Web" presentation, 332
    PHP server-side language, 422
    polyfills, 377
    ProtoFluid, 347
    right-to-left languages, 141
    showform.php script, 420
    SitePoint, 520
    Stack Overflow, 520
    Sublime Text editor, 29
    table structures, 489
    text editors, 29
    TextMate, 29
    TextWrangler, 28
    Typekit service, 356–357, 359
    validating code, 515

scripting best practices, 501

scripts

adding embedded, 502

Google Closure Compiler, 501

loading external, 499

YUI Compressor, 501

search engine optimization (SEO), 12

section element

versus **article** element, 69, 73, 283

example, 74

terminology, 50

using, 72–74

using with **role="main"**, 69

sections, defining, 72–74

secure server, using, 431

Seddon, Ryan, 377

select boxes

creating, 438–439

grouping options, 439

option element, 438–439

select element, 438

size attribute, 438–439

selectors. *See also* attribute selectors

combining, 238–239

constructing, 214–215

grouping, 237

semantics

accessibility, 11

displaying HTML, 12

importance of, 11–12

screen readers, 12

semicolon (;), using with CSS properties, 205

SEO (search engine optimization), 12

server, transferring files to, 525–528

server side vs. client side, 421

Sexton, Alex, 377

shims, using for progressive enhancement, 376–377

showform.php script, downloading, 420

sidebar, **aside** as, 76–77

simulators, using with mobile devices, 347

SitePoint, 520

sites

HTML 5 Outliner, 52

loading, 528

planning, 26

sketching out, 26–27

small caps

removing, 271

using, 271

small element, 8, 132

Sneddon, Geoffrey, 52

Snook, Jonathan, 254

source code, saving, 40

source element

media attribute, 460

type attribute, 460

using with multiple media, 460

using with **video** element, 461–462

spacing

controlling, 264

fixing between lines, 123

span element

versus **div** element, 85

using, 134

spans, creating, 134–135

src attribute

audio, 471

contents, 15

video, 454, 460

Stack Overflow, Web resources, 520

stacking order, specifying, 315, 317

start tags, including in elements, 13

strikethrough, applying, 126

strong element, 110

versus **b** element, 110

versus **i** element, 110

versus **mark**, 117

nesting, 110

style element, **@import** rules in, 206

style rules

adding comments to, 182–183

cascading, 185–187

constructing, 181

creating, 237

declaration blocks, 181

inheritance, 185–186

location of, 187

selectors, 181

specificity, 186–187

style sheets. *See also* external style sheets

alternate, 210–211

@charset declaration, 199

CSS reset, 290

vertical-align property *(continued)*
    super value, 322
    text-bottom value, 322
    text-top value, 322
    top value, 322
video
    adding to Web pages, 453
    adding with Flash fallbacks, 463–466
    autoplay attribute, 455–456
    books, 487
    controls attribute, 455–456
    coupling with SVG (Scalable Vector
        Graphics), 486
    embedding YouTube, 484
    hyperlink fallbacks, 461–462
    looping, 457
    multiple sources, 459
    object element for Flash fallbacks, 463–466
    online resources, 487
    preload attribute, 454
    preventing preloading, 458
    specifying poster images, 457
    using with **canvas** element, 485
video attributes
    autoplay, 454–456
    autoplay and **loop**, 457
    controls, 454–456
    height, 454
    loop, 454
    muted, 454
    poster, 454
    preload, 454
    src, 454, 460
    width, 454
video element, using with **source** element,
    461–462
video file formats
    converting between, 452
    H.264, 452
    MP4, 452
    Ogg Theora, 452
    WebM, 452–453, 455, 457
"Video for Everybody," 466
Video for Everybody Generator, 466
"Video on the Web," 487
View Source command, using, 39

viewports
    features of, 339
    meta element, 339
visibility property, 324
    collapse value, 326
    hidden value, 326
visited links, 230
visitors, allowing to upload files, 442
Visscher, Sjoerd, 287
VoiceOver screen reader, 91
void elements, omitting end tags from, 511

W

WAI-ARIA. *See* ARIA (Accessible Rich Internet
    Applications)
WAV audio file format, 468
wbr element, 137
Web design. *See* responsive Web design
Web Font Specimen, 357
Web fonts. *See also* fonts
    bold formatting, 366–369
    browser support, 355
    demo.html file, 358–359
    downloading, 358–359
    .eot (Embedded OpenType), 354
    features of, 354
    file types, 354
    finding, 356–357
    @font-face feature, 355
    incorporating into Web pages, 361–362
    italic formatting, 366–369
    legal issues, 355
    managing file sizes, 365–369
    quality, 357
    rendering, 357
    self-hosting, 356
    services, 356–357, 370
    styling, 365–369
    subsetting, 365–366
    .svg (Scalable Vector Graphics), 354
    TrueDoc, 354
    .ttf (TrueType), 354, 359
    using, 362–364
    using for headlines, 369
    .woff (Web Open Font Format), 354

THREE WAYS TO QUICKSTART

The ever popular Visual QuickStart Guide series is now available in three formats to help you "Get Up and Running in No Time!"

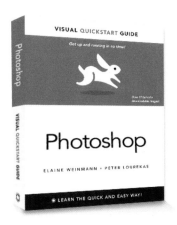

Visual **QuickStart Guide Books**

The best-selling Visual QuickStart Guide series is available in book and ebook (ePub and PDF) formats for people who prefer the classic learning experience.

Video **QuickStart**

Video QuickStarts offer the immediacy of streaming video so you can quickly master a new application, task, or technology. Each Video QuickStart offers more than an hour of instruction and rich graphics to demonstrate key concepts.

Enhanced **Visual QuickStart Guide**

Available on your computer and tablet, Enhanced Visual QuickStart Guides combine the ebook with Video QuickStart instruction to bring you the best of both formats and the ultimate multimedia learning experience.

Visit us at: Peachpit.com/VQS

VISUAL QUICKSTART GUIDE